THE NATIONAL TRUST BOOK OF THE
COUNTRYSIDE

THE NATIONAL TRUST BOOK OF THE
COUNTRYSIDE

Introduction by Nick Baker

Foreword by Adrian Phillips CBE

THE NATIONAL TRUST

First published in the United Kingdom in 2009 by National Trust Books
10 Southcombe Street,
London W14 0RA
An imprint of Anova Books Company Ltd

ISBN 9781905400690

A CIP catalogue for this book is available from the British Library.

15 14 13 12 10 09
10 9 8 7 6 5 4 3 2 1

Authors: Jane Eastoe and Matthew Oates
Project Manager: Jilly McLeod
Copy Editor: Katie Hewett
Consultant: J. Edward Milner
Consultant: Steve Parker
Layout designer: Mark Holt
Proofreader: Betsy Hosegood
For illustrators, photographers and picture libraries see Picture Credits.

Reproduction by Dot Gradations Ltd, London
Printed by A. Mondadori Printing, S.p.A., Italy

This book can be ordered direct from the publisher at the website
www.anovabooks.com, or try your local bookshop. Also available at
National Trust shops.

Chapter Openers:
Page 12: A view of a field of haystacks at Cherhill Down, Wiltshire, in summer.
Page 14: The spectacular cliffs of the Seven Sisters on the South Downs west of
Eastbourne in Sussex.
Page 64: The sun shining through the woodland canopy at Alderley Edge in
Cheshire.
Page 112: A rolling field of scarlet poppies, near Alfriston Clergy House in East
Sussex.
Page 140: Looking south west at Cherhill Down, between Calne and Beckhampton
in Wiltshire, with the Lansdowne Monument, built 1845 in memory of the
economist Sir William Petty, in the distance.
Page 156: Carneddau, Snowdonia. In the mountains of Snowdonia, showing Tryfan
to the left, the Glyder Fach and Y Garn, the snow covered peak to the right and
Llyn Ogwen with a light covering of ice.
Page 176: Coastal heath covered in common heather, bell heather and gorse, lining
the coastal path in late summer on the Great Hangman with the Little
Hangman near Combe Martin and the North Devon coast.
Page 194: Situated in the Wasdale valley in Cumbria, Wastwater is 4.5km (3
miles) long, 0.75km (½ mile) wide and 85m (260ft) deep, and the deepest of all
the lakes in England.
Page 240: Walkers on the Cantilever, the Glyders, Snowdonia National Park,
Wales.
Page 242: The view north-west from Pencarrow Head to Great Lantic beach near
Fowey in Cornwall.
Page 272: Bluebells carpet the ground layer among the beeches in Dockey Wood on
the Ashridge Estate in Hertfordshire.
Page 300: Snow and ice in the midst of winter at Wicken Fen in Cambridgeshire.
Page 312: Gritstone rock formations overlooking moorland at Kinder Scout in the
Peak District with Swines Back beyond.
Page 324: Barrow Bay on Derwentwater in the Lake District, Cumbria, looking
towards the snow-covered fells in the distance
Page 346: View from Stackpole Head on the Stackpole Estate in Wales looking
north towards Barafundle Bay beach.
Page 362: Sunset at Murlough Bay, looking north-west towards Fair Head in
Northern Ireland.

Contents

Foreword

Many of the stunning photographs in this book are of National Trust properties. They remind us, powerfully, that the Trust is not only responsible for an unrivalled collection of Britain's historic buildings, but that it also owns – and protects – many of the most beautiful landscapes of these islands. They include magnificent mountains and upland moors, as well as wetlands, downland, heathland, parkland, and farmed and wooded landscapes, to be found everywhere from remote rural areas to the edges of great cities – and mile upon mile of fine coast.

The value of such places are many. Some 43 per cent of the water surface area of England and Wales drains through Trust properties. Their soils and trees absorb and store carbon on a scale we are only now beginning to understand. No other landowner has anything like the variety (and rarity) of wildlife in its care. The Trust's countryside is a treasure house of vernacular heritage as well. Thousands earn their living from the Trust's land. And, of course, the scenic beauties of the Trust's landscapes are sought out by millions.

The accumulation of this great national institution began in 1895 with the acquisition of less than 2ha (5 acres) of Welsh coast, followed in 1899 by a small area of Wicken Fen in Cambridgeshire. More iconic places followed: Box Hill (1914), Hatfield Forest (1924) and the Farne Islands (1925), for example. But protecting isolated 'beauty spots' was not enough. The National Trust saw the need to care for whole landscapes, nowhere more so than in the Lake District. The Trust's countryside holdings grew too as large estates came to it, along with the fine country houses that it saved from neglect or demolition and kept intact with their indigenous contents. In 1965, the National Trust launched Enterprise Neptune, a visionary project that has saved hundreds of miles of coast from development. Through other large and small acquisitions, the Trust now owns more than a quarter of a million hectares (618,000 acres) of countryside (about the size of Oxfordshire) and 1150km (714½ miles) of coastline (about as far as Bologna is from London).

The management of such a large estate would always be a huge responsibility. But for the Trust it is even more complex. It has to balance its duty to conserve nature and landscapes with providing public access. It has to run a business-like operation – for example on its many tenanted farms – and yet be alive to wider social and environmental expectations. Above all, it has to think long term and about the nation's needs as a whole. Moreover, because the Trust has become a national institution, it manages its countryside, landscape and wildlife very much in the public eye: a little like the BBC, the Trust is a body about which everyone (not only its members) feels a sense of ownership and is ready with criticism too. So its standards must be exemplary. It cannot cut corners or sell assets as others might – its unique power to provide permanent protection through inalienable ownership means it has huge obligations.

The Trust has to meet these high demands at a time when the pressures on the countryside are unprecedented. Endangered species and habitats, and historic features, are threatened by the demands for homes, jobs and transport – and all this when the climate itself is changing, the sea beginning to encroach and the global and national economy seemingly more unpredictable than for generations.

We have been very fortunate in Britain to have been served by an institution like the National Trust, which has such respect for the past, and such a strong sense of responsibility towards the future. While huge and complex threats now confront it, the Trust's record gives reason to hope that, in another hundred years, there will still be landscapes and wildlife in the countryside of England, Wales and Northern Ireland that can delight the human spirit.

Adrian Phillips CBE
National Trust Board of Trustees

Right: Formby, in Merseyside, is one of the few places left in the UK where the native red squirrel can be seen.

Introduction

'What's my favourite place on earth?' is probably the question most frequently asked of me. Having been fortunate enough in the last 15 years to have visited every major continent, travelled to some of the most inaccessible and rarely seen corners of the world, climbed their mountains and dived their oceans you might expect me to divulge a location most exotic and exclusive. But the truth is I have no favourite place; it's an impossible question to answer. However, if there is such a location, I will tell you this much; it is definitely to be found somewhere in the group of islands that I and 63 million other souls call home; a place called the British Isles.

It is comprised of over 6,000 islands; from the largest and greatest of Britain and Ireland to many smaller fragments, some of them no more than mere splinters of rock. They have been millions of years in the making; born of volcanic activity, river and estuary sediments or comprised of the bodies of a multitude of hard-shelled creatures they have been moulded, squeezed, etched, pounded and squashed by rivers, seas and ice ages – if every rock or speck of dirt we tread on could tell a story, what an adventure it would be. Much of this book reveals the British countryside as it is now, but, as with so many things, it helps our understanding if you can fully appreciate the background to the scene set before us today and one that is still as dynamic as ever.

As a naturalist I have often asked myself why I love Britain so much. It is certainly not the most biodiverse place on earth and although it does have its endemic species it is not the tropics by any standards. We have the great ice sheets of the last glaciation some 15,000 years ago to thank for this limitation of animal and plant species in relation to the rest of continental Europe.

The glaciation from millennia ago acted like a giant biological etch-a-sketch: the ice sheet crept down from the north, smothering most of the land and turned the remaining ice-free southern portions into barren, cold tundra. It was not until the ice retreated that things really started warming up, but this colonisation of wildlife from the continent was cut short after about 8,000 years when the thaw caused the sea levels to rise and cut off the tip of what was a peninsula. It was a small temporal window and many of the slower species did not get across before the rise in sea levels divorced us from the European mainland and formed these islands.

But for all that, this is still a wondrous place with wildlife and landscape that are dear to me, and I know, to many others. I've been scampering around the hedgerows, dipping my net into its ponds and streams and rock pools along its shores for as long as I can remember. I feel close to it and the familiar everyday creatures and plants continue to fascinate me in the same way as they have always done – it is my comfort zone; I belong here.

Other than this familiarity, the other thing that stops me buying a biodiverse slice of a Costa Rican rainforest and spending the rest of my life in it is that even with the rest of my life I will never get to know it with anywhere near the intimacy that I could get to understand my own patch of the planet. It is with the same sense that I feel sorry for Americans and Australians – imagine living in such an incredibly large and diverse place that you will never stand a realistic chance of getting to know it all that well. They are just too vast, while our islands are perfect and getting to know them well is an achievable goal.

However, do not confuse the word achievable with boring – every bit of the 313,400km² (121,000 square miles) plus that comprise the surface area of our islands is still very much full of adventures and discoveries, and this book is ideally placed to help you tackle some of them and inspire you to find your own. While there is still no way anybody could ever know everything, or see every place, breath in every atmosphere, or watch every bird – we can all realistically get a feel for it before its soils reclaim our bones.

Just think of what is possible: you could swim with a basking shark, the second biggest fish in the world (and believe me it is every bit as special and memorable as sharing a moment with a mountain gorilla). If this seems too big, try the other end of the scale – what about snorkelling with one of our two species of seahorse? How about an adrenalin-soaked moment watching a peregrine falcon strike, like a steely arrow, through the heart of a couple of million starlings as they congregate around a winter roost? If you need something curious to ponder, how about the massive and still largely secretive migrations of our eels, salmon and sea trout, an exploding bombardier beetle, a totally aquatic moth, a Cornish lumpsucker or maybe a contemplative moment lying in a field of ling heather or bluebells? Whatever your fancy, this book will help you find it or put a name to a face or flag to a flower.

The book is divided into two major sections: the first describes the 'flavours' of the land; the major habitats and landscapes, such as mountains and forests. What lies beneath our feet affects what we see at eye level; the different soil types as well as the moisture content it holds have a profound effect on what roots plunder its

Right: Part of the Snowdonia National Park in north west Wales, Glyder Fach is the second highest mountain of the Glyderan. Glyder means a heap of stones.

loam and sod, and this in turn affects what grows here and the ecosystems stacked upon its geological shoulders.

From the limestone cliffs and grasslands to the remnant of the original 'wild wood', from the lofty peaks of Ben Nevis at 1344m (4409ft) to the lowest of our wet fen lowlands at 4m (13ft) below sea level, each habitat is described in great detail, and while no book can realistically show you everything, this one covers most of the ground. The book is an informative delight, ideal for dipping into and a source of inspiration for those wishing to know these islands better.

The second half of the book gives you a tour of the key landscapes of each of our regions, from an exploration of the Lake District to why the White Cliffs of Dover are white. Within its pages we discover not just the essence of what makes each place so unique, but we dig a little further and discover how it functions. It is not a field guide but a way to truly understand the land beneath our feet.

Nick Baker
Naturalist and Broadcaster

The Countryside Code

There is a great need in these modern times to reconnect our lives to the landscape. This has to start with an understanding of the land. The National Trust works hard to do this, encouraging people to connect with the land but also to conserve and appreciate it. It asks people to abide by the Countryside Code when enjoying the land around them. Scotland has its own Outdoor Access Code, as does Northern Ireland. Particular areas and some National Trust properties may have separate byelaws that may restrict a small number of activities.

1. **Shut gates after you** Using gates and stiles is highly recommended and is easier than clambering over walls, which can damage hedges and fences. Shutting gates after use also prevents any livestock escaping.

2. **Keep dogs under control** Even the best-behaved and best-loved dogs will be seen as a predator by the rest of the natural world. Dogs and dog walkers are welcome at National Trust coast and countryside sites, but there are occasions when a minority of dog owners cause problems for other visitors and vulnerable wildlife. To avoid distressing livestock or wildlife keep dogs on leads and under close control at all times. Particularly observe local notices on the need to keep dogs on a lead at sensitive times of the year, such as during the breeding season for ground-nesting birds, when sheep are lambing or deer are having calves. You may also need to abide by seasonal

access restrictions on popular beaches in the summer. Where access for dogs has been restricted, the Trust attempts to find suitable alternative locations to walk a dog nearby. Please also bear in mind that dogs should not be left in cars on hot days and dog mess should be taken away with you.

3. **Keep to paths** By keeping to the path, you not only avoid trampling and disturbing many habitats but you can also move quietly and quickly and in doing so enhance your chances of seeing wildlife.

4. **Do not pick flowers** To help maintain the beautiful plantlife, try to enjoy flowers in their habitat and leave them where they are so they can flourish and grow. Use a notebook or a digital camera to capture specimens for later identification back at home.

5. **Take all litter home** That means everything, including apple cores and banana peels. Take pride in leaving the place exactly as you found it.

6. **Be careful with fire** Any unguarded naked flame, from matches, cigarettes and barbecues is capable of untold damage if the conditions are right. Forest or grassland fires can be disastrous for many lives both wild and human.

7. **Be careful on the roads** In the countryside the roads become narrower and more winding and therefore more dangerous. So be aware of this if you are walking or driving on them.

Right: Field of corn marigolds at West Pentire, near Newquay in north Cornwall. Poet Laurence Binyon was inspired to write For the Fallen *here in 1914.*

Part One

Landscape and Wildlife

Coasts

Our Coastal Heritage

Incredible as it may seem, you are never more than about 110km (70 miles) away from the coast in Britain, though it may not always feel that way in a queue of traffic on a sunny bank holiday. The village of Coton in the Elms, near Tamworth in south Derbyshire, takes the record for the greatest distance, located, as it is, 117km (73 miles) from the coast.

The coastline of mainland Britain stretches some 17,820km (11,073 miles); however, if you include the 1,000 or so islands dotted around our shores this figure almost doubles to 31,368km (19,491 miles). Thanks to this vast number of islands, the UK is among those countries with the longest coastline in Europe. It also contains a wide variety of landscapes and wildlife habitats, from the

towering 100m (328ft) chalk cliffs at Dover, through the salt marshes of Llanrhidian on the Gower Peninsula, to the magnificent sandy beach of Portstewart Strand in Northern Ireland.

The majority of Britain's islands – 790 of them – are located off the Scottish mainland, most within the Orkneys, Hebrides and Shetland Isles, accounting for almost two thirds of Scotland's coastline. The White Cliffs of Dover are the nearest point of Britain to the Continent, with only 34km (21 miles) separating the chalk cliffs at South Foreland from those at Cap Blanc Nez near Calais; about 20,000 years ago, before the formation of the English Channel, these two points were, in fact, joined by land.

Protecting the coast

Shaped by the deposition and erosion of rocks during the earth's history, our coastline is constantly shifting and changing due to the effects of tides, waves and weather. It can provide terrifying examples of the forces of nature, swinging from peaceful tranquillity to wild drama in a matter of minutes. We cannot tame the sea but, through careful management, coastal landowners can help to protect our coastline from the forces that threaten it.

Left: The ragged coastline of Lundy offers spectacular scenery and habitat, with inlets where seals pup, where seabirds nest and exposed rocks are rich in lichens and algae.

Right: Whitford Burrows, on the Gower Peninsular, consists of wind-blown sand over a sand bar. Farmed for its flora, it is a dynamic place that will always change radically.

Below: Classic lower salt marsh developing at Northey Island, with the lowered sea wall in the middle distance.

Since 1965, the National Trust's Neptune Coastline Campaign (originally called Enterprise Neptune) has been raising funds to acquire stretches of coastline, such as the iconic Rhossili Beach on the Gower Peninsula in Wales. The campaign has raised more than £45 million to help save some of the UK's most beautiful coastal locations, promoting access where possible and providing long-term protection from threats such as pollution, climate change, erosion and inappropriate development. Thanks to its success, the National Trust now owns and manages over 1130km (700 miles) of coast – almost 10 per cent of the total coastline of England, Wales and Northern Ireland.

Coastal climate

The UK lies on the same latitude as parts of northern Canada, yet our climate is much warmer. A contributory factor is the warm ocean currents of the North Atlantic Drift (an extension of the Gulf Stream that flows from the Florida Strait) which enfold the UK and keep average temperatures 10°C (18°F) higher than they would otherwise be at this latitude, resulting in mild winters and warm, moist summers. The North Atlantic Drift crosses the Atlantic and passes up the west coast of Britain, via southern Ireland, to western Scotland, enabling subtropical plants to grow in the Scilly Isles, Cornwall and southern Ireland, and palm trees to flourish on the west coast of Scotland. (In contrast to the same latitude in northern Canada, where the seas freeze over.)

Our climate is also affected by the fact that we are an island nation: because the sea warms up and cools down more slowly than the land, winters in the UK are kept relatively mild and summers relatively cool.

Glendurgan Garden

Cornwall's characteristic valley gardens, such as these at Glendurgan, near Falmouth (shown below), depend on the warm climate produced by the North Atlantic Drift. Lying in a sheltered coastal ravine, the gardens support exotic plants from all over the tropics, which flourish in a sub-tropical microclimate. However, climate change heralds new and diverse challenges: while a decline in frosts will benefit the established plants, and encourage earlier leafing and flowering to enable the garden to be open all year round, stormier weather, heavier rains and more frequent and intense drought will present problems. Worse, pests and diseases are increasing in such gardens, which require new biological control methods. New shelter belts are urgently needed. Moreover, plants that were formerly well-behaved may now become invasive, both within and outside the gardens.

Winds and Tides

Along with the effects of ocean currents and our island setting, the prevailing south-westerly winds that hit our shores have a major impact on the UK's climate. The winds pick up humidity crossing the Atlantic Ocean; when they reach higher ground on the south-west coast, the air rises and cools and the water carried by the winds falls as rain, which explains why the east coast tends to be drier than the warm and wet south-west. The winds also help to erode the geological profile of the coast. The famous White Cliffs of Dover, for example, depend on regular surface erosion, in the form of cliff slumping, for their sparkling whiteness. Without this, they would turn green with vegetation. Parts of the cliffs are protected from erosion by concrete sea defences and will change colour.

The wind will also create surface waves in the sea by steadily pushing on the water, causing it to rise and fall. While tides can be predicted with a reasonable degree of accuracy, the effect of the wind can alter the predicted height of the water. A classic example of the effects of high winds combined with high tides is the devastating storm surge of 1953, which battered the eastern coast of Britain. Reaching a height of 2.97m (nearly 10ft) at King's Lynn in Norfolk, the surge killed over 300 people, sweeping away coastal defences and promenades in its path, and flooding almost 100,000ha (250,000 acres) of land.

The tides

Tides are created by the gravitational pull of the moon and, to a lesser extent, the sun, acting on the earth's oceans. High and low tides occur alternately on the coast of the United Kingdom, approximately every 12 hours and 25 minutes – that is, two high tides every 24 hours and 50 minutes. Spring tides, when the tide reaches its maximum ebb, occur twice a month about two days after the full moon and two days after the new moon, when the gravitational pull of the moon and sun is combined. In contrast, neap tides, when the ebb and flow of the water is at its lowest (between the spring tides), occur during the first and last quarter of the moon. Tidal equinoxes – the highest and lowest tides of the year – occur around 21 September and 21 March, when the hours of daylight are more or less equal to those of darkness.

The tides are influenced by a number of complex factors, including ocean currents, centrifugal forces (created by the earth spinning on its axis), and the coastal landscape. When a tidal wave enters a shallow region of the coast, or a river estuary, its form becomes distorted. This can cause a more rapid flow and a slower ebb which can, in extreme cases, lead to a wall of water, or tidal bore, that moves rapidly up the estuary, such as occurs on the Severn and Trent rivers.

Above: The White Cliffs of Dover are important for seabirds, flowers and splash-zone algae. Without erosion, averaging at 50cm (20in) per year, they would become the Green Cliffs of Dover.

Right: Souter Lighthouse, near Sunderland, was the world's first lighthouse to use alternating electric current to warn shipping of the dangers of The Leas and the notorious currents nearby.

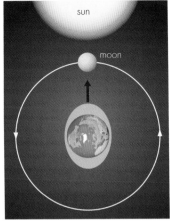
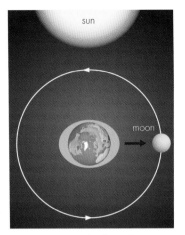

spring tides (highest)   neap tides (lowest)

Above: When the sun, moon and earth form a line at both the new moon and the full moon each month, the sun reinforces the tidal pull of the moon and high spring tides occur. When the sun and moon are at 90 degrees, viewed from the earth, the sun cancels the moon's gravitational pull and the tide range is at its lowest – a neap tide.

Right: A global first, SeaGen's 16m (52ft) rotors only run at certain times. Efforts are made to prevent seals and fish making contact with the blades.

Tidal power

Balancing our urgent needs for sustainable energy with conserving the unique importance of estuaries is extremely difficult. The energy produced by tidal movements is immense and could provide at least 20 per cent of Britain's energy needs. The National Trust and other environmental organisations are closely involved in the Severn Tidal Power Feasibility Study, examining options for generating electricity from the Severn's vast tidal range. Many of the options being considered are not financially or environmentally viable, given the high investment costs and the likely damage to marine habitats. In contrast, a scheme launched at Strangford Lough, Northern Ireland, in 2008, could prove a turning point in the search for a cost-effective and environmentally friendly way of harnessing the power of tides. The world's first commercial-scale tidal-stream turbine has been installed in the mouth of the lough, which has one of the fastest tidal flows in the world. Anchored in place via a single pile in the seabed, the generator, called SeaGen, is designed to produce 1.2mw of electricity – enough to power 1,000 homes. The obvious advantages of tidal power over wind power lie in the fact that, unlike the wind, tides are predictable, and the generators, if based upon the prototype used at Strangford Lough, may prove a lot less unsightly than wind-powered generators and have less impact on wildlife and marine habitats.

Life in the tidal zone

The height of the shoreline can vary between high and low tide by 10m (30ft) or more, creating an ever-changing environment that poses enormous challenges for wildlife. In order to survive, the plants and animals that inhabit the inter-tidal zone have had to adapt to the rhythm of the tides and the constant threat from pounding waves, dehydration, extremes of temperature, and predation. Many creatures, such as shellfish and worms, survive by burying themselves in the sand and mud – it may look like there is little life on a sandy beach, but dig down using a small spade or fork and you will reveal a wealth of wildlife just beneath the surface. Many of these burrowing animals are filter feeders, sifting small particles of food from the water when the tide is in. On rocky shores, rock pools act like natural aquariums where plants and animals can flourish when the tide is out (see page 26).

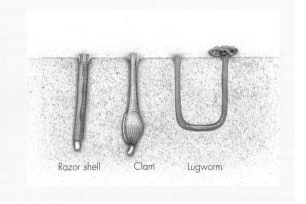

Razor shell   Clam   Lugworm

Shaping the Coastline

Pounded by the sea, battered by the winds, and at the mercy of frost, ice and coastal currents, our coastline is an immensely dynamic environment, constantly being shaped and reshaped by the forces that assail it. These powerful forces have helped to create many of Britain's distinctive coastal features, from sand bars, spits and mud flats, to arches, stacks and caves. They also threaten human communities, habitats and wildlife. The natural process of coastal erosion eats away at cliffs, causing the coastline to retreat – sometimes sweeping houses, even whole villages, into the sea – while the effects of climate change and rising sea levels could have more devastating effects in the future.

If climate change and global warming continue as expected, we could witness more frequent and more violent storms, and a sea level rise of 1m (3ft) by the year 2100, resulting in increased

Below: Newlyn harbour, Cornwall, in a Force 12 gale. Climate change modelling predicts a significant increase in storminess, at a time when sea level is likely to rise significantly.

flooding and coastal erosion and much less deposition around our shore. It is estimated, for example, that 70 per cent of Wales' coastline could be severely affected; among many precious sites, the stunning dunes of the Gower Peninsula could be threatened and the magnificent beaches of Marloes Sands in Pembrokeshire, along with many others, may simply disappear.

The National Trust, which manages one sixth of the Welsh coast, including these two sites, is seeking sustainable ways to address the future impact of erosion and sea level rise – both in Wales and elsewhere in the UK – favouring adaptation over interference, allowing time and space to adjust to changes in the coastline and work with the forces of nature.

Coastal erosion and accretion

Our coastline is hugely dynamic, with some stretches continually being worn away (erosion) and others built up (accretion). The patterns change throughout time. At sites with high cliffs, particularly those made of softer rocks such as chalk and

limestone, the relentless force of the wind, waves and water-born boulders crashing against the cliff face gradually erodes the rocks at the toe of the cliff, resulting in an overhang. Freeze-thaw, in which water in the rock freezes and expands, causing fragments of rock to break away, also contributes to the process of erosion. Eventually, the overhang collapses and crashes into the sea below. For a while, this

Above: Looking east along the Jurassic Coast World Heritage Site from the summit of Golden Cap, Charmouth, Dorset. The WHS designation is exclusively due to the outstanding geology and geomorphology (landform processes).

Left: A spectacle rock pinnacle along the long distance coastal path at Stackpole, Pembrokeshire. The Stackpole Estate is a National Nature Reserve, featuring not only coastal paths but also sandy beaches, ancient woodland and a tiny harbour.

Below: The natural limestone arch on the Jurassic coast at Durdle Door, near Lulworth, Dorset has been formed over centuries due to the erosion of rock around it. Eventually the overhang will collapse, leaving a pillar much like those at The Needles off the Isle of Wight.

Birling Gap

At Birling Gap in Seven Sisters, East Sussex (shown below), the chalk cliffs are eroding steadily and naturally, but the softer rocks of Birling Gap combe are eroding faster, through periodic section collapse. It would be impossible to hold back nature here: two cottages have already been demolished and the others are threatened, along with the hotel, although the National Trust continues to maintain access to the beach.

landslip provides some protection for the cliff until it, too, is washed away. The resulting sediment is transported farther down the coast by the currents and accretion occurs where it is deposited back on to the shore, for example, on beaches and salt marshes.

Over time, these processes have smoothed out soft-rocked coastlines and added thousands of hectares of land elsewhere. It has been estimated that around 15 million cubic metres (500 million cubic feet) of soil is cut away from the coast of England and Wales each year, although much of this is deposited back on to the shore again. At Selsey Bill, in Sussex, for instance, around 180m (200yd) of land has been lost in the last 20 years, and medieval Dunwich, once the second largest town in East Anglia, now lies under water, 1.5km (1 mile) off the Suffolk coast. Conversely, Smallhythe Place in Kent was originally called Port House and served a thriving shipyard, when parts of what is now Romney Marsh were under water. The house now lies

15km (over 9 miles) inland, stranded by a combination of natural accretion and land reclamation for agricultural use. Similarly, Rye in East Sussex, once a port almost surrounded by sea, now lies more than 3.5km (2 miles) from the coast.

Waves at work

Waves are a forward movement of energy, not water – the water droplets are moving in a circular motion as a wave passes. As the wave approaches the shore water builds up and breakers form, primarily at an angle to the shore, generating a longshore current. Waves travel in straight lines and their force travels at right angles to the line of the waves. Waves bend obliquely as they meet shallower water. They come on to the shore at an angle, carrying sand, mud and silt with them from further up the shore in a process known as longshore drift. Waves that carry and deposit sediment in this way are called 'constructive' waves. 'Destructive' waves tend to be larger and to break vertically on the beach; these waves drag material away from the beach and can cut away cliffs, causing landslides. The process of longshore drift then carries and deposits the debris further along the coast.

Breakwaters are often constructed to prevent the excessive drifting of material along a beach; sand and shingle piled up higher on one side of the breakwater than the other bear witness to the effects of these barriers. While breakwaters may protect one stretch of coast, they starve the shoreline further down the coast of any supply of sediment, resulting in erosion of the beach as material is washed away but not replaced. Similarly, hard defences built out of concrete or stone, designed to hold back the sea and protect the coastline from erosion, can also have a damaging knock-on effect further down the coast. East Head in Sussex, for example, is being starved of its essential supply of sand and shingle from the shoreline to the east, due to the hard defences protecting houses on the Manhood peninsula.

Above: Groynes at East Head on the West Sussex coast. Groynes attempt to slow erosion of the area in which they are placed but often only move sand and shingle from one area (erosion) to another location (deposition).

Right: The Leas, 5km (3 miles) of geologically important magnesian limestone cliffs on the edge of South Shields, Tyne and Wear, include remnants of fossilised desert sand dunes topped with layers of black bituminous mud.

Rocky Coasts

Steepled cliffs and rock-formed coastlines, shaped over millennia, offer us much of our most awesome, wonderful and varied scenery. Many of the cliffs and rocky islands that surround our coasts were shaped into their current form by direct glacial action during the last Ice Age, as the great ice sheets periodically advanced across much of the land, stretching as far south as London. As the glaciers advanced and retreated, they carved out many of the highs and lows of our landscape, both inland and along the shore. Some 10,000 years ago, temperatures started to get warmer and the last of the glaciers melted, causing sea levels to rise and flood the lower coastal land, isolating the higher ground as peninsulas or strings of islands.

Cliffs

Around 4,000km (2,500 miles) of UK coastline have been characterised as cliffs; they can be loosely classified as hard or soft, though in reality many lie in between, dependent on their geology. Cliffs may form where a 'fault' in the Earth's crust has allowed a section of rock to be pushed upwards, or where softer rocks have been eroded by the waves and weather. Hard cliffs are steeply sloping or vertical and are principally formed of rocks such as granite and basalt that are capable of withstanding the elements. Soft cliffs are formed of rocks such as sandstone, shale and limestone; they are vulnerable to erosion and prone to frequent landslips. The highest cliffs occur where Atlantic breakers eat into the hilly coastline – the tallest in the British Isles are the Cliffs of Moher in Northern Ireland, which are composed largely of shale and sandstone and tower up to 214m (702ft) above sea level.

Hard igneous rocks – such as the granite cliffs of Cape Cornwall or the gabbro of St David's Head in Pembrokeshire – erode very slowly and relinquish little ground, despite facing the full blast of the Atlantic. By contrast, the cliffs of soft chalk that make up the Seven Sisters in Sussex, or the softer clays of parts of the Yorkshire coast, erode rapidly, sometimes losing a metre or more of ground every year.

Sculpting the rocks

Soft cliffs made of sedimentary rocks are prone to crack under pressure and form fault lines. These are weak points at the mercy of the sea, which erodes the cliff to carve out caves. On promontories, caves on either side may be cut so deep that they join together, forming an arch; with further erosion, the arch collapses to form a stack – an isolated needle of rock that serves to indicate the original coastline. Britain's most iconic stacks are the Needles, on the Isle of Wight, which will ultimately be destroyed by the very forces that created them. Where areas of soft rock are sandwiched between hard rock, the soft rock will erode first, creating a bay with the hard rock forming headlands, jutting out into the sea on either side.

Above: Ancient metamorphic rocks at Pen Anglas, just west of Fishguard on the dramatic Pembrokeshire coast. As the name suggests, metamorphic rocks are rocks that have been changed by heat and intense pressure from an earlier type.

Above: Giant's Causeway is an example of igneous rock. The 40,000 or so reddish-black hexagonal basalt columns were produced by the sudden cooling and solidification of volcanic lava. The Causeway itself is quite small but surrounded by towering cliffs.

Above: Burton Bradstock cliffs along the Dorset coast consist of sands left over from an ancient delta, capped by weak limestone. These are sedimentary rocks – those formed on ancient sea beds, deserts, lakes and deltas.

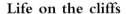

Life on the cliffs

Coastal cliffs provide important habitats for wildlife, especially for nesting birds and specialised plants that can survive the harsh conditions. Many cliffs, such as the White Cliffs of Dover, are designated Special Sites of Scientific Interest (SSSIs) due to their rare flora and fauna – the National Trust and other conservation organisations strive to preserve these precious habitats by protecting cliffs from damaging and unsightly coastal development. Cliff faces that are exposed to the prevailing winds dry out quickly in summer and become drenched with salt spray during winter gales. There is little soil, except where pockets have accumulated on ledges and in crevices. Only low-growing plants with deep roots and thick, glossy leaves that withstand the drying effects of the wind – such as rock samphire, thrift and scurvy grass (a member of the cabbage family) – are found here.

On the cliff tops, depending on the type of soil, plants such as red fescue and Yorkshire fog may form patches of springy turf. Flowers such as thrift, sea campion, roseroot, stonecrop and rock samphire carpet the ground in spring and summer, attracting a wealth of insects including grasshoppers, beetles, butterflies and moths. The larger, less steep stretches of cliff slope have a history of grazing, as suggested by old field system walls. Traditionally, grazing occurred during periods of high population pressure, war or agricultural profitability, punctuated by eras of neglect. These old grasslands are biologically very rich, but the wildlife interest depends on regular cutting and grazing, or thuggish vegetation such as bracken and scrub takes over. Grazing must be carried out by animals well adapted to the conditions, not least to ensure good standards of animal welfare.

Birds of rocky coasts

It is difficult to imagine cliffs without seabirds, and a nesting cliff in the height of the breeding season is one of the most exciting wildlife spectacles that Britain has to offer. Relatively few stretches of coast in England, Wales and Northern Ireland support large numbers of breeding seabirds, but where cliffs offer the right combination of protection from predators, rocky ledges and access to a good food supply, then the crush can be extraordinary.

Above: Yellow lichens and pink sea thrift encrusting rocks above the splash zone at Stackpole Head, Pembrokeshire.

Left: Jointed limestone with a large sea cave at Stackpole, Pembrokeshire. These sea caves are important roosting sites for bats.

Guillemots and razorbills lay their eggs on bare rock, always choosing ledges on the most precipitous cliffs. They arrive at their nesting site from late winter onwards and, as the available space is gradually used up, the colony becomes busier and noisier by the day. Cliff ledges are also used by the kittiwake, one of seven species of gull that breed around our coast. The kittiwake breeds in colonies, and gets its name from its piercing 'kitti-week' call, which in volume is more than a match for its noisy neighbours.

The short turf of cliff tops provides a nesting site for the colourful puffin which, like the guillemot, spends much of the year far out to sea, coming ashore for a short period to breed. Because these birds nest in burrows on slopes near the cliff tops, rather than on inaccessible ledges, their eggs and young are more at risk from predators such as foxes. Research found that a catastrophic plummet in the

Right: Puffins visit the United Kingdom to breed in spring and summer, nesting in old rabbit burrows.

numbers of puffins and Manx shearwaters on the island of Lundy, in the Bristol Channel, was due to severe predation by up to 10,000 black rats – itself a rare species in today's British Isles. The National Trust, RSPB and other conservation organisations established the Seabird Recovery Project, which has eradicated the rats and saved seabird populations.

Rocky shores

Rhythmically washed by the waves, rocky shores vary from wide, almost flat pavements of rock slabs stretching out into the shallows, to tumbledown jumbles of boulders, hollows, jagged edges and rounded humps. The latter, in particular, support a wealth of wildlife, particularly where rock pools form. Here, stealthy shrimps stalk for food, tiny fish dart in the shadows, and brightly coloured sea anemones wave their stinging tentacles over rocks that are thinly coated with sheets of algae. Sea anemones use their tentacles to trap

Below: An ecosystem in its own right, the rock pool holds a multitude of creatures and plants from different species of small fish and crabs to rock-hugging barnacles and limpets, among others, though the less tenacious are redistributed with every tide. Most are highly vulnerable to marine pollutions, 80 per cent of which emanates from the land.

Edible crab

Mussels

Fifteen-spined stickleback

Sea lettuce

Common starfish

Goby

Shanny

Butterfly blenny

Hermit crab

Sea oak

Spiny starfish

Beadlet anemone

Periwinkle

Shore crab

Limpets

Common prawn

Watch for Wildlife

Seaweeds, a form of algae, are widespread on rocky shores, where the rocks provide firm anchorage. Species of seaweed and other wildlife occupy different zones on the shore, depending on how tolerant they are to various factors such as periodic desiccation and dramatic temperature change, caused by the ebb and flow of the tide. Look out for different coloured horizontal bands of seaweed across the shore – these are indications of the different zones. The upper shore is home to **spiral wrack** and **channelled wrack**, as well as **barnacles**. Lower down, on the middle shore, **knotted wrack** and **bladder wrack** may be found, along with **dog whelks** and rough **periwinkles**, with **barnacles** jostling for space among the **limpets**. The lower zone supports the richest life, being the most constantly washed by the waves – here, **oarweed** forms dense beds and creatures such as **sea anemones** and **starfish** abound in rock pools.

Bladder wrack

Starfish

and kill their prey. When they are left out of the water by the falling tide, they withdraw their tentacles into the centre of their bodies, turning into miniature, jelly-like volcanoes.

Elsewhere, the rocks may be covered in winkles, barnacles and limpets. The limpet's conical shell, along with the similarly shaped shell of the barnacle, is able to resist the pressure of the largest waves. The shell of the limpet has an irregular edge that fits precisely into the depression in the rock that is the limpet's home. When covered by the tide, a limpet moves around over fairly large distances, scraping algae off the rock. As soon as the tide begins to fall, it returns to its home, locking itself against the rock if touched. By contrast, barnacles are permanently cemented to the rock. They feed on minute animals that they catch by waving their long, feathery arms in the water.

Rocky platforms

The sea is at its most destructive where large waves dash against the cliff, carrying boulders and pebbles in the swash, which further help to break down the rock face. After a long time the cliffs become eroded to form a low expanse of flat rock called a wave-cut platform, which is usually exposed at low tide. One of the best examples of this feature is to be found in Robin Hood's Bay, in North Yorkshire, where the sedimentary rock has eroded layer by layer.

Beaches

Beaches are landforms created by the action of waves and currents depositing material – whether sand, shingle or pebbles – on to the shore. They are composed of particles of rock, formed by cliff erosion and ceaseless waves slowly grinding boulders into pebbles and sand, and may also contain fragments of shell and coralline algae. A beach is constantly shifting through the year as tides and storms bring seasonal changes to the landscape. Heavy storms can carry sand away from the beach, uncovering rocks or shingle, while smaller summer waves redistribute the sand, lifting it up and depositing it back on the beach further along the shore in a process called longshore drift (see page 22).

The steepness of a beach is determined by the beach's composition, the hardness of the underlying rock, and the volume of water coming on to the shore. Waves coming on to an exposed sandy shore on the edge of an open sea or ocean tend to be large and powerful, pushing huge amounts of water up on to the beach, of which only a small proportion can soak away into the sand. As the waves recede, the backwash carries sand particles held in suspension away from the beach into the shallows, creating a gently sloping shore. As the beach extends seawards and its slope declines, the waves begin to break further and further out at low tide, eventually forming a broad sandy beach that is ideal for surfing.

Below: Rhossili Bay on the Gower Peninsula, South Wales, showing a classic storm beach backed by an extensive terrace of soft deposits that have been washed down from the hill over time.

Left: The long stretch of unspoilt sandy beach at Formby, in Lancashire, periodically reveals its hidden secret. Patches of prehistoric mud, sand-baked by the sun 5,000 years ago, are fleetingly exposed by the ebb and flow of the tide, unveiling the footprints of mammals, birds and humans who roamed the shores during the Bronze Age. Evidence of red deer, wild boar, oyster catchers and children have all been revealed, only to be destroyed within a few hours by the incoming tide.

Waves coming on to shores edging more enclosed seas are smaller and less powerful. This means more water drains away; as it does so it deposits its sandy load and the beach consequently becomes steeper. The composition of the beach also has an impact on the beach's gradient as this determines how much water drains away. Shingle beaches allow more water to drain away and so tend to be steeper, whereas sandy beaches have poorer drainage and so slope more gently.

Clean waters

Around 50 per cent of the UK's biodiversity is found in the sea, and keeping our seawater clean is essential for conserving wildlife and maintaining a healthy marine environment. Clean water for bathing and watersports is also vitally important for tourism. Over recent years, water quality has been improving as less untreated sewage is sent out to sea. The Marine Conservation Society's Good Beach Guide, which records and reports on seawater quality, has done much to improve standards and the number of beaches recommended for bathing has quadrupled since records started in 1987.

Above: Shingle ridge at Orford Ness in Suffolk. Coastal erosion here is so rapid that the lighthouse is under very real threat of demolition by the sea.

Legislation has helped to reduce water pollution over the last few decades, but much remains to be done. Pollution from agricultural run-off, untreated sewage and other hazardous substances that have drained into rivers and then to the sea, damages aquatic ecosytems and can make swimming off the coast rather unpleasant. Improving water quality at source will help lessen damage and the impact of climate change. Our demand for water has a huge effect on the coast; turning on a tap or flushing a toilet starts the flow of waste water through the sewers and treatment plants to the sea.

Beaches are rich in wildlife, although it may not appear so at first. Vast numbers of bivalve molluscs, such as **razorshells**, **cockles** and **clams**, and marine worms such as **ragworms**, **lugworms** and **fan worms**, lie hidden from view, buried in the damp sand to avoid desiccation at low tide. Look out for telltale signs that give away their presence. Curly worm casts, for example, indicate the presence of **lugworms**. The casts are made of excavated sand or mud, formed as the worm digs out its U-shaped burrow. Jets of water squirted into the air indicate bivalve molluscs, which swiftly pull their trunk-like siphons back into their shells as you approach, ejecting any water from inside.

Cockles

Empty seashells are a further indication of life beneath the waves or under the sand – shells to look out for include those of **thin tellin**, **striped Venus**, common **necklace shell**, **great scallop**, **common whelk** and **razorshell**. **Mermaid's purses** can often be found along the shoreline after a storm. These are the egg cases of **certain fish**: the brown rectangles with long curly tendrils belong to the **dogfish**, while the smaller black rectangles are the empty egg cases of **rays** and **skates**. Birds are abundant, attracted by the rich pickings to be found beneath the waves or buried in the sand. A variety of gulls, plus numerous waders such as **dunlins**, **knots**, **lapwings**, **curlews**, **redshanks**, **ringed plovers** and **oystercatchers** gather along the shoreline to feed, while **terns** can be seen hovering over the sea, ready to dive down and snatch fish out of the water. The constantly shifting sand and shingle make it difficult for plants to take root. Only specialised species with deep roots and resistance to salt spray, such as **sea holly** with its striking blue flowers, can successfully inhabit beaches.

Tern

Dunes

Sand dunes are the fastest changing of all coastal habitats. They tend to form on exposed shores with regular onshore winds (blowing from sea to land), where the waves, tides and currents bring a regular influx of sandy sediments. When sand dries on an exposed, windy beach, it may be whipped up by the onshore winds and driven inland across the surface, coming to rest where obstacles such as pebbles, bits of wood, even old shoes block its path. As the sand piles up around these obstacles, it forms mounds, which may become colonised by pioneer plants such as sand couch grass and lyme grass, along with other salt-tolerant flowers including sea sandwort and sea rocket.

Below: Beaches and dunes are constantly shifting and eroding due to natural processes, though these are set to become more extreme as a result of climate change. The sands at Formby, Lancashire, may recede by over 400m (1,300ft) within the next 100 years. The National Trust, which owns the site, recognises this as a natural process and aims to let the dunes move back naturally, rerouting the coastal path and moving the car park as necessary.

These early, or embryo, dunes grow to about 2m (6ft) and are the first stage in the formation of a mature dune system; they are fragile and constantly shifting, migrating inland at the mercy of strong winds, and sometimes being washed away by the tide. Conditions are harsh for the plants that live here – they have to endure salt spray, drying winds, extremes of temperature and immersion in sand; those species that do survive, however, help to trap the wind, increasing the rate at which sand collects. Furthermore, sand couch grass has an extensive root system that is highly effective in binding the sand and stabilising the dunes. Well-developed embryo dunes are, however, an increasingly rare sight today as coasts become starved of new sand deposits.

As the embryo dunes merge and grow beyond the reach of the highest spring tide, plant succession occurs. The pioneer plants die out, no longer able to reach the water table, and marram grass becomes the dominant species, safe from inundation and stimulated by burial in the sand. The marram encourages substantial accretion

(build-up) of sand, which, in turn, stimulates plant growth, and its extensive root system and underground stems bind the sand and stabilise the dunes as they continue to grow. The marram grass also adds much-needed nutrients and organic matter to the environment. Such marram-dominated dunes are known as fore dunes, or yellow dunes (named after their large expanse of bare sand) and they form the most widespread dune community around Britain's coast.

Dunes in old age

As the dunes grow taller – reaching up to 30m (100ft) in some cases – and the ground becomes more stable, the vegetation again changes. Sheltered from strong winds, richer in nutrients and organic matter, and with better water retention than younger dunes, these old, or grey, dunes support a wide range of plants and animals. Marram grass, starved of a new supply of sand, gives way to red fescue, bloody crane's-bill, viper's bugloss and common centuary, and mosses such as screw moss and lichens fill in the gaps between the higher plants (the latter giving the dunes their grey colour). Where leaching turns the sand acidic, heathers, gorse and bracken may dominate, and the dunes may eventually be lost to pine woodland.

The valley between and behind the dunes, and the dry land beyond, is called the slack – here, underlying deposits or groundwater may be exposed, and nutrients leached from the surrounding dunes may accumulate, making the area rich in plant and animal life.

Above: Coastal heath at Dunwich on the Suffolk coast. Specialist invertebrates abound, dependent on both the vegetation and the bare sand. The soft acidic sand cliffs are, of course, being eroded rapidly.

Left: Sea bindweed growing in bare sand, like a pale pink version of the closely related morning glory. This is quite a local plant, of shingle and sand dunes.

A tendency to be waterlogged encourages marsh plants such as yellow irises, reads and rushes to grow in the slack, and certain species of snail and spider, along with the rare natterjack toad, may be found taking advantage of the damper environment.

Conserving dunes

Attitudes to the conservation of sand dunes have changed in recent years. In the 1970s the trend was to try to prevent dune erosion and encourage sand accumulation by building boardwalks, which improved public access while acting as a sand barrier. Today, however, it is acknowledged that a healthy dune system is by its very nature mobile. Path systems may still be used to ease movement through a dune, but are no longer designed to prevent natural erosion.

To maintain biodiversity and prevent woodland taking over, the correct level of animal grazing is key to retaining the balance of a stable dune – over-grazing can lead to erosion whereas under-grazing can allow scrub to develop. Selecting the correct animal and breed to manage and protect the balance of the dunes is therefore essential.

A living larder

Few animals live on the open, shifting sand of dunes. But where plants hold the sand together, plant-eating and predatory insects such as grasshoppers, crickets and ground beetles are common. It is here that the sand wasp nests, excavating its shallow burrow in which to house its eggs. Before laying its eggs, the parent wasp stocks its nest with a paralysed caterpillar, thus providing its larvae with a ready store of fresh food.

Sand wasp

Saltmarshes and Mudflats

Saltmarshes are a type of coastal wetland, found in sheltered bays and especially estuaries where they mark a transitional area between the sea's saltwater and the dry land. A saltmarsh occurs where tidal and wave actions are gentle, and where fine sediments – mainly sands and silts – are continually brought in by the tides and currents. The sediments accumulate over centuries, first forming a mudflat, but as the process continues the surface of the deposits rises so that only the highest tides cover it. Where the muddy surface is exposed to the air, between high and low tide, plants gradually gain a foothold and almost imperceptibly the mudflat becomes a marsh, populated with clumps of greenery.

At the same time, in an estuary, the river brings fine sediments picked up during its inland journey. As the river waters trickle out on to the flat marsh they lose speed and deposit their sediments, adding to those coming in from the sea. However, in times of flood, especially in winter, the river's rise in level and surging flow may wash away some of these sediments. Similarly, a combination of high tides and powerful waves whipped up by high winds can have a destructive effect. As a result, a saltmarsh is an ever-changing mosaic of pools, creeks, channels and low mounds, formed and destroyed by both sea and river, where plants alternately thrive and are then swept away.

The twice-daily tidal surge brings a regular supply of sediments and nutrients into the salt-marsh system, supplemented by the periodic river flooding, resulting in a biologically rich habitat. The higher inland parts of saltmarshes form rich grazing land, renowned for producing tasty lamb, though much has been claimed for intensive agriculture.

Wildlife of saltmarshes

Salt-tolerant or halophytic plants (those that can withstand total or partial immersion in saltwater) are the first pioneer species to indicate that a saltmarsh is developing. Seaweeds such as *Enteromorpha* or hollow green weed appear first, followed by eelgrass (the only flowering plant to grow in the sea), glasswort and cord grass, which gradually raise the surface of the marsh and help with stabilisation and sediment deposition. Other plants gaining a roothold are sea lavender, sea aster and sea purslane.

The salt-tolerant plants attract worms, shellfish, fish, crabs and shrimps, which in turn draw wading birds. First seen in the UK as recently as 1989, the little egret is found in saltmarshes and estuaries in increasing numbers on the south and east coasts. The bar-tailed godwit is a winter visitor from the far north, as is the black-tailed godwit, although some pairs of the latter are resident and breed during summer. At high tide throughout the year, waders such as dunlin, redshanks and curlews that have been feeding on mudflats may use the saltmarsh to rest and preen.

Saltmarsh is a very rich habitat for wildlife, yet it is inconstant and ever-changing. Much of our saltmarsh, especially along the East Anglian coastline, is being eroded away, trapped in front of a sea wall protecting land claimed for agriculture. Saltmarsh inland of a sea wall is likely to dry out and lose its character.

Above: Since 1989 the little egret has become a familiar sight along the edges of southern estuaries, a beneficiary of milder winters.

Left: Tidal saltmarsh in Chichester Harbour, West Sussex, where gently moving seawater deposits fine sediments, leading to the gradual development of further vegetation.

Mudflats

Mudflats, like saltmarshes with which they are often associated, are generally found in sheltered areas such as bays and particularly estuaries. They form where muddy sediments such as silts and clays deposit in relatively calm waters, but where the action of tides, waves and currents is too vigorous to allow the surface of the sediment to rise high enough for plant colonisation and saltmarsh formation. As a result, mudflats are largely devoid of vegetation.

The muddy sediments have a high organic content that is washed in from the sea by tides and currents, and from rivers. The tiny edible particles provide food for worms such as lugworms and ragworms, also shrimps, prawns, crabs and sand hopper-like amphipods such as the mud shrimp, plus many kinds of shellfish including cockles, tellies and spireshells. On some mudflats shellfish live at incredible densities – a hundred or more within the area of a footprint. In turn, these detritus-feeders support predatory animals, such as sea bass, flatfish and other fish that come in with the tide. The mudflats also provide feeding and resting areas for internationally important populations of migrant and wintering waders and waterfowl.

Mudflats are widespread in the UK with significant examples in the Wash, the Solway Firth, the Mersey Estuary, Bridgwater Bay and Strangford Lough. Some of our best-known mudflats are found at Morecambe Bay in Lancashire, where the fast-moving tides are said to come in as fast as 'a good horse'. Like saltmarshes, mudflats are important in helping to prevent coastal erosion as their long, low, imperceptibly sloping profile causes waves to lose energy gradually and peter out before reaching dry land. However, they are under threat from rising sea levels, pollution, dredging for shipping and land claim for urban development and agriculture (although

Hot mud

As part of its drive to reduce its carbon footprint, and incorporate the latest renewable energy technology into its properties, the National Trust has made an interesting use of the surrounding mudflats at its Brancaster Millennium Activity Centre in Norfolk. The Trust has installed a ground-source heat pump linked to 1km (nearly two-thirds of a mile) of plastic piping unobtrusively buried under the mudflats (which are a natural store of geothermal energy). In a process similar to a refrigerator in reverse, this system transfers heat from the mud to supply underfloor heating to the building.

Left: Mudflats lie under shallow seas where water movement is too strong for saltmarsh formation. Being rich in nutrients and specialist invertebrates, they are major feeding grounds for coastal birds. Indeed, our mudflats attract birds from all over Europe.

land claim has slowed considerably in recent years) – even fishing and bait digging can have an adverse impact. To help protect them, mudflats have been made a priority habitat under the government's UK Biodiversity Action Plan, which aims to conserve Britain's precious biodiversity. The aim is to create and restore enough inter-tidal areas over the next 50 years to offset predicted losses due to rising sea levels.

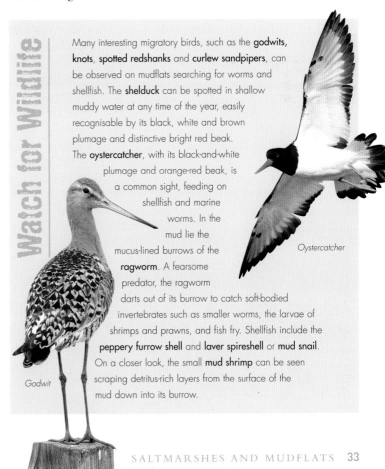

Watch for Wildlife

Many interesting migratory birds, such as the **godwits**, **knots**, **spotted redshanks** and **curlew sandpipers**, can be observed on mudflats searching for worms and shellfish. The **shelduck** can be spotted in shallow muddy water at any time of the year, easily recognisable by its black, white and brown plumage and distinctive bright red beak. The **oystercatcher**, with its black-and-white plumage and orange-red beak, is a common sight, feeding on shellfish and marine worms. In the mud lie the mucus-lined burrows of the **ragworm**. A fearsome predator, the ragworm darts out of its burrow to catch soft-bodied invertebrates such as smaller worms, the larvae of shrimps and prawns, and fish fry. Shellfish include the **peppery furrow shell** and **laver spireshell** or **mud snail**. On a closer look, the small **mud shrimp** can be seen scraping detritus-rich layers from the surface of the mud down into its burrow.

Oystercatcher

Godwit

Coastal Wildlife

The different faces of our coast – cliffs, islands, sand dunes – are the result of geology, weather conditions and exposure to the ever-pounding sea. Coastal wildlife has adapted to this challenging environment. Salt water and shifting habitats make survival difficult for plants, but there are fascinating flowers and seaweeds to be found. Many birds that spend the year at sea migrate to our shores to breed. Rock pools offer a tantalising glimpse of life beneath the sea, and the tides reveal the marine life that can be seen at different times of the day.

Sea kale

Plants

Yellow-horned poppy
(Glaucium flavum)
This is a beautiful seaside plant with the classic papery four-petalled, yellow flowers and grey foliage. The leaves and stems are sturdier than the field poppy to better withstand sea breezes. The flower lasts for just one day then ripens into a curved seedpod with a horned tip. The pods can be up to 30cm (12in) in length and are the longest of any British plant. This poppy grows on shingle banks around the coast, but is not commonly seen.

Wild cabbage
(Brassica oleracea)
The wild cabbage is the ancestor of modern cultivated vegetables such as cabbages, kale and cauliflower. It has rosettes of deeply lobed, grey-green leaves that, unlike cultivated cabbage, do not form a heart, and throws up tall spikes of yellow flowers. The plant is found on cliffs on the south-east coast, and in Yorkshire and Wales.

Sea kale
(Crambe maritima)
Sea kale is a cabbage-like plant that mostly grows on shingle beaches above the high-tide mark. The silvery blue leaves, which grow up to 30cm (12in) long, are thick and waxy with wavy edges, and the small white flowers are borne in flat-topped clusters from June to August. The seeds form in globular pods.

Below: Yellow-horned poppy forms impressive local colonies on shingle. The leaf rosettes can be seen year round and the flowers from May to October.

Sea sandwort
(Honckenya peploides)

This is a discreet, low-sprawling plant with fleshy stems and clusters of yellow-green leaves that forms a dense mat on sand dunes, shingle and sandy beaches. It bears tiny white flowers from May to August, which ripen into pea-like yellowish green fruits. Sea sandwort, although rather unobtrusive, plays an important role in the stabilisation of sand dunes.

Hottentot fig
(Carpobrotus edulis)

Also known as *Mesembryanthemum*, this plant originates from South Africa but has naturalised along the warm south coast of Britain where it grows on rocky cliffs and dunes. It has fleshy leaves that are triangular in section, and bears yellow or pink daisy-like flowers from May to August. This alien plant is highly invasive and a great threat to native cliff flora, and so conservation organizations keep it under strict control wherever it is accessible.

Sea rocket
(Cakile maritima)

Sea rocket is a low-sprawling plant that can be found growing above the high-tide line on sandy and shingle beaches, along with all kinds of flotsam and jetsam. It has fleshy, deep-lobed leaves and clusters of pink, white or lilac flowers borne at the end of the stems from June to August.

Scurvy grass
(Cochlearia officinalis)

A salt-tolerant plant able to survive where many others cannot, scurvy grass is found in salt marshes and on cliff ledges. It is not a grass but a flowering plant related to wild cabbage, with heart-shaped, fleshy green leaves that form dense mats, topped with four-petalled white flowers on the tips of short spikes. The leaves are rich in vitamin C and were once used by sailors suffering from scurvy to treat their vitamin deficiency, hence the name.

Sea campion
(Silene uniflora)

Sea campion can be found on shingle, stony beaches and on cliff tops around the coastline. It is a low-growing, cushion-forming plant with fleshy oval leaves. The white flowers, which appear between June and August, are borne on delicate upright stems and the calyx is swollen to form a distinctive pink-veined bladder at the base of the petals.

Above: Fragrant sea campion attracts bees and night-flying moths, seen here growing on a shingle beach at Abbotsbury, Dorset.

Right: Sea sandwort is one of the pioneer plants that trap sand and contribute to dune formation.

Salt toleration

Most flowering plants will die if exposed to salt water for even short periods of time, but there are a few species, such as glasswort, sea sandwort and sea kale, that actually thrive in habitats with a high salt content. Known as halophytes, these plants may be found in salt marshes, where they tolerate the saline soils and occasional inundation by seawater, and along the high-tide mark on sandy or shingle beaches, where they are periodically drenched by salt spray.

Sea beet
(Beta vulgaris subsp. *maritima)*
Sea beet is a common perennial that bears a resemblance to its close relative spinach, but with larger, tougher, shinier leaves. It has insignificant clusters of green flowers that are borne on tall spikes from May to August.

Sea purslane
(Atriplex portulacoides)
Sea purslane grows in low spreading mats at the edges of salt marshes and along the high-tide mark around the coast, especially in southern England and western Scotland. It has grey stems and paddle-shaped, succulent, silvery green leaves. The flower buds are pink and spikes of insignificant yellow flowers appear from July to October.

Glasswort or marsh samphire
(Salicornia agg.)
Also known as marsh samphire, glasswort is a succulent plant that handles partial submersion in seawater and grows in salt marshes and mud around the south and east coast. It forms tussocks of fleshy, short-jointed stems up to 30cm (12in)

Above: Glasswort, also known by the common name marsh samphire, is seen here growing on the tidal saltmarsh at Morston Harbour in Norfolk.

Left: Tree mallow, commonly found in the south and west, is creeping towards more northerly locations as temperatures rise. Its invasion of Craigleith Island in Scotland has halved the puffin population.

tall and has tiny inconspicuous flowers that appear from August to October. The ashes of this plant are rich in sodium carbonate, or soda, and were once widely used in the production of glass – hence the plant's common name, glasswort.

Tree mallow
(Lavatera arborea)
This tall, imposing plant has stiff stems that reach up to 1.2m (4ft) tall. The stems bear thick, hairy leaves and form spikes of dark-veined purple-pink flowers that bloom from June to September. Tree mallow is found in localised spots around Britain, mainly on the south and west coast, and around the shores of Ireland. A steep decline in puffin numbers on the island of Craigleith, off the east coast of Scotland, has been traced to an invasion of tree mallow, which grows in the manure-rich entrances to the puffins' burrows and prevents the birds from breeding.

Sea holly
(Eryngium maritimum)
Sea holly is a distinctive coastal perennial that grows 20–60cm (8–24in) tall on sand

and shingle beaches all around the UK, although it is no longer as common as it once was. The spiny, holly-like leaves are a pale grey-blue in colour and in July and August the thistle-like flower heads appear, surrounded by a whorl of brilliant blue leaf bracts. In Tudor times the roots were believed to be an aphrodisiac and in the 17th and 18th centuries they were candied and used to make sweets.

Rock samphire
(Crithmum maritimum)

Rock samphire is a bushy succulent plant that grows on cliffs, rocks and shingle on southern and western coastlines. It has branching tubular stems with narrow, fleshy leaves that are triangular in cross section, and umbels of yellow-green fennel-like flowers that bloom from June to August. Rock samphire was once

Above: Sea holly has intricate and extraordinary flowers that resemble blue snowflakes. Excess salt is secreted through their leaves and removed by wind and rain.

hugely popular as a pickle and, in King Lear, Shakespeare makes reference to the perilous practice of sending children down cliffs to collect it: 'Halfway down, hangs one that gathers samphire; dreadful trade!'

Wild carrot
(Daucus carota)

The root of the wild carrot is a very pale orange and is the ancestor of the cultivated carrot. It is common seaside plant, sending up white, domed flower heads on tall, hairy stems on chalky and sandy soil. The flowers and foliage bear some resemblance to cow parsley but are less delicate and lacy.

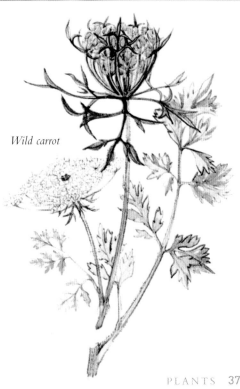

Wild carrot

Thrift
(Armeria maritima)

This lovely plant forms dense carpets of green, topped by a haze of pink, which drapes over cliff tops and rocky ledges. The grassy, narrow leaves grow in clumps, about 15cm (6in) tall, above which the globular pink flower heads rise on slender stems from April to July. Thrift is common on grassy cliffs around the UK coastline and is sometimes found in salt marshes.

Sea bindweed
(Calystegia soldanella)

This creeping perennial sends out stems up to 60cm (2ft) long, bearing long-stalked, kidney-shaped leaves and funnel-shaped, pink and white striped flowers that bloom from June to August. It grows on sand dunes around much of the coast, its stems often buried in the sand and its fleshy roots helping to stabilise the dunes; occasionally it can also be found on stabilised shingle.

Sea aster
(Aster tripolium)

The sea aster is a close relative of the Michelmas daisy that bears similar

Above: Sea aster is a salt-tolerant perennial found in salt marshes and on rocky cliffs. It is a source of nectar for late butterflies.

Right: Close view of a fine display of pink thrift on the cliffs and boulders of Wembury Bay on the Yeam Estuary, east of Plymouth. The bay is sheltered by the headland of Heybrook.

Below: Sea bindweed does not have tendrils like other forms of bindweed. Stems are often buried in the sand or shingle, as here on coastal dunes in Norfolk.

clusters of multi-petalled, daisy-like lilac flowers with yellow centres from July to October. The plant ranges in height from 15–45cm (6–18in) and has fleshy foliage that forms mats from which the flower spikes emerge.

Eelgrass
(Zostera marina)

Eelgrass, despite its name, is not a grass. Rather, it is the only flowering plant to grow in the sea, thriving on muddy and sandy shores, usually below the low-tide mark. It has long, ribbon-like leaves that grow up to 1m (3ft) long, and is an early coloniser in the development of salt marshes, helping to trap mud and silt and so accelerate the build-up of deposits. Eelgrass is the favourite food of the Brent goose, which winters in Britain and Ireland.

Marram grass
(Ammophila arenaria)

Marram grass is one of the first plants to colonise accreting (growing) sand dunes and can be seen all around the UK coastline. It is defined as a xerophyte – a plant that can withstand arid conditions. It produces tussocks of rigid, in-rolled spiky leaves from 60–120cm (2–4ft) long and forms dense networks of fibrous roots, which help to stabilise the sand dunes. The typically white grassy flower heads appear between June and August.

Seaweeds

There are around 800 species of seaweed in the United Kingdom. They do not produce flowers or embryos and are without true roots. There are four main groups: green seaweeds, the ancestors of green land plants that are found on the shoreline, often in rock pools; red seaweeds that grow in shallow water; brown seaweeds, the most common, that are found in deeper water; and the rare blue-green species. Colours within the groupings are variable. Brown species can appear olive green and decaying seaweed turns orange, which can be confusing. All seaweeds bleach to white when they are dead.

Seaweeds have a stalk that is attached firmly to the rock by means of a holdfast. The thallus has jelly-like cell walls, which give protection against the waves. On either side of the mid-rib are small air bladders that increase buoyancy and bring parts of the plant nearer to the surface of the water and light, sufficient to drive photosynthesis. The fronds of the seaweed release eggs and sperm into the sea for fertilisation. Each plant will produce millions of eggs, though only a few will germinate. Seaweeds also reproduce by the vegetative process of spore formation. Some drape over rocks, providing shade and protection for delicate shore animals, others can be found in rock pools. Seaweed must be able to locate secure footholds if it is to flourish, which is why so little is found on mobile shingle beaches. If you are collecting seaweed to eat remember that it takes its food from the water around it, so only gather seaweed when you know that it

is in clean and unpolluted water and rinse thoroughly before use.

Green seaweed

Sea lettuce
(Ulva lactuca)
The sea lettuce resembles its namesake, and can be found on rocks in sheltered bays, in rock pools on the upper and middle shores and on mudflats.

Gutweed
(Enteromorpha intestinalis)
The fronds of gutweed are long, green tubes that do resemble intestines as its Latin name suggests. It is found in sheltered estuaries and rock pools high on the shore.

Red seaweed

Purple laver
(Porphyra umbilicalis)
Commonly found from autumn to spring on the upper or middle shore, purple laver is used to make laver bread in Wales, and can be chopped up small and added to salads. In Japan it is known as 'nori'. It has broad, leafy, dark red fronds that look like wet tissue paper.

False Irish moss
(Mastocarpus stellatus)
Reddish-brown to purple in colour and comprising channelled fronds that widen from a narrow stem or stipe. False Irish moss was used during the Second World War as an emulsifying agent in place of agar, which was usually imported from Japan.

Below: The bright green ruffle-edged leaves of sea lettuce are rich in protein, minerals and vitamins, especially iron. Sea lettuce can thrive in moderate levels of nutrient pollution; it is therefore regarded as an indicator species.

Coral weed
(Corallina officinalis)
Coral weed has delicate, upright fronds that are made up of fine segments, giving a feather-like appearance. Ranging in colour from pale pink to purple, it is characteristic of rock pools on the middle to lower shore.

Dulse
(Palmaria palmate)
Dulse fronds are dark red to red-brown with divided tips, they are 50–80cm (20–30in) long, and project from a holdfast on rocks or other species of seaweed. Dulse can be eaten raw.

Carrageen
(Chondrus crispus)
A small, purple-red seaweed that turns a yellow green when exposed to strong sunlight. It has short, narrow to broad fronds and can be found on rocky shores and in pools. It has been used to gel blancmange.

Brown seaweed

Channel wrack
(Pelvetia canaliculata)
Found at the top of the shoreline, channel wrack has long, multi-divided stems, each tipped with lumpy and bulbous frond tips, the reproductive parts. It can turn black on long hot days, but will recover its colour after immersion.

Knotted wrack
(Ascophyllum nodosum)
Also known as egg wrack, this species grows further down the shore in the

inter-tidal zone. It lives for a long time and will grow for up to 13 years – it grows one large single air bladder per year, so its age can be calculated by counting the air bladders. It is a deep olive green and has segmented fronds that can reach 2m (6½ft).

Bladder wrack
(Fucus vesiculosus)
This common, easily identifiable seaweed is found further into the inter-tidal zone. It has small air bladders in pairs on the branching fronds that can be popped. It has brown-green fronds that can exceed 1m (3¼ft) in length.

Above: Seaweed grows in tidal zones and both channel wrack (top) and spiral wrack (bottom) live at their limits. These seaweeds are able to stand periods of dehydration when the tide is out because they can revive and hydrate in about 25 minutes when the tide comes in.

Kelp
(Laminaria digitata)
Also known as oarweed, kelp has broad, flexible, olive-green fronds that can reach up to 2m (6½ft). It grows in the deepest water, where it can develop underwater forests, and is often only revealed during spring tides.

Birds

Divers

Perfectly designed to spend most of their lives in the water, divers divide their time between floating on top and diving beneath it. They can reach depths of 9m (30ft) and will remain under the water for up to one-and-a-half minutes. They are strong fliers but look very ungainly on land. They breed in the north on lochs and small islands and visit offshore fishing banks in winter.

Red-throated diver
(Gavia stellata)

The smallest diver seen in British waters, at around 60cm (2ft), the red-throated diver has dark grey wings and back, a paler grey head and neck and a white chest with a rusty red triangular flash at the throat. Its slender grey beak is up-tilted. It nests on lochs in Shetland, Orkney, the Outer Hebrides, western Scotland and north-west Ireland. In winter it can be seen in sheltered waters around much of the British coast.

Above: A red-throated diver takes off from a lake. Note the feet are placed characteristically far back; these birds cannot walk on land, but propel themselves forward on to their chests using their feet. The bill changes colour from black in the summer to pale-grey in the winter.

Right: The great northern diver hunts for fish under water and can reach depths of 60m (200ft).

Great northern diver
(Gavia immer)

A winter visitor to the UK, the great northern diver is most common around the northern and western Scottish islands, but also off the coast of Cornwall. At around 90cm (3ft) it is the largest of the divers and a solitary bird. It has a black neck divided by two collars of black and white, a black back dotted with white squares and a large sharp beak.

Black-throated diver
(Gavia arctica)

A rare bird with only around 200 breeding pairs left in the larger Scottish lochs, it overwinters around the coasts of Britain and Ireland. The black-throated diver has a soft grey head and neck, a white breast and a black back decorated with white squares and dashes. Black-and-white stripes follow the line of the neck and its eyes are red.

Red-necked grebe
(Podiceps grisegena)

All three species of coastal grebe found in the UK are scarce. The red-necked grebe is most likely to be seen in the south and east in the summer months, and on the east coast in winter. It has a brown body, a black cap and off-white cheeks; the neck and breast turn red during the summer. The bill is sturdy and black-tipped with a yellow base.

only return to the nest at night, remaining on the sea during the day in large flocks to deter predatory birds. Most birds migrate to South America in July, returning to breed in late February and March.

Gannet
(Morus bassanus)

A large seabird that undertakes spectacular dives for fish, dropping from the sky like a stone, head first with folded wings, at speeds of 100kmph (62mph), and reaching depths of 9m (30ft). Around 1m (3¼ft) in length, the gannet has a wingspan of around 1.8m (6ft). It is white with black legs and wingtips, the beak is pale blue, edged in black, and the head and neck are flushed a pale yellow. The largest breeding colony in mainland Britain is at Bempton Cliffs, Yorkshire, and there are more off the coasts of Scotland and Wales. Outside the breeding season the birds can be seen offshore all around the coast.

Black-necked grebe
(Podiceps nigricollis)

In summer the black-necked grebe has dull red plumage on its flanks, a bright red eye and beautiful yellow ear tufts that contrast with its black face and neck. In winter the flanks and lower half of the head are white. It nests on lochs in Scotland in summer and winters along the south-west coast of England.

Slavonian grebe
(Podiceps auritus)

The Slavonian grebe's summer plumage is similar to the black-necked grebe with red flanks and yellow ear tufts that extend around to the back of the head. However, the Slavonian grebe's neck is reddish rather than black, and in winter it has more white on its face and a pale tip on its bill. A rare breeding bird in Scotland in summer; wintering birds can be seen around the British coast.

Fulmar
(Fulmarus glacialis)

The fulmar looks like a small, plump seagull, though it is in fact a relative of the albatross. It has a snowy white head and undersides, and a soft grey back and wings. Its short,

Above: The Slavonian grebe has a striking summer plumage, seen above, though it is more commonly seen in winter with black-and-white plumage. The eyes are ruby red.

Right: The fulmar, pictured here in the Shetlands, is part of the petrel family and flies with a stiff wing action. It lives far out to sea except when breeding.

stout bill is grey and yellow. Fulmars breed on ledges and crevices on rocky cliffs, especially in seabird colonies along the north coast of Scotland and the Scottish Isles. If disturbed when nesting they vomit fetid-smelling oil over the intruder.

Manx shearwater
(Puffinus puffinus)

The manx shearwater is a distinctive bird that forms a cross-shape in flight as it glides with slim, straight wings. It is all black above and all white below. It is usually seen out at sea, except in the breeding season when it nests in burrows on islands on the north and west of Scotland. Adult birds

Petrels

Leach's petrel

Petrels spend their time out at sea, flying so low over the water that their feet splash across the surface, feeding on fish and plankton. Their name is thought to have derived from that of St Peter, alluding to their apparent ability to walk on water. They breed on offshore islands, on the north and west Scottish coast, in rock crevices, between boulders, or in rabbit burrows. The **storm petrel** (*Hydrobates pelagicus*) is the UK's smallest seabird, about the size of a sparrow, with a square tail, while **Leach's petrel** (*Oceanodroma leucorhoa*) is somewhat larger, approximately the size of a starling, and has a forked tail. Both are black with a white rump, with black beak, feet and eyes.

Cormorant
(Phalacrocorax carbo)

Cumbersome in flight and almost prehistoric in appearance, the cormorant is glossy black in colour, with a green or purple sheen to the feathers and a small black crest on its head. It has a white thigh patch and bare patches around the beak and eyes. It is a large bird measuring 1m (3¼ft) long and has a wingspan of 1.2–1.5m (4–5ft). Like its close relative, the shag, the cormorant swims with just its head and neck above water, and sits on rocks with wings outstretched to dry, as its plumage is not as well waterproofed with oil as other seabirds. It can be seen all around UK coasts and estuaries, where it breeds in colonies at the foot of cliffs or on islands and rock stacks.

Above: The plumes of the little egret were fashionable as hat decorations between the 17th and 19th centuries, so much so that hunting caused an alarming decline in numbers.

Shag
(Phalacrocorax aristotelis)

Smaller and more solitary than the cormorant, the shag can be seen flying low over the water, alone or in small groups. It has dark green plumage, a curling crest on its head, and a yellow line around its beak. Like the cormorant, it can often be seen perched with its wings outstretched to dry. It breeds in large colonies on Orkney, Shetland, and the Inner Hebrides but can also be seen around the coast of Wales and the south-west of England.

Little egret
(Egretta garzetta)

The little egret arrived in the UK as recently as 1989, but it is now quite often seen on south and east coastal estuaries, mudflats and salt marshes. A member of the heron family, it is snowy white with plumes on its head, back and chest. It has a long black beak and legs and yellow feet. It wades through the water hunting for fish. Its numbers are swelled in autumn and winter by visiting birds.

Barnacle goose
(Branta leucopsis)

The barnacle goose, like the brent goose, spends October to March in the UK, on

Brent goose
(Branta bernicla)

Smaller than the barnacle goose, the brent goose winters on estuaries and salt marshes, mainly on the east and south-east coast of England and Northern Ireland. It flies north in summer and can be seen flying in beautiful V-formations. It has a black head, beak and neck, a dark grey back and wing tips and a white stripe at its rear. A shooting ban helped save these geese from extinction.

Shelduck
(Tadorna tadorna)

The shelduck lives in estuaries and marshland around the coast where it searches for food in muddy shallow water. It has a black neck and head and a beautiful red beak. The body is white with a brown band around the breast and on the wings.

Wigeon
(Anas penelope)

The wigeon is medium-sized duck with a brown head, a pink breast, grey back, white undersides, a white stripe along the wings and black wing tips. Large numbers overwinter on the coast all around the UK, but some breed in central and northern Scotland. The wigeon is very sociable and prefers to gather in large flocks.

the western coast of Scotland and the coast of Northern Ireland, flying to the Arctic for summer. It prefers marshy sea meadows and salt estuaries where it feeds on vegetation, roots and flowers. A medium-sized goose, at around 60cm (2ft), it has a long black neck, topped with a distinctive white head, and black beak and eye markings. It has a grey back, striped with black bars and black legs and feet. It flies in noisy groups that seem to yap rather than honk.

Above: An adult pair of wigeon in flight. The bird is migratory and breeds principally in the northernmost areas of Europe and Asia, venturing south for the winter.

Below: An adult female shelduck nursing a creche of ducklings, including her own. The birds build nests in rabbit burrows, hollow trees or under bushes and lay 8–10 white eggs. In summer they migrate in huge numbers to North Sea estuaries to moult and grow new feathers.

Eider
(Somateria mollissima)

A true seaduck, the eider is rarely found away from the coasts, as it depends on shellfish for food. The UK's heaviest duck, it wears a black cap, has a white face and neck and a black underside, wings and tail. It breeds in large colonies in Scotland, northern England and Northern Ireland, but during winter it is found all around the British coast.

Common scoter
(Melanitta nigra)

Despite its name, the common scoter is now on the RSPB Red List of Threatened Species as its numbers have substantially declined. It is a sociable duck that can be seen bobbing at sea in large groups in winter, where it is vulnerable to oil spills, or flying in long lines. It is black all over apart from a small yellow patch on the top of its bill. It breeds in June and July on

Above: The oystercatcher has a strong beak, enabling it to prise open or smash the shells of bivalves. Despite its common name it does not eat many oysters.

Below: The avocet had been extinct in Britain, but returned after World War Two to breed on reclaimed land that had been returned to saltmarsh to deter German invaders.

small lochs in the north and west of Scotland. At other times of the year it can be seen around the UK coast, but notably in Carmarthen and Cardigan Bays, the Moray Firth and the north Norfolk coast.

Long-tailed duck
(Clangula hyemalis)

A brown- or black-and-white seaduck with long, elegant, upward-curving tail feathers and a pink stripe across its beak. Long-tailed ducks breed north of the Arctic Circle but overwinter around the north and east coasts, notably in Northumberland and northern Scotland.

Oystercatcher
(Haematopus ostralegus)

A distinctive wading bird that can be seen on almost all UK coasts. It passes its time on the shoreline, or in shallow water, dipping its beak and looking for shellfish. It has a black head, neck, back and wings, a white underside, a long orange-red beak and long pink legs and feet.

Avocet
(Recurvirostra avosetta)

This elegant bird, the symbol of the RSPB, was once in serious danger but successful protection and conservation projects have enabled numbers to increase. It has a white body with a black veiled hood and black markings around its wings. It stands on long

grey legs and sports a distinctive, long, upturned black beak.

Ringed plover
(Charadrius hiaticula)
A small bird, around 20cm (8in), the ringed plover has a brown back and a white underside and wears a black eye mask and black bib. The legs are orange, as is the beak, which in summer is tipped in black as though dipped in ink. It also sports a pair of beautiful white eyebrows and breeds on beaches around the coast.

Grey plover
(Pluvialis squatarola)
The grey plover is a common sight on beaches, salt marshes and estuaries. As its Latin name suggests, it is a plump bird, perched incongruously on a long pair of pale blue legs. Its underside is silver spotted with black and it has a black face, neck and body spotted with beige; in the summer it looks a browner grey. The wing undersides

are black, as is the beak. Birds feed at a distance from each other.

Knot
(Calidris canutus)
With relatively short legs, the knot has a grey head, neck and back, and is white below. In summer the chest, face and belly turn an impressive brick red. In flight it has a wing stripe and white rump. The beak is black and the legs green. Knots form dense flocks and can be seen in estuaries in winter, which they visit after breeding in the Arctic.

Above: The sanderling is a winter visitor from the sandpiper family – a group of waders and shore birds which feed on molluscs, plants, small fish and insects.

Left: A flock of knots. The bird can be seen in muddy estuaries between August and May; largest numbers appear between December and March.

Sanderling
(Calidris alba)
As the name indicates, this bird hunts in the sand and shingle along the shoreline for shrimp. It has a pale grey back, white undersides, a black beak and short legs.

Purple sandpiper
(Calidris maritima)
A winter visitor from the Arctic, the purple sandpiper is dark grey above and grey-white below, it has bright orange legs and a black and orange beak. It hunts through seaweed and stones looking for invertebrates. Purple sandpipers are found in Orkney, Shetland and the east coast of Scotland.

Turnstone
(Arenaria interpres)

Turnstones scurry over the ground turning over stones when hunting for invertebrates. The cock has a brown and black back, a black-and-white chest, and white undersides. It has a black beak and orange legs. Turnstones can be found on sandy, rocky and muddy coastlines. They breed in the Arctic, but birds visit throughout most of the year, some spending the winter, and non-breeding birds may stay through the summer.

Dunlin
(Calidris alpina)

The dunlin has a brown back and a grey head, both of which are speckled with brown. Its underside is white with a black splodge on its belly when breeding. Its legs and long, down-curved beak are both black. The dunlin is present all year round, but numbers increase in winter due to visitors from overseas.

Curlew sandpiper
(Calidris ferruginea)

This species is similar to the dunlin, only rather more streamlined, and with a longer neck, legs and beak and a white rump in flight. The curlew sandpiper only visits the

Above: A turnstone displays summer plumage. The bird likes to forage in flocks; it consumes crustaceans, molluscs, worms, insects, plant matter and carrion.

Below: The curlew sandpiper in near summer plumage wades through mud hunting for snails, worms and flies as the tide retreats. Young birds may remain for a year before migrating to breed.

UK while migrating from Siberia to South Africa in August and September where it is most commonly seen on salt marshes in east England. It mixes with the dunlin, but feeds like the curlew, wading in deep water to look for food in the mud below.

Redshank
(Tringa totanus)

A medium-sized wader, 30cm (12in) long, the redshank has a brown speckled back and a grey speckled breast. Its wings have white rear edges, its legs are bright orange, and its orange beak, tipped with black, is slightly upturned. Widespread around the coasts of the UK, the redshank can live in large flocks in winter, and is very noisy when disturbed.

Spotted redshank
(Tringa erythropus)

Most spotted redshanks pass through the UK in September, but the few birds that remain in coastal wetlands during winter do so in Essex, north Kent, Hampshire and west Wales. Virtually black in summer, in winter spotted redshanks are pale grey with dark grey speckles on their back and wings. Legs are bright orange, and the beak is long and black with an orange stripe and slightly turned down at the tip.

It is most common in the north and west, but can be found all around the coast.

Whimbrel
(Numenius phaeopus)
The whimbrel resembles the more common curlew, but it is around 15cm (6in) smaller, and also has a more distinct dark eye stripe. Most birds are passage migrants around British coasts, seen mid-April to August, but some pairs are now breeding in Shetland and Orkney.

Black-headed gull
(Larus ridibundus)
A common species, the black-headed gull has moved along estuaries into cities, and is now scavenging in most urban areas as well as following the plough in fields. It tends to remain in limited feeding areas and does not mix with its neighbours. Despite their name, black-headed gulls actually have a chocolate-brown (rather than black) hood in summer, which turns to a dark smudge in winter. Wings are grey, undersides white, and legs are red.

Greenshank
(Tringa nebularia)
This bird has a longer neck and legs than the redshank and is slimmer in build. It has a dark grey back and white undersides, green legs and a slightly upturned beak. It eats fish, snails and worms and can be found on estuaries, salt marshes and seashores throughout the UK, as well as at inland lakes and freshwater marshes. The birds breed from April to August on moors in northern Scotland. They overwinter in Africa and can be seen along the coast travelling between these two areas in April and May, and in July, August and September returning to the sun.

Bar-tailed godwit
(Limosa lapponica)
The bar-tailed godwit arrives in the UK in July and August to overwinter on coastal estuaries. It departs in March and April. Its plumage is grey-brown in winter, but turns to chestnut-red in spring. It has long black legs and feet and a pink and black beak, and feeds with its beak in the mud, hunting for worms and molluscs.

Black-tailed godwit
(Limosa limosa)
Characterised by a very long, straight bill that is pink at the base and black at the tip, the black-tailed godwit has a grey-brown head, back and breast, white undersides, a white tail with a black band and black legs. Look for them in coastal estuaries and salt marshes in the south of England and notably on RSPB coastal reserves.

Curlew
(Numenius arquata)
The UK's largest wader at 48–57cm (19–22in) the curlew has a solid body, which balances on amazingly long, thin legs. It can be seen wading through the shallows or poking around in mud on the shores of estuaries and salt marshes, looking for invertebrates and molluscs. The curlew has brown feathers and a cream underside both speckled with brown. The legs are grey and the black beak long and downward curving, with a small stripe of orange on the underside.

Above: Black-tailed godwit can be seen year round in the UK, but breeding pairs are rare. Migrants from northern Europe visit to spend the winter and can be seen around the coast.

Right: The numbers of curlew are in decline, it is believed due to the effects of agricultural intensification. The bird gets its name from its echoing 'curl-oo' call.

Skuas

Skuas are the pirates of the skies and pursue other birds to steal their food. They are not daunted by size and will chase terns and gannets with equal enthusiasm. Their hunt is so aerobatic that the birds they are chasing often vomit their catch. They breed in colonies on moorland, often miles from the sea. The **great skua** (*Stercorarius skua*) measures almost 60cm (2ft) and as well as fish will take birds as large as puffins as prey. They are unafraid of man and will dive-bomb anyone who gets near to their nests. Skuas breed on rocky coastal islands before flying to Spain and Africa to pass the winter, but can be seen along the east and west coasts as they migrate in spring and late summer. The great skua looks somewhat like a brown gull but has white flashes on its wing tips. The **arctic skua** (*Stercorarius parasiticus*) is much smaller than the great skua at 45cm (18in), but is faster and more threatening in flight. There are two forms of adult plumage, a sooty brown dark phase, and a pale phase with a dark cap, back and wings but a pale neck and underside. Its central tail feathers project beyond the end of the tail. A passage migrant in spring and autumn, it also breeds in Shetland, Orkney and the north of Scotland.

Arctic skua

Herring gull
(Larus argentatus)

This is the species that makes the call we most commonly associate with seagulls. Distinguishing features include its yellow eyes, bright pink legs and bright yellow beak with a red dot near the tip. Its black wing tips are marked with large white spots. The herring gull nests on rocky ledges, roof tops and on the ground on moorland.

Above: A great black-backed gull in flight with a fish in its beak. Gulls usually pair in March and large groups gather in selected breeding sites; pairs preen, sleep and feed and begin courtship rituals. The female circles the male, brushing his chest feathers with her beak and he feeds her regurgitated fish.

Common gull
(Larus canus)

Similar to the herring gull, but less common inland, the common gull is smaller and has yellow-green legs and black eyes. The white spots on its black wing tips are smaller than those of the herring gull. It breeds on moorlands and northern coasts.

Great black-backed gull
(Larus marinus)

The largest species of gull found around the UK, at nearly twice the size of the black-headed gull, the great black-backed gull measures 61–74cm (24–30in). Its body is white, but its wings are black, tipped with white; the beak is yellow with a red spot at the tip and the legs are pink. It does not nest in colonies but selects isolated spots on islands, rocky cliffs and moorland.

Lesser black-backed gulls
(Larus fuscus)

Similar to the herring gull, the lesser black-backed gull has yellow legs and dark grey wings. Birds are resident all around the coast, breeding takes place on the Scottish coasts and many birds from Scandinavia arrive in October to overwinter.

Kittiwake
(Rissa tridactyla)

The only species that truly lives up to the moniker of 'seagull', the kittiwake is rarely seen on the shore, often only being seen in open sea. It is a medium-sized, white gull with pale grey wings tipped with black triangles. It has dark eyes and legs and a yellow beak. The kittiwake breeds in seabird colonies around the coast in summer and spends the winter out in the Atlantic.

Terns

All terns are summer visitors, coming to the UK to breed, migrating from as far as Australia, Africa and Antarctica. The common tern, arctic tern, little tern and sandwich tern are found around the coast and on offshore islands, as well as at rivers and canals. They are light and graceful birds that swoop around like maritime swallows. Terns feed by diving into the water for small fish.

Common tern
(Sterna hirundo)
The common tern is silver-grey with a white chest and a black cap, its coral beak is tipped with black, and it has coral legs. Breeding birds should not be disturbed as they respond aggressively to intruders.

Arctic tern
(Sterna paradisaea)
The arctic tern arrives in the UK as late as May or June after its long journey from the

Above: A little tern adult feeding a chick. Courtship involves the male offering the female a fish from his beak.

Antarctic. Similar to the common tern, its body is a darker grey and its beak has no black tip. It is less widespread than the common tern and breeds along the coasts of Scotland, Northumberland, the Northern Isles, north Wales and Northern Ireland.

Little tern
(Sterna albifrons)
As its name suggests, the little tern is smaller than other members of its family at just 25cm (10in). It has a white body, grey wings and back, a black cap, and a black-tipped, yellow beak. Its beachside nesting

Left: A sandwich tern parent with chick. The birds breed in dense colonies, often with black-headed gulls, relying on volume of numbers and the gulls as a defence against its predators.

sites have made it a vulnerable species.

Sandwich tern
(Sterna sandvicensis)
Named after the Kent market town where it used to breed, the sandwich tern is still only found along the south-east coast, where it feeds on sandworms, sprats and whiting. It is a little whiter than the other terns, but wears the family black cap with a tiny frill of feathers at the back of the head. The legs and beak are black, the latter tipped with yellow.

Auks

Four species of auk – the 'penguins of the Northern Hemisphere' – reside in the UK: razorbills, guillemots black guillemots and the puffin. These birds spend most of their lives at sea, only coming to land to breed on or below steep cliffs in the north and west.

Guillemot
(Uria aalge)
A dark brown bird with a long beak; one form wears a discreet circling of white around the eyes like feathered eyeliner. Underwater, guillemots work as a team, chasing shoals of fish together, on land they nest in noisy colonies. They can be found on sheer cliffs at sites around the UK with large colonies at Bempton Cliffs in Yorkshire, Fowlsheugh in Aberdeenshire and Marwick Head in Orkney.

Black guillemot
(Cepphus grylle)
The black guillemot has black feathers all over, save for a large white patch on the centre of its wing, and bright red feet. Unlike the sociable guillemot, it is often seen alone or in small groups. It nests on rocky beaches in Shetland and Orkney; it can also be seen on the Cumbrian coast near to St Bees, on the Isle of Man, and along the coastline of Northern Ireland.

Below: The black guillemot dives for fish and crustaceans as well as molluscs and plant material. These birds gather in huge nesting colonies between March and late July.

Above: The distinctive puffin is unique in its ability to hold a number of fish crossways in its beak at one time, allowing it to extend foraging trips longer than other birds.

Razorbill
(Alca torda)
Present on the coastline only during the breeding season from March to the end of July, the razorbill is a stocky bird with the look of a small penguin or large puffin. It has a black head and back and black wings edged with white. It has a broad beak with a white stripe as well as a delicate white line from eye to beak. It nests on cliff ledges or between large rocks at the cliff base around the coast of the UK.

Puffin
(Fratercula arctica)
The puffin breeds in large colonies on cliff tops on northern, western and eastern coasts, either digging burrows on grassy slopes, or by requisitioning rabbit burrows. It has a black back and wings, a grey head with a white patch around the beak, eyes and cheeks and black eye make up. The large triangular beak is striped red, grey, white and yellow and its feet are orange.

Rock dove
(Columba livia)
The ancestor of the domestic pigeon, the rock dove feeds on seeds, grain, shellfish and

seaweed. In coastal regions it lives on northern islands and rocky cliffs and nests on cliff tops and in caves. It is similar in shape to the wood pigeon, but has a blue grey body, a grey head and beak, and a white rump. The eyes and legs are both red.

Rock pipit
(Anthus petrosus)
The rock pipit is found along the shores of Britain, notably in Wales, Cornwall and Scotland, where it can be seen sorting through stones or seaweed along the shoreline, hunting for small invertebrates, tiny fish and seeds. It is an olive brown on the back and neck and a dirty white underneath, the whole being flecked with dark streaks.

Chough
(Pyrrhocorax pyrrhocorax)
The chough belongs to the crow family though it is slightly smaller at around 40cm (16in). It has glossy black feathers, red legs and a bright red, long, curved beak. It can be found on the west coast of Northern Ireland, west Wales, the Isle of Man, and some of the Inner Hebridean Islands, where it puts on wonderful aerial displays, swooping and diving on the cliff top.

Mammals

Bottle-nosed dolphin
(Tursiops truncates)

The bottle-nosed dolphin is most commonly seen in summer off the south and south-west coasts in bays and estuaries. It has a dark grey body, with a light underside, and can grow to 3.5m (11½ft). The bottle-nosed dolphin can remain submerged in water for up to 20 minutes before surfacing for air. It has a short snout and a steep forehead and a prominent, curved fin on its back. Dolphins live in sociable groups, with schools working together to catch small fish, shrimps, crab and squid, and to deter their natural predator, the shark. Pollution and overfishing is believed to be responsible for their recent decline in numbers.

Common porpoise
(Phocoena phocoena)

The common or harbour porpoise lives in small groups and can be seen all around the UK and notably off the south-west coast of Wales. It can reach nearly 2m (6½ft) in length and live for 15–25 years. It looks somewhat like a dolphin – grey above, paler below – but it has a blunt head with no beak and a smaller dorsal fin. It feeds on significant numbers of small fish such as herring and sprat.

Killer whale
(Orcinus orca)

The killer whale can be seen all around the British coast and particularly off the west coast of Scotland. The largest member of the oceanic dolphin family, it has a black back, white chest and sides, a white patch above and behind the eye, and a large dorsal fin. Males are larger and heavier than females: they can measure a startling 8m (26ft) and weigh in the region of 8 tonnes (8,000kg). In British waters seals are their main food source, but they will also take porpoises, dolphins, birds and fish.

Minke whale
(Balaenoptera acutorostrata)

The minke whale can be found along the Atlantic coast and in the northern part of the North Sea, but it is most commonly seen off the north-west coast of Scotland from April

Left: A bottle-nosed dolphin breaching Chanonry Point, Black Isle on the Moray Firth. Dolphins surface several times a minute for air, but can submerge for up to 20 minutes.

Below: Half of the world's population of grey seals is found around the coastline of the UK.

to September. They are solitary creatures but can be found in larger groups where food is concentrated. Males can measure 8–10m (26–33ft) in length and typically weigh 4–5 tonnes by maturity. The body of the minke whale is black or dark grey above and white underneath, and it has two blowholes and 50–70 grooves on the underside of its throat.

Common seal
(Phoca vitulina)

The common or harbour seal is grey, brown or tan, mottled with dark spots. It has distinctive V-shaped nostrils and a mouth that appears to smile. Adults can reach an impressive 2m (6½ft). They can often be seen basking on sand or mud banks on eastern coasts, notably off the Wash, north-west Scotland and all around the Irish coast.

Grey seal
(Halichoerus grypus)

The grey seal is principally found on islands off the north and west coasts, with large colonies on the Farne Islands off the Northumberland coast, Lambay Island off the coast of Dublin, and Ramsay Island off the coast of Pembrokeshire. They are best observed in winter, basking on rocks. The grey seal is dark grey on its back and light grey underneath, all spotted with irregular blotches. It has small, widely spaced eyes, a long, blunt-ended muzzle and nostrils that form a W-pattern. Females, or cows, grow to around 2m (6½ft), the males, or bulls, are much larger and can reach 3m (10ft) in length.

Fish

Five-bearded rockling
(Ciliata mustela)
This long, slender fish can be found in rock pools, around pilings and in hollows on the sea floor. The five-bearded rockling can reach up to 25cm (10in) in length, it has a brown body and five barbels on its head, two on the nose and one under the chin. The dorsal fin is set in a small depression on the back, and runs along the last two-thirds of the body, with a matching fin on the underside.

Shore rockling
(Gaidropsarus mediterraneus)
Less common than the five-bearded rockling, the shore rockling lives in similar habitats, and looks much the same, except that it has just three facial barbels and is larger, reaching 40cm (16in).

Fifteen-spined stickleback
(Spinachia spinachia)
This is the marine species of stickleback, sometimes known as the sea stickleback, which can be found all around the UK coastline, although it is rarely seen around the South East coast. It lives in rock pools and in seaweeds at the low-water mark. The sea stickleback has a long, slender, brown or olive-green body of up to 19cm (7½in) that narrows to the tail fin. It has 14–17 spines situated in front of the dorsal fin. It has a tapering snout and small eyes and lives on worms and crustaceans.

Wrasse

The UK boasts a few colourful representatives of the wrasse family, which is principally a tropical or sub-tropical fish.

Wrasse have thick, fleshy lips, and a set of large, strong teeth that are used to feed on molluscs, such as crab and shrimp. Juveniles act as cleaner fish, helpfully removing dead skin and parasites from other fish.

Ballan wrasse
(Labrus bergylta)
Common in UK waters, ballan wrasse have been known to grow to 60cm (2ft). Colouration varies according to age and sex: younger fish are shades of green, while older fish are red-brown or dark green with many white spots. They can be seen off rocky shores in the south west and the young can be seen in rock pools.

Left: The three-bearded shore rockling at low tide. Adult fish are dark brown and live on the sea floor.

Below: The male corkwing wrasse builds nests from seaweed in inter-tidal crevices.

Corkwing wrasse
(Crenilabrus melops)
The corkwing wrasse does not grow as large as the ballan wrasse, and is usually less than 15cm (6in) in length. It can be seen in lower shore pools and out to depths of 50m (165ft). Although colour can vary, corkwing wrasse are usually greenish brown, and male fish tend to be more brightly coloured. All have a brown spot in the middle of the tail and a black squiggle behind the eye. When sleeping, or in danger, the black spot is obscured by black bars.

Lesser weever fish
(Echiichthys vipera)
This brown fish lies half-buried in sand in shallow water, moving in and out with the tide, waiting for small fish and shrimp to come along. It leaves its poisonous spiny dorsal fin raised above the sand as an effective defence mechanism. The lesser weever fish ranges in colour from yellow to light brown on the back, with darker spots towards the sides and belly, and it can grow to 15cm (6in). The mouth is large and the eyes set towards the top of the head.

Sustainable seafood

The National Trust believes that many seafood species are at risk from overfishing. In line with their food policy, the Trust seeks to use seafood from sustainable and responsibly managed stocks in its restaurants, following the guidelines of the Marine Conservation Society. Those guidelines recommend the best seafoods to choose in respect of sustainability of supply, environmental impact on marine habitats and other species, and avoidance of unnecessary or inefficient transportation. Many other retailers and restaurants are starting to put in place similar guidelines to ensure that their fish and seafood is sustainably harvested. Consumers are becoming more discerning and are interested in where their food has come from and how far it has travelled, how it has been treated and whether it was wild or farmed.

Common blenny or shanny
(Lipophrys pholis)

The common blenny or shanny is a common rock pool or shoreline find. It has slimy skin and is coloured grey, green and brown with blotchy markings to help provide camouflage. It grows to around 15cm (6in) long, and has large eyes and mouth, with a steep forehead. Rock pools provide its home base in summer, and it will venture out only at high tide, but in winter shanny move to the shallows to avoid being tossed around by

Above: The shanny is a rock-pool dweller that uses its paired fins to crawl into crevices to hide. It eats green seaweed, barnacles and other invertebrates and rests on rocks out of the water when the tide is out.

Below: The shore clingfish (see page 56) is a common find in Cornish rock pools and, like the goby, it can survive periods out of the water, where it can be found clinging to the undersides of rocks by means of a suction cup on its pelvic fins. It has a distinctive duck-like profile.

winter storms. They eat barnacles and other invertebrates as well as seaweed.

Butterfish
(Pholis gunnellus)

The butterfish is covered with mucus and is extremely slippery – hence its common name. This is a small, eel-like fish with large fleshy lips that commonly grows to 25cm (10in). It is dark red-brown in colour, with 9–15 white-edged dark spots, and it has a long dorsal fin running the entire length of its body. The butterfish eats worms and crustaceans and is found hiding in seaweed or crevices in rocks on the lower shore.

Lesser sand eel
(Ammodytes tobianus)

The lesser sand eel, which despite its name is a fish and not an eel, is an important food source for both seabirds and other fish. This long, thin fish has a prominent lower jaw, and is coloured a greenish-yellow on its back, yellow on its upper sides and silver on its lower sides and belly. Juveniles can be seen swimming in large shoals in rock pools with sandy bottoms or around rocks. Adults spend much of their time buried in the sand.

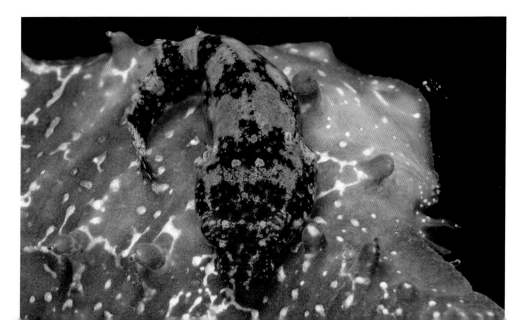

Goby

Gobies form one of the largest families of fish. Most are on the small side, measuring less than 15cm (6in). They are an important food source for commercially important fish such as cod and haddock. Gobies are notoriously difficult to differentiate, but in general they have blunt heads with large eyes and lips, and two dorsal fins that are divided into two sections. They live in shallow marine habitats and can be found in sandy shallows, sandy rock pools and estuaries, and eat small crustaceans and worms.

Common goby
(Pomatoschistus microps)
Measuring only around 7cm (2⅔in), the common goby is grey or sandy-coloured and has darker blotches along its back and fainter ones along the side of the body. It is found in pools on sandy shores and on estuaries.

Rock goby
(Gobius paganellus)
The male rock goby turns black when guarding his eggs, but is more usually black or brown with many white blotches that make him appear silvery grey. Rock gobies can grow to 12cm (5in) long and can be found in rocky areas near the shore.

Above: The rock goby hides under rocks and in crevices in rock pools. It prises barnacles off rocks with its teeth.

Below: The two-spot goby has false eye-spots on its dorsal fin designed to fool other fish that they are in the presence of a much larger specimen.

Sand goby
(Pomatoschistus minutus)
Pale grey or brown in colour with darker markings on its sides and a creamy white belly underneath, the sand goby can reach 10cm (4in) in length. Males have a distinctive blue spot to the rear of the dorsal fin when breeding. This species can be found in sandy shallows and sandy rock pools as well as in estuaries in the autumn.

Two-spot goby
(Gobiusculus flavescens)
Slimmer than many gobies, the two-spot goby is mottled, red-brown in colour and has a large black spot at the base of the tail fin. Males have a second, smaller spot at the base of the pectoral fin. The dorsal fin is banded in red and all the markings become brighter in the males during the breeding season. They can be found in small shoals in seaweed-filled rock pools.

Shore clingfish
(Lepadogaster lepadogaster)
The shore clingfish, also known as the Cornish lumpsucker, is an inter-tidal species that can be found in rock pools and seaweed-covered shorelines between the high- and low-tide lines. The body can reach 15cm (6in) long, and is flattened, while the head is broad and the snout resembles a duck's bill. The body colour varies from reddish to green with irregular brown markings and there is a blue spot behind each eye.

Invertebrates

Coastal butterflies

The coastal landscape offers some of the best butterfly and moth habitat in the UK, despite the fact that it is often exposed. Sand dunes, cliff slopes with grass and bracken and sheltered sea combes are all important, though no butterflies and only a few specialist moths live in salt marshes. Some 39 species of butterfly can be seen along the British coasts, with coastline owned by the National Trust being particularly important for the Glanville fritillary, dark green fritillary, silver-studded blue and, curiously, the wood white. The last is normally associated with sheltered woodland rides but also occurs along the South Devon coast. Many top holiday beaches are backed by important Trust-owned butterfly sites; for example, beaches at Holywell and Kynance in Cornwall, Woolacombe in north Devon, Studland in Dorset, Compton on the Isle of Wight, Oxwich on the Gower, Brancaster and Winterton in Norfolk and Murlough in Northern Ireland.

Clouded yellow
(Colias croceus)

This splendid butterfly is a master mariner, capable of serious migrations. There are descriptions of swarms flying low over the sea to British shores. Until recently it was a periodic immigrant, but it now appears to be surviving increasingly mild winters along our south coast and may be becoming a true resident. These fast-flying butterflies settle with their wings closed, revealing green-yellow undersides that contrast with the gold with black trim uppersides. They are seen mostly during August and September along the foot of south-facing slopes.

Small blue
(Cupido minimus)

The UK's smallest butterfly lives mainly on downland but also occurs sporadically in sheltered places along the coast, where its foodplant, kidney vetch, grows. The uppersides are very dark, and the undersides

Fritillary butterflies

Several species of these orange-and-black chequered butterflies occur along the coast. The most special is the **Glanville fritillary** (*Melitaea cinxia*), named after the 18th-century collector Lady Eleanor Glanville. It is effectively restricted to the Isle of Wight coast, where it flies in late May and June. Many of its colonies are threatened by heightened erosion caused by increased storminess associated with climate change. It breeds on a common grassland weed, ribwort plantain. The **dark green fritillary** (*Argynnis aglaja*) is widespread along the coast, breeding on violets under bracken or among rough grass. This large and powerful butterfly, with silver and green hind wing undersides, can be seen in July visiting tall flowers such as knapweeds and thistles. In May and June, colonies of the delicate small **pearl-bordered fritillary** (*Boloria selene*) occur in similar habitats along the south-western and Welsh coasts.

Dark green fritillary

Glanville fritillary

Left: A pair of silver-studded blue butterflies mating. Females lay eggs singly on the larval foodplant; the eggs overwinter before the larvae emerge the following spring.

grey with a few black spots. It flies during June, resting at night and in rough weather among tall grasses.

Silver-studded blue
(Plebejus argus)

Male silver-studded blues have bright blue upper wings with a broad black border; the females are brown with a row of red spots. They can be found in colonies on the coasts of England and Wales.

Above: The grayling is one of the family of brown butterflies that have markings that resemble eyes. When threatened by a predator it opens its forewings to expose the eyespot and startle its attacker.

Grayling
(Hipparchia semele)

This magician of a butterfly is primarily a coastal species, breeding on fine grass tussocks and sand sedge on bare cliffs and dunes. Graylings settle only with their wings closed, on bare ground, into which they blend perfectly, tilting themselves to avoid casting a shadow. The wings are a meditation in delicate browns and greys. These butterflies fly in July and August.

Cream-spot tiger moth
(Arctia villica)

This moth is so gloriously coloured that is it sometimes mistaken for a butterfly. The hindwing is yellow spotted with black; the forewing provides camouflage, and is black spotted and blotched with cream. The cream-spot tiger moth flies at night and can be seen in southern England, South Wales and East Anglia; it is often disturbed along coastal paths at dusk in June.

Jersey tiger moth
(Euplagia quadripunctaria)

Similar in appearance to the cream-spot tiger, the hindwings of the jersey tiger are yellow or orange with black spots, while its forewings are black with broad, cream, diagonal stripes. It is seen along the south coast of Devon and Dorset later in the year – in August – and it flies by day.

Scarce blackneck moth
(Lygephila craccae)

The scarce blackneck has the most beautiful lacy, grey to brown wings, with four dark marks along the front edge of the forewing, and a deep black collar behind the head. It lives on coastal cliffs and rocky areas where landslips encourage its food source, wood vetch, to grow. This is a rare species, as its habitat is constantly eroding, but there are several strong colonies in north-west Devon, Cornwall and Somerset.

Kelp flies
(Coelopa frigida)

Coelopa frigida is the largest and most common species of kelp fly, which can be spotted in swarms around seaweed. This flat-blacked fly is just 6mm (¼in) long and has brown legs and transparent wings. It lays its eggs on rotting seaweed, which its larvae eat, aiding the decomposition process.

Inter-tidal invertebrates

Common winkle
(Littorina littorea)

The winkle or common periwinkle is a common, and edible, seaside snail. It has a small, concentric-ringed, spiral shell in dark grey to light brown that can be rubbed smooth with age. It feeds on seaweed.

Limpets

Limpets are rock-clinging snails with ridged, conical shells. They breed in September and October, dispatching eggs into the sea. Larvae hatch after 24 hours and after 10 days a shell develops. Limpets feed on algae on the rocks and help to keep them clean. The shell of the **common limpet** (Patella vulgata) grows to fit a space on the rock. The animal will venture about 1m (3¼ft) from this spot to feed when covered by water. The **slipper limpet** (Crepidula fornicata) was introduced from America in the 19th century. It has a kidney-shaped shell that can grow to 4cm (1½in) long. Slipper limpets gather together in piles and, remarkably, change sex as they age; the bottom layers are females and the smaller and younger limpets on top are all males.

Common limpet

Common cockle
(Cerastoderma edule)

Finely ribbed with concentric circles across its ribs, the common cockle comes in a variety of creamy brown tones. Cockles live in large colonies (in densities of 10,000 per m²/yd²), just beneath the surface, in damp sand or sandy mud above the low-tide mark.

Oyster
(Ostrea edulis)

The native oyster has a flattened and irregular, round grey or brown shell that can grow to 10cm (4in). It can live for 12 years and the ridges on its shell indicate growth. A large, single muscle clamps the two halves of shell together and these are surrounded by gills through which the oyster filters food particles from the water. Oysters live in large colonies known as oyster beds offshore on rocky coasts.

Left: The common winkle feeds by grazing the surface of the rocks on which it resides; it moves using a mucous-covered foot.

Left: The common cockle feeds by siphoning plankton from the surrounding water and conceals itself in sand by burrowing with its one foot. It attempts to escape predators by straightening and bending the foot to 'leap'. The foot is generally as long as its heart-shaped shell.

Razor clam
(Ensis siliqua and Ensis arcuatus)

Razors are bivalves that live in burrows in the sand. They have long, thin shells from which they extend a strong, muscular foot that is used for rapid digging – they can be out of sight in seconds. At high tide they come closer to the surface of the sand and push out a siphon for feeding and breathing.

Thin tellin
(Angulus tenuis)

Thin tellin shells are found littered along the shoreline of coasts all around the UK. This bivalve has a fan-shaped shell, with concentric ridges, in pink, white, beige, yellow and grey. The connecting ligament between the two shells is very strong, so it is commonly found intact, although the shell is brittle and breaks easily. The thin tellin lives in wet sand from mid-shore outwards. It extends a siphon outside its shell to feed on larvae.

Whelks

Whelks are scavenging sea snails that feed off dead meat; dozens can be found snacking on a dead crab. The shell of a whelk is a distinctive whorled spiral in cream and brown covered in horizontal ridges. Hermit crabs often take over an empty shell. Whelks feed by means of a siphon, which extends out of the shell. The egg cases of the whelk are a common sight on the seashore. Commonly known as 'mermaid's necklaces', they are a white or yellow spongy mass of capsules, and are laid on eelgrass.

Common whelk
(Buccinum undatum)

The common whelk is the largest British whelk. It can reach 12cm (4¾in) long and lives on the lower shore.

Common dog whelk
(Nucella lapillus)

The common dog whelk is much smaller and is common on rocky shores where it feeds on barnacles.

Netted dog whelk
(Nassarius reticulatus)

The netted dog whelk is the smallest British whelk at just 2.5cm (1in) and lives on sandy shores below the low-tide mark.

Mussels

Mussel beds occur below the low-tide mark, as mussels need to be covered by water, and feed constantly. Any mussels living higher up the shore will remain small as their feeding patterns will be restricted. The shells are blue-black or black-brown in colour, and are almost straight on one side and curved on the other; they are generally around 5cm (2in) in length, though they can grown much larger. They are often crusted with barnacles. Mussels are delicious, but can easily be contaminated, even when living in clean seawater. Water contaminated with faeces contains harmful bacteria and viral pathogens, which can be 100 times more concentrated in bivalve molluscs than in the surrounding water. It can take an oyster one week to cleanse itself after contamination, but it can take a mussel three months – which is why they are best not collected from the seaside. Mussels bought from fishmongers may have lived in the sea, but they will have been through purification tanks before being sold. The **common mussel** (*Mytilus edulis*) lives in colonies on rocks or timbers, such as pilings, and can be found all around the coast. The **horse mussel** (*Modiolus modiolus*) has a dark purple-blue shell and can grow to an impressive 23cm (9in). It is found most commonly on northern and western coasts on the lower shore or offshore. The largest British mussel is the **fan mussel** (*Pinna fragilis*), which is found offshore and can grow to 30cm (12in). It is shaped like an elongated triangle, coloured from yellow-brown to dark brown and is very brittle, breaking easily on the shore. Fishermen used to believe that this mollusc fed upon drowned people and refused to eat it.

Common mussel

Crabs

Some 50 species of crab live around the coasts of the UK; some pass their time far out at sea, others prefer rock pools. Crabs have four pairs of legs and two front pincers that can be used for swimming or digging. Their soft bodies are enclosed in a hard shell and their eyes are positioned on stalks. Impressively, they can shed damaged limbs and grow replacements.

Green shore crab
(Carcinus maenas)
The most common species of crab. It grows to around 6cm (2½in) in size and its shell can be green, brown or red. The green shore crab is found in all kinds of marine habitats, including mud and sand, as well as rocky shores.

Edible crab
(Cancer pagurus)
The edible crab is the largest British crab with a shell up to 25cm (10in) wide. It has a flat, smooth, red-brown shell, the edge of which is crimped like a piecrust, and its claws have black tips. Small edible crabs can be seen in rock pools; larger ones are generally found offshore.

Velvet swimming crab
(Macropipus puber)
Hairs on the top of the shell used for collecting silt give the velvet swimming crab its 'velvety' appearance. It has flattened back legs, which it can use as swimming paddles. This crab is found on rocky lower shores.

Spider crab
(Macropodia rostrata)
Spider crabs are often found on the lower shores and in rock pools, where they use seaweeds and sponges for camouflage, hence their other name of 'decorator crab'. Their legs are long and spider-like and the shell is roughly triangular.

Broad-clawed porcelain crab
(Porcellana platycheles)
A small crab 1.5cm (½in) long, the broad-clawed porcelain crab, has a flattened, almost circular body with a dense fringe of hairs

Left: A green shore crab adult, on a seaweed-covered beach, Norfolk.

Below: A common hermit crab needs a regular shell upgrade – if the crab becomes too cramped it is vulnerable to predators as it will not be able to completely withdraw to protect itself.

around the edges. The large, flat claws are also hairy. This species of crab is common on rocky coasts.

Hermit crab
(Pagurus bernhardus)
Despite its name, technically the hermit is not a true crab, as it has just two pairs of legs and one set of pincers. It does not grow a shell of its own, but uses first winkle shells, then whelk shells for protection, with its tail twisted down to fit the spiral. The shells are exchanged regularly as the crab's size increases. Hermit crabs are found on sheltered shores and in rock pools.

Common lobster
(Homarus gammarus)
The common lobster is characterised by a blue body and a pair of massive pincers on its front walking legs. Size varies enormously: the largest specimens, which

can reach up to 1m (3¼ft), are probably around 50 years old. Lobsters live in holes and excavated tunnels at the lower shore and outwards to sea depths of 60m (200ft) – the bigger lobsters live further out to sea. Lobsters most commonly caught in lobster pots are around 15cm (6in) long and are approximately four to five years old.

Acorn barnacle
(Semibalanus balanoides)
Related to crabs and lobsters, the acorn barnacle is a crustacean that can be seen encrusting rocks and timbers all around the coast. Its shell comprises six plates with a diamond-shaped opening. When the tide is in, the barnacle pokes its six feathery legs outside its shell and uses them to sieve the water for minute plankton. It is found on all coasts apart from the South West.

Edible shrimp
(Crangon crangon)
Less transparent than the common prawn, the edible shrimp can grow up to 9cm (3½in) long. It is found on muddy or sandy shores and it can change colour to match its surroundings. It has five pairs of legs: the

Prawns

Prawns can be found in rock pools all around the coast and are most abundant in autumn. The front two pairs of legs have pincers that enable them to move food around, the rear three are used for walking. Prawns swim using flaps under their abdomen and their tail. They eat plant and animal debris and fish eggs. The **common prawn** (Palaemon serratus) is the largest prawn, and can grow as large as 11cm (4¼in). It has a translucent grey-brown body (prawns only turn pink when they have been boiled), black eyes on stalks and five pairs of legs. The smaller **chamaeleon prawn** (Hippolyte varians) can change colour from green to brown according to the colour of the closest seaweed. Shrimps and prawns are different creatures, the prawn having an entirely different gill structure.

Common prawn

Above: The edible or brown shrimp buries itself in the sand to avoid predators and to ambush prey – it consumes any animal material.

rear four pairs are used for walking and swimming, while the front pair has pincers, enabling it to collect worms, crustaceans and dead animal and plant matter for food.

Common sandhopper
(Talitrus saltator)
The common sandhopper spends much of its time buried in burrows in the sand or hiding under stones and seaweed. It is a green-brown or grey relative of the shrimp just 1.5–2.5cm (½–1in) long. It is most active at night and feeds on decaying seaweed on the shoreline at low tide.

Sea slater
(Ligia oceanica)
A marine relative of the wood louse, the sea slater ranges from green to grey in colour, reflecting its habitat. It has an oval-shaped, flattened body, seven pairs of legs and two projections at the tip of the abdomen. It has long antennae that curve out sideways from the head to the shoulders and large black

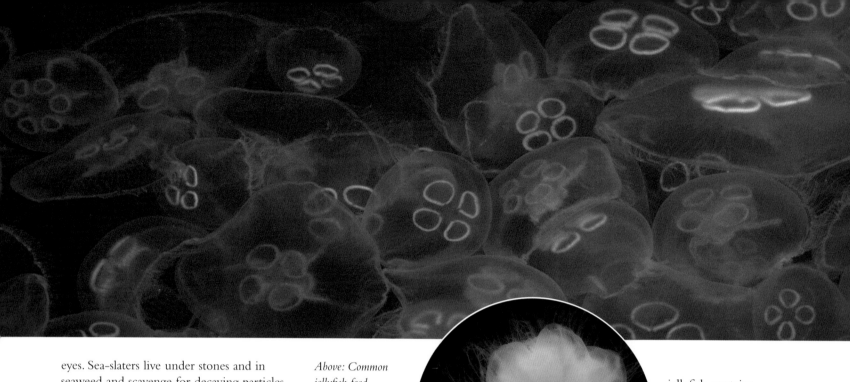

eyes. Sea-slaters live under stones and in seaweed and scavenge for decaying particles of animal matter. They are active at night.

Jellyfish

The jellyfish is a marine invertebrate consisting of two bell-shaped layers of cells. It has a veil of stinging tentacles, and when the stinging cells are triggered, coiled threads carrying poison are discharged, a process that is used to stun prey prior to feeding. Contained within the fringe of stinging tentacles and surrounding the mouth, are longer tentacles that direct plankton, fish or shrimps towards the mouth. The coloured parts of the jellyfish can either indicate the reproductive organs or be light-sensitive pigment spots that ensure the jellyfish keeps its upper side turned toward the surface. Jellyfish species around the UK are not dangerous to humans, although they are toxic, and stings can cause severe and painful allergic reactions. Most jellyfish have a lifespan of just ten weeks, and dry out rapidly and die if they become stranded. They can congregate in large swarms or blooms, often where food is plentiful.

Common jellyfish
(Aurelia aurita)
A flat blob of translucent jelly, 8–20cm (3–8in) in size, the common or moon

Above: Common jellyfish feed principally by trapping microscopic plankton in the film of mucus that is secreted over the surface of the bell, then picked off by the tentacles beneath.

Right: The lion's mane is the largest known species of jellyfish; the tentacles of the largest species can trail as long as 30m (100ft) and their stings are toxic.

Sea temperature

Jellyfish tend to bloom when sea temperatures warm up so recent longer and milder winters have increased the period in which they are active. In the last few years, some species have been recorded as blooming as late as November. Species of jellyfish with powerful stings which are usually native to the Mediterranean, such as the **Portuguese man of war** (Physalia physalia) and the **mauve stinger** (Pelagia noctiluca), are being increasingly spotted on the UK coast due to warmer sea temperatures.

jellyfish contains four pink or violet horseshoe-shapes. It does not have tentacles and does not sting. It is seen most frequently between May and August.

Compass jellyfish
(Chrysaora hysoscella)
Distinguished by the 16 V-shaped markings on its dome and its 24 tentacles, the compass jellyfish can grow to 30cm (1ft) in diameter and can be seen around most of the UK coast between July and October.

Lion's mane jellyfish
(Cyanea capillata)
A yellow, red or orange jellyfish that is variable in size. Specimens have been recorded with a bell diameter of 2.5m (8ft) with tentacles trailing 30m (100ft). In British waters they are more commonly a modest 50cm (20in), and pulsate just below the surface of very cold water, on the west coast of Scotland and the northern North Sea. Their frequency decreases the further south you travel.

Beadlet sea anemone
(Actinia equina)
The sea anemone is a predatory animal related to corals and jellyfish. The beadlet

sea anemone is one of the most common species to inhabit UK coastal waters. It attaches itself to rocks by means of an adhesive foot called a basal disc. A small creature, up to 5cm (2in) high, it is a ruthless stalker, yet it looks like an innocent underwater flower, with its red tentacles waving and a ring of bright blue spots at their base. Out of the water it resembles a blob of red jelly.

Lugworm
(Arenicola marina)

Most of us have seen worm casts on wet sand, but may never have seen an actual lugworm, which can be as long as 25cm (10in), and as wide as an adult's little finger. Lugworms live in U-shaped burrows with a cast at the surface marking one end, and a blow hole marking the other. They are reddish brown and found on sandy shores. Fisherman dig up the worms for bait and some wading birds like to snack on them.

Common ragworm
(Nereis diversicolor)

An active predator, the common ragworm is 8–10cm (3–4in) long, and has a long, flattened body with a distinctive red blood

Below: The ragworm feeds on mud, but is a fearsome predator and will dive out of its burrow to snare soft-bodied invertebrates when food is scarce.

vessel running down the middle. Ragworms live in mucus-lined U- or J-shaped burrows in sandy and muddy estuaries. They are popular as bait with fisherman and wading birds are its main predator. They can bite when they are handled.

Starfish

There are over 2,000 species of starfish around the world; just seven are common in rock pools and seas around the United Kingdom. Typically starfish have five arms radiating from a central disc, however limb numbers are variable and starfish have the capacity to shed an arm if injured and can then grow another one or two to replace it. They live on oyster and mussel beds, prizing shells apart with their suckers to snack on the contents and can push their stomachs out of their mouths to enable them to digest prey too large to swallow.

Common starfish
(Asterias rubens)

Pale orange in colour, the common starfish is studded all over with white dots or pedicellariae, which prevent encrusting creatures from taking hold. It can range in size from 10–40cm (4–16in) and is found on rocky shores.

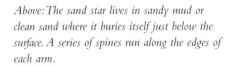

Above: The sand star lives in sandy mud or clean sand where it buries itself just below the surface. A series of spines run along the edges of each arm.

Sand star
(Astropecten irregularis)

Similar to but smaller than the common starfish, growing up to 20cm (8in) across, the sand star is found on sandy floors where it burrows into the sand and feeds off worms and molluscs. It is widespread in sand and on the lower shore.

Spiny starfish
(Marthasterias glacialis)

This species is found in gravel and sand, often among rocks, and can reach a whopping 35cm (14in). It is variable in colour, from purple to white, grey, yellow and green. The spiny starfish feeds on common starfish as well as crabs and other shellfish.

Common cushion star
(Asterina gibbosa)

A small starfish 5cm (2in) in diameter, the common cushion star has a distinctive pentagonal outline and short arms. Colour is variable and cushion stars can be mottled grey, brown or green. It is commonly found under rocks and seaweeds on the lower shore.

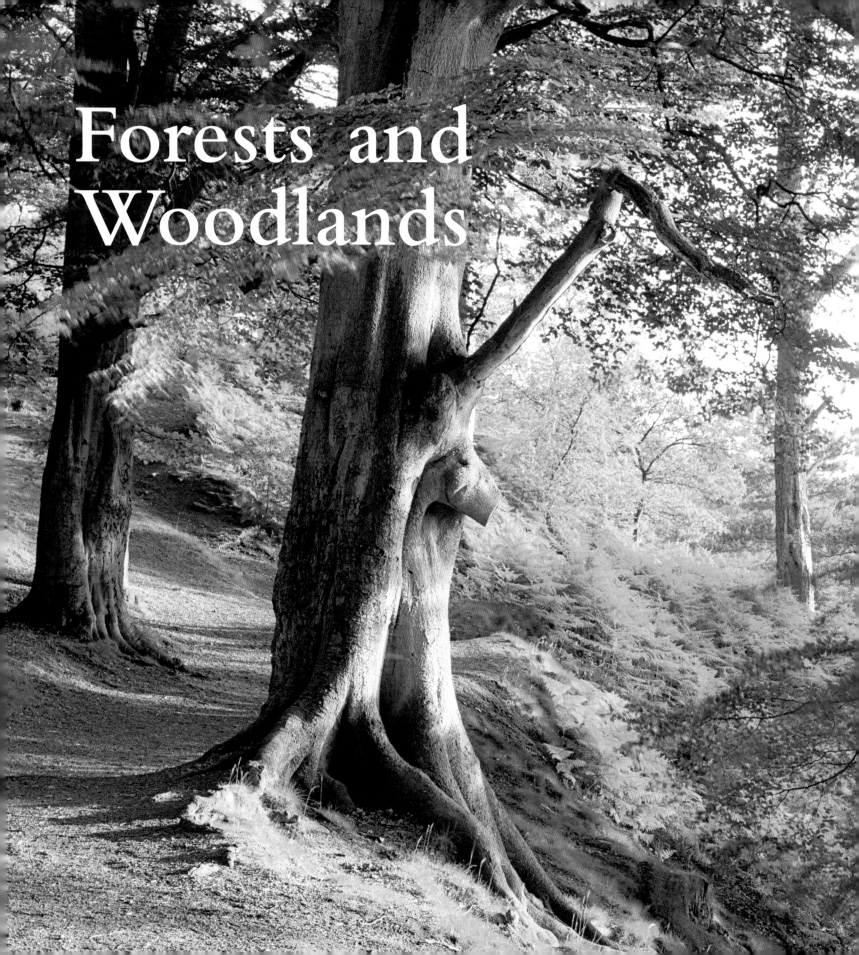

Forests and Woodlands

Ancient and Modern Woodland

Today, woodland covers less than 12 per cent of our land, far less than most other countries in the European Union. However, our varied geology, topography and climate, together with centuries of diverse management, means that we have a wide range of woodland types. Throughout lowland Britain, woods dominated by a single species of tree, such as oak or ash, can be found, while in the south mighty hangers of beech clothe chalk and limestone hillsides, their thick canopies creating a dense shade where little else can grow. Other woodlands are made up of a mix of tree species – oak, beech, ash, hazel, lime, willow, yew and many others. Some of these woods are dark and tangled, while others, such as the Caledonian Forest in Scotland, or the New Forest in Hampshire, have boggy glades and open stretches of grassland, kept clear of saplings by grazing animals.

Ancient woodland

Nearly all of Britain's woodland has been greatly modified by humans since prehistoric times, and only the most inaccessible slopes bear fragments of the original, untouched ancient woodland. However, the term 'ancient woodland' means any wooded site that has held a continuous cover of woodland for at least the last 400 years.

Characteristically, ancient woodland is dominated by big trees such as oak and beech; it also has a wider variety of trees than other types of woodland, including some less-common species such as aspen and wild service, as found in parts of the Sussex Weald. On chalk and other limestones – for example, on Box Hill in Surrey – other trees are common, including ash, field maple, native box, yew and the remains of elm. Many types of ancient woodland support spectacular arrays of spring flowers, such as bluebells and wood anemones, which thrive before the leaf canopy grows over and the forest floor darkens through late spring and early summer. Many spring insects are associated with these flowers, including several types of butterfly and hoverfly, as well as other insects, birds, spiders and fungi.

In many areas, ancient woodland shows evidence of intensive management; abandoned 'coppice with standards' contains many-stemmed trees and bushes, especially hazel or hornbeam, with taller, single-stemmed oaks (standards) dotted about. Examples of this type of woodland can be found in south Cumbria, Oxleas

Below: The ancient sessile oak woodland of Horner Wood, on the Holnicote Estate on east Exmoor, is of national importance for lichens growing on the twisted trunks, and also for bats.

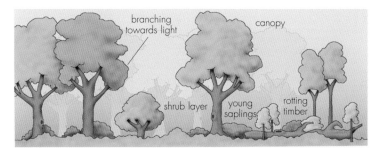

Above: Trees regenerate quite differently in unmanaged ancient woodland (top), with saplings appearing in gaps left by fallen trees, while coppicing in ancient woodland (bottom) allows light through the canopy to promote new growth.

Right: Old parkland in the Peak District, which has been planted over a medieval ridge-and-furrow system. Parkland is really a form of pasture woodland.

Wood in Greenwich and on the National Trust's Mottisfont Estate in Hampshire. In some places, coppice woodland occurs without standards, such as the hazel plantations in Hampshire and Spanish chestnut coppice in Kent, at Scotney and Sissinghurst.

Another traditional method of management was called 'wood pasture', or 'pasture woodland', in which trees dotted around grassland were cut, or pollarded, at 2.5–3m (8–10ft) above the ground so that the regenerating shoots were out of reach of grazing animals. On large estates, such as at Windsor Great Park, Epping Forest and Hatfield Forest, ancient pollards – mainly oak but also hornbeam, field maple and some other trees – grow distinctively, with all the branches beginning at the top of a short, thick trunk.

Fruit trees, too, have been cultivated in orchards for hundreds of years, often spread quite wide apart to get the most light and with grass between that could be cut for hay or grazed by sheep. Like wood pasture, many traditional orchards are centuries old and can have a rich flora of mosses, lichens and wild flowers, as well as specialist insects, including some that depend on mistletoe, itself a feature of old orchards.

Hatfield Forest

In historic terms the word 'forest' refers to land containing some trees, with defined boundaries, reserved for royal hunting, but it has come to mean any large area of wild woodland. Hatfield Forest, near Bishops Stortford on the Hertfordshire and Essex border, was declared a royal forest in the early 12th century. Since 1924, it has been owned and managed by the National Trust and is truly remarkable in that it retains all the elements of a medieval forest, including ancient coppices (shown below), wood pasture, timber trees, scrub, deer and cattle. A Site of Special Scientific Interest and a National Nature Reserve, with some trees over 600 years old, the area is of enormous historical and ecological importance. As well as preserving this unique environment by continuing the traditional practices of grazing, coppicing and pollarding, the Trust also protects the Forest from over-development and resists development in the surrounding area, such as housing developments and the expansion of Stansted Airport.

Secondary woodland

In numerous places, such as many of the old heather-clad heaths of south-east England, trees have taken over in the absence of grazing or cutting to form relatively new 'secondary woodland'. Here, the spring flowers are often poor – it takes much longer for these to arrive than for trees to colonise – and tree species are often few in number, mainly oak, ash, birch, hawthorn and sycamore. As a result, the associated wildlife is usually less varied.

Plantations

Woods where trees have been planted in distinctive rows are easily identified as plantations, often belonging to the Forestry Commission but also, in some cases, under private ownership. Here, the main function of the wood is the production of timber; the trees are frequently fast-growing alien species, especially North American conifers, and there are often only one or two types. These dense woods can be very dark at all times of the year, and have few, if any, woodland flowers or other wildlife – there is too little light for much life to survive. In some places new trees have been planted into existing woodland, so there may be some trees – even ancient pollards – that have survived from what was there before.

Woodland Ecology

The ecology of woodland is perhaps best understood in terms of a series of layers – the tree canopy, the shrub layer or understorey, the field layer and the ground layer. Each layer is characterised by its own range of plant and animal species that interact with each other and their environment to form a complex web of processes that make up a functioning ecosystem.

Woodland layers

The uppermost level is the canopy layer, made up of the foliage of the main forest trees. In the summer, the trees manufacture organic matter (in the form of sugars) from water and carbon dioxide using the energy from sunlight; in other words, the canopy is the powerhouse for the whole ecosystem. In the canopy there are many insects, including caterpillars, sawflies and aphids feeding on the leaves, while predators, such as spiders and birds, feed on these insects.

Below the main canopy there is often an understorey of smaller trees and bushes, such as holly and hawthorn, that make use of the lower levels of light trickling through the canopy; often these plants benefit from glades formed when mature trees die back. This zone also contains the main trunks of the bigger trees, which provide a range of habitats, such as rot holes and hollows for insects, birds and small mammals. Many beetles live at this level, and their larvae are one of the main sources of food for woodpeckers and other birds.

The field layer, comprising flowers and seedlings, is often intermittent; in the deeper shade few plants can survive. This zone contains many small creatures including beetles, millipedes, harvestmen and spiders, as well as those insects that descend from higher levels to visit the flowers, pupate in the soil, search for food, or lay their eggs, while predatory creatures such as spiders hunt and prey on them.

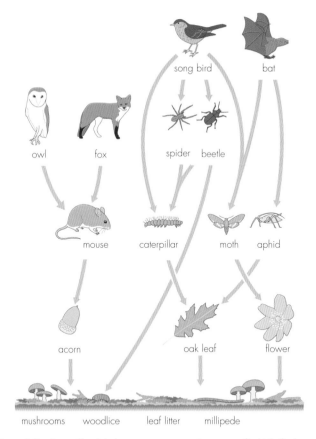

Above: Mixed woodland is home to many species, some of which feed on trees and plants while others are predators and parasites. When the animals and birds at the top of the food chain die, their bodies decompose and feed insects, fungi and ultimately the trees. So the process continues.

Left: Bracket fungi and lichens on a fallen oak trunk. A succession of fungi, lichen and insects (especially beetles) colonise the trees and then fade away as the wood rots. The fungi and insects play key roles in wood decay.

In the spring, before the trees have unfurled their leaves, most of the sunlight reaches the ground; it is these conditions that allow spring flowers such as bluebell, ramsons and wood anemone to flourish. The plants flower briefly and disappear, all their effort concentrated into a period of no more than three spring months. Where gaps in the canopy allow it, some grasses and other woodland flowers can thrive.

Large and small mammals, such as deer, badgers, rabbits and wood mice, live on the field and ground layer, feeding on the lower vegetation and nuts falling from oaks and beech trees. In a few places wild boar have now become re-established in English woodlands; these are foraging omnivores and, like badgers, disturb the woodland soil, so providing a suitable habitat for germinating seeds. Many fungi associated with both living and dead trees erect fruiting bodies above the ground – our familiar mushrooms and toadstools – which are eaten by insects and woodland mammals.

Nature's recyclers

The minerals required by the woodland ecosystem are brought up from the soil or even from underlying rock by the roots of the trees. Woodland soil, which varies according to the nature of the rock beneath, is usually covered with a layer of leaf litter – dead leaves and parts of trees that fall and slowly decay. Both the litter layer and the soil beneath are teeming with life; bacteria and fungi break down the dead organic matter, while all sorts of tiny creatures, such as earthworms, snails, woodlice, millipedes and mites, graze on the dead leaves and decaying organic matter. Others, such as beetles and spiders, feed on these tiny creatures and are, in turn, eaten by birds. Some of these birds also use the trees for nesting.

When a tree dies the decomposers move in, starting with the fungi, beetles and flies. It has been estimated that 80 per cent of the beetles in woodland depend on dead wood, which is often scarce or of the wrong type (species) in secondary woodland and plantations. This whole suite of decomposer species, together with the predators that feed on them, make use of the organic matter produced ultimately by the canopy leaves. At the same time, decomposition of dead material releases minerals back into the soil. Some of these minerals are lost as water runs off into streams but most are recycled and taken up by the roots of trees and smaller plants, usually through their mycorrhizae (fungi that form a close relationship with the roots of plants, especially trees). These myrcorrhizal fungi are incredibly important, being fundamental drivers of woodland ecology; yet we scarcely see them.

Above: Spring in the Cotswold beech woods, with a dense carpet of wild garlic (ramsons) on which breeds a special hoverfly Portevenia maculata.

Plantations, especially single species (monocultures) on impoverished soil, tend to have very few and less varied fauna and flora, though they are not without specialists, such as conifer aphids and birds such as the goldcrest and sparrowhawk. In many cases, the plantations have failed to produce worthwhile timber. The Forestry Commission is now leading an initiative to remove ailing plantations created over valuable wildlife sites and restore the former habitat, especially to restore native woodland on ancient woodland sites.

Upsetting the balance

In our highly modified, if still-beautiful woods, natural processes, checks and balances have been grossly distorted or broken by man's impact. Many woods now consist largely of trees of the same height, with a dense canopy. This is especially true of plantations and secondary woods, but also of ancient woodland sites where intensive management suddenly lapsed, such as at the Horner and Watersmeet woods on Exmoor, which were intensively managed until around the First World War. Addressing these issues is a major challenge, especially on steep slopes, though in time the woods will manage themselves as individual trees collapse, or storm damage occurs. Deer (shown right), which have no natural predators since the wolf was eliminated, and which are often non-native, are a major issue, as high numbers prevent natural regeneration by nibbling and destroying the shoots of young trees.

Woodland Habitats

Various types of 'natural' woodland are found in Britain, although the term is more correctly 'semi-natural' woodland given that virtually all our woodland has been influenced to some degree by active management. Each type supports its own characteristic plants and animals, the richness of wildlife influenced by the type and number of tree species and the age of the trees, which in turn affect the amount of sunlight penetrating the canopy and the quantity of dead or decaying wood that litters the ground. The large quantity of decaying wood found in ancient woodland, for example, accounts for the rich variety of insects and fungi found in these woods. The following are just some of the many different types of woodland habitat to be found in the UK.

Beech and birch woodland

Beech woods are characteristic of the landscape of some of our southern limestone hills, notably the Chilterns and Cotswolds. These woods are not natural in origin but are the result of forestry practices. Indeed, beech is not a true native apart from, perhaps, in the south east. Crucially, beech will not successfully regenerate in established beech woods; instead it is replaced by ash, which then nurses the next generation of beech in alternate cycles. This process is evident today in many beech woods that were damaged by the great storms of 1987 and 1990 as a result of the shallow-rooted nature of the tree.

Above: Ashridge Estate in Hertfordshire features ancient beech woodland where beech and ash flourish.

Right: Some wildlife typical of mixed woodland through the seasons.

Beech comes into leaf fairly early and casts a heavy shade, which means that the understorey and field layers are usually sparse and simple. Locally, holly and yew regenerate well under beech; indeed, yew is taking over spectacularly in many storm-damaged beech woods. The ground flora in beech woods encourages certain types of species, including rare orchids, and often lots of fungi and lichens, and supports an important insect fauna, especially those associated with dead wood. But the future of beech woodland is far from secure. Young beech trees are devastated by grey squirrels and the rise in temperatures due to climate change may well make southern England less suitable for this beautiful but problem-prone tree.

Oak and hazel woodland

Oak and hazel woods are typically managed as coppice with standards (single-stemmed oaks), such as found in the woods of south Cumbria. The oak is renowned for having the greatest number of associated insect species of any native tree, although the rare goat willow has almost as many. In typical coppice woodland the tall oak trees are the only single-stemmed trees, standing tall among a dense growth of understorey consisting largely of multi-stemmed coppiced hazel. These woods are the habitat of dormice, which eat hazel nuts and buds, flowers and fruits

Healthy woodland

A good indicator of the health of woodland is the presence and condition of tree seedlings (like this common oak seedling, shown below). In many woods the few seedlings that do exist get browsed by deer and keep having their top shoot removed; some, like holly and hawthorn can survive for many years like this but hazel and birch soon give up and die. In a healthy wood there should be a new generation of seedlings waiting for the chance – given more light – to shoot up and join the canopy, though this may only be necessary every 50 or so years. Unfortunately, in too many woods today most of the seedlings of the main trees do not survive – if they germinate at all – and so as the wood ages its composition may change. Often this is because many woods have far more deer in them than is healthy. To encourage essential regeneration and maintain healthy woodland, landowners may manage deer populations by selective and humane culling.

Left: A classic hazel coppice with oak standards. For centuries much of our lowland woodland looked like this – now it is largely a feature of woodland nature reserves.

Below: The common dormouse is a scarce nocturnal inhabitant of ancient woodland and hedges. It prefers dense shrub, where it can forage for fruits, berries, nuts and insects.

in season, and are rich in spring flowers such as yellow archangel, violets and ramsons (wild garlic). Among the hazel trees may also be found ash (either coppiced or grown as standards), wild service, field maple and occasionally crab apple. Because there is not a complete canopy (except where the wood has been abandoned), light reaches the ground at all times of year, so there is a much greater diversity of plants and animals to be found here than in a beech wood.

Alder carr

Wet woodland, or carr, occurs on poorly drained or seasonally wet soils, such as damp river valleys and marshes, usually with alder, birch and willows as the predominant tree species. Many alder woods are ancient and have a long history of coppicing – sometimes to make charcoal for gunpowder and fuel. They are often associated with ash and goat willow, and may contain pools fringed with reeds and sedges, and areas of enormous grass tussocks. This is the habitat of many specialist insects, such as craneflies and snail-killing flies, as well as birds, such as the moorhen and marsh tit. Large areas of alder woodland can be visited around the Norfolk Broads, on the Crom Estate in Northern Ireland and Bramshaw Commons in the New Forest. Because of threats to its diverse fauna and flora, wet woodland is one of the habitats covered by the UK Biodiversity Action Plan, whereby landowners such as the National Trust work to protect these precious environments, not least because of their role in natural water purification and preventing flooding and siltation.

Native pinewoods

In some parts of the Highlands of Scotland the remaining one per cent of the ancient Caledonian pine forest can still be seen, dominated by Scots pine but with some broadleaved trees such as aspen, birch and rowan. There is often open woodland with dense heather and bilberry below, completely enveloping fallen tree trunks and single branches, and, as the trees drop vast quantities of pine needles, the soil can be submerged under a deep layer of sphagnum moss and pine needles. This is the home of rarities such as the pine marten, the capercaillie and the Scottish crossbill, as well as unusual insects such as the Kentish glory moth and various hoverflies. Many of these forests are overrun by a large number of red deer. Scottish landowners are working towards the possibility of restoring other animals that used to live in these woods hundreds of years ago, most realistically the beaver and lynx.

Left: Saturated alder carr woodland is often home to myriad mosquitoes, biting flies and insectivorous birds.

Right: Little now remains of the formerly vast Caledonian forest, like this pine forest in the Highlands.

Woods and Forests Through History

Thousands of years ago much of the British Isles was covered with woodland, but probably not by dense, dark forest. Recently, the Dutch ecologist Frans Vera has demonstrated that the wildwood, as it is known, was largely open with grassy areas grading into land scattered with patches of trees. Streams and rivers had densely wooded fringes, and woodland extended up the slopes of mountains, giving way to a woody scrub zone above the tree line. This wildwood was the natural vegetation that had developed after the last ice age.

About 5,000 years ago, people began to change things, felling and burning trees to make way for crops and villages, and harvesting the wood for fuel, fencing and building materials. Early settlers also kept animals that grazed on seedlings and foliage, which compounded the loss of ancient woodland by discouraging natural regeneration. As a result it is estimated that by the Iron Age (c. 500BC) about half of Britain's native woodland had already disappeared. The Domesday Book – a detailed survey of English towns, villages, houses, people, animals and land compiled in 1086 at the request of William the

Royal forests

Large swathes of woodland, often incorporating areas of moorland and heath, were designated 'royal forest' by William the Conqueror. Here, the king's right to hunt took precedence over all other activities. All game and timber within these forests became the property of the king and severe penalties were imposed on anyone trespassing. Local people were only allowed to collect small branches for fuel or making tools and baskets; in some places they were granted permission to graze their animals. Successive monarchs used the royal forests as a source of revenue and sometimes sold off parcels of land when they were short of cash. One of the best surviving examples of royal forest is the New Forest in Hampshire, which William the Conqueror designated in 1079.

Conqueror for the purpose of taxation – shows that approximately 80 per cent of native woodland had disappeared, with only a fifth of England's landscape still covered in woodland.

Woodland resources

Managed woodland provided a valuable resource; as well as using timber for building houses and boats and constructing fences, people used the underwood (small-size timber, branches and twigs) as a major source of fuel, as bedding for livestock, and for making a wide range of everyday objects from tables to tool handles. In addition, stock could be grazed among the trees, pigs fattened with nuts, fruits gathered and woodland animals and birds hunted for food. Early on, people had devised ways to manage woodland to provide for their basic needs. As early as 3000BC it was found that cutting trees such as oak, ash and hazel close to the ground would produce many new shoots, resulting in a multi-stemmed tree that provided useful and easily harvested wood, and by Roman times coppicing was widely practised. It was to remain fundamental to the rural economy until the early 20th century.

Left: The intricate timber-framed house at Speke Hall, Liverpool, illustrates the extent to which woodland products were formerly used in building work. Timber beams were often reused and recycled as houses were rebuilt or remodelled, although they were often more susceptible to fire than other types of construction materials.

Trees for profit

As the demand for wood increased, private landowners began to transform their estates by planting trees on a commercial scale, encouraged by prominent citizens such as John Evelyn whose great treatise on trees and forestry, *Sylva*, was first published in 1669. Thanks to pioneers such as William Windham who, at his estate at Felbrigg Hall in Norfolk in the 1670s, became one of the first to establish a plantation purely for profit, the 18th century became one of countrywide forestation. Many of these plantations were run primarily to supply timber – especially oak – for boat-building in general and specifically the Navy's ship-building programme, which burgeoned during the Napoleonic Wars. Further pressure was put on the timber industry by the Industrial Revolution when demand for wood increased enormously, initially for fuel, but later, as coal took over as the main fuel source, for wooden pit props for coal mines and charcoal for forges and iron foundries.

Just as coal replaced wood for fuel, by the middle of the 19th century iron and steel began to supplant timber in ship-building. As country people migrated to the industrial cities and industrial manufacturing practices caused traditional country crafts to go into decline, many areas that were previously managed as coppice woodland were abandoned. Meanwhile, Britain became increasingly dependant on imported timber, such as softwoods from Scandinavia and North America, and hardwoods from the tropics.

During the First World War, when vast quantities of timber were needed for building trenches and as pit props for increased coal

Above: The 18th-century woodland landscape around Dunham Massey in Cheshire was designed for aesthetic reasons but also as a natural wood resource.

Right: A charcoal kiln in the Forest of Dean, c. 1910. The traditional practice of charcoal burning used to be widespread and benefited many flowers, birds and butterflies that favour young, open woodland.

production, the demand for wood soared once more. With cheap imports no longer available, the government soon recognised the strategic importance of self-sufficiency in timber production, so in 1919 they established the Forestry Commission to grow timber trees as a crop. Native trees, such as oak and beech, took too long to mature, and even Britain's only native tall conifer – the Scots pine – was slower growing than other conifer species, so the Commission concentrated on fast-growing imported species such as the Douglas fir, lodgepole pine and Sitka spruce. They soon faced opposition from country-lovers who argued that these alien plantations were defacing the landscape, especially in much-loved areas like the Lake District and the New Forest. Today, with many of their plantations fully mature, the Forestry Commission's approach has widened. Trees for timber are still planted in large numbers, but there is more concern now for both landscape and wildlife conservation, and most of their forests and woodlands are open to the public.

Managing and Conserving Woodlands

The 20th century saw a revolution in woodland management in the British Isles, with the widespread introduction of non-native species. These were used either to create new plantations on formerly open land or planted into existing woods. Not all of these plantings were successful as the locations or soil types were sometimes unsuitable for particular species. This introduction of non-native trees had a severe impact on wildlife, for example, populations of butterflies associated with open woodland clearings collapsed, the high brown fritillary declining by 84 per cent in under 30 years. Some butterflies, together with songbirds associated with dense 10–25 year old plantations, fared well for a while until the young plantations began to mature into conifer monocultures.

Worse, when areas of tall conifers are cleared only a few tough and ubiquitous plants flourish, such as bracken and brambles, as opposed to the diverse ground flora that thrives when broad-leaved trees are felled. The associated birds and insects are similarly affected. Also, many woods that were not turned into new plantations were simply neglected and became overgrown, and so failed to act as reservoirs for the myriad animals associated with open woodland. Non-native species, notably rhododendron (*Rhododendron ponticum*), which grows best on acid soils, invaded many woods, leading to huge expense for conservation organisations that had to remove this highly invasive alien shrub.

Woodlands conservation

But all is far from lost. Woodlands are hugely dynamic systems and much of the wildlife associated with them has immense powers of recovery, given remnant populations to act as sources. The Forestry Commission (FC) has been running a conservation scheme called PAWS – Plantations on Ancient Woodland Sites – which aims to restore suitable broad-leaved woodland to ancient woodland sites that were planted up with conifers during the 20th century. This

Above: The pearl-bordered fritillary was widespread, and common in clearings in woods until the 1970s, but has now disappeared from over 60 per cent of its former localities, despite conservation efforts.

scheme is proving highly successful on land owned by both public and private bodies. Now, the FC is also looking at removing plantations that were created on former open habitats such as heathland and downland. So wildlife associated not just with woodland is also benefiting from more enlightened, broader-minded woodland thinking.

The great storms

The great storm of 16 October 1987 marked a watershed in thinking about trees – in woods, parks, gardens and the open countryside – with the joint realisations that nothing is immortal and nothing can be taken for granted. The storm felled some 15 million trees in southern England, with the bulk of the damage occurring on young forestry plantations, such as Alice Holt forest in Surrey (shown below). The impact on historic landscapes and gardens was perhaps more severe, with famous National Trust gardens such as Nymans in East Sussex being devastated. During another great storm on 25th January 1990 a further three million trees were felled.

These events, seemingly catastrophic at the time, revealed the ability of woods to look after themselves, for these wind-blown woods have regenerated spectacularly. Many were cleared and replanted, though those where natural regeneration was allowed to take place seem to have fared best. At Toys Hill woods, near Sevenoaks in Kent, for example, the National Trust planted some new trees but left other parts of the area to regenerate naturally; Toys Hill has now reasserted itself as a beautiful wood, with the hulks of the fallen monoliths peacefully rotting on the ground, providing a great source of dead wood for beetles and other decomposers.

Today there is a huge interest in woodland conservation, as illustrated by the success of the Woodland Trust. The Forestry Commission itself is now an ardent conservation organisation; it still has obligations to provide timber and produce revenue from its woods, but is now doing so in a more sustainable manner.

The future

Our woodlands and woodland wildlife are entering a radical new era – a time of new problems but also of great opportunity. The only certainty is change, possibly quite radical change; some aspects of woodland ecology will benefit, others will be adversely affected. Climate change, with milder winters, hotter summers, and more extreme weather events, will pose many challenges. It may well release into our countryside a new generation of non-native invasive plants (many of them currently behaving themselves in gardens), and will undoubtedly bring in new insect pests and plant diseases. As examples, the oak processionary moth *(Thaumetopoea processionea)* will invade the UK, with the capacity to defoliate oaks en masse, while new *Phytophora* diseases are already affecting trees and shrubs such as horse chestnut, alder and, incredibly, rhododendron.

At the same time, a burgeoning human population facing an energy crisis will make new demands on our forests and woods. The search for sustainable energy will embrace woods and it may be that many plants and animals thriving in woodland clearings will, in the future, resurge in woods that are actively managed for wood fuels. Indeed, wood fuel is the great white hope of woodland nature conservation.

Left: A typical pine plantation on an ancient woodland site. These areas are being restored to broad-leaved woodland.

Right: A volunteer clearing invasive rhododendron. Huge swathes of countryside have been cleared of this oppressive shrub.

Heritage Trees

The UK is believed to have more ancient trees than any other European country. Some species of tree have life spans that stretch across millennia. Yews can live for several thousand years – at 3–5,000 years old, the Fortingall Yew in Perthshire is believed to be the oldest tree in the UK. Oak and sweet chestnut can survive for 800 years or so, while many other species live to 400 or 500 years. The National Trust cares for more ancient trees than any other individual owner. If you want to walk among ancient trees, here are the stories and locations of some of the National Trust's most famous specimens.

The Ankerwycke Yew at Runnymede, Berkshire

This aged tree, thought to be at least 2,000 years old, is said to have witnessed the oathing and sealing of Magna Carta by King John in June 1215, and to be the location where Henry VIII met Anne Boleyn in the 1530s. At that time the river Thames followed a different course so that Runnymede and Ankerwyke were on the same side of the river. This venerable yew grows in the grounds of the ruined Priory of Ankerwycke and measures an impressive 9.4m (31ft) in circumference.

The Borrowdale Yew, Cumbria

This is one of the four ancient yews celebrated in Wordsworth's 1803 poem *Yew Trees*:

'But worthier still of note
Are those Fraternal Four of Borrowdale,
Joined in one solemn and capacious grove;
Huge trunks! – and each particular trunk a growth
Of intertwisted fibres serpentine'

One of the four went down in a great storm in 1883, though the three others still survive. The Borrowdale Yew is female and boasts a large hollow that fits four people. Although it was damaged in a storm in 2005, the tree continues to thrive.

The Clumber Park Lime Tree Avenue, Nottinghamshire

This is the longest tree avenue of its kind in Europe. Planted in about 1840, it is over 3km (almost 2 miles) long and consists of 1,296 common limes planted in a double row on each side of a drive. Records from 1906 relate that the trees were suffering from insect attack. To alleviate this, black grease bands are painted round the trunk of each tree to prevent the female winter moth climbing up the trunk and laying her eggs in the canopy, which then is stripped bare by her larvae.

Above: One of the three remaining Borrowdale Yews, which have attracted visitors since at least the late 18th century. Yew is the oldest living tree in Britain.

Left: The early Victorian lime avenue of the hybrid European lime at Clumber Park, near Worksop. In 2007, two species of fungi new to Britain were found here.

The Crom Castle Yews, Co. Fermanagh

One of the most impressive trees in Northern Ireland grows near the ruins of old Crom Castle on the Crom Estate. This huge 'tree' is actually two yews, thought to have been planted close together in the 17th century.

Mottisfont Abbey Plane Tree, Hampshire

Trees dominate the grounds of Mottisfont Abbey in Hampshire. Ancient specimens of English oak, sweet chestnut, green and purple beech, hornbeam and others, reveal their years through girth and spread. The 'Great Plane' *(Platanus* x *acerifolia)* is reputed to be one the largest of its kind in the country, with branches covering an area of some 1,500m² (16,000ft²).

Isaac Newton's Apple Tree at Woolsthorpe Manor, Lincolnshire

One of the most historically important trees in Britain, this has been a celebrated national treasure for over 300 years. It is believed to be a descendant of the apple tree that inspired Isaac Newton in 1665 when the 'notion of gravitation came to mind' after he watched an apple fall.

The Original Irish Yew at Florencecourt, Co. Fermanagh

Originally a freak of nature, this peculiar Irish Yew *(Taxus baccata* var. *'fastigiata')* caught the eye of a farmer some time around 1770 due to its graceful upright shape, which was very different from the norm. The farmer dug out the tree and gave it to the Earl of Enniskillen who had it planted on his estate, where it flourished and attracted the attention of the horticulture community which took cuttings. Soon known as the 'Florencecourt Yew', its popular shape led to the tree being commercially propagated in 1820. Though not as impressive as it once was, the tree is known affectionately as the mother of all Irish yew trees.

The Spanish Chestnuts at Croft Castle, Herefordshire

This famous avenue of pollarded sweet chestnuts stretches for 1km (nearly two-thirds of a mile) to the west of the castle. The tale of the chestnuts' origins suggests that the nuts were salvaged from the wrecks of the Spanish Armada some time after 1588, making some of the trees over 400 years old and nearing the end of their normal life. The trees are now gradually succumbing to fungal attack, probably associated with old age, and sooner or later a replacement set of chestnut trees will have to be planted.

The Tolpuddle Martyrs' Tree, Dorset

This world-famous sycamore tree marks the site where the Tolpuddle Martyrs met in 1834 in an attempt to form one of the world's first trade unions, against a background of falling wages and harsh employment laws. The

meeting led to the martyrs' deportation, which was followed by a pardon and, ultimately, the foundation of the Trade Union Movement. The tree was dated for the first time in 2005 by the National Trust. Using special dating techniques, it was possible to work out that the tree is likely to have started life in the 1680s, more than 150 years before the meeting that made it famous.

The Wild Cherry at Studley Royal Water Garden, North Yorkshire

One of Britain's largest wild cherries, this tree grows near Fountains Abbey in the grounds of Studley Royal in arguably England's most important 18th-century water garden. A highlight of this World Heritage Site, the wild cherry is 5.7m (18ft 8in) wide and is an amazing sight, especially when in flower, even though it recently lost its top and classical shape during a severe storm.

Above: A descendant of one of the apple trees under which Isaac Newton discovered gravity.

Left: One of the historic sweet chestnut trees at Croft Castle, near Leominster, at the end of its natural life. Dead trees are important for wildlife, especially fungi.

Wildlife of Forests and Woodlands

Only about 33 species of tree are native to the UK, the other hundreds of species having been introduced over the centuries. Some, like the horse chestnut, were introduced as ornamental trees for parks and gardens, others for commercial purposes such as for their timber (conifers and walnut), fruit (plums and apricots), or nuts (Spanish or sweet chestnut). The following is a selection of the species of tree you are most likely to encounter, along with some of the wildlife – flowers, fungi, birds and mammals – that inhabit our woodlands.

Plants

European larch
(Larix decidua)

Although the larch is a member of the pine family, it is deciduous and loses its leaves in winter. The twigs carry knobs from which clusters of bright green, soft, needle-like leaves will appear; these darken with age but turn yellow before falling in autumn. The flowers appear before the needles in April; the male flowers are yellow tassels while the female flowers are orange pink and upright – both appear on the same twig. When fertilised they rapidly form flat-topped brown cones.

Douglas fir
(Pseudotsuga menziesii)

This is a mighty evergreen, which grows to 55m (180ft) in the UK but which can reach 100m (330ft) in its natural home on the west coast of the United States. The tree prefers wet, sheltered sites, and has downward-curving branches that carry single, lemon-scented needles, with two white stripes underneath. Both male and female flowers can be seen at the tips of shoots, and the barrel-shaped cones hang downwards from the branches.

Pine

Pine is among the most commercially important timbers and is used in furniture, flooring, panelling and window frames. Trees generally grow to around 25m (80ft) and achieve a diameter of about 1m (3ft). The branches are arranged around the trunk in a tight spiral. New shoots appear in spring, commonly called candles because they are paler than the rest of the tree, and point upwards. Most pines have both male and female cones on the same tree.

Above: The Scots pine is readily identifiable by its tall, straight and rather bare trunk – the foliage stands away from it and is rounded or flat topped.

Left: The European larch can survive very cold temperatures and is often seen high on the tree line on mountains as well as in woodland. The seeds are an important food source for the lesser redpoll and the siskin.

Spruce

The spruce is a cone- or triangular-shaped evergreen that carries green needles. Flowers appear in May; the male flowers are yellow and the female flowers are red. When fertilised they develop into downward-pointing cones. The **Norway spruce** *(Picea abies)* is better known today as a Christmas tree, but it is also grown for timber, as well as to fulfil the demands of the festive season. **Sitka spruce** *(Picea sitchensis)* has sharper needles than the Norway spruce, and its cones have wavy scales, unlike the more rounded scales of the Christmas tree. It also grows much faster, and can reach heights of 50m (164ft), compared to the 42m (138ft) attained by the Norway spruce.

Sitka spruce

Birch

Common or silver birch

The birch is a strong tree, rarely planted by foresters as it has little timber value. However, it spreads readily without assistance, can grow to 30m (100ft), and colonises wasteland. It is important because its light and open leaf canopy allows flowering plants, mosses and grasses to thrive underneath, which in turn provide food for a wide variety of insects, birds and animals. Birch is tough and hardy, and grows further north and higher up mountains than most other broad-leaved species, apart from mountain ash. The **common** or **silver birch** *(Betula pendula)* has distinctive white bark on its trunk, but darker, whip-like twigs, which were used to make brushes called besoms. The leaves are small, serrated, pale-green ovals that turn golden in autumn, some of which loiter on the branches late in autumn, looking like jewels on a necklace. The smaller **dwarf birch** *(Betula nana)* is commonly found in Scotland.

Scots pine
(Pinus sylvestris)

Native to the UK, the Scots pine has grey-brown, deeply cracked bark, lightening to orange near the top of the long, bare trunk, and is topped by a flat or rounded mass of foliage. The dark green or blue-green needles are arranged in spirals. Seed cones are red on pollination, and mature to a yellow-brown over the course of around two years, when the seeds are released.

Lodgepole pine
(Pinus contorta)

An import from Canada, the lodgepole pine has a long, straight trunk, and can comfortably reach 30m (100ft) or more in height. It has straight, sharp green needles and the scales of the cone each have a sharp prickle. The cones, which are covered in a sticky pitch, need extreme heat to open. In the wild this occurs naturally with forest fires. This tree was readily planted in bogs during the mid-20th century but efforts are now being made to remove plantations and restore bogs that are valuable for wildlife.

Aspen
(Populus tremula)

There are many different varieties of poplar, a member of the willow family. Aspen, a form of poplar, was one of the original trees of the wildwood and is believed to be one of the first trees to have migrated north after the Ice Age, along with birch. Deer do not like to eat it, which may in the long term have helped the species to flourish. The aspen will grow to 20m (66ft) tall. The green leaves are softly serrated circles, held on delicate flattened stems, and flutter and tremble in the slightest breeze. The male catkins are pale purple and the female catkins are green.

Leaves, flowers and fruit

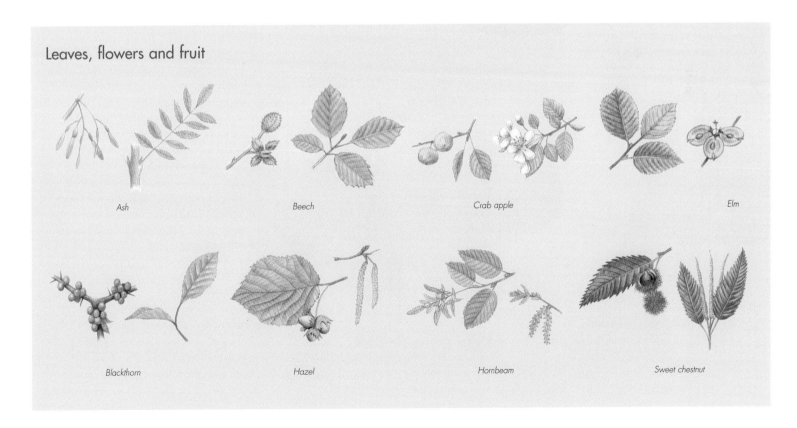

Ash

Beech

Crab apple

Elm

Blackthorn

Hazel

Hornbeam

Sweet chestnut

Goat willow
(Salix caprea)

The sallow or goat willow is better able to withstand dry conditions than other members of the willow family. It produces either male or female plants. The male flowers are immediately recognisable: they start grey before puffing up into yellow, pollen-tipped balls of fluff – what we know as 'pussy willow'. The female catkins are greenish white in colour, but still splendid to look at. The catkins appear very early in spring on the bare branches. The grey-green, toothed oval leaves have a downy underside.

Hornbeam
(Carpinus betulus)

Similar to the beech in appearance, the hornbeam has smooth, grey-green bark. The leaves are broad ovals with narrow veins and toothed margins, and first appear in May, somewhat later than the beech. Yellow-green male catkins and erect, pink female flowers are borne on the same branch. Winged papery bracts contain a small ribbed nut and hang in green clusters. Hornbeam is a slow-growing tree, which

Above: Beech woods are at their most spectacular at bud break in April and in October when the leaves are changing colour. Climate change is impacting on the trees whose shallow roots are affected by drought.

Above left: Hazelnuts are held in a short, leafy husk until ripe, around 7–8 months after pollination, when they fall to the ground.

was commonly pollarded for its hard timber; this was used for butcher's chopping blocks, ox yokes and cogs for mill machinery. It is most frequently found in the south east.

Hazel
(Corylus avellana)

In the past hazel was an important economic crop and was commonly grown in woodland for coppicing every seven years. This would encourage the plant to send up a series of new shoots that had many uses, including clothes pegs, hurdles and kindling. Hazel has large, heart-shaped leaves with toothed margins. The flowers appear in February; the male flowers are long, yellow catkins and female flowers are swollen buds with crimson tassels. Hazelnuts or cobnuts are a valued food source for birds and squirrels.

Beech
(Fagus sylvatica)

The beech is an imposing tree that will reach heights of around 30m (100ft). Beech has smooth grey bark and zigzag-shaped twigs that contain alternate buds. Male catkins are purple-brown, while female catkins are green and bud shaped. The pale green, oval leaves appear towards the end of

Oak

Oak is a valuable source of fine timber and was pollarded in wood pasture and used to make timber frames for houses, hulls for ships, fence posts and rails, floorboards, church pews and pulpits. It is also a valuable tree for fauna, supporting some 500 species. Oak has pale grey, deeply fissured bark and a distinctive irregular branching pattern. The distinctive wavy-edged leaves, the emblem of the National Trust, emerge from mid-March to April. Three species are common in the UK. The **common** or **English oak** (Quercus robur) and the **durmast** or **sessile oak** (Quercus petraea) are both native trees. The former is commonly found in the drier southern and eastern regions, the latter dominates areas in the more acid north and west. The **Turkey oak** (Quercus cerris) is an import. Each species can be readily distinguished from the other: the common oak has acorn cups with stalks; the sessile oak has cups without stalks; and the leaf lobes on the Turkey oak are jagged zigzags rather than wavy, and its acorn cups are bristly. Identification can become difficult if English and sessile oak grow close together as they can hybridise.

Common oak

Elm

The bark of the elm is smooth and grey in youth but becomes browner and rougher with age. The branches curve upwards and become brittle over time. The leaves are irregular ovals and are toothed in some varieties. The flowers appear in February or March, before the leaves, and appear as red-purple fuzz on the bare twigs. There are a number of species in the UK, most notably the **English elm** *(Ulmus procera)*, the **Scots** or **wych elm** *(Ulmus glabra)* and the **smooth-leaved elm** *(Ulmus carpinifolia)*. Identification is difficult as all species hybridise. The tree is a favourite nesting site for owls, rooks and kestrels, and is the main foodplant of white-letter hairstreak and large tortoiseshell butterflies, which have suffered with the decline of the elm due to Dutch Elm Disease.

English elm

catkins in July. Spiny, lime-green seed cases contain 3–7 nuts, but not until the tree has reached 30–40 years of age. Sweet chestnut can have a long life span, but in managed forests it is commonly coppiced on a 12–16 year rotation, and used for fencing.

Crab apple
(Malus sylvestris)

Crab apple comes into leaf late in the season, towards the end of April, and flowering follows rapidly in May. The bright green, oval leaves stand on a long stalk. The five-petalled flowers are flushed red on the outside and are white on the inside. The mature twigs carry spines. The greenish yellow apples provide a reliable food source for many insects and birds and, after they fall, mammals will take the fruit.

April and in autumn they turn a beautiful golden orange. Beechnuts appear in the autumn but the tree generally only produces a good crop approximately every 5–8 years. Birds and mammals will feast on the nuts, given the opportunity.

Below: The sweet chestnut produces edible seeds, which were highly prized by the Romans. They can be ground into flour, or used as a distinctive flavouring in desserts and cakes.

Sweet chestnut
(Castanea sativa)

The Romans are believed to have introduced this tree to the UK some 2,000 years ago. It now grows wild across England but is less common in Scotland and Ireland. The bark is beautiful and becomes deeply fissured with age. The tree has long, toothed, green leaves, that turn golden in autumn, and produces both male and female flowers on yellow

Orchards

With more than 100 traditional orchards in its care, the National Trust is working to revive the fortunes of orchards, helping to provide good-quality habitats for wildlife. The gardens contain a diverse range of fruit trees including apple, plum, damson, pear, cherry, apricot, quince and fig, some as much as 200 years old. Nectar and pollen support a variety of insect life, birds thrive on fruit and seeds and the nesting sites offered by the trees, and mammals and amphibians also benefit from the stability and security of the habitat. The meadows that underly orchards also sustain a rich diversity of plant life including wild flowers, fungi and lichens. Orchard highlights include Acorn Bank in Cumbria, Brockhampton in Herefordshire, Llanerchaeron in Wales, Cotehele in Cornwall, Lyveden New Bield in Northamptonshire, Killerton in Devon, Hugheden Manor in Buckinghamshire, Lacock Abbey in Wiltshire, and Felbrigg Hall in Norfolk.

English cox

Wild cherry
(Prunus avium)
Wild cherry has reddish purple bark with a beautiful sheen. The leaves are long, serrated ovals with pointed tips and carry 2–5 bright red glands at their base. In late April the tree is smothered with small, five-petalled white flowers. When fertilised, the flowers develop into small, shiny black fruit, the ancestor of the sweet cherries, that are popular with birds. The tree produces an attractive red hardwood that is used for making musical instruments and furniture.

Bird cherry
(Prunus padus)
Smaller than the wild cherry the bird cherry reaches 10m (33ft). It can survive in wetter conditions and is found in the north of England and Scotland. It has grey bark and smaller flowers than the wild cherry, carried in spikes. The fruit, beloved by birds, is very astringent to taste.

Holly
(Ilex aquifolium)
Holly can be seen in woodland right across the country, and its prickly, glossy green leaves are instantly recognisable. The leaves last for 2–4 years and are immediately replaced on falling. The insignificant

Opposite: The wild cherry carries an abundance of white flowers in early spring and in autumn the leaves turn to vivid shades of gold and red. The fruit is the ancestor of the cultivated cherry.

Below: The lime tree produces scented flowers in June and July, which attract masses of bees. The flowers are also used to make a tea, tilleul, which is still very popular in France.

white flowers appear in May or June. Each bush is single sex and needs other bushes nearby for pollination if it is to produce berries. The berries start green and ripen to a vivid red by November and are appreciated by wood pigeon, starlings and thrushes.

Sycamore
(Acer pseudoplatanus)
The sycamore is not thought to be native to Britain, although it is unclear when it arrived. It is a vigorous, deciduous tree, which tolerates wind and pollution, thrives in a range of soils, and self-seeds easily. It carries pairs of five-lobed, dull green leaves. The greenish yellow flowers hang in clusters in June and are followed by the brown, wing-like seeds that spin down in autumn.

Field maple
(Acer campestre)
The field maple is the UK's only native maple. The young shoots are red-brown, and the brown and green buds sit in opposite pairs. The distinctively shaped, five-lobed leaves are soft green at first but take on a reddish hue as they develop. The green flowers hang in inconspicuous clusters and develop into small, swirling helicopter blades.

Small-leafed lime
(Tilia cordata)
The small-leafed lime is believed once to have been a dominant tree in English forests, but is very sensitive to browsing animals. The grey bark has a strong fibre that was once used to make ropes. The lime-green, heart-shaped leaves appear in April and May. Small clusters of yellow-white flowers appear in June and July and the fruit that follows in September is small, hard and ridged. Woodpeckers are very partial to the sap and will drill holes to get at it.

Woodland tree diseases

In recent years, trees at many sites around the UK have been affected by fungal-like plant diseases *Phytophthora ramorum* and *Phytophthora kernoviae*. These cause the death or decline of some woody plant species, and in the UK are most commonly found on rhododendron, viburnum, magnolia and camellia. *P. ramorum* is also known as Sudden Oak Death, a name originating from the United States, where the disease was identified on tan oaks (Lithocarpus) in California in the 1990s. The disease has not affected any British oaks.

The diseases have already had an impact at several National Trust properties where gardeners have worked to control the spread of the disease through clearance of affected areas. The challenge is to save rare and historically important plants that make up the special character of individual gardens and, equally importantly, to find ways of dealing with the diseases while managing the gardens in a way that minimises the loss of character or their special historical significance. When an outbreak is confirmed at a National Trust site, control measures are implemented following DEFRA guidelines.

The National Trust has also introduced a number of measures to combat the spread of the diseases, including securing funding for research, a long-term programme of clearance of *Rhododendron ponticum*, which acts as a host for these two diseases, and the establishment of an action group to co-ordinate efforts across the gardening sector in tackling these plant diseases. Biosecurity in gardens and nurseries is vital.

Above: The wood anemone can form large colonies that spread by means of underground stems called rhizomes. The face of the flowers, which bloom from March to early May, will follow the course of the sun through the day.

Wood anemone
(Anemone nemorosa)

The wood anemone used to carpet the woodland floor but it is seldom seen today. It is a beautiful perennial that flowers in early spring before the leaf canopy appears to shade it in March and April. The flower is white, with 6–8 petals, and the leaves are deeply indented and fern-like in appearance. The plant reaches heights of 7–15cm (3–6in). The seeds develop in clusters and lure the ants that carry them some distance from the parent plant.

Lesser celandine
(Ranunculus ficaria)

A member of the buttercup family, the golden yellow petals of the lesser celandine are instantly recognisable, as this is one of the country's most widespread wild flowers. The flowers, which appear as early as February, carry 8–12 petals, compared to the five petals of the buttercup. The heart-shaped leaves resemble those of ivy. The plant is easy

Ash
(Fraxinus excelsior)

When ash develops into a mature tree, it has a large spreading crown, creating a familiar landscape silhouette. The wood is tough; indeed the handles of implements that were once made from ash are now almost all made from metal. The wood is still used for hockey sticks, billiard cues, polo sticks and cricket stumps. The tree's down-curving branches carry black buds from which nondescript green catkins sprout, and are followed by nine, oval, tooth-edged leaves. Paper-thin winged seeds appear in September and often loiter on the tree until winter.

to spot when flowering in spring in damp and shady woodland.

Wood violet
(Viola riviniana)
Violet is a creeping hardy perennial that reaches just 15cm (6in) in height. It has heart-shaped leaves and carries deep purple flowers, with three petals above and two below, on delicate stems. It can be distinguished from its close relative the sweet violet *(viola odorata)* by its flowers, which bloom much later in May and June, and its lack of perfume. It favours damp conditions and, when it is established, it will self-seed and send out runners to establish a clump of flowers.

Red campion
(Silene dioica)
Red campion is a woodland beauty and was named after Silenus, the drunken companion of Bacchus. The flowers have five, deeply divided petals and appear from May through

Above: The wood violet, or common dog violet, is the most common of the wild violets and the earliest to flower; it used to feature in Easter bouquets.

Right: The bramble is an important food source for a wide variety of creatures; the fruit is consumed by wasps, greenbottles, butterflies, birds and foxes.

Below: Mammals and birds enjoy the fruit of the wild strawberry and spread the seeds in their droppings.

to September. The long oval leaves, and the tall stalks and buds, are all hairy. White campion *(Silene latifolia)* is also found in woodland and, when growing together, the two varieties can hybridise to form pale pink flowers.

Herb robert
(Geranium robertianum)
Herb robert is a relative of the cultivated geranium, and forms similar clumps of deeply toothed green leaves that gradually turn red as the summer progresses. The plant grows up to 45cm (18in) tall and produces small, five-petalled pink flowers on tiny, slender stems. The flowers develop into pointed fruit that resemble a crane's bill.

Bramble
(Rubus fruticosus)
The bramble must be one of our most familiar plants. Its unruly, prickly, arching stems can grow to 3m (10ft) tall and it roots from the tip of these fruiting stems. Flowers are white, flushed with pink, and appear from May to September. The green fruit appears from July to October, rapidly ripening to a deep purple-black. Blackberries are a favourite with all kinds of birds, insects and mammals.

Wild strawberry
(Fragaria vesca)
This low-growing perennial herb is not a hybrid of the modern cultivated fruit, but a plant in its own right. It has deeply veined, serrated leaves and white, five-petalled flowers that appear in clusters in late spring and throughout the summer. The small red fruit develops from early summer through to early autumn and is hidden under the leaves. Wild strawberries grow in both woodland and hedgerows.

Wood spurge

Above: Sloes, the astringent blue-black fruit of the blackthorn, should not be picked until after the first frosts. The skin wrinkles slightly at this time and the fruit becomes sweeter.

Below: Dog's mercury is regarded as an indicator of ancient, semi-natural woodland. Ants disperse its seeds; they are attracted to elaiosomes, structures rich in lipids and proteins that are attached to the seed.

Blackthorn
(Prunus spinosa)

Blackthorn is a native plant, with delicate white flowers that appear in late February or early March, long before the leaves. If the flowers emerge even earlier, after a warm spell at the beginning of February, this is known as a 'blackthorn winter'. The leaves are small, oval and toothed and have a hairy underside. The fruit, or sloe, is blue-black. The wood is hard and tough, and was traditionally used to make the Irish cudgel, the shillelagh.

Ivy
(Hedera helix)

Ivy is a woody climber. Non-flowering shoots carry the familiar five-lobed, deep green leaves. Flowering shoots have larger, elongated oval shapes. The flowers appear in September and are followed by berries that are initially a dull yellow, ripening to black. Birds utilise this providential food supply in mid-winter.

Dog's mercury
(Mercurialis perennis)

Dog's mercury is an easy plant to overlook as it does not have any showy flowers. It grows in same-sex clumps about 30cm (12in) tall in deep shade, and the light green, oval leaves are veined and toothed. It flowers from March to May; the tiny green male flowers can be seen growing on spikes and have long yellow-green stamens, the female flowers are harder to spot as they are hidden among the leaves. The plant has an unpleasant smell when rubbed and is poisonous.

Wood spurge
(Euphorbia amygdaloides)

Wood spurge can be found in damp woodland and in recently coppiced woods. It has hairy, upright, reddish stems surrounded by whorls of green leaves, and between March and May is topped with flowering, kidney-shaped bracts containing several small male flowers and one female flower. As with all euphorbia the milky white sap is toxic and can cause skin irritation. Wood spurge is most common in southern England.

Primrose
(Primula vulgaris)

Clumps of primroses are all too rare today; they can be found in woodland edges and woodland clearings, or damp and shady hedgerows although agricultural chemicals have almost eliminated them from hedges. The primrose is a low-growing perennial with rosettes of deeply veined, oval leaves. The pale yellow, gently scented, five-petalled flowers grow on delicate hairy stems and appear in early spring.

Yellow pimpernel
(Lysimachia nemorum)

Yellow pimpernel looks very similar to the creeping jenny that is found in our gardens. This perennial has creeping stems that carry pairs of oval or heart-shaped leaves. The

small, five-petalled, star-like yellow flowers are carried on fine stems and can be seen from May to September. Yellow pimpernel spreads to form clumps and is found in damp woodland.

Foxglove
(Digitalis purpurea)

The foxglove enjoys light shade and is often seen on the edges of woodland or in clearings. It can reach a height of nearly 2m (6½ft). In its first year it forms a rosette of large leaves, and the following spring it sends up a flower spike that carries purple bells, freckled with brown spots inside. The Latin name refers to the shape of the flowers that fit over the human finger. Similarly, the common name is believed to be derived from 'folk's gloves', and has nothing to do with the fox. All parts of the foxglove are poisonous.

Yellow archangel
(Lamiastrum galeobdolon)

Yellow archangel is immediately recognisable as a dead-nettle. The plant has toothed, dark green leaves, and the upright stem carries whorls of small, red-streaked, yellow flowers that sit at the base of the leaves, and appear between May and June. The leaves have an unpleasant smell when crushed. Yellow archangel likes damp, shady habitats and is often found in coppices.

Far left: Foxgloves are often found on the edges of woodland, where their bright spikes of purple bell-shaped flowers attract bees and other insects. Bees love the nectar from foxgloves and crawl deep into the flower, covering their legs in pollen in the process.

Left: The flowers of the yellow archangel are small, but if you take a closer look you will see that they are streaked throughout with dashes of red, and are a lure for early bees.

Ground ivy
(Glechoma hederacea)

This plant has a highly misleading common name, given that it neither resembles, nor is related to, ivy. It is actually from the mint family, though it has no minty smell. Ground ivy is a creeping perennial with reddish stems that root at the leaf nodes. The leaves are kidney-shaped and green, often with a purple hue, and have large, rounded teeth and deep veins. The tiny, purple-blue hooded flowers appear in whorls around the stem from March to June. Ground ivy has anti-inflammatory and expectorant properties and was used to treat bronchitis and urinary tract infections.

Wood sage
(Teucrium scorodonia)

Wood sage grows in clumps in woodland, favouring birch and oak forests and is related to the dead-nettle. The heart-shaped and wrinkled, sage-like leaves ring the tall stems that are topped with whorls of insignificant yellow-green flowers from July to September. Birds enjoy the seed. The plant was once widely used as a herbal astringent as well as a calmative and diuretic.

Bugle
(Ajuga reptans)

Bugle is a perennial herb and can be seen in clay woods throughout the UK. It has stiff, dark, upright stems that carry purplish green leaves. Tubular blue flowers are carried in the leaf axils from May to July. Bugle spreads by creeping stems and forms large mats on the woodland floor. It was once used to treat wounds and was grown for this purpose in country gardens.

Giant bellflower
(Campanula latifolia)

The giant bellflower grows in damp, shady woods and hedgerows in England. It is a relative of the garden favourite, Canterbury bells, and produces tall, impressive flower spikes that carry pale blue, bell-shaped flowers. The oval leaves are spaced alternately down the stem.

Above: The giant bellflower is an impressive sight in flower; established clumps can reach over 1m (3ft) in height and carry beautiful blue bell flowers.

Below: The flowers of the bugle are an important food source for woodland insects; here a pearl-bordered fritillary enjoys its nectar.

Opposite: The UK's native bluebell woods are estimated to represent 29–49 per cent of the entire world population of the flower and thus are of international importance. Do not be tempted to pick the flowers or dig up the bulbs.

Bluebells

There are few things more beautiful in spring than a bluebell wood. In the dappled shade of the newly emerging leaf canopy, the intensity of the blue haze is truly astonishing. Bluebells are slow to establish themselves, so when the floor is carpeted, it is indicative of ancient woodland. The juicy white bluebell bulb throws up a succulent stem surrounded by 3–6 strap-like leaves. The flower spike produces

Bluebells

small, bell-like flowers that hang in a line, causing the stem to droop, so that the deep blue, six-petalled flowers hang down like bells. The flowers have a sweet perfume that is strongest on warm days. Bluebells appear before deciduous trees come into leaf and the flowers open in April and May. When the bluebell is established few other flowers can compete. There is some concern that the native **bluebell** (Hyacinthoides non-scripta) is under threat from the **Spanish bluebell** (H. hispanica) and the **hybrid bluebell** (H. non-scripta x hispanica). Bluebells that appear in parks and gardens are often the larger Spanish bluebell. These have hybridised with the native bluebell to produce the hybrid bluebell that is now more common than its Spanish parent. It is very difficult to tell the different varieties apart by sight but the perfume is a giveaway – only the native bluebell has a wonderful scent.

Elder
(Sambucus nigra)

The elder is a large deciduous shrub or small tree with brittle wood and straggly growth. It has oval serrated leaves and flat heads of tiny creamy white flowers that appear in late spring and early summer. The flowers have a subtle flavour, often likened to that of Muscat grape, and can be used to flavour syrups, cordials, desserts and jam. The berries that follow ripen to a deep purple black and hang downwards when fully ripe. Elderberries are rich in vitamin C and can be used to make jams and conserves.

Honeysuckle
(Lonicera periclymenum)

Wild honeysuckle is commonly found in woodland where it twists around shrubs and branches, always in a clockwise direction. It is often one of the earliest plants to grow leaves, with some appearing in late February. From June onwards, it produces small trumpet flowers with long curled-back petals, in a range of colours from cream through to red. Many night-flying moths are attracted to its nectar and white admiral caterpillars feed on its foliage. Bright red berries appear in autumn and winter.

Moschatel
(Adoxa moschatellina)

Moschatel is a curious little flower with a distinctive musky scent, most noticeable when dew is falling. It carries clusters of

Above: Moschatel often flowers around Easter – hence one of its common names, Good Friday plant. The flowers are followed by a drooping green fruit.

Right: Elderflowers have a sweet perfume and a tree in full bloom is a thing of beauty. Elderberries hang down when fully ripe and are a valuable food source for birds.

Ramsons

deeply lobed leaves and sends up succulent flower spikes in April and May. Five pale green flowers are carried at the top of each spike. Four are tightly packed around the stem, while the fifth is right at the top and faces skywards – hence one of the plant's other common names, town-hall clock.

Ramsons
(Allium ursinum)

Wild garlic or ramsons can be found on the fringes of woodland, where you can often smell it before you see it. Ramsons is a bulbous perennial, with broad odorous leaves like spears, and white starry flowers that bloom in umbels. The leaves appear from March onward and flowers follow from April to June.

Snowdrop
(Galanthus nivalis)

The wild snowdrop is sometimes known as Candlemas bells, perhaps because it flowers around Candlemas (2 February), and was commonly planted round churches. It is generally agreed that the snowdrop is not a native plant as it is first mentioned in Gerard's Herbal of 1597 as a cultivated rarity. The first record of wild snowdrops comes from the 1770s, and notes their presence in woods in Gloucestershire and Worcestershire, where some of the best displays of snowdrops can still be found. The snowdrop has bell-shaped flowers that can appear from Christmas to March, depending on local temperatures, with three white outer petals and three white inner petals tipped with green. The flower hangs like a bell from a delicate grey-green stalk.

Daffodil
(Narcissus pseudonarcissus)

The wild daffodil or Lent lily is the ancestor of the cultivated daffodil we know today. It is slighter than cultivated varieties and has a nodding head. The pale yellow outer petals form a halo around a darker yellow trumpet and are surrounded by tall, strap-like, grey-green leaves. A spread of naturalised daffodils that do not appear to have been planted can be indicative of ancient woodland. The native species can hybridise freely with cultivars, which is why the National Trust removed introduced varieties at Ullswater in Cumbria, where William Wordsworth composed 'Daffodils' (1804).

Above: Wild snowdrops are not a native plant to the UK, but they are happy to establish large clumps in the right location. Sometimes called Candlemas bells, many woods throughout the country now boast beautiful displays of flowers in January and February.

Orchids

There are 54 species of orchid that grow in the UK. Orchids can be identified by their flowers, which have three petals, one of which, the lip, gives each species its own distinctive characteristics. The stamens and the stigma (male and female parts) are not separate as in other flowers, but are instead fused in a central column. Some orchids, such as the **bird's-nest orchid** (Neottia nidus-avis) are saprophytes, obtaining their energy from dead vegetation. The leafless bird's-nest orchid grows in deep woods, favouring beech, in heavy shade. It sends up a spike of brown flowers in June and July that can blend into the leaf litter around it. Its common name is derived from its thick mass of untidy roots. The **early purple orchid** (Orchis mascula) is a beauty and, as its name suggests, it is the first orchid to bloom. It has a rosette of 4–8 blunt-tipped, spotted leaves at its base, and flowering leaves on each tall flower spike, which can grow to 60cm (2ft). There are 20–30 purple-pink or white flowers on each spike that appear from April to July. The plant can be found in broad-leaved, undisturbed, ancient woodland all over the country, though it is less common in the north east.

Early purple orchid

Woodland fungi

The terms mushroom and toadstool are not scientific and are open to loose interpretations. Fungi with fruiting bodies and a centrally placed cap are commonly called both mushrooms and toadstools. Fungi rely on organic matter for nutrients. Some feed on dead plants and animals and are known as saprophytes, which are important in the recycling of animal and plant matter into the food chain. Other types of fungi feed on living plants and animals and are called parasites. Woodland fungi are immeasurably valuable as they clear up rotting and dead organic material and recycle it into productive soil. There are around 1,000 fungi large enough to be spotted by the human eye in the UK; of these, 250 are relatively common, more than enough to fill a field guide. They can be found in gardens, hedgerows and grasslands, but are most common in mature woods and forests. The names alone are enticing – have you ever seen an amethyst deceiver, a destroying angel, a shaggy ink cap, jelly ear, chicken of the woods or a giant fairy club? Do not attempt identification from a button mushroom, which is an immature fruiting body – use ones that are fairly open. Here is a selection of the most common fungi you are likely to encounter in woodland.

Above: Honey fungus is a destructive parasite that is common in forest and woodland and can be devastating in gardens and parks. The damage is out of sight, beneath the bark and in the roots and trunk.

Jelly ear
(Auricularia auricula-judae)
This fungus is delightfully easy to identify for, as its name suggests, it looks like a reddish-brown gelatinous ear growing out of a tree trunk. It grows in clusters on branches, or stacked upon tree trunks, often on elder. Its relative *Auricularia polytricha* is used in Chinese cooking, where it is commonly dried until it is black and then used as flavouring. Jelly ear can be found throughout the year but is more common in October and November.

Chanterelle
(Cantharellus cibarius)
The chanterelle is a beautiful mushroom with a distinctive egg-yolk yellow flesh. It is delicious and is much prized in France where it is known as *girolle*. It has a distinctive perfume of apricots or ripe plums. The chanterelle is seen from June to October, and instead of gills it has blunt ridges, which flare upwards and outwards to the lip of the horn so that the centre of the cap is inverted. The chanterelle can be found in mixed and coniferous woods and grows close to beech, birch, or on mossy banks.

Honey fungus
(Armillaria mellea)
As the name suggests, honey fungus is a warm golden honey colour, and is studded with brown scales that cluster toward the centre of the cap. It favours broad-leaved trees, notably oak and beech. Its thick, black rhizomorphs invade the roots of woody plants, and the fruiting bodies appear in September, and die back after the first frosts. Honey fungus can reach 15cm (6in) in height and the cap can range from 5–15cm (2–6in).

Fairies' bonnets
(Coprinus disseminatus)
A lone fairies' bonnet is not much to get excited about – a small, ridged, shell- or

thimble-shaped cap perched on a delicate stem. The beauty of this mushroom is that it is rarely seen alone, but springs up in spectacular colonies on the rotting stumps of deciduous trees, between August and November.

Fly agaric
(Amanita muscaria)

The quintessential, highly toxic fungus of fairy stories. Its red or orange cap, ringed with white spots is instantly recognisable, although rain can wash the spots away. It commonly grows to 15cm (6in) tall and can measure the same across the cap. It grows in mixed woodland and is often seen near birch and pine trees between August and November.

Verdigris agaric
(Stropharia aeruginosa)

This blue-green fungus is even more exotic than the fly agaric. When young, the cap is topped with white scales, and white flaking scales also cover the stem. Verdigris agaric is common in woods and meadows.

Deathcap
(Amanita phalloides)

The name tells you the most important thing you need to know about this fungus; it is deadly poisonous. It is found with broad-leaved trees, notably oak, but also under other deciduous trees. The cap and

Above: Fly agaric is enveloped in a white veil when young; this splits, revealing an almost round cap, dotted with warty white spots. It spreads and flattens into a mature cap and the spots, which can be washed off by rain, diminish in size.

Below: The cep is an easy species to identify – the gills are a foamy, spongy mass, which mark it out as part of the Boletus family.

stem are both yellowish green in colour and the cap has lines that radiate from the centre. The flesh is white and it has a rather unpleasant, sickly smell.

Cep
(Boletus edulis)

The cep or penny bun is better known by its Italian name *porcini*. The cep is found

in woodland clearings between August and November and has a smooth, dry, polished top, which looks rather like a bun, and which measures 8–30cm (3–12in) in diameter. The cap starts to look increasingly polished as the fungus ages. The underside is a mass of yellowish, sponge-like pores; the stem is short, swollen and fawn and white in colour.

Earthball
(Scleroderma citrinum)

This fungus is associated with birch and oak and is often found growing in woods and forests from August to November. It looks like a warty, dirty-white potato and can reach 10cm (4in) in diameter. When cut, the fruit body is black, and this helps to differentiate it from the puffball.

Stinkhorn
(Phallus impudicus)

This is an unusual-looking fungus. It starts to grow as a striking, white, egg-shaped capsule that ruptures to reveal a white stalk topped by a dark brown, slimy and unmistakably graphic, phallic head. It emits a foul smell that attracts flies, which in turn, disperse the spores. The stinkhorn is a common species, and can be found in a wide variety of woods, often close to buried, rotting wood, in summer or autumn.

Birds

Sparrowhawk
(Accipiter nisus)

With a body length of around 38cm (15in), the sparrowhawk has a grey-blue back, head and wings and speckled underside. The male of the species tends to be smaller than the female and hunts for small birds in woodland, while the female hunts larger prey – and is able to catch birds up to pigeon-size – across open countryside. The sparrowhawk was common in the UK until the 1950s when numbers started to decline due to the use of a pesticide that was later banned; however, the species is no longer regarded as under threat. Numbers increase in winter when migratory birds arrive from Scandinavia.

Goshawk
(Accipiter gentilis)

Larger and rarer than the sparrowhawk, the goshawk was once used in falconry. Females can measure as much as 66cm (26in) in length. Males are smaller reaching around 50cm (20in) in length. The head, back and body is grey or brown, while the throat, chest and undersides are white speckled with brown, and the eyebrows are white. The goshawk was extinct in the UK in the 19th century, after persecution from egg collectors and gamekeepers, but it has been reintroduced. There are approximately 400 pairs breeding in the UK but their eggs are still stolen today.

Right: The sparrowhawk flies swift and low when hunting. It eats its kill on the ground, spreading its wings around it like a cape.

Grey partridge
(Perdix perdix)

The partridge is a medium-sized game bird with brown plumage broken by chestnut bars on the flanks and a chestnut tail. The head is orange, the bib is white, and the breast sports an inverted, brown horseshoe shape. The grey partridge lives in copses and hedgerows and enjoys young shoots, leaves, grain and seeds and a variety of insects, slugs, snails and spiders.

Birdsong

Birdsong is highly distinctive: there are mating serenades, territorial calls, calls for nestlings and fledglings and graded danger warnings. An extraordinarily lovely birdsong may well alert you to the presence of a mature bird; birdsong is a learned skill and the oldest birds have the greatest vocal range. Male birds make the most melodious calls that are true birdsong. Learning to identify most calls is not difficult. Sound recordings are available on CD and DVD, and many websites, notably that of the Royal Society for the Protection of Birds (RSPB), have clips of birdsong that you can play to help you identify the calls of individual birds. Alternatively, join a guided walk with an expert. Visual recognition helps too. Verbal translations of birdsong are interesting but difficult to make sense of in the field; for instance, the song of the yellowhammer is often interpreted as 'a-little-bit-of-bread-and-no-cheese'.

Nightingale

Pheasants

It is believed that the Romans introduced the **common pheasant** *(Phasianus colchicus)* to Britain, but the bird originated in the Caucasus. The male is around 82cm (32in) long and has richly coloured plumage with chestnut, golden brown and black markings on its back, iridescent green feathers on top of the head, red wattles around the eyes, and a glorious flourish of tail feathers. The hen's plumage is, inevitably, darker and drabber but it allows her to blend in beautifully with leaf litter. The **golden pheasant** *(Chrysolophus pictus)*, which has beautiful red plumage, and **Lady Amherst's pheasant** *(Chrysolophus amherstiae)*, which has black and white head plumage, were introduced in the 18th century and are now recognised as wild British birds.

Pheasants live in woods and hedgerows and their diet includes seeds, fruit and leaves, as well as a variety of insects and worms. They are vulnerable to predators such as foxes, weasels and stoats, but also to humans; the pheasant is the most hunted bird in the world.

Common pheasant

Woodcock
(Scolopax rusticola)

The woodcock lives in deciduous woodland and conifer forests, and flies at dusk to nearby damp and boggy spots, where it forages using its long beak to hunt for worms and insects. The best time to attempt to see it is on spring evenings when males put on mating displays. The woodcock's brown, russet and buff feathers provide perfect camouflage against the woodland floor. The bird's call sounds almost like the croaking of a frog.

Stock dove
(Columba oenas)

The stock dove looks much like the pigeons that are found in cities. However, it is a far

more solitary bird, and is rarely seen in groups. It is grey in colour with a pink flush on its breast, a green tinge to the back of the neck, and dark wing tips and tail. The call is quite distinct from the usual 'coo-coo' of the wood pigeon, and sounds rather as if the bird has a sore throat.

Owls

Owls are often heard hooting at night. It is a rare treat to catch sight of one, as usually they roost by day, and hunt at night. They swoop silently down on their prey, picking it up with their talons. The light-sensitive eyes are forward looking but the owl has the ability to turn its head around an impressive and disconcerting 180°. The catch is eaten whole with the indigestible parts such as fur and bones being regurgitated later as pellets.

Tawny owl
(Strix aluco)

The tawny owl is our most widespread owl, though it is not found in Ireland, or the north west of Scotland. With a body length

Above: The long-eared owl utilises discarded stick nests of magpies, hawks and ravens in woods.

of around 38cm (15in), it is chestnut brown above and a paler buff colour underneath, and is mottled all over with grey and dark brown streaks. The tawny owl has a blunted, heart-shaped face and pale feathers ring its dark eyes. Tawny owls eat small birds, rodents, insects and frogs, and perch on hunting stations waiting patiently for something to move below.

Long-eared owl
(Asio otus)

The long-eared owl appears longer and leaner than the tawny owl, and has less rich colouration, mixing pale, warm brown tones with buff, white, dark brown and black. Its eyes are a distinctive orange. Its 'ears' are not ears at all, but tufts of feathers that only stand to attention when the bird is frightened. Long-eared owls hunt over open countryside, emitting long, gentle hoots, looking for voles, a favourite snack, but will also eat other rodents and birds.

Wren
(Troglodytes troglodytes)

The wren is one of the smallest British birds at just 9cm (3½in) long. It has a red-brown coat, and bars on its upturned tail, wings and flanks, and a very piercing song for such a small bird. Wrens suffer in hard winters; they usually roost in open bushes overnight, but when it is very cold they seek shelter and huddle together for warmth. The birds are insect eaters, and their habit of searching for food in rocks and crevices helps to explain their Greek name 'troglodytes', which means 'cave dweller'.

Dunnock
(Prunella modularis)

The dunnock has similar markings to a house sparrow, but its black bill is narrower and blunter. It has a blue-grey eye-stripe on the head, a grey throat and breast, and its back feathers are brown, streaked with darker brown tones. It is a shy bird and hides away in the undergrowth of woods, hedgerows, parks and gardens throughout the UK. The dunnock is not as common as it once was: this is believed to be due in some part to changes in woodland practices and loss of hedgerow habitat.

Robin
(Erithacus rubecula)

The robin, arguably Britain's favourite bird, lives in woods and hedgerows. It is also among our most familiar native birds, with its bright orange-red breast, brown back and grey bib. The plumage becomes

Far right: The wren is famed for its long, sweet warbling song. It can be heard year round but is at its most beautiful in spring.

Right: The robin is a fearless bird that will fight to the death to maintain its territory. A successful adult can live for ten years.

Woodpeckers

Great spotted woodpecker

The **great spotted woodpecker** *(Dendrocopos major)* is our most commonly seen species. It is small in stature, around the size of a blackbird, and has flamboyant monochrome markings on its head, back and wings, a white chest and belly, with bright red patches at the back of the neck, and at the rear end. Its elastic tongue can extend four times the lengths of its beak. Much of the drilling noise made by the woodpecker serves merely to help the bird maintain its territory by warning off other birds. Great spotted woodpeckers nest inside tree trunks, pecking out holes, and eating the grubs and insects they find in the trees, as well as ones they find on the ground. The **lesser spotted woodpecker** *(Dendrocopos minor)*, looks similar to the great spotted, but is around the size of a sparrow. It is the least common woodpecker, found mainly in the south of England. The **green woodpecker** *(Picus viridis)* has a distinctive, repetitive, laughing call that has given it the common name of the 'yaffle'. It is the largest of the woodpeckers with a green back and wings, a pale buff body and cheeks, yellow rump, grey rings around the eyes and a distinctive red hood. Green woodpeckers are often seen perching on tree trunks or upright branches with their beaks pointing upwards. They live on ants and larvae. The green woodpecker is rarely seen in the north of Scotland or Ireland.

dowdy in summer and the birds look down at heel. It is approximately 12–17cm (5–7in) in length. A small number of birds, notably females, migrate to southern Europe for winter, and some birds from mainland Europe migrate to the UK for winter.

Nightingale
(Luscinia megarhynchos)
The nightingale is a shy bird with a fondness for concealing itself in the centre of large bushes – so you are more likely to hear one than to see one. It is a migratory bird, arriving from central Africa in April and departing between July and September. Its famous song is valued for the range of notes that few other birds can reach. Nightingales sing at their best from April to June. Most common in the South East, the nightingale looks somewhat like a large, drab robin, with a brown head and back and a pale grey breast and underside. It eats insects and berries.

Song thrush
(Turdus philomelos)
The song thrush may sing throughout the year, notably in the evening when it repeats clear phrases from a treetop. It is a medium-sized bird with a mottled plumage, darker above and paler below, with speckled breast and brown beak. Thrushes eat a varied diet

Above: The song thrush population has halved in recent years, especially on farmland. The RSPB have put the bird on its 'red' protection list, making its conservation the highest priority.

Below: Willow warblers feed on insects and can often be seen fluttering around the tips of branches, searching underneath the leaves for aphids. It is often confused with the chiffchaff, but has paler legs, longer wings and a more defined stripe above the eye.

and particularly enjoy snails, whose shells they smash on stones specifically chosen for this purpose. Around half of the population is believed to be migratory, coming to winter in Britain from northern Europe.

Mistle thrush
(Turdus viscivorus)
The mistle thrush is similar to the song thrush, but is browner, considerably larger, and is far less common. The undersides of its wings flash white when in flight. Its name comes from its fondness for mistletoe berries.

Blackbird
(Turdus merula)
The blackbird is a member of the thrush family and is the only one with a different plumage for male and female. The cock is black with a yellow eye ring and beak and the hen is a mottled dark brown with a brown bill. The blackbird has a beautiful song, best heard from March to early July, and a distinctive staccato warning cry. The blackbird is omnivorous and will eat insects and worms as well as fruit, seeds and berries. Our native birds are joined each winter by migrants from Europe.

Warblers

Warblers are a large group of British birds, most of which are summer visitors that migrate to Africa in autumn. Species can be difficult to differentiate, but those seen in forests and woodland are the leaf warblers *(Phylloscopus)* and scrub warblers *(Sylvia)*.

Willow warbler
(Phylloscopus trochilus)
The most common British warbler, the willow warbler arrives to breed in mid-April, and keeps itself very busy hunting for insects and berries. The willow warbler has a dull green back and a pale underneath, its breast is yellow and it has a yellow stripe above the eye.

Chiffchaff
(Phylloscopus collybita)

The chiffchaff looks similar to the willow warbler, but the latter sings a song of descending notes whereas the chiffchaff repeats a two-note call. It can be seen across the UK, though less frequently in the north of Scotland, and a few birds overwinter in the south of England instead of migrating.

Wood warbler
(Phylloscopus sibilatrix)

The largest of the leaf warblers, and similar in appearance to the willow warbler, the wood warbler features a brighter yellow chest and eye stripe, and a white belly. It is found most commonly in oak and beech woods in the north and west and notably in west Wales. Its call is a vibrating trill.

Blackcap
(Sylvia atricapilla)

Scrub warblers, such as the blackcap, live principally in hedges, but this bird is the exception. It is principally grey, with darker grey or light brown wings, but its distinguishing feature is a black cap, worn low over the eyes by the male, or a copper-brown one worn by the female. The blackcap has a beautiful fluting song that rings out through the woods; indeed, it is sometimes called the 'northern nightingale'.

Garden warbler
(Sylvia borin)

Despite its name, the garden warbler is actually more common in woodland, but is hard to see because it is so shy. It is a small, inconspicuous brown bird with little in the way of markings to aid identification, but its song is rather lovely, and similar to that of the blackcap.

Goldcrest
(Regulus regulus)

The goldcrest can be found in coniferous forests where it hunts for small insects and spiders. It is the smallest British songbird but it is quite fearless despite its diminutive size. Its back is greenish brown and its undersides are buff-coloured. The head is black with a striking yellow or orange stripe through the centre. The tail and wings are marked with dark brown stripes. The goldcrest suffers badly in hard winters.

Pied flycatcher
(Ficedula hypoleuca)

The pied flycatcher is found in woodlands on the west of the UK, but not in Ireland. It is a migratory bird, flying in from West Africa in April and departing in October. Migrants from Scandinavia can also be seen along the eastern coast in spring and autumn. The pied flycatcher is principally

Above: The wood warbler has a long shivering song which it sings from its arrival in April until June; it falls silent in July and departs in September.

Below: The male blackcap lives up to his name but the female, in contrast, wears a chestnut cap.

black above and white underneath, with a white patch on its wing, and two white spots above the bill. It sits high on a perch, looking for insects to catch, and will also eat seeds.

Long-tailed tit
(Aegithalos caudatus)
Despite its name, this bird is not a member of the tit family, though it looks and behaves like one. The long-tailed tit is a very small bird with a white cap, a pale chest flushed with pink, buff undersides, black wings and a long black tail. It is highly sociable, living in noisy groups and hunting for insects.

Nuthatch
(Sitta europaea)
The nuthatch has the distinctive skill of being able to run down trees head first – it does this by clinging on to the bark with its toes. It looks somewhat like a small kingfisher and has a blue-grey head, back and wings, white stripe on its cheeks and a distinctive black stripe like a mask across its eyes. The undersides are a rusty brown. The nuthatch is more common in southern Britain, but it is creeping northwards, although local populations always suffer in hard snowy winters as the bird is unable to find the nuts, seeds and insects it relies upon.

Tits
A feature of the diminutive tit family is that it has a distinct cap, of varying colours, on top of its head. The **crested tit** (Parus cristatus) is found only in coniferous woodland in northern Scotland. It has black-and-white markings on its face, a distinctive crest on top of its head, and a neat black bib under its bill. The back and wings are brown and the chest and undersides a warm buff colour. It scours tree trunks and branches, carefully looking for insects and seeds. Despite their names, the **marsh tit** (Parus palustris) and the **willow tit** (Parus montanus) both live in woodland, though the willow tit prefers a damper environment. Both species have a coal-black cap, white face, grey back and wings, and a pale underside. They are very hard to differentiate from one another except for their calls. They eat insects, fruit and seeds. The **coal tit** (Parus ater), also likes woodland, both coniferous and deciduous. It has a black head with white cheeks, a warm corn-coloured breast, a grey back, a white spot on the nape of the neck and grey wings barred with white.

Coal tit

Treecreeper
(Certhia familiaris)
The treecreeper is not rare, and is found over most of the UK wherever there are woods, but you have to look hard to spot it spiralling busily up (but never down) the trunks of trees. It is a small and insignificant brown-and-white bird, with a dark speckled back, head and wings, and pale undersides. The treecreeper uses its long, pointed bill to extract food from the crevices of tree bark where it hunts for insects. It also eats seeds.

Jay
(Garrulus glandarius)
The jay is a member of the crow family, but looks rather more exotic than its relatives. Its body is a pinky-brown, with a paler head that is speckled with black. It has white on the wing and rump, and the edges of the wings are marked by bright blue and black bars. Jays steal eggs and nestlings from other birds, and adore acorns, which they hide away like a squirrel, a practice that has contributed to the spread of oak woods.

Rook
(Corvus frugilegus)
The rook is a large, black bird whose inky black feathers have a purple sheen. Grey or white patches can be seen on its face, and around the long, pointed beak, and it has shaggy feathers around the top of its legs. The rook is an intelligent and sociable bird that lives in colonies high up in trees in small copses close to farmland or villages. Rooks eat grain, fruit, snails, worms and insects and sometimes carrion.

Finches

Finches are seed-eating birds with distinctive short, sturdy bills. Twelve species of finch are found in the UK. They are sociable birds, hunting for food by day in flocks, especially in autumn and winter, and returning to the roost at night. They court by touching bills – an apparent kiss.

Chaffinch
(Fringilla coelebs)
The chaffinch is arguably the most common bird seen in woodland, hedgerows and fields throughout the UK, though it is less common in Scotland. The male bird has a pink cheek and breast, a blue-grey head and neck, and a chestnut back. White flashes can be seen on the shoulder, wings and tail. The female has yellow-brown plumage above, and brown below, with similar white flashes to the male bird. The chaffinch population increases in winter with millions of birds visiting from western Europe and Scandinavia.

Hawfinch
(Coccothraustes coccothraustes)
The largest of the finches, the hawfinch spends its days perched high up in trees. This shy bird has a large head, thick neck and a powerful bill, which it uses to eat large

Above: The chaffinch enjoys open woodland and nests in joints in tree branches. The exterior of the nest is decorated with lichen and moss to act as a camouflage.

Below: When extracting seed from a cone, crossbills move from the bottom upwards in neat spirals, prising open the scale with their beaks and then removing the seed with their tongues.

seeds, such as beech and hornbeam nuts, hips, haws and fruit stones. It has an orange-brown head and breast and wears a grey scarf; the wings are black and white, the back brown. This is not a common bird, but it can be found in woods in parts of England, most notably the south east, the Home Counties and the Welsh borders. You see it most when wandering alone in woods.

Crossbill
(Loxia curvirostra)
The crossbill is found in coniferous forests. It is a remarkable-looking bird, with a bill that crosses at its tip, allowing it to prise open fir cones to obtain seeds. It is noisy and

sociable. The males are very easy to spot as they are a distinctive orange-red all over, save for brown wings and tail; the females are a greenish brown.

Bullfinch
(Pyrrhula pyrrhula)
The male bullfinch has a rose-pink breast and cheeks, a grey back, white rump, and a black cap and black wings, which feature a single white stripe. Bullfinches feed on tree seeds, notably ash, on the edge of woods, and supplement this diet with flower buds, favouring fruit trees that they can easily strip of valuable buds. They are found all over the UK, more commonly in the south, but numbers have declined severely.

Lesser redpoll
(Carduelis cabaret)
The lesser redpoll congregates in large groups, favouring birch woods and conifer plantations, and is more commonly found in the north and east of England. Its key feature is the flash of red on top of its head that is more pronounced in the male in the breeding season. Its back and wings are striped in brown, the under parts are white and there is a dab of black under the chin and a faint blush of pink on the upper breast. It enjoys birch and alder seeds, but will eat grass and weed seeds and insects.

Above: The brambling arrives from its breeding grounds in Scandinavia and Siberia to spend the winter in the UK; it can be seen from mid-September through to March or April.

Left: In the 1950s the bullfinch population was so large that fruit growers were allowed to trap them. It is now in decline.

Brambling
(Fringilla montifringilla)
A sociable bird that lives in large groups, the brambling passes the winter in the UK, favouring beech woods. It looks somewhat like the chaffinch, and the two birds often flock together. The male has an orange chest, a white rump, dark spotted flanks and a grey and brown back, with orange and brown wing stripes. Summer colouration varies.

Siskin
(Carduelis spinus)
A small, busy bird with a yellow-green body and a black bib and crown. Flashes of yellow appear on the wings and on the forked tail. The siskin is seen all over the UK, on the edges of woodland and in conifer plantations, but is more common in Scotland and Wales. It consumes the seeds of conifer, birch and alder. Many birds are resident throughout the year but in winter numbers are swelled by visitors from Europe.

Mammals

Bank Vole
(Clethrionomys glareolus)

The bank vole is about 10cm (4in) long. It has chestnut-coloured fur with a grey belly, a blunt snout, tiny ears and a short tail. It feeds on buds, leaves, fruits such as hips and haws, fungi, bulbs and insects. The bank vole is very nimble: it can run, climb, tunnel and swim. Left to their own devices, bank voles will live for a maximum of two years, but with a huge number of predators, many only survive for a few months.

Mice

Mice are nocturnal animals that eat seeds, grains, shoots, buds, berries, fruits, nuts, snails and insects. They make burrows, often amongst tree roots, which contain grassy, mossy nests and a larder to see them through winter. They can live for up to 18 months, but most only last a matter of a few months, as so many carnivores are dependent on them for food.

Right: The yellow-necked mouse is found in old woodland and hedges in southern England. It nests under tree stumps and occasionally in tree crevices.

Woodland mammals

Many woodland creatures are extremely shy, some are nocturnal, and all require stealthy observation. Winter is often the best time to spot them, as the undergrowth has died down and they have less cover to hide behind. Tracks in the mud and snow give away their presence, and droppings and food remnants also offer clues. Some mammals are so rare you would be very fortunate to catch even a glimpse of them. The **pine marten** *(Martes martes)* is one of these. It looks a little like a large weasel and hides away deep in pine forests and woodland. The **Scottish wildcat** *(Felix sylvestris)* is the last native wildcat to survive; it resembles a large tabby cat and is on the verge of extinction. The now misnamed **common dormouse** *(Muscardinus avellanarius)* is heavily protected by law. Other mammals, like the **New Forest pony** *(Equus caballus)*, are easy enough to see but only in their particular habitat where they have lived wild for over 1,000 years.

Scottish wildcat

Wood mouse
(Apodemus sylvaticus)

The wood mouse has a body length of 9cm (3½in), with a tail half as long again. It has large ears and protruding eyes. The fur on its back is a warm red-brown, its belly is grey-white, and it has a patch of yellow on its chest. The hind legs are longer than the forelegs. The wood mouse operates out of a series of tunnels, the entrances to which are often marked with a mysterious pile of stones.

Yellow-necked mouse
(Apodemus flavicollis)

The yellow-necked mouse grows to 10cm (4in) and has longer, red-brown fur on its back than its more common relative the wood mouse. It also has a whiter belly and a yellowish collar around its neck. It is found in woods only in southern England and Wales.

Squirrels

Squirrels are adept climbers with long bushy tails, sharp teeth and a keen sense of smell that they utilise to locate buried nuts. They are very dexterous and can be seen using their forepaws much like hands to hold food. Contrary to popular opinion, squirrels do not hibernate in winter, though they do bury food when plentiful to ensure survival. Spring is a difficult time and squirrels rely on leaf buds for food.

Red squirrel
(Sciurus vulgaris)

The red squirrel can be found in pine forests in Scotland, Wales, Northern Ireland and in the north of England, as well as on the Isle of Wight, which still has no grey squirrels at all. There is usually just one pair per acre. The red squirrel is around 20cm (8in) tall, and has russet-red fur with a white chest and belly, and red ear tufts in winter. It enjoys pine seeds, buds and shoots and acorns. You have a better

chance of seeing red squirrels if you follow these tips: look for them in the morning or later in the afternoon; try not to make too much noise; look up (they live in trees most of the time); listen for the falling rubbish from squirrels eating; look for evidence of squirrels feeding around pine trees – they eat pine cones in a very distinctive way; in autumn look near sweet chestnut and beech trees – they like the nuts these trees produce; stop still as soon as you spot one.

Grey squirrel
(Sciurus carolinensis)
Larger than the red squirrel, reaching 25cm (10in) in height, with grey fur and a white chest and belly, grey squirrels are found virtually all over England, Wales and central Scotland.

Badger
(Meles meles)
The badger is around 90cm (3ft) long with a solid body, short tail and short, powerful legs with strong claws. Its coat is covered in white hairs that are tipped with black. The head is white with the distinctive black stripe that runs from each eye to ear; the undersides and legs are black. The male has a thicker neck and broader head than the female. The badger builds a sett, a series of chambers and tunnels, around 10–20m (30–65ft) in length with several entrances. Badgers are sociable – as many as 19 can live in one sett – though the core is commonly two males and two females. They leave the sett after sunset to hunt; badgers eat snails, wasps, earthworms, mice, windfall fruit, elderberries, acorns, blackberries and grass. Man is its worst enemy – badger hunting led to the 1992 Protection of Badgers Act, which makes it illegal to kill, injure or take a badger or to interfere with its sett.

Above: Red squirrels do not hibernate but they are able to stay in their nests for several days when the weather is bad, feeding mainly on seeds, nuts, cones and fungi. Their diet varies according to the season and can also feature flowers, shoots and leaves.

Right: Badgers line their sleeping chambers with leaves and grass. They drag any of their old, soiled bedding out of the sett.

Conserving red squirrels

The threat posed to red squirrels by grey squirrels is potentially lethal. The greys carry a squirrel pox to which they are immune but reds are not. Squirrel pox is often the likely cause when red squirrel populations decline after greys invade. The National Trust is working in partnership to keep grey squirrels out of both Brownsea Island in Dorset and the Isle of Wight. These two islands, currently free from greys, are red squirrel havens. In the north of England, where red squirrels are severely threatened by greys, the Trust is supporting an initiative to set up 16 refuge areas for them where greys are controlled.

As red squirrel numbers dwindle, the five National Trust sites with red squirrel populations are becoming increasingly important havens for Britain's only native squirrel. As well as the island sites mentioned above the others are: Formby, Merseyside; Mount Stewart, Co. Down; and Wallington, Northumberland.

Bats

Bats are the only mammals that can fly; they hunt for insects on the wing, mostly at dawn and dusk, and this is the best time to observe them. They have very poor eyesight and navigate using echo-location: they squeak, at a pitch too high for the human ear to detect, and the sound is reflected back at them, so they can detect their prey, or an obstacle in their path. Bats have elongated fingers, and these mark the outside frame of the wing, which is connected to the ankle by a sheet of skin. They hang upside down when resting, as they are unable to support their limbs in any other position, and they hibernate in caves and tunnels in winter.

The 17 species of British bat, and their roost sites, are protected from disturbance by law. Examples of disturbance include: entering a loft which is a roost site; timber treatment; fitting loft insulation; attending to wiring or piping; storage use; pest control; other building work in a bat roost. When bats are hibernating, the presence of a person or their lights can cause them to wake up. This

wastes energy, which cannot be replenished in the depths of winter when feeding is impossible. Roosts are protected whether bats are present at the time or not.

Brown long-eared bat
(Plecotus auritus)
A relatively common bat, the brown long-eared bat has a body length of up to 5cm (2in) and a wingspan of 28cm (11in). The fur is a mid-brown, the face is pink-brown, and the wing membrane is grey-brown in colour. It has impressively large, glistening ears. Brown long-eared bats roost in tree holes in woodland fringes, caves and tunnels. They feed off moths but will take caterpillars and spiders from branches.

Above: Brown long-eared bats can emerge around 20 minutes after sunset, but they sometimes spend over an hour grooming themselves after waking, in preparation for flight.

Left: The whiskered bat is occasionally seen in the day, but usually emerges at sunset. It follows a regular route in hunting for food, taking small insects in flight and sometimes snatching spiders from foliage.

Whiskered bat
(Myotis mystacinus)
The whiskered bat is 9cm (3½in) long and has a 23cm (9in) wingspan. The upper body is dark brown, while the underparts are greyish white and covered in long fur. The face is grey-black as are the wing membranes. Whiskered bats hunt for moths, midges and beetles, with a slow and fluttery flight, in woods, parkland, open country and gardens, and roost in buildings. They hibernate in caves, tunnels and cellars.

Leisler's bat
(Nyctalus leisleri)
Leisler's bat is rare, but can be found in wooded areas, parks and gardens in central

England and Ireland, where it hunts for midges, beetles and moths. It has a body length of around 5cm (2in) and a 22cm (8½in) wingspan. It has long grey-brown fur, a screwed-up, dark grey face, with a distinctive furry snout and dark grey wing membranes.

Noctule bat
(Nyctalus noctula)
One of the largest British species, and the first to emerge at dusk, the noctule bat has a body length of around 8cm (3in) and a wingspan of 35cm (14in). It has golden brown fur, which extends on to the wing membrane, a paler underside, and dark brown face and wing membranes. Noctule bats favour woodland habitats and roost in tree hollows, but numbers have declined due to loss of habitat, and they suffer badly in cold winters.

Deer

Hunting deer was, for centuries, the exclusive preserve of the royal court. William the Conqueror went so far as to introduce the death penalty for anyone found breaking this law. Such harsh penalties were later abolished but deer remained under protection until the 19th century. The red deer, which lives on moor and mountain, and the roe deer are both natives. Fallow deer are believed to have been introduced by the Romans, sika deer were introduced to parks in the 19th century, and muntjac were introduced to Woburn Park in Bedfordshire from China in the early 20th century. Deliberate releases and escapes have led to feral populations. Reindeer were hunted in Scotland in the 12th century, and disappeared due to this and loss of habitat. They were reintroduced in 1952, and a controlled herd of 150 can now be found in the Cairngorms.

Fallow deer
(Dama dama)
The fallow deer is the largest woodland species and can reach up to 90cm (3ft) at shoulder height. It has a red-brown coat, marked with spots on the back, which can be white to black. There is a distinctive white, heart-shaped patch, ringed with black, on its rump. The antlers are flattened unlike those of other deer. Fallow deer live in isolated, single-sex groups for most of the year; male and female groups join together for the rutting season from September to mid-October.

Below: Fallow deer will forage by day in a peaceful, secluded environment, emerging from the woods to feed on grasses, young leaves and rushes.

Roe deer
(Capreolus capreolus)

Hunted to extinction in England by the 18th century (but still found in Scotland), the roe deer was gradually reintroduced to England, and now thrives in woodland. A roe deer will reach around 60cm (24in) at the shoulder. It is brown in colour with a black muzzle and a white patch on its rump. The buck's antlers are small and upright. Roe deer feed on grass, leaves, herbs and brambles.

Sika
(Cervus nippon)

The sika deer stands around 70cm (27in) at the shoulder, and its brown fur is spotted in summer and plain in winter, when its coat darkens. It has a white patch on its rump that is edged in black. The white tail sometimes has a black stripe. Sika can

be found dotted around the country in open woodland, notably Scotland, the New Forest and the Lake District. They eat grass, shoots, and shrubs, notably heather, and can strip bark. They hybridise with red deer, and it is feared that there are now no pure-bred red deer left in Britain.

Reeves' muntjac
(Muntiacus reevesi)

This is a diminutive, slightly hump-backed deer, and at just 50cm (20in) in height at the shoulder, it is around the size of a large dog. The coat is russet brown in summer and grey brown in winter, and it can have white marks on its neck and chin. Hidden under the tail there is a white patch on the rump that is exposed when the deer is frightened. It eats grass, shoots from trees and shrubs, herbs, heather and ivy and it often strips tree bark.

Above: The diminutive muntjac likes dense woodland. It is around both day and night, but is virtually impossible to spot at night. It has a distinctive bark, which is most commonly heard around breeding time.

Below: The roe deer is active at twilight (crepuscular) but will forage at night in the months from September to April when food is scarcer.

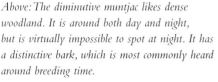

Management of deer

The National Trust manages between 4,000 and 5,000 deer in parks across the UK. Mature deer have no natural predators and, as a result, populations can increase and cause damage to wild-plant communities and crops. Numbers of most deer species are increasing and there is a growing risk of a high level of damage to woodland ecosystems, including the destruction of young trees. Consequently the National Trust finds it necessary to manage the numbers of wild deer in order to maintain populations of deer in a healthy condition, to maintain wild-plant communities and to maintain the historic landscape. This is achieved through a combination of measures: habitat management; protection of vulnerable areas or plants by the use of fencing or guards; the use of reflectors and other methods to reduce road casualties; and culling. The National Trust is aware that there is public concern about the killing of deer and its aim is to conduct all operations in a safe and humane manner; any culling is carried out with full regard at all times for the safety of visitors and staff, the welfare of livestock and other animals and the swift and clean despatch of culled deer.

Invertebrates

Violet ground beetle
(Carabus violaceus)

The body of the violet ground beetle has an iridescent sheen, and the wing cases and thorax are edged in violet. Violet ground beetles are large beetles that hunt for small insects by night, consuming large quantities of pests. By day they can be found concealed under leaf litter, stones and logs.

Rose chafer
(Cetonia aurata)

Chafer beetles are characterised by a broad head shield, and antennae that broaden out at the ends into flaps or fans. The rose chafer is found in Britain and Ireland but is absent from Scotland. Its head and body are bronze-green in colour and its back is often marked with white flecks. The larvae live in rotting wood.

Noble chafer
(Gnorimus nobilis)

The noble chafer occurs in old orchards, open woodlands, and pasture woodland. The larvae develop in rotting wood and wood mould from old standing trees, especially fruit trees (plum, apple, pear, damson and cherry), but also willow and oak. Adults have been found during the daytime on flowerheads, especially of the larger umbellifers. The noble chafer has been rare in Britain for over a century but appears to have undergone considerable decline in range. It is currently found in Hampshire, Worcestershire, and also in Oxfordshire and Herefordshire.

Stag beetle
(Lucanus cervus)

The largest beetle in the UK at around 6–9cm (2½–3½in) long, the stag beetle is found in southern England, and is now rare. It has an impressive set of antler-like jaws that the larger males use for fighting in the mating season. The head and thorax are black, the body is brown, and the antlers and wing cases a rusty brown. The larvae are cream with an orange head and legs. They live for around six years, feeding on rotting wood, and when they are fully grown they pupate in soil in the summer and emerge as a beetle a full year later.

Above: The violet ground beetle is a friend to the gardener for it eats numerous garden pests as it hunts by night. It is one of the larger beetles and can grow to 3cm (1¼in).

Left: Male stag beetles have large and distinctive antler-like mouthparts, which are used for fighting other males. Females have smaller mandibles, but are more likely to give a sharp nip. It is essential that small amounts of dead and dying timber are left in woodland to enable this species to survive.

Purple hairstreak
(Quercusia quercus)

The purple hairstreak butterfly is found in woodland containing oak, though it is hard to spot as it spends much of its time high in the tree tops, hunting for honeydew, and is most active in early evening. The male butterflies have a purple sheen to their upper wings; the hind wings have two orange spots and a small tail.

White admiral
(Limenitis camilla)

The white admiral is found in woodland in southern England. Its upper wings are inky-black with white bands and are tipped with white dashes. The white admiral feeds on honeydew and bramble blossom. It is the most graceful of our butterflies in flight.

Purple emperor
(Apatura iris)

This spectacular butterfly is rare, but worth looking out for in oak woods in central and southern England. It is the second largest butterfly found in the UK. The wings appear brown, until the sun shines on them, when they are transformed into iridescent purple triangles. The wings have a sprinkling of white spots and two orange rings or eyespots on the rear wings. The butterflies can be seen from late June until early August and they feed on tree sap and honeydew as well as extracting nutrients from rotting animal remains and dung.

Silver-washed fritillary
(Argynnis paphia)

Fritillaries are orange-brown butterflies with dark spots. The silver-washed is the largest of the group and can be seen south of Cumbria between July and September in deciduous woodland, feeding on brambles and thistles. The dark brown spots on the wing are evenly spaced and the rear wings are scalloped. The undersides of the wings are green with silver streaks.

Above: The female purple hairstreak has black wings marked with a bow of iridescent blue or purple. It lays its eggs at the base of oak buds.

Right: The white admiral has black wings with white bars. The undersides, which are seen here as the butterfly settles on a thistle, are a tawny mix of amber, cream and black. It lays its eggs on woodland honeysuckle.

Speckled wood
(Pararge aegeria)

Speckled wood butterflies have brown wings; the upper wing features cream spots with a dark eyespot near the tip, the lower wing has a row of dark eyespots. These butterflies can be seen flying in the dappled sunlight of woodland from March to October and feed on honeydew.

Green oak tortrix moth
(Tortrix viridana)

This moth breeds primarily on oak trees, and can be something of a pest as its caterpillars can completely defoliate trees, especially in certain years. It is a small moth, with shimmering leaf-green wings, and flies exclusively at night, though it can be spotted sunning itself on leaves during the day.

Winter moth
(Operophtera brumata)

These moths are active during the winter from October to February; the females are virtually wingless and wait for the males in trees – they are particularly partial to oak. The male moths have delicate grey-brown wings with very faded and intricate zigzag patterns.

Wood ants

The presence of wood ants indicates healthy woodland, as these ants like their habitat to be well-managed, and can be

Southern wood ant

found in coppiced woods and clearings. Wood ants are a valuable asset within a wood as they disperse seeds, eat insects that damage leaves, such as moth caterpillars, and contribute to nutrient recycling as well as being a food source for various birds. Their main food is honeydew and the ants will make trails to bountiful trees. They also eat small invertebrates and can be seen marching through the woodland in columns, making a rustling noise as they go. Wood ants range in size from 0.5–1cm (⅕–⅜in) long and have a brown head and thorax, and a black body. The **northern wood ant** *(Formica lugubris)* and the **Scottish wood ant** *(Formica aquilonia)* are found in Cumbria, Northumberland and Scotland, while the **southern wood ant** *(Formica rufa)* is found in the Midlands and southern England.

European hornet
(Vespa crabro)

The hornet is the largest UK wasp. The queen measures 2.5–3.5cm (1–1⅖in) long, and the workers are slightly smaller. Hornets make an impressive noise and look fearsome but they are actually quite difficult to antagonise. The hornet builds a nest in hollow trees, chewing wood into a paste to make the papery combs. The nest eventually contains 100–200 hornets. Adults feed on nectar and rotting fruit, while the larvae are fed on other insect larvae and flies. Hornets can be seen in central and southern woodland in the UK between April and October. Several species of fly and even moth mimic hornets, such as the hoverfly *Volucella zonaria* and the hornet clearwing moth.

Black snake millipede
(Tachypodoiulus niger)

The black snake millipede or white-legged millipede is found throughout the UK. It lives in bark, moss or leaf litter and

Above: Hornets are shy and peaceful creatures who will avoid conflict and back away from a perceived aggressor, but will defend their nest.

Right: Woodlice moult regularly as they grow, shedding their skin in two parts and eating it. It is especially vulnerable to attack at this time.

consumes dead and living plant material – it will climb trees in search of food. It has around 100 pairs of white legs that contrast with the black body. It moves slowly and winds up into a spiral coil when alarmed.

Common centipede
(Lithobius forficatus)

The common centipede has around 15 pairs of legs. It has a red-brown segmented body with one pair of legs per segment. It has poor eyesight and relies on two sensitive

antennae to find its way around. It hides in dark, damp places during the day, but hunts ground insects by night, which it paralyses with venomous fangs. Centipedes can be found in England and Wales, but are unusual in Scotland.

Smooth woodlouse
(Oniscus asellus)

This common arthropod is related to crustaceans that live in the water. It obtains oxygen by using gills on its back legs and survives only in cool, damp places. The smooth woodlouse has a distinctive oval-domed, armour-like back. Woodlice hide by day under stones and logs, and scavenge for food, including rotting wood, leaves and plant material, by night. They provide a valuable service recycling decaying material and putting nutrients back into the soil.

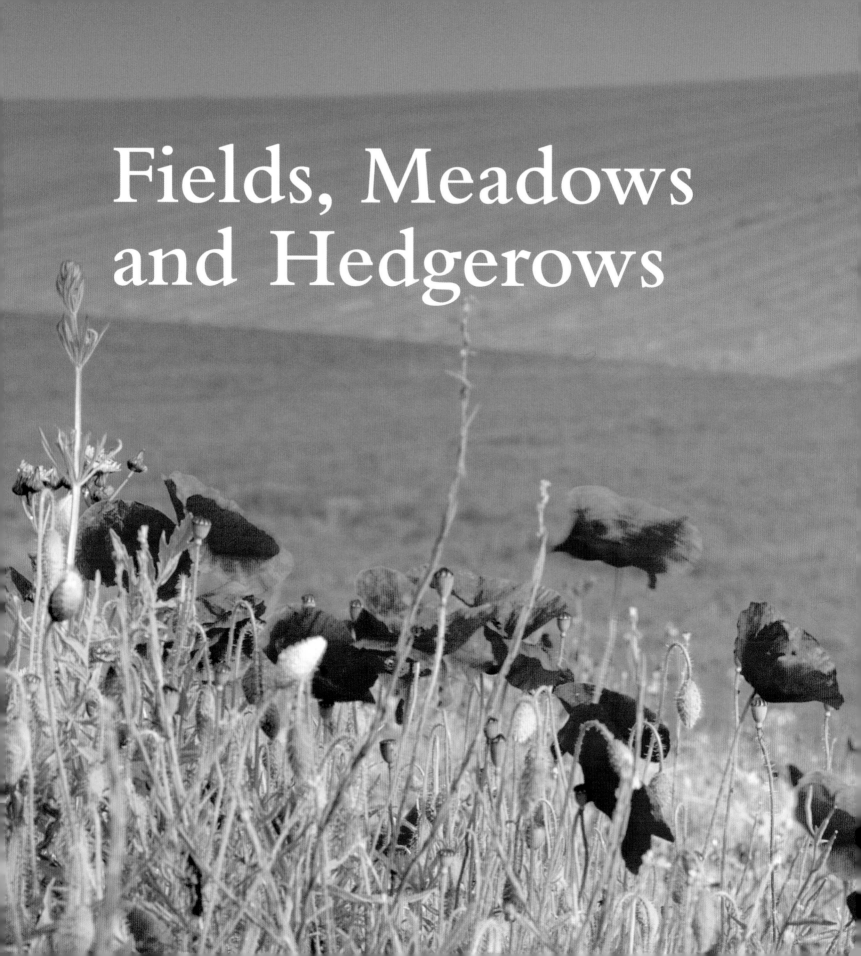

Fields, Meadows
and Hedgerows

Our Green and Pleasant Land

Fields, more than any other feature, have long been a characteristic element of the British landscape. They dominate the scenery and have formed the matrix of much of the English countryside since the enclosures acts of the 18th century; the field patterns in some areas of ancient countryside are much older.

Different regions have been given their own identity by the method used to divide the fields, be it hedges, walls, earth banks, or merely fences. In some regions, such as Worcestershire and West Sussex, hedges are studded with oak trees, giving the impression of wooded landscapes when viewed from the summits of distant hills. In other regions, such as the slopes of the Pennine hills, fields are bordered by low, grey stone walls and appear open, bleak and windswept.

The size of the fields can also add to the character of the countryside. In some districts the fields tend to be small, giving the impression of intimate, compact landscapes, while in others, they are larger, presenting an open vista. Of course, many were enlarged during the great agricultural changes of the late 20th century – at the expense of the established intricacy of smaller field systems.

The changing nature of fields

Until the last 50 years, both arable and pasture abounded in season with wildlife. Arable fields were often plagued by arable weeds,

Right: This Lakeland valley field system, near Derwentwater, consists mainly of fertilised agricultural rye grass, hence the uniform colour. In Wordsworth's time several different greens would have showed.

Below: Large arable fields at the foot of the South Down escarpment near Lewes, East Sussex. Formerly, sheep and cattle would have alternated between the downland slopes and the fields but that crucial relationship has ceased.

Above: Corn poppies flower along the field edge in stark contrast to the pure barley crop behind the flowering linseed.

Left: Crop spraying. Today, conventional arable crops are treated with fertilisers, insecticides and fungicides to reduce or eliminate the growth of other plants, mainly arable weeds. This has increased yield dramatically, but to the detriment of biodiversity.

many of which grew as annuals. At certain times of year these fields could be yellow with corn marigolds or crimson with poppies – the seeds of which are poisonous to people and farm animals. Today, such vistas are rare, seen mainly on organic farms or occasionally on conventional farms when sprays have failed in wet summers. A great many birds and small mammals fed and bred in these weed-infested arable fields, on the abundant insect life, on the weed seeds, and at times on the actual crops. Predators consequently flourished. Such fields were, of course, inefficient for food production, a fact that first became apparent during the Napoleonic Wars (1803–15) and then again, increasingly and intolerably so, during the First and Second World Wars.

Today, arable fields are virtually weed-free, kept so by efficient herbicide sprays designed to target specific plants or groups of plants, such as thistles and black grass. At best a small number of low-growing, short-lived weeds subsist at ground level. Corn marigold, formerly a serious 'problem' in many districts, was

controlled early on by a herbicide so powerful that it has long been banned. What used to be a veritable pest is now a rare plant. Indeed, arable weeds comprise a group of the British flora that has declined most, albeit with some justification.

Protecting our arable heritage

Nowadays many of our traditional arable weeds are some of our rarest plants. Their glorious names – pheasant's eye, shepherd's needle, Venus's looking-glass and weasel's snout to name but a few – are now more likely to be found in books rather than in the field. However, this decline has not made front-page news. But the associated loss of farmland birds is openly regretted – so much so that birds are now recognised by the government as indicators of environmental quality. The change in farming practices has meant that new arable weeds have begun to replace the traditional ones; the one that is flourishing most in today's countryside is wild oilseed rape – look on disturbed ground on any road verge. This weed is, though, of some benefit to cabbage white butterflies, whose caterpillars feed on it.

Some 80 per cent of National Trust land is farmed, much of it under agricultural tenancies that give the landlord little say in how the land is managed. Consequently, the bulk of the Trust's arable land is indistinguishable from other mainstream commercial farmland. But the EU's set-aside scheme and, in particular, the government's Countryside Stewardship scheme of the 1990s, helped to create more varied conditions, notably along the margins of many fields. The latter scheme is now being replaced by the Environmental Stewardship schemes; at a time of radical change, it cannot be overstated how much depends on these schemes. The fate of so much of our wildlife hangs on this thread of hope, as does the very integrity of our countryside. Never before has the Trust's voice been so important, as massive new pressures are developing on the countryside. Foremost among these are climate change and the need to use land to lock up carbon, the necessity of ensuring cleaner water and air, suburbanisation stimulated by human population growth, and a new round of agricultural intensification that includes biofuels.

Conservation in action

Some National Trust farms seek to conserve elements of our traditional arable field flora and fauna, usually along specific field margins or in certain fields. The Trust does, though, run a small farm on the North Cornwall coast specifically as an 'arable weed farm'. This farm, at West Pentire near Newquay, is managed for a staggering 81 species of arable weed; the tiny fields are sown with a weak barley crop that is periodically harvested by a small, old-fashioned combine harvester – assuming

Left: Venus's looking glass, now one of the rarest of our arable weeds.

Below: Corn marigold flowers prolifically at West Pentire Farm, on the north Cornwall coast. Although growing these weeds constitutes 'bad farming' it is actually a skill in its own right, which shows how fields would have looked in the past – when things had gone wrong.

Farmland birds

A Victorian naturalist would not believe the paucity of bird life that exists on modern farmland; in his day an abundance and diversity of bird life on farmland was regarded as a birthright. The writer and naturalist William Henry Hudson (1841–1922), one of the founders of the Royal Society for the Protection of Birds (RSPB), would be appalled. The figures, so well determined by the RSPB and the British Trust for Ornithology (BTO), are shocking. Crucially though, the potential – for not so much a recovery or restoration as a new coalescence – is still there. Demonstration farms run by the likes of the RSPB and the Game Conservancy Trust prove that bird life and farming can be compatible to a fair extent. These organisations have proved, for example, that the native grey partridge does not need to be a rarity, and that even the elusive stone curlew (shown right) can fare well in arable fields.

the machine will start! Paradoxically, it has been found that it is essential to use a grass-killing herbicide to control couch grass, which would otherwise smother the annual weeds. Rarities here include corn spurrey, night-flowering catchfly, small-flowered catchfly, Venus's looking glass, western ramping fumitory and several species of poppy.

Further west, close to St Just and Land's End, there is another Trust reserve, this for one of the most glamorous of arable flowers, purple viper's-bugloss, which makes a particularly lurid display when its bright reddish purple flowers are mixed with corn marigold. Elsewhere, there are many good examples of where individual farm tenants are doing their bit, most notably at the aptly-named Labour In Vain Farm at West Bexington on the Dorset coast. There, despite marginal economics, the Trust's inspired organic farm tenants purposefully cultivate certain fields to perpetuate annual plants such as the round and sharp-leaved fluellens, nit grass (the flowers really do look like head lice) and the rare blue-flowered form of the familiar scarlet pimpernel.

Meadows and Pastures

Traditionally, meadows and pastures teemed with wild flowers and animals. The dominant colours of our landscape were totally different – they were infinitely varied and changed radically at intervals during spring and summer. Our green fields are now the same monotone throughout the year, particularly as increasingly mild winters ensure that grass does not get scorched by cold and grows all year round, at least in the warm south and the lowlands. As recently as the mid-1980s, pastures turned grey and brown in severe winter weather. Now, most of our grass fields are constantly the same colour, except when hung with morning dew, tinged with raindrops, whitened by frost, or turned brown by summer drought.

Moreover, during the spring and early summer in particular, our old meadows scarcely looked green, but shone yellow, first with dandelions and then with buttercups. In high summer they were studded purple and crimson with knapweeds and red clover, and in late summer they were dotted with yellow again, with the likes of smooth hawk's-beard. In June, some fields turned white with pignut or the ridiculously-named corky-fruited water dropwort, two standard flowers of clay meadowland, both of which are now scarce.

The challenge of uniformity

That is how the countryside looked for several centuries, as illustrated by the scatter of ancient meadows. However, the 20th-century agricultural revolution – which was far more radical than those of the 18th and 19th centuries – has changed the composition of much of our grasslands and, crucially, has made most of our fields homogenous. Today, our grasslands – yesterday's buttercup meadows in the main – consist primarily of a single species of grass, rye grass, of which new and improved strains are continually being produced. This is often accompanied by agricultural strains of white clover, which fixes nitrogen in the soil. This mix is kept uniformly lush by regular doses of artificial fertiliser, known as NPK and consisting of nitrogen (N), phosphate (P) and potassium (K). This chemical mixture, usually applied twice a year, effectively changes the soil from being driven, ecologically, by micro-organisms, especially fungi – as is the natural state of soil – to being driven chemically, and with bacteria. The difference is massive: one works naturally, the other artificially.

Numerous other complications exist; for example, concentrated foods given to animals (as pellets or nuts) add extra nutrients to the ground after they have passed through the animal, especially phosphates. Animal medications, many of them preventative,

Left: Small pearl-bordered fritillary butterfly feeding on pignut flowers. Both were formerly widespread in damp meadows.

Below: During the 20th century the UK has probably lost more buttercup meadows than any other major habitat, replaced wholesale by the ubiquitous rye grass.

also add extra chemicals to the soil. The National Trust has effectively had to ban one particular group of chemicals used to treat internal parasites, as the residues kill off invertebrates that break down dung and as such are key elements of the food chain. A critical equilibrium has been disturbed.

Worse, most of the plants associated with old grassland depend on low levels of fertility, and are instantly out-competed once the fertility of their soil base is increased. The main exceptions here occur in flood plain meadows that are naturally fertile. Also, of course, farmyard manure, mostly generated from dairy cattle or beef cattle wintered in sheds or yards, was painstakingly applied to accessible land. This means that level fields close to farm buildings tended to receive a lot of manure, and have long been of a fairly uniform green colour. However, as a nation we really need to discuss what we mean by England's green and pleasant land – the National Trust has a fundamental role to play in that crucial debate.

Improved versus semi–natural grasslands

Nature conservationists make a fundamental distinction between modern 'improved' grasslands, reseeded with rye grass and dosed up with artificial fertiliser, and the older, more natural grasslands. The latter are technically not truly natural, as they are the by-products of past agricultural and land use practices that were benign or even beneficial, so conservationists term these 'semi–natural grasslands'. These are our downs, hay meadows, grazing fields and upland pastures.

The National Trust's Biological Survey Team, which surveys and produces reports on all the Trust's countryside properties, uses a simple grassland classification system based on the diversity of plants growing in a field. Fields are graded 1–4 depending on how floristically rich they are or whether they have been heavily improved by artificial fertilisers, G1 being the most diverse and G4 the least. At present, 90 per cent of the Trust's permanent pasture fields are heavily improved (G3 and G4) and only 1.3 per cent are unadulterated meadows (G1). These proportions will be worse outside National Trust land.

But all is far from lost – the dynamism of our countryside and of nature itself are not to be underestimated, and the potential for the development of meadowland rich in wildlife is enormous. Everything depends on what we as a society want, and are prepared to accept or allow. The key point is that in terms of wildlife and aesthetics our countryside is being sold woefully short.

Right: A monoculture of vigorous rye grass, the main constituent of modern grass fields, stretches as far as the eye can see. It can be cut for silage (fodder) two or three times a year, and grazed by cattle and sheep. Rye grass pollen is also one of the major causes of hayfever.

Watch for Wildlife

Flower-rich meadows may be increasingly uncommon but those that still exist are a naturalist's and an artist's paradise. Look out for the bright yellow of the **meadow buttercup** and its relative, the **bulbous buttercup**, which prefers drier habitats. Other yellow flowers include the locally common **cowslip** with its distinctive bell-like flowers, and **yellow rattle** whose name is derived from the noise made by the ripe seeds when the dead flower head is shaken. At the opposite end of the spectrum, the 'ragged' pink flowers of **ragged robin** can be seen in damp meadows, and the thistle-like flowers of **common knapweed** attract many different insects including the **marbled white butterfly**. Also popular with butterflies is **lady's smock** or **cuckooflower**. It has pale lilac or white flowers and is the main foodplant of the **orange-tip** and **green-veined white butterflies**. Rich splashes of purple are added to the palette by the 'bottle-brush' flowers of **great burnet**, spikes of **betony**, pin cushions of **devil's-bit scabious** and the thistle-like flowers of **saw-wort**. The bright violet-blue flowers of **meadow cranesbill** are characteristic of meadows in central and northern England. Display accents of white are provided by umbels of **cow parsley** and **alexanders**.

Ragged robin

Orange-tip butterfly on cowslip

Meadowland survivors

Despite the impact of recent farming methods, there are still pockets of meadowland – traditional hay or grazing fields – here and there. Some fields have survived, perhaps because the ground was just too wet to plough or drain, too distant from the farm buildings, or because a farming family held on to the old ways. Many such fields are now nature reserves, owned by the likes of the Wildlife Trusts, RSPB and the National Trust. Some of the richer or more extensive meadowland systems are National Nature Reserves, while a high percentage is protected as Sites of Special Scientific Interest (SSSIs). Areas of impeded drainage are especially important for flowers in old meadows. Here, in these boggy places, flowers like bugle grow alongside a great diversity of sedges and rushes, both large and small. Often these damp areas move about, and come and go. Such changes are due to hydrological movement underground, fluctuations in water tables, and old field drains blocking up or being replaced. River margins and old ditch systems are also important, holding a huge range of semi-aquatic and truly aquatic plants.

Managing meadows

Traditionally, meadows were managed primarily either as grazing land or as hay meadows, though the latter were often grazed late in the summer after the cut fields had re-grown – partly in order to provide them with nutrients via animal dung. Without the right amount of dung, hay meadows gradually become unviable; the volume of grass diminishes, fewer and fewer bales are produced, and the fields have to be managed as grazing meadows for a while, until nutrient levels build up a little.

Today's nature conservation movement has classified meadows into various types. There are two major types of conservation value: upland hay meadows, which are found in decreasing number in the

Below: A female green-veined white butterfly visiting lady's smock flowers in an organic hay meadow. The caterpillars of this and the orange-tip butterfly feed avidly on this plant, which has been ousted from most meadows by modern agricultural methods. The main problem is that artificial fertilisers make the grasses grow vigorously and suppress delicate flowers.

Farmland insects

Modern farmland is not a rich habitat for insects, though the opposite was true in bygone days. Arable fields in particular support few resident insects, partly because of the use of insecticidal sprays designed to control insect pests such as aphids. Happily some modern crops are attractive: the pale blue flowers of linseed, for example, attract various bees and hoverflies; the flowers of broad beans, or field beans as they are termed, are attractive to hive and bumble bees. The honey bee (Apis mellifera) also loves the flowers of red clover and lucerne.

Hedges are the second most important farmland habitat for insects, though much depends on the condition and botanical composition of the hedge. In early spring, blackthorn blossom attracts a profusion of small winged insects, mainly hoverflies (shown below) and mining bees, some of which are seldom seen away from this blossom. Sallow (or pussy willow) flowers are also valuable spring nectar sources. In May, hawthorn blossom is visited by a large number of flies, bees, bugs and beetles, and by moths at night. Of course, the most favoured high-summer source of nectar in hedgerows is bramble, which is one of the best bee, hoverfly and butterfly flowers in the countryside.

Above: This heavy clay pasture, below Burrow Mump in Somerset, has a tendency to become waterlogged. Such fields are only fit for grazing animals during the summer and early autumn.

Right: Tractors are used for efficiently topping outgrown grass fields, such as this field at Sissinghurst in Kent, to produce low, young grass that is more suitable for grazing cattle and sheep. The finely chopped grass tops act as a mulch on the cut grass.

likes of the Yorkshire Dales, and lowland meadows, which is a rather broad category that includes riverside and floodplain meadows, and largely consists of meadows on heavy clays that were too difficult for the plough.

Cutting or grazing is crucial to the survival of these meadows, or brambles, bracken, scrub and trees become established. Grasses are particularly well adapted to grazing because they grow, not from the tips of their leaves like most flowering plants, but from the leaf bases, close to the ground. So, even if a grass blade is almost wholly bitten off, it still continues to grow. Moreover, cutting or grazing causes grasses to 'tiller' – that is, grow in a prostrate manner and produce more leaves close to the ground.

Hedgerows

Many hedges were originally planted as barriers to prevent farm animals from straying, while some are the remains of ancient woodland where trees were cleared for pasture or crops, leaving only a narrow strip as a barrier. Others were planted as boundaries, such as parish boundaries, or in response to the Enclosure Acts. These acts – passed from the 1750s onwards and affecting over a fifth of England's landscape – allowed for the enclosure of large tracts of arable, waste and common land. Whereas many people, notably the Northamptonshire poet John Clare, raged against the Enclosure Acts, it should be recognised that hedges have been important landscape features and habitats for a considerably long time.

Havens for wildlife

From a wildlife angle, hedgerows can be immensely rich habitats in their own right, and can also provide vital connectivity through landscapes dominated by modern, commercially managed farmland, especially for woodland animals. The more hostile the countryside is to wildlife, the more valuable hedgerows become. Even hedges comprised of a single species of shrub can be important wildlife sanctuaries, especially the blackthorn hedges that characterise so much of lowland England on clay soils. The richest hedges, however, contain several species of shrub and tree, brambles and roses, and a number of plants normally

Right: Wildlife in hedgerows is extremely varied and is now thriving. It is set to increase even further now that farmers are being subsidised to cut hedges less often as part of various Environmental Stewardship schemes. Taller and thicker hedges will gradually change the look of the British landscape.

associated with woodland; they are also thick, even outgrown, and vary greatly in height. Above all, they are dense. Such hedges moulded many a naturalist. Some of the hedges on the National Trust's Golden Cap estate, on the West Dorset coast, are so wide and dense, containing such a diversity of shrubs, that they support strong populations of dormouse, a creature normally associated with dense old woodland.

Hedgerow maintenance

Hedges were designed to contain farm animals and mark ownership boundaries, but became heavily and wondrously exploited by wildlife. The alternatives were walls, ditches and shepherding, but walls need abundant,

Long-eared bat

Tiger moth

Blackthorn

Linnet

Orange-tip butterfly

Spindle

Fox

Brown hairstreak

Jack-in-the-hedge

Yellowhammer

Bank vole

Skylark

Grey partridge

accessible stone and ditches are viable only in low-lying areas with high water tables. However, keeping hedges stock-proof was laborious and costly work; indeed, for centuries farm workers spent much of the winter months managing hedges, walls, ditches and drains. But there were always problems; for example, sheep can gradually denude a hedge, eating out the bottom growth and slowly eroding it as a stock-proof feature.

Barbed wire was patented in 1874, and the barbed wire fence became a dominant feature of the British countryside during the 20th century, making hedges effectively redundant. Where hedges were retained they no longer needed to be stock-proof because they could be fenced on either side and kept as token landscape features.

Then along came the mechanical hedge-cutter, powered from a tractor power take-off (PTO) shaft. The first versions consisted of reciprocal cutter blades that gave a clean cut but left the farmer with myriad lying stems to clear up. Today's hedge-cutters are fiercely strong flails that pulverise stems up to several centimetres in diameter, leaving nothing that needs to be tidied up, and commonly with arm-reaches of

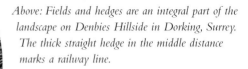

Above: Fields and hedges are an integral part of the landscape on Denbies Hillside in Dorking, Surrey. The thick straight hedge in the middle distance marks a railway line.

Left: Traditional hedge-laying involves skilfully cutting partly through thick hedge stems, and laying and binding the stems down to create a stock-proof barrier, in a manner that stimulates re-growth.

up to 7m (23ft). These machines now determine how our hedges look: narrow, low and horribly stark, providing little cover for nesting birds and far greater opportunities for egg predation.

Conserving the brown hairstreak

The plight of the brown hairstreak (shown below) illustrates the potential of hedges, and farmland in general, for wildlife. The brown hairstreak is a rare butterfly that breeds on blackthorn, and other members of the plum family, found in hedgerows and woodland edges. As a result the survival of this species is directly affected by hedge removal and the frequency and extent of hedge cutting. Once widespread in England and Wales, the loss of habitat and intensive hedgerow management has caused a huge decline in numbers. Populations have remained in the Weald of Surrey and Sussex, Wiltshire, Oxfordshire, Warwickshire, parts of Devon and Somerset and south-west Wales.

Redressing the balance

The government has recognised this parlous state, and during the 1990s produced funding schemes to produce better-looking hedges. Much of the money went into restoring traditional hedge-laying, but this may well have accidentally reduced the number of tall thick hedges in the countryside. Now, two Environmental Stewardship schemes both target the conservation of hedges. Farmers can now receive subsidies to cut hedges every other year or every third year. These initiatives could make a monumental difference to the appearance and biodiversity of the landscape.

Like all farmland habitats, hedgerows could – and arguably should – be better havens for wildlife than they actually are. This can readily be done without jeopardising food production and farmers' livelihoods. The simple truth is that the farmed landscape of much of the UK is a parody of the potential that could be realised within the parameters of food production and other land use aims, and, by not doing more to redress the balance, we are selling nature, the countryside and ourselves short.

Wildlife of Fields, Meadows and Hedgerows

Species-rich or 'improved' grassland is a naturalist's paradise. Sadly, due to the intensification of farming practices, much of our grassland has been 'improved' with seeding or fertilisers. However, fine examples still exist across the country, and although the species vary according to location and soil type, our traditional summer meadows are a spectacular sight. Hedgerows provide a natural barrier to our grasslands and also offer protection to numerous plants and animals. Many hedgerow species are also found in woodland and are cross-referenced accordingly.

Plants

Spindle
(Euonymus europaeus)

The common name of this species comes from the fact that its hard wood was used to make spindles, a tool for spinning thread. Spindle grows in hedgerows or as a straggly tree. It can be confused with dogwood, but can be recognised by its four-angled twigs, and its bright pink seed cases. Its greenish white flowers open in May.

Hawthorn
(Crataegus monogyna)

The oldest and most common hedgerow plant, hawthorn is seen right across the country. Its tiny, white five-petalled flowers appear in May and June. The small leaves are deeply lobed with indentations almost reaching the midrib. The berries or haws appear at the end of the summer and are relished by many birds, especially thrushes and blackbirds.

Dogwood
(Cornus sanguinea)

This plant's common name is believed to derive from the fact that butchers made skewers, or dags, from its tough wood. Dogwood has pale green oval leaves with wavy margins and carries tiny white, domed flowers. The flowers turn into bitter black berries, which the birds enjoy. The bare twigs and stems turn red in winter.

Privet
(Ligustrum vulgare)

A common hedgerow shrub, wild privet is most frequently seen in southern England on chalky and calcareous clay soils. It has lance-shaped leaves on short stems that sit opposite each other on the twig. In

Below: Hawthorn flowers cluster together, with 16 or more in a bunch. The berries that follow start green but by September turn a brilliant scarlet, later darkening to magenta. They persist on the leafless branches into December.

hedgerows wild privet is often a mass of frothy white flowers, which are followed by shiny black berries, popular with birds.

Wayfaring tree
(Viburnum lantana)

Sometimes known as the cotton tree – a reference to the fine hairs that cover the twigs, shoots and leaves – the branches of the wayfaring tree shoot almost up from the base with very little trunk. It carries heart-shaped, fleshy, serrated leaves and white flowers supported in domed clusters.

The berries start yellow and ripen to black. Unpleasantly sour, they are not eaten by birds if food is plentiful.

Old man's beard
(Clematis vitalba)
Also named traveller's joy by John Gerard, the 16th-century botanist, and otherwise known as wild clematis, this remarkable climber will scramble over hedgerows until little can be seen of the supporting plants. Common and widespread in the south, it is rare in the north. Greenish white flowers appear in July and August. In autumn it is covered with beautiful feathery, grey-white seed heads.

Meadow buttercup
(Ranunculus acris)
The meadow buttercup is the tallest and most common yellow buttercup and is found primarily in grassland habitats. Flowering from May onwards, it is distasteful to stock, and therefore flourishes when grazing animals remove

the competition by eating out the palatable grasses.

Bulbous buttercup
(Ranunculus bulbosus)
The bulbous buttercup favours drier habitats than the meadow buttercup, and the sepals are turned back along the stem.

Lady's smock
(Cardamine pratensis)
The pale lilac or white flowers of lady's smock are familiar along lanes, in damp fields and in woodland clearings. It is one of the first flowers to bloom in its habitat, coinciding with the call of the cuckoo in April and June, and so is also known as cuckooflower. Lady's smock is the main foodplant of the orange tip and green-veined white butterflies.

Jack-in-the-hedge
(Alliaria petiolata)
Also known as garlic mustard, this is a plant you can expect to have a powerful aroma.

Above: Jack-in-the-hedge can grow up to 120cm (4ft). The garlic-flavoured leaves were once commonly used as a culinary flavouring.

Below: The four-petalled lilac flowers of lady's smock are 15–60cm (6–24in) tall and form dancing drifts that bleach white in the sun to resemble scraps of linen – hence the common name.

Poppies

Common in the south and east, the large scarlet flowers of the **common poppy** (*Papaver rhoeas*) can be seen growing on farmland and roadsides in June and August. Its flat-topped seed pod is hairless. As its name suggests, the **bristly poppy** (*Papaver hybridum*) has egg-shaped seed pods covered with bristles. The flowers are smaller than the common poppy and dark red in colour. A local species in the south, the bristly poppy is rare in the north. The **long-headed poppy** (*Papaver dubium*) is the most common poppy species in the north. The pale red flowers are smaller than the common poppy and have no black patch at the base.

Common poppy

The leaves are either triangular or heart-shaped with toothed margins. The flowers appear in April and May and are small and white with four petals. The bright orange seed pods are much enjoyed by the caterpillars of the orange-tip butterfly.

Sweet violet
(Viola odorata)
Like the primrose, the sweet violet has suffered from intensive farming practices. It is a local plant of woods and hedgerows in England and Wales. It has heart-shaped leaves and carries highly perfumed flowers, with three petals above and two below.

Ragged robin
(Lychnis flos-cuculi)
The 'ragged' pink flowers of this species are prominent between May and July in damp meadows and along rides in wet woods. Its leaves are narrow and grass-like, and each of the five petals is divided into four unequal lobes, which gives the flower its untidy appearance.

Meadow cranesbill
(Geranium pratense)
With its bright violet-blue flowers, meadow cranesbill is a characteristic local plant of

Above: The sweet or common violet was heavily cultivated in Victorian times when it was fashionable for ladies to wear a tiny corsage of these sweetly perfumed flowers.

Below: The pretty cup-shaped blue flowers of the meadow cranesbill bloom between June and September. The veins on the flowers are said to direct bees towards the nectar.

roadsides and meadows, in central and northern England and Scotland. The name 'cranesbill' derives from the fruit, which has five segments that curl upwards from the base when ripe, and end in a pointed 'beak'.

Wood cranesbill
(Geranium sylvaticum)
Wood cranesbill has deep, reddish-purple flowers with five petals and the leaves are deeply divided into 5–7 lobes. It is now very localised in northern meadows and woodland and is more likely to be seen on a roadside verge than in a real country meadow. Like meadow cranesbill, wood cranesbill does not occur in the south.

Tormentil
(Potentilla erecta)
A trailing plant found in grassy places, as well as heaths and moors, tormentil produces small, yellow, buttercup-shaped flowers on long, slender stalks from May onwards. The leaves comprise three toothed leaflets that appear to have fives lobes because of two leaf-like stipules at the base.

Lady's mantle
(Alchemilla vulgaris agg.)

Lady's mantle is one of an aggregate of species associated with upland grassy areas, and is scarce in the south and east. All species have toothed leaves with 7–11 lobes. The tiny clusters of greenish yellow, petalless flowers appear between May and September.

Great burnet
(Sanguisorba officinalis)

Growing up to 90cm (3ft) tall, great burnet is a robust plant of old hay meadows, which produces dark purple, 'bottle-brush' flowers between June and September. It is rather localised in damp, grassy places in central and northern England.

Cow parsley
(Anthriscus sylvestris)

Cow parsley is a perennial with a deep taproot. It starts sending up pretty, bright green, fern-like young leaves in December, which are welcomed by hungry animals. The plant will reach heights of 1m (3¼ft), with hundreds of tiny flowers clustered together in umbrella-like umbels that form a flat dome on the tops of the hollow, ribbed stalks. The seeds follow and are shaped like a bird's beak.

Hedge parsley
(Torilis japonica)

Hedge parsley will reach up to 90cm (3ft). It is similar to cow parsley, but it is pink and has fewer and larger flowers in its umbels. It

Above: Cow parsley turns the May hedgerow into a foaming mass of white flowers. Whistles and pea shooters can be made from the plant's hollow stem.

blooms far later in the season, from July to September. The leaf is also similar to that of cow parsley, but the flowers have a small burst of green bracts at their base. The seed pod is bristly and clings to clothing, fur and feathers, effectively distributing the seed.

Wild roses

There are over 100 species of wild rose in the UK with five main species: the **dog rose** *(Rosa canina)* which is the most common, **sweet briar** or **eglantine** *(Rosa rubiginosa)* which has a wonderful apple fragrance, the **downy rose** *(Rosa villosa)*, the **field rose** *(Rosa arvensis)* and the **burnet rose** *(Rosa pimpinellifolia)* which has dark purple hips. These poetically named plants decorate the hedgerow with perfumed flowers, which are a lure for many insects, followed by orange and red hips, which are a rich supply of food for birds. Wild roses range from 1–5m (3–16ft) in height and the stems carry some vicious thorns. The pretty five-petalled cup-shaped flowers have yellow stamens and vary in colour from white and pink through to yellow and red-flushed flowers. These are followed by plump, orange, red or purple rose hips.

Burnet rose

Alexanders
(Smyrnium olusatrum)

This is a tall, hardy biennial that can reach 1.5m (5ft) high. It has large, glossy, serrated leaves and tall flower stems topped with white umbels, which in turn produce black seeds. Alexanders appears in March and flowers in May; the black seeds, a useful indicator for the novice, are visible by late June and July. The plant is commonly found on the roadside and beside hedgerows, especially in coastal regions.

Corky-fruited water dropwort
(Oenanthe pimpinelloides)

This gloriously named plant used to be common in damp, clay meadows in southern Britain. It has small lace-like flowers that occur in clusters, technically known as umbels, like cow parsley. These appear in July and August.

White bryony
(Bryonia dioica)

White bryony is a common sight in the somewhat neglected hedgerows of southern England. Bryony is a perennial with tough, hairy stems. It sends out long coiled tendrils by which it supports itself as it grows; these spiral coils change direction in the middle.

The green leaves have five or seven lobes and resemble vine leaves. The five-petalled white flowers grow in clusters from May to August; the female flowers develop bright red berries, which are an emetic and highly poisonous.

Stinging nettle
(Urtica dioica)

Nettles can reach 2m (6½ft) high and are a common sight beside the hedgerow. Perennial and annual varieties can be seen – both have veined and toothed leaves covered with fine brittle hairs, like hollow needles, at the base of which is formic acid. The hairs break on contact and release the acid on to the skin. Cattle are immune to the sting and will happily eat the plant. It bears tiny greenish white flowers from June onwards.

Cowslip
(Primula veris)

Formerly common in meadows and downland, this quintessential plant of the English spring, with yellow bell-like flowers,

Above: Nettles are rich in iron and vitamin C and are said to be useful in treating anaemia.

Left: Hedge bindweed twines around stalks and twigs in an anti-clockwise direction. The growing tip can encircle a twig in just one hour.

Opposite: The cowslip has suffered from modern farming methods but was once common in meadows.

is now very local, though often abundant where it occurs. Some theories hold that its name is derived from its habit of germinating where cattle hooves have poached the ground.

Hedge bindweed
(Calystegia sepium)

Bindweed is a climbing perennial that will reach heights of around 3m (10ft). The leaves are shaped like long arrowheads; the flowers are large white bells that appear from July to September. It has stout underground stems that will produce new plants if any part is broken off, and it is via this method that it spreads most successfully.

Yellow rattle
(Rhinanthus minor)

Some meadowland plants are canny, and in particular yellow rattle, whose name is derived from the noise made by the ripe seeds when the dead flower head is shaken. It is a semi-parasite of grasses, meaning that it partly extracts minerals and water from the roots of grass plants, thus stunting the grass. Although this can cause problems for the farmer, by reducing the quantity and quality of grass, it allows many small plants to flourish in the absence of competition from the more vigorous meadow grasses. Flushes of yellow rattle tend to occur in cycles, often on the back of dry springs, or after drought summers.

Orchids

Orchids are more sensitive than many other meadowland flowers, and are easily damaged by grazing with too many animals, or by grazing at the wrong time of year, and can be out-competed by tall grasses, if grazing is inadequate. The principle orchids of lowland meadows are the **green-winged orchid** *(Anacamptis morio)*, a small purple plant of early spring, and the marsh orchids, a complex group of species, sub-species and hybrids that keep many a keen botanist occupied of a summer's afternoon. Notable examples are the **southern** *(Dactylorhiza praetermissa)* and **northern** *(Dactylorhiza purpurella)* **marsh orchids**. Plant taxonomists periodically alter the identification and classification rules governing orchids, meaning a new set of species, sub-species and variants have to be learnt, thereby adding to the confusion.

Green-winged orchid

Betony
(Stachys officinalis)

Common in grassland and woodland in England and Wales, betony produces spikes of reddish-purple flowers from June onwards. Stalked leaves appear wide apart on the stem lower down, with unstalked leaves beneath the flowers. Although more sensitive to grazing than most grasses, classic meadowland wild flowers, such as betony, can tolerate significant amounts of grazing.

Hedge woundwort
(Stachys sylvatica)

The stems of this plant are hairy, and the small, oval-toothed leaves, reminiscent of the nettle, are similarly hirsute. They smell foul when crushed. The two-lipped, purple-red flowers emerge in whorls of six in July and August on a spike that can reach 90cm (3ft). Each flower produces four tiny nut-like fruits that nestle in the flower bracts.

Goosegrass
(Galium aparine)

Goosegrass is a pale green perennial with long stems around which at intervals are whorls of 8–10 small pointed leaves. The stem, leaves and seeds are covered in tiny, hooked hairs that enable the plant to cling on to anything and everything. The flowers are tiny circles of white petals.

Devil's-bit scabious
(Succisa pratensis)

A tall, purple, pin-cushion flower of late summer and early autumn, with narrow deep green leaves, devil's-bit scabious grows in old meadows, downland and woodland rides. Its flowers are popular with insects and its leaves are the food plant of the marsh fritillary butterfly and other rare insects.

Right: Betony was once commonly used as a medicinal herb to treat a great range of illnesses.

Common knapweed
(Centaurea nigra)

This is a classic plant of meadows and downs that flowers from July to September. Insects love its pink, thistle-like flowers. The plant itself only thrives where summer grazing is light, and does best under winter grazing or cutting regimes.

Saw-wort
(Serratula tinctoria)

The beautiful, purple, thistle-like flowers of saw-wort appear late in the summer. It occurs in damp meadows on neutral clays,

Above: The flower heads of purple saw-wort turn a bright straw colour once the flower has died. Long-tongued bees and butterflies enjoy its nectar.

and also on some southern downs, in a diminutive form.

Snake's-head fritillary
(Fritillaria meleagris)
One of our rarest meadowland plants, although it is frequently grown in gardens, the snake's-head fritillary is very much a specialist of old meadows in the Thames floodplain, where few of its old meadows survive. The plant produces bell-shaped, chequered purple and white flowers in April.

Autumn crocus
(Colchicum autumnale)
Also known as meadow saffron, this is a large and distinctive plant that produces leafless mauve crocus flowers in late summer, though they tend to flop and be damaged by slugs or birds. The blue-green leaf clumps appear earlier and are more prominent.

Black bryony
(Tamus communis)
Black bryony is a perennial climber that can reach heights of 1.8–3.6m (6–12ft) as it winds itself around other hedgerow plants, always in a clockwise direction. It has pretty, shiny, heart-shaped leaves and tiny six-petalled yellow-green flowers that appear on delicate stems from May to July. Bright red poisonous berries follow the flowers.

Grasses

Modern meadows consist of monocultures of agricultural rye grass, sometimes with white clover. Old-fashioned meadows host a dozen or more grasses, with resonant names such as crested dogstail, false oat grass, meadow foxtail, rough and smooth meadow grasses, sweet vernal grass, timothy and Yorkshire fog. A multitude of wild flowers grew among these natural grasses, whereas few are now able to survive amongst the vigorous, all-consuming rye grass.

Grassland fungi

Meadows that have not been treated with artificial fertilisers are great for fungi, but even small quantities of fertiliser can wipe out traditional meadowland species, such as the **field mushroom** *(Agaricus campestris)* or **horse mushroom** *(Agaricus arvensis)*, as they are extremely sensitive. A series of unimproved fields can support over 100 species of fungi, including many beautiful waxcaps and spectacular earth tongues. Waxcaps appear on short grass in autumn. Two common species are the **pink** or **ballerina waxcap** *(Hygrocybe calyptriformis)*, which comes complete with a delicate waxy pink tutu, and the **blackening waxcap** *(Hygrocybe conica)*, which turns from yellow or orange to black as it ages. The **fairy ring champignon** *(Marasmius oreades)* is also found in meadows and grasslands where its presence can be detected by circular rings of dark green grass. The mushroom itself has a small, smooth, brownish, slightly-bell-shaped cap. The **parasol mushroom** *(Macrolepiota procera)* has a large flat cap, never less than 8cm (3in) in diameter. The dark centre of the cap is surrounded by grey brown scales. This species is mostly found in October in pastures, hedges, open woodland and grass verges. **St George's mushroom** *(Calocybe gambosa)* has a flattish cap with a wavy margin. It can be white or buff in colour and has a diameter of 5–12cm (2–5in). The stem and gills are both white. This mushroom appears around St George's Day, April 23rd, and is visible until June. The **giant puffball** *(Lycoperdon gigantea)* is a truly astonishing fungus – a mighty white football of a mushroom that can suddenly appear at the edge of a wood between July and November, measuring anything from 15–75cm (6–30in) in diameter.

Parasol mushroom

St George's mushroom

Birds

Grey partridge
(Perdix perdix)
This native partridge, mainly of lowland arable farmland, is now quite rare. Many farmers are now actively conserving it through careful management of arable field margins and the grey partridge is making a welcome return. It is a plump bird with an orange face, striped flanks and a chestnut tail.

Stone curlew
(Burhinus oedicnemus)
A rare summer visitor to bare-ground places in southern Britain, often breeding in large arable fields in the south east. They are incredibly well camouflaged against stony soil. The RSPB has been leading a successful campaign to work closely with farmers to increase numbers of stone curlew. It has sandy-brown plumage with darker flecks, large yellow eyes that help it find food when it is dark, and long yellow legs.

Wood pigeon
(Columba palumbus)
A plump, blue-grey pigeon with a pink-tinted breast, its mournful call can be heard as, 'It is going to rain', repeated several times. In cold winter weather wood pigeons gather into sizeable flocks to feed in fields and on beechnuts in woods.

Above: The grey partridge consumes grains and seeds, leaves, flowers, shoots and a good range of insects, slugs, spiders and snails.

Collared dove
(Streptopelia decaocto)
This relative newcomer first appeared in the UK in the early 1950s, but has spread virtually throughout the country. Now one of our most common birds, the collared dove is found in most of the countryside, except extreme upland areas. It is characterised by its grey-pink plumage and dark stripe on the neck.

Skylark
(Alauda arvensis)
The skylark is another countryside bird that has suffered a terrible decline. Not only has it inspired some of the country's most famous writers, Shelley and Wordsworth among them, it has also been immortalised by composers in works such as Ralph Vaughan-Williams' *The Lark Ascending* (1914). The survival of the skylark requires lighter grazing regimes that produce tussocky fields, ideally under organic or low-input farming systems.

Swallow
(Hirundo rustica)
In summer, the distinctive, red-throated swallow skips over the fields in pursuit of small flies. Look out for its long forked tail and dark blue back. Swallows arrive in March and migrate south to Africa in October. They can be seen across the whole of the UK.

Redwing
(Turdus iliacus)
A small thrush with red patches under its wings, the redwing arrives in mid-autumn and leaves in March, feeding mainly on winter berries. It also flies in the night, and its clear piping call is a familiar sound on winter evenings.

Fieldfare
(Turdus pilaris)
A winter visitor to open fields, this large thrush-like bird has a distinctive grey head, and maroon-brown back. Fieldfares spend the winter in flocks and often mix with redwings. In late March fieldfares fly north to their breeding grounds.

Whitethroat
(Sylvia communis)

The whitethroat is not partial to our cold British winters and takes off to Africa, Asia or India for some winter sun – a journey of around 3,200km (2,000 miles) – before returning in April to breed in overgrown hedgerows. It is brown above and buff below with a white bib, rusty brown wings and white outer tail feathers. The male has a grey head and the hen a brown one; both have a grey-brown beak and legs.

Rook
(Corvus frugilegus)

The rook is a highly intelligent and sociable bird that lives in colonies high up in hedgerow trees. The rook is a large, black bird whose inky feathers have a purple sheen. It has grey or white patches on its face, and around the long bill, and it has shaggy feathers around the top of the thighs.

Above: In December the redwing can be found snacking on holly berries, seen here in Leicestershire.

Below: Swallows gravitate towards areas of pasture that are near water and feed their young on the small insects that are found there.

Starling
(Sturnus vulgaris)

This familiar, dumpy bird is black with a metallic purple-green, flecked plumage. One of the most beautiful sights in the countryside are tornado swirls of evening starlings homing in to roost communally.

Linnet
(Carduelis cannabina)

The linnet is one of the smaller members of the finch family. The cock has a crimson breast and crown, a grey-blue head, a chestnut back and white bars on its wings and to the sides of its tail. The hen is a much duller speckled brown. The linnet is widespread across the UK except for the highlands of Scotland.

Greenfinch
(Carduelis chloris)

A common bird of the countryside, the greenfinch has the trademark stout bill of the finch family, and is olive green with yellow streaks on the wing bars, chest and the sides of the tail. The beak and legs are flesh-coloured. The hen is a subdued version of the cock bird with fewer yellow feathers.

Yellowhammer
(Emberiza citrinella)

The yellowhammer enjoys a quiet existence in rural hedgerows, well away from human settlements. The male boasts a splendid covering of yellow feathers – with a bright yellow head and breast streaked with chestnut and brown, and black-streaked back and wings. The female has fewer yellow feathers and more brown markings, with white feathers along the edges of her tail.

Mammals

Hedgehog
(Erinaceus europaeus)

The hedgehog has suffered from the large-scale destruction of so many miles of its natural hedgerow habitat. It is grey-brown in colour; its upper surface is covered in sharp, pointed, yellow spikes and the spineless parts of the body with coarse hair. The spines are actually hollow hairs stiffened with keratin. It is quite noisy and snuffles and grunts through the undergrowth.

Mole
(Talpa europea)

The mole originated in wood and grasslands but has adapted to hedgerow life over the years. It has a cylindrical body, a long pointed snout and a club-shaped tail. The very fine and velvety black or dark-grey fur that can rub either way without causing discomfort, allows the mole to reverse through his tunnels. The mole is almost blind, but has good hearing, a strong sense of smell and sensitive whiskers on its head and pink snout.

Pygmy shrew
(Sorex minutus)

Five species of shrew exist in the UK and it is the smallest, the pygmy shrew, which is most widespread. The back of the pygmy shrew is grey-brown in colour, while its underside is white and has dense, velvety fur. It has a distinctive, long, tapering snout and razor-sharp, needle-like teeth with orange-red tips. Its tail comprises two-thirds of its total length.

Field vole
(Microtus agrestis)

There are two species of vole found in fields and meadows. As its name suggests, the field vole lives among rough grass, in tunnel systems. It has grey-brown fur and a very short tail.

Right: The bank vole is the smallest vole in the UK. It looks like a mouse but has a blunt nose, rather like a hamster.

Below: Moles will bite the head end off a worm to prevent it from struggling, tie the remainder in a knot and store it in his larder until required.

Bank vole
(Clethrionomys glareolus)

The brown bank vole is a common hedgerow mammal that feeds on buds, leaves, fruits such as hips and haws, fungi, bulbs and insects. It will make a food store in autumn to help it through the winter.

Harvest mouse
(Micromys minutus)

The harvest mouse is the UK's smallest rodent. It has orange-brown fur and a long tail that helps the mouse to climb among plants – usually cereal crops – where it also builds its nests.

Wood mouse
(Apodemus sylvaticus)

The long-tailed field mouse is also known, perhaps more accurately, as the wood mouse, as it is primarily a nocturnal creature of areas with trees and bushes.

Rabbit
(Oryctolagus cuniculus)

Modern farmland is a poor habitat for mammals, not least because of the long-established and necessary practice of controlling problem species. Herbivores, notably rabbits, can seriously damage arable crops and newly sown grass fields. Nonetheless, rabbit burrows occur in hedge banks and in soft, dry ground. Often these diggings are in woodland close to farmland, over which the animals range to feed.

Above: Rabbits emerge from their burrows to feed at dawn and dusk. They are voracious eaters and are said to consume as much as 450g (1lb) of greens in a single day – the damage they can do to arable crops and the surrounding countryside is considerable.

Stoats and weasels

Stoats and weasels are seldom seen, and the pitiful squeal of a hunted rabbit is often all we know about their presence. We rarely see them for more than the odd moment, as they use cover to great effect and move fast. These small, agile and ferocious predators now exist only in small numbers. The **stoat** (Mustela erminea) is the larger of the two and always has a distinctive black tip to its tail. As well as being the smaller of the two, the **weasel** (Mustela nivalis) has a shorter tail.

Weasel

Brown hare
(Lepus europaeus)

The brown hare causes little damage to farm crops (though hares can damage young trees, when eating bark in cold winter weather). Hares are quite common in the arable lands of eastern England, though they tend to occur only at low population density, and are scarce further west.

Badger
(Meles meles)

Badger setts can be used for decades, though there is also a scatter of satellite or outlier burrows that are used intermittently. Like rabbits, badger setts also occur in hedge banks and in soft dry ground. Badger populations have increased over much of the UK greatly in recent years, partly because of the 1982 Badger Protection Act, which was introduced to curtail badger-baiting.

Bats

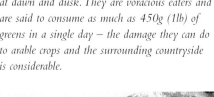

Several species of bat hunt over farmland. Some feed on winged insects that breed in woods and hedges, others on dung beetles and craneflies (daddy-long-legs) that emerge from grazed fields. Some, like the **noctule bat** (Nyctalus noctula), roost in trees, others like the **serotine bat** (Eptesicus serotinus) and the **pipistrelle** (Pipistrellus pipistrellus) roost primarily in buildings. Old farm buildings can be important to them, as well as the barn owl and swallow. Hedges can provide crucial roadmaps and hunting grounds for bat foraging expeditions, and hedgerow trees much-needed midnight resting places en route.

Noctule bat

Invertebrates

Cockchafer
(Melolontha melolontha)
The cockchafer, or maybug, is a large beetle, 3.5cm (1⅜in) in length, with a reddish-brown, squat body and clubbed antennae. It lives in the soil for several years, feeding on underground root systems, and flies in May and early June.

Grasshoppers and crickets

There are 30 species of grasshoppers, groundhoppers and crickets in the UK, some more common than others. They are diminutive in size, a maximum of 3.5mm (1⅜in) long. As a general rule, grasshoppers have short antennae; crickets have long, fine ones, but there are exceptions. Crickets tend to be nocturnal. Both have large heads and strong biting jaws. When they are picked up, grasshoppers spit out a brown liquid known as tobacco juice as a defensive measure. The legs are well developed and carry claws; they are capable of transporting the grasshopper 20 times its own body length in one jump. The **meadow** (Chorthippus parallelus), **common field** (Chorthippus brunneus) and **common green** (Omocestus viridulus) **grasshoppers** are widespread throughout Britain, the latter two also being found in Northern Ireland. The **common groundhopper** (Tetrix undulata) is restricted to southern England and Wales, but is widespread throughout Ireland. The most common and widespread crickets are the bush-crickets, such as the **dark bush-cricket** (pholidoptera griseoaptera), which is common in hedgerows and rough grassland throughout England and Wales.

Common green grasshopper

Garden chafer
(Phyllopertha horticola)
The greenish-tinged garden or common chafer is much smaller than the cockchafer. It, too, feeds on roots underground and can be seen in flight throughout May and early June.

Clouded yellow
(Colias croceus)
The flashing golden wings of the clouded yellow butterfly provide one of the most special late summer sights, as the males patrol clover fields. It is primarily a migrant species, though it has been breeding along the south coast for the last few years, due to milder winters.

Above: The clouded yellow is famous for spectacular mass migrations from North Africa, Southern Europe and the Middle East called 'clouded yellow years'.

Cabbage white butterfly
(Pieris brassicae and Pieris rapae)
There are two cabbage whites, the large white (P. brassicae) and the small white (P. rapae). These species breed on a wide range of plants from the cabbage family, both wild and cultivated. They are also partially migratory, with invasions coming across the English Channel in hot summers. The large white has black margins on the forewings and the females also have a black spot. The small white female boasts two spots, while the male has just one.

Brown hairstreak
(Thecla betulae)

An archetypal hedgerow butterfly, the brown hairstreak is rare, elusive and indolent. These butterflies spend hours sitting around on ash trees in late summer, imbibing a sticky secretion from developing buds. Eggs are laid on blackthorn twigs in hedgerows and hatch the following spring. However, the majority are destroyed when hedges are cut, so what should be a widespread butterfly remains rare.

Small copper
(Lycaena phlaeas)

The tiny and fiery small copper is a typical inhabitant of the traditional meadow. Its

Above right: The wing colour of the male gatekeeper, or hedge brown, is brighter than that of the female. They feed on flat-topped flowers when they are fully open.

Below: The small copper enjoys sun bathing and can often be seen basking in the sun, but it will defend its territory against any passing insect.

upper wings are orange with dark brown markings; under wings are orange and grey-brown. It is a fast-flying species found in a range of open-country habitats.

Common blue
(Polyommatus icarus)

The common blue is a classic butterfly of the traditional meadow. It is likely that it, along with the meadow brown and the small copper, has declined more than any others during the 20th century, as the direct result of the loss of traditional meadowland.

Small tortoiseshell
(Nymphalis urticae)

The small tortoiseshell is an adaptable butterfly that can be found in a wide range of habitats across the UK but it favours hedgerows in particular. It breeds in nettle patches in sunny places. Recently, this

standard butterfly of gardens and farmland has started to become scarce in southern England. It is not yet known why. It has orange-brown wings with dark brown, pale yellow and white patches of colour on the forewing and blue marks on the margins.

Red admiral
(Vanessa atalanta)

The red admiral is probably the best-known British butterfly. It is dark chocolate brown or black in colour with red or orange bands and white markings. Despite it being such a familiar sight, it actually has great difficulties surviving our winter. Luckily the resident population is swelled by the arrival of immigrants from mainland Europe in May, as they migrate northwards.

Gatekeeper
(Pyronia tithonus)

The gatekeeper is an archetypal hedgerow butterfly and ubiquitous species of scrub edges. Its other common name is, appropriately, the hedge brown. It is common in late July and August in the south, and breeds on grasses in the base of hedges.

Above: The spectacular magpie moth has many forms of wing patterning, but maintains its white wing background with contrasting black spots and a yellow-orange stripe. It can be seen on the wing from June to August.

Below: Antler moths can be seen flying both by day and night in warm weather.

Meadow brown
(Maniola jurtina)

The meadow brown is the most common hedgerow species of butterfly, enjoying the sheltered environment. It can also be seen in old fields in high summer, bobbing among the grasses. It has velvety mole-brown wings with flashes of dull orange highlighting a dark spot. The males are paler and appear washed out compared to the females.

Barberry carpet moth
(Pareulype berberata)

Hedgerow species, such as blackthorn, hawthorn, sallow and bramble, are all-important foodplants of the caterpillars of several hundred different types of moth. A number of rare moths are strongly associated with hedges, especially blackthorn. One remarkable moth that has a strong association with hedgerows is the barberry carpet moth, a moth so rare that it is afforded special protection. Its caterpillars feed only on barberry (the wild flower *Berberis vulgaris* as opposed to the cultivated forms), a thorny hedge plant similar to the

common buckthorn. However, it was found that barberry harbours wheat rust in winter, so it was assiduously grubbed out from hedges – hence the rarity of the moth. Now, of course, farmers grow varieties of wheat that are resistant to wheat rust, so both plant and moth can safely return.

Chimney sweeper
(Odezia atrata)

One of the most distinctive day-flying meadowland moths is the chimney sweeper, a small black moth with pale wing tips that flies in June. Its caterpillars feed on the flowers and seeds of pignut, a low-growing plant with lace-like flowers and an edible tuber. The moth is common in northern England but local in the south.

Magpie moth
(Abraxas grossulariata)

The magpie moth is a boldly patterned species with black splodges on a creamy white background and a wavy orange stripe on its forewing and head; the caterpillars are similarly patterned. Birds do not like the taste of this moth and its colouring warns them away; even spiders will not eat it and remove it from their webs. The

caterpillars are partial to blackthorn, hawthorn and hazel, and are common in hedgerows.

Large yellow underwing
(Noctua pronuba)

The common large yellow underwing can occur in abundance in old meadows. This yellow and brown moth is readily flushed off lawns by advancing mowers.

Setaceous Hebrew character
(Xestia c-nigrum)

A prolific moth of fields, old and new, is this gloriously named setaceous Hebrew character, a dull, grey species that flies in late summer and autumn.

Antler moth
(Cerapteryx graminis)

A large number of moths breed in old meadows, including several whose larvae can occur in such profusion that whole meadows, or even hillsides, can be denuded of grass. Such events are rare these days, but the antler moth, whose name is derived from the antler-shaped marking on the upper-sides of its forewing, still occasionally occurs in profusion.

Autumn cranefly
(Tipula paludosa)

The caterpillars of some insects feed underground on plant root systems. The most profuse of these is the common autumn cranefly, which occurs in super-abundance during September and comes into houses at night.

Cross spider
(Araneus diadematus)

The cross spider, or garden spider, is one of the most common species of spider. It is either yellow or grey and is easily identifiable, being marked with a series of white dots that make up a cross on its abdomen. It spins circular orb webs of around 40cm (16in) and can be found either hanging head down in the centre, or concealed from sight on a retreat line, which allows it to drop back on to the web in a moment.

Money spider
(Linyphia triangularis)

The money spider is extremely common and boasts around 250 species, including the ubiquitous *Linyphia triangularis*. Money spiders are generally around 2mm (¹⁄₁₆in) long, but can be a little larger. It utilises all sorts of vegetation as web support – anything from grass to trees – where it spins a horizontal sheet or hammock web surrounded by a tangle of numerous lines. The tangled lines catch the prey, usually aphids, mosquitoes and midges, which then fall into the web below, where they are caught and devoured.

Slugs and snails

Slugs and snails do well on moist hedgerow floors, hidden beneath undergrowth, where they form an important food source for birds and hedgehogs. They emerge at night when the humidity is greater or will venture forth in the daytime after a shower of rain. Their moist bodies are susceptible to water loss, so damp conditions allow them to explore with confidence. In hot weather snails retreat into their shells where they plug up the aperture to retain moisture, while slugs slither into dark, damp places. Snails hibernate in the autumn and emerge in spring to mate. Slugs are active all year round but will burrow into soil in very cold or hot weather.

Red slug
(Arion rufus)

The large red slug is one of our most familiar and widespread slugs. Growing up to 12cm (4¾in) long, the orangy-red form is common in southern regions, whereas

Above: The cross spider, or garden spider, eats its own web every day, a process that takes just a few minutes. It spins a new web each morning.

Above left: There is considerable colour variation in the shell of the white-lipped snail – it frequently features yellow stripes, as shown here.

further north the black form (*Arion ater*) prevails. When the slug is alarmed it contracts into an almost spherical ball, often rocking from side to side.

Brown-lipped snail
(Cepaea nemoralis)

The brown-lipped snail is commonly found in gardens and woodlands, as well as hedgerows. It has a pretty, thin, glossy shell in pale pink or yellow with no more than five banding patterns in brown. The key to identification is that the lip of the mouth of the shell is brown.

White-lipped snail
(Cepaea hortensis)

The white-lipped snail is similar to the brown-lipped snail but has a white lip at the mouth of the shell.

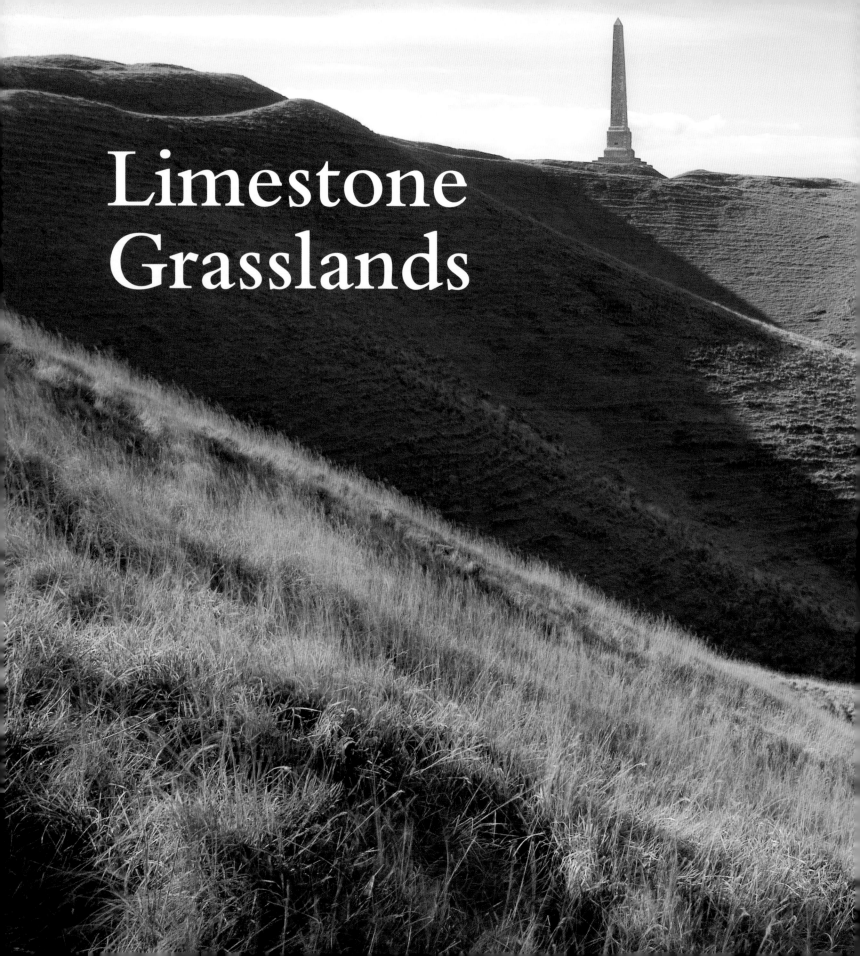

Limestone Grasslands

Our Chalky Downlands

The grasslands of the UK's chalk and limestone countryside are renowned for their scenic beauty and wildlife. The springy downland turf, studded with ant hills, harbours some of our most colourful and precious flowers, which in turn support an unusually rich insect fauna, including many of our most special butterflies. The longer grass, and even the scrub, sustains other specialists, making downland one of our islands' richest wildlife habitats.

Surprisingly, though, these grasslands are essentially man-made, the product of centuries of grazing by sheep and cattle, and constant attacks against invading scrub by downland shepherds. Without these activities woodland would soon re-establish, as has indeed happened in many places. Today, these grasslands are largely restricted to steep slopes that proved too difficult to plough or reseed with agricultural grasses.

As the name suggests, limestone rocks are rich in lime, or calcium, and are known as calcareous rocks. There is a broad range of calcareous rocks in the British Isles, together with associated soils. The calcium content of these rocks varies considerably, as does the amount of impurities. Occasionally, calcareous soils occur over underlying neutral or even acidic rocks, usually as wind-blown sands that have been deposited over differing geology, or washed down and deposited by rivers. The opposite occurs too; for example, much of the carboniferous limestone of the Mendip Hills in the south west, and that in northern England, is overlain by acidic peat. And there can be calcareous peat too, created by the percolation of alkaline water, as in the Test and Itchen valleys in Hampshire.

There are four major types of limestones in England, Wales and Northern Ireland, plus some mildly calcareous clays and a whole host of weak limestones that occur locally, sometimes as single hill outcrops, and also some calcareous sands. Largely, though, we are concerned with the chalk and carboniferous, Jurassic and magnesium limestones, plus a range of local geologies and soils that host a number of plants strongly or wholly associated with calcareous soils. This calcareous geology is essentially composed of sedimentary rocks, formed from calcium-rich shells of sea creatures on ancient long-gone sea beds. Their legacy is truly immense, incorporating many of the most diverse and deeply valued habitats and landscapes in the British Isles.

Above: The exquisite pasque flower is one of the rarest of our downland plants, growing only on well-grazed slopes in southern England.

Left: The Devil's Dyke, a historic beauty spot on the South Downs above Brighton, is the largest chalk combe in Britain. It was formed by solifluction — when saturated soil slowly washes away under tundra conditions. The slopes support rich chalk grassland.

With the exception of some calcareous fens, which can be quite rich in nutrients, calcareous grasslands are – and must remain – of low fertility. If the fertility increases, then many elements of the flora and fauna decline or disappear; they are out-competed by more vigorous grasses and die out.

Wildlife of downlands

Plants that love lime-rich soils are termed calcicoles, and those that cannot tolerate such conditions are called calcifuges. Lime-loving vegetation can be incredibly rich in terms of the number of plant species; it is reputed that downland can contain as many as 40 species of plant per square metre (10ft²), though few botanists have bettered 30. Of course, these listings include plant species existing in a non-flowering, vegetative state, and it takes a true botanical expert to identify such species. In addition, the less pure limestones, notably carboniferous limestone, contain many impurities and pockets of leached soil; in such conditions plants of neutral or acidic conditions grow, often close to true calcicoles situated in pure limestone pockets. The overall effect is truely wonderful.

Effects of climate change

We now know that there is a pattern over most of the UK of hotter, drier summers, milder, wetter winters, more storms with heavy rainfall, and higher sea levels and increased wave heights. These trends, which are projected to continue, will be punctuated by more extreme weather events, affecting water tables and accentuating soil erosion. Such changes are likely to impact on chalk downland through altered patterns of vegetation growth as the habitat becomes wetter or drier, increased gorse, bracken and scrub growth, and increased soil erosion. If carefully maintained, however, our downland can remain a robust habitat; the National Trust aims to achieve this with its dual policies of establishing and maintaining suitable grazing regimes, and controlling scrub and invasive species.

Limestone grasslands suddenly explode into flower in May, when yellow colour dominates; first with cowslips and then with bird's-foot trefoil, horseshoe vetch and common rockrose late in the month. Pinks and reds dominate in June, with carpets of wild thyme, often on ant hills, and tall spikes of sainfoin and the common spotted, fragrant and pyramidal orchids. July and August belong to the purples of the thistles, including the delicate ground thistle, a downland speciality, and the purples and blues of the common and greater knapweeds, fellwort and devil's-bit, field and small scabiouses, alongside the deeper blue of the round-headed rampion in the south east. By this time the grasses have lost their colour in the summer sun and by September the downs often look straw coloured.

Left: Some of the classic elements of downland wildlife. The rich and varied flora is maintained by grazing, including by rabbits, and supports an exceptionally rich insect fauna, which in turn attracts predators.

Kestrel

Marbled white

Common rockrose

Greater knapweed

Chalkhill blue

Fragrant orchid

Cowslip

Rabbit

quinancywort

Meadow pipit

Wild thyme

Mother shipton moth

Horseshoe vetch

Hawthorn

Common lizard

Downland Management and Conservation

If left to nature, our limestone grasslands would revert to woodland, albeit slowly and via a lengthy scrub phase. The agricultural depression of the 1920s and 1930s, and the introduction of myxamatosis to control rabbit populations, gave us an insight into this process. Numerous areas of downland turned into hawthorn forest or ash woodland. The National Trust owns woods which used to be downland: Smithson Hill, for example, on the north Chilterns escarpment, was a renowned site for the pasque flower, a plant of short downland turf, but over the last 80 years it has developed into a dense wood, and is probably now not reclaimable as downland, and not just because of the steepness of the slope.

Left: The belted Galloway is a hardy, traditional breed of cattle, suitable for steep slopes and low-quality vegetation.

Below: Fontmell and Melbury Downs, south of Shaftesbury in north-east Dorset, is the largest area of chalk grassland owned by the National Trust and one of the richest for flora and fauna. It is home to a staggering 37 species of butterfly.

The battle with scrub

Of course, it is relatively easy to cut a few trees or bushes down, should that be deemed desirable, and there are several chemicals that successfully kill large cut stumps. The problems are the issue of scale, the resource implications and, crucially, the fact that flower-rich limestone grassland does not instantly return; rather the reverse in fact, for brambles and tree saplings instantly fill the empty space, and are significantly harder to eliminate than the original trees and mature bushes. In nature conservation, one often swaps one set of problems for another, and nowhere is this truer than in the clearance of scrub and trees from limestone grassland, or indeed from heathland: the plants fight back – viciously; where there was one problem stem there are now many. The aftercare is actually harder, more labour-intensive and resource-demanding than the initial cutting work.

Although there is no simple panacea or instant-fix remedy, the nature conservation movement is extremely good at clearing

moderate scrub cover and gradually restoring limestone grassland. Such work does, though, go through a messy phase and the scars left by initial clearance are ugly. The work necessitates the unwelcome noise of chainsaws, the removal or burning of cut material, either the use of herbicide or repeat-cutting by machine (or both), and invariably the use of grazing stock – cattle, sheep, ponies or even goats. Grazing usually requires fencing, often in relatively small paddocks in which the animals are able to concentrate their efforts to maximum effect. The wellbeing and care of such animals is paramount, and currently all farm stock owned by the National Trust is run either to organic standards or to the RSPCA's Freedom Food standard, or both. The perpetuation of public access to grazed sites is also a major objective for the National Trust.

Conservation through grazing

One critical element in grassland restoration management is the choice of grazing animal. This is partly a matter of species (cattle, sheep, equine or other), for the various species behave, feed and impact on vegetation differently. Choice of breed is also crucial in the more challenging scenarios, particularly where the quality of grazing is poor. The National Trust uses older, more traditional breeds as they are best adapted to coping with such vegetation, avoiding potentially poisonous plants, and are sure-footed in difficult terrain. Belted Galloway cattle, Exmoor ponies and Beulah sheep all have good proven track records in nature conservation grazing. But choosing the right animal goes deeper than species and breed, as it is important to use animals of an appropriate background that are best adapted to dealing with the vegetation, topography and climate. Finally, the social structure of the group of grazing animals is vital: young stock needs older, calmer and more experienced leaders (such as matriarch cows) to show them how best to cope.

The National Trust does not graze sheep on nature conservation sites with heavy public access, as the issues involving dogs are too great – for the Trust, for the sheep, for the dog owners and perhaps for the dogs themselves. In such situations small and docile breeds of pony or cattle are used; Exmoor ponies and Galloway cattle, for example, are virtually oblivious of dogs and of people, but are also capable of looking after themselves should the need arise. Thus, the Trust grazes Exmoor ponies on the downland cliff tops east of Dover and on the North Downs west of Dorking, while Galloway cattle graze the downs near Reigate and in the Cotswolds. Wherever possible, of course, commercial farm livestock are used, though it is often the case that older breeds such as Aberdeen Angus cattle fare better, and make a more suitable impact, than modern commercial breeds.

Right: The National Trust is a major partner in the large blue recovery programme, running Collard Hill in the Polden Hills as an open-access site where people can readily see this once-extinct jewel. The Trust also runs two large blue sites on the north Cornwall coast and in south Dartmoor.

Downland chalk marks

The southern chalk downs are renowned for their chalk figures, many of which are of uncertain origin. These are scrapings rather than carvings, where the turf has been removed on exposed escarpment slopes to create a white figure. A few, notably the white horse at Uffington in Oxfordshire (shown right), seem to be of prehistoric origin, whereas some, like the Fovant badges near Salisbury, are relatively recent – in this case the badges of Great War regiments, plus some more recent additions. Many, such as the White Horse at Cherhill, in north Wiltshire, are only some 300 years old, while Dorset's famous Cerne Abbas giant cannot be traced back beyond the late 17th century, and may even be a caricature of Oliver Cromwell. Conserving these marks is hard work, for they green over naturally, so that clean chalk has to be compacted in regularly.

Wildlife of Limestone Grasslands

Chalk or limestone grassland, or downland, is a precious wildlife habitat, often with every 1m² (10ft²) supporting over 30 species of wild flower. Downland is a habitat created by, and dependent on, the grazing of domesticated stock or rabbits. Without grazing, even the steepest slopes revert to woodland, as happened widely after myxomatosis decimated the rabbit population during the early 1950s. Modern management regimes ensure satisfactory conditions for specialist plants and insects, including several types of orchid and the scarce adonis and chalkhill blue butterflies.

Plants

Grasses

A whole host of grasses occur on our limestone grasslands, often as dominant species. Such grasses, along with a range of small sedges, which are often overlooked as grasses, strongly help to characterise limestone grassland. Many are coarse thugs that will readily choke out finer grasses, sedges and herbs, and suppress mosses and lichens, unless controlled by effective grazing. Several of these grasses are genuinely beautiful in their own right but do require an element of discipline. It is highly likely that nitrogen deposition is encouraging these vigorous grasses to become over-dominant.

Tor grass
(Brachypodium pinnatum)
One of the main coarse grasses of limestone grassland, tor grass is stiff and virtually hairless. It is a creeping species that often forms yellowish patches. Leaves are narrow and green, sometimes with an orange tint. One of the species apparently thriving due to nitrogen deposition, there is strong scientific evidence from Holland,

Right: Red fescue is common in many habitats due to its adaptability. It is a key food plant for the gatekeeper butterfly and is part of a family of tufted grasses, being closely related to the common rye grass.

suggesting that tor grass becomes increasing dominant and difficult to control given a dose of airborne nitrogen.

Upright brome grass
(Bromus erectus)
This stiff, slightly hairy grass bears bunches of long-stalked purple-green flowers, each of which ends in a bristle. Together with tor grass, upright brome grass can dominate large areas of downland in southern England, but these species seldom occur together outside the Cotswolds. With the

correct management, such as grazing by the right type of animal in the correct manner, these dominant grass species can co-exist peacefully with a host of more innocent plants.

False oat grass
(Arrhenatherum elatius)
A tall, broad-leaved grass that can be highly invasive on deeper soils, false oat grass has shining green or purple-green, two-spiked flower heads. It is widespread and common in grassland and on roadsides.

Wood false-brome grass
(Brachypodium sylvaticum)

A yellowy grass that invades downland alongside scrub and is disliked by grazing animals. It has drooping soft green leaves.

Red fescue
(Festuca rubra)

Red fescue is a fine, low-growing grass that supports quite a rich flora and fauna unless allowed to become too dense, thick or ungrazed. It has narrow, dark green leaves and reddish flowers that appear between May and July.

Blue moor grass
(Sesleria albicans)

The dominant grass on many of the limestones in northern England and southern Scotland, blue moor grass requires sensitive grazing to prevent it, and its dead litter mass, suppressing other plants. The small, egg-shaped blue-green flower heads sit at the top of the stalk and appear in April and May.

Wild flowers

Assuming appropriate levels of fertility, and that any scrub and grazing issues are appropriately addressed, limestone grassland can – and will – support an unrivalled delight of specialist wild flowers. The vast majority of these limestone grassland flowers are long-lived perennials, capable of withstanding summer drought and even prolonged heavy grazing.

Pasque flower
(Pulsatilla vulgaris)

A rare purple spring flower of close-grazed downs, pasque flower can be found at some places in south and east England, but is more commonly seen growing in garden rockeries.

Above: The common rockrose provides bees with a valuable source of nectar and a few species of beetles and butterfly larvae feed on its foliage. It sheds its leaves in times of drought and can withstand both drought and frost.

Below: The hairy violet looks similar to the sweet violet, but does not have its heady perfume. The flower, as its common name suggests, has conspicuous hairs under the leaf and on the stem.

Hairy violet
(Viola hirta)

The most common violet of spring downland, the hairy violet flowers between March and May. The leaf undersides and stalks have prominent hairs. Unlike the sweet violet (*Viola odorata*) it is unscented and has no runners. It is the foodplant of the dark-green fritillary butterfly.

Common rockrose
(Helianthemum nummularium)

A classic plant of old downland throughout England, common rockrose is a low-growing plant whose five crinkly yellow flowers open with the sun and close up when it is overcast. It has narrow leaves that are green above and white below.

Milkwort

Two species of milkwort occur on downland. **Common milkwort** (*Polygala vulgaris*) can be blue, mauve or white, and is common and widespread. The flowers of the rarer **chalk milkwort** (*Polygala calcarea*) are always gentian blue in colour. This species is largely restricted to the Cotswolds and Wiltshire.

Common milkwort

Fairy flax
(Linum catharticum)

Perhaps the most notable of the short-lived downland plants is fairy flax, a tiny white flower of high summer. The clusters of small white flowers with green sepals grow on fine stalks with opposite pairs of small, green flowers. These are the flowers of Cicely Mary Barker's *Flower Fairy* books, and of the poetry of John Clare.

Bird's-foot trefoil
(Lotus corniculatus)

This familiar plant abounds on most downs. A member of the pea family, it has small yellow- and reddish-tinged flowers that appear in June and July. It is the main food plant of the common blue and dingy skipper butterflies.

Horseshoe vetch
(Hippocrepis comosa)

A plant of old downland that has no history of ploughing, the flowers of the horseshoe vetch resemble bird's-foot trefoil, though without the red buds; the alternately paired leaves are distinctive. The flowers have a strong, sweet smell. Horseshoe vetch is the food plant of the adonis blue and chalkhill blue butterflies.

Sainfoin
(Onobrychis viciifolia)

A prominent plant with racemes of deep pink flowers that appear in June, sainfoin was formerly grown as a fodder crop and to fix nitrogen in the soil, like clover, and now occurs largely as a naturalised escapee.

Birds-eye primrose
(Primula farinosa)

Birds-eye primrose is an exquisite pink primrose of damp calcareous grasslands

Above: The bird's-eye primrose is a pretty pink or lilac flower with a distinctive yellow eye in its centre. The rosettes of leaves are covered in a mealy white powder.

Left: Sainfoin is in the legume family and has a tall hollow stem. Ruminant animals adore it and, taste aside, it has beneficial non-bloating properties; bees enjoy the nectar and birds and rodents consume the seeds in autumn.

in northern Britain that flowers in June and July. The clusters of pink flowers grow on tall stems. The leaves are small, narrow and bunt-ended, and grow in a rosette at the base.

Cowslip
(Primula veris)

In spring, cowslip abounds on many downs, particularly those grazed by cattle. Sheep readily eat the flowers and so must not be grazed on cowslip downs in spring. The flowers of cowslip are bell-shaped and yellow and carried on tall stalks. The basal leaves grow in a rosette.

Thistles

Several types of thistle flower on limestone grasslands between June and September, of which the most notable is the low-growing **dwarf thistle** (Cirsium acaule) – the bane of many a summer picnic in local places in south and east England and south Wales. The most delightful of the thistles is another low-growing plant, the **carline thistle** (Carlina vulgaris), a straw-coloured plant that flowers from July to September, and looks like it belongs in a dried-flower display. **Tuberous thistle** (Cirsium tuberosum) is a rare downland thistle, restricted to a few nature reserves in the south and east. It has a habit of hybridising with more common species and this has caused a decline in numbers.

Carline thistle

Autumn felwort
(Gentianella amarella)

A late-flowering downland plant, the autumn felwort has a rarer cousin that grows in the Chiltern Hills, the Chiltern gentian (*Gentianella germanica*), and a diminutive relative of the driest slopes, early gentian (*Gentianella anglica*), which is only found on chalk downland south of the River Thames.

Wild thyme
(Thymus polytrichus)

Wild thyme is a woody, creeping, mat-forming perennial with small, short-stalked leaves and dense, reddish-purple flower heads that appear between June and September. It is a widespread and often common species.

Above: There are three species of thyme in the UK. Large thyme is an intensely fragrant plant and is beloved by bees, hoverflies and butterflies.

Below: Common knapweed can be found in grassland, on roadside verges and alongside hedgerows. The fragrant purple-pink flowers are incredibly attractive to bumblebees, hoverflies, butterflies and some day-flying moths.

Large thyme
(Thymus pulegioides)

Large thyme has larger flowers and is generally more upright than wild thyme. It is found mainly in the south and east and is rare elsewhere.

Round-headed rampion
(Phyteuma orbiculare)

The pride of the Sussex Downs, the round-headed rampion has dark blue, pin-cushion flowers, that appear in July and August. Growing up to 50cm (20in) tall with oval leaves in a basal rosette, it is found on chalk downs in the south of England.

Squinancywort
(Asperula cynanchica)

A tiny but exquisite little plant, with carpets of delicate pink-white, star-shaped flowers, squinancywort is found locally on chalk and limestone grassland in the south of England. It flowers between June and September.

Common knapweed
(Centaurea nigra)

Many limestone grasslands are studded with mauve and purple knapweeds during the summer months. This common species has long grooved stems and narrow leaves while the flowerheads are pink-purple with brown bracts.

Greater knapweed
(Centaurea scabiosa)

Not as widespread as the common knapweed, this species is commonly found in parts of the south and east. It also has purple flowers but these are bushier than those of common knapweed. Both species are greatly favoured by bees and other insects.

Birds

Hen harrier
(Circus cyaneus)
Occasionally in winter the hen harrier hunts over the more extensive of the Wiltshire and Dorset downs. Males are grey above with a white belly and black wingtips; females and young birds are brown with darker stripes on the wings and tail.

Great bustard
(Otis tarda)
Limestone grassland is not especially renowned for rare bird and mammal species, but the iconic great bustard is now being reintroduced to Ministry of Defence land on Salisbury Plain. This bird needs huge areas of uninterrupted landscape to survive and is partially migratory.

Turtle dove
(Streptopelia turtur)
A rapidly declining summer migrant that nests in dense scrub, and also in some woodlands, the turtle dove was formerly quite widespread on scrubby southern downland. Its soft and continuous cooing is distinctive.

Barn owl
(Tyto alba)
Barn owls hunt over large areas of rough downland at night, as this is the habitat of their favourite prey, the field vole. With its distinctive pale face and belly and grey-brown back and wings the barn owl is always a delight to see. Once a declining species due to intensive farming, numbers have started to grow.

Skylark
(Alauda arvensis)
Open limestone grassland can support large populations of skylark, especially where there is short grass with frequent longer tussocks, the favoured nesting situation. It has a distinctive, high-pitched aerial song that may last up to 10 minutes.

Above: Great bustard eggs have been hatched in the UK this millennium for the first time since 1832, when Queen Victoria was a young girl.

Below: The barn owl does not hoot, but emits screams, hisses and snorts. Rodents are their preferred food and a breeding pair and their young can consume over 4000 prey in one year.

Meadow pipit
(Anthus pratensis)
A cousin of the skylark, this little bird occurs in lonely open places where its distinctive call is part of the spirit of place. It has brown, streaked plumage with a paler belly.

Nightingale
(Luscinia megarhynchos)
Some scrub-infested downs can be important for the nightingale, a rapidly declining bird. Summer visitors to the south and east of England, they arrive in April and leave at the end of the summer. Slightly larger than the robin, the nightingale is known for its beautiful song.

Dartford warbler
(Sylvia undata)
Burgeoning gorse scrub now means that the Dartford warbler is now quite frequently encountered on downs and other limestone hills in central southern England, such as the Mendips. This bird, and its beloved gorse, have benefited from milder winters. Dark blue-grey above with a reddish breast and a slight crest on its head, the Dartford warbler has a long tail and orange legs.

Corn bunting
(Miliaria calandra)
Important populations of some of our deeply valued bird species can occur on limestone grassland, but usually when this grassland occurs in a mosaic with scrub, woodland or farmland. Thus, the fast-disappearing corn bunting is more of a species of chalky arable fields of southern England than a true downland species.

Mammals

Field vole
(Microtus agrestis)

Rougher limestone grassland will support huge populations of the field vole, which forms the primary food of the barn owl and kestrel. Field voles have yellowish-brown fur and measure about 14cm (5½in) from head to tail.

Bank vole
(Myodes glareolus)

The scrub margins of limestone grasslands host the ubiquitous bank vole. Bank voles are slightly smaller than field voles, with chestnut brown fur and more prominent ears.

Dormouse
(Muscardinus avellanarius)

A small nocturnal mammal, the dormouse occurs on a surprising number of southern downs, where young, dense flowering scrub occurs – the flowers are an important food source in spring. The stoat and weasel are major predators of small mammals like the dormouse.

Rabbit
(Oryctolagus cuniculus)

For almost 200 years the rabbit was the primary grazing animal on many downs, until the disease myxomatosis was introduced in 1953, and populations plummeted. Rabbit populations remained low for almost 40 years, but have recently recovered in many areas. On many southern downs the recovery only started with the advent of mild winters in the late 1980s. The drought summers of 1989 and 1990 also aided the return of rabbit-grazed downland. Rabbits love grasslands that have been heavily grazed by sheep, as sheep nibble close to the ground,

Bats

Limestone grasslands are not especially important to bats. There are, however, some exceptions. For example, Rodborough and Minchinhampton Commons, National Trust limestone grassland sites near Stroud in the Cotswold Hills, form an important site for the **greater horseshoe bat** (*Rhinolophus ferrumequinum*) and the **lesser horseshoe bat** (*Rhinolophus hipposideros*). The name is derived from fleshy growths around the nose. These bats hibernate in old stone mines and old buildings in these areas, and are especially fond of the nocturnal dung beetles that breed in cow pats on the commons. The lesser horseshoe bat is found in west England and Wales while its larger and much rarer relative is found only in south west England and Wales.

Greater horseshoe bat

Below: Brown hares are solitary creatures except during the breeding season; boxing commonly occurs when a female tests her male's determination and also tells him she is not ready for mating.

Left: Field voles mark the trails to their tunnels with scent to warn off other voles. Kestrels look for the UV light that radiates from these scent markings to locate prey.

making the turf perfect for rabbits. Today, farmers and conservationists have to be careful about grazing downs too heavily with sheep, lest rabbits move in and take over.

Brown hare
(Lepus europaeus)

The brown hare occurs on many lowland limestone grasslands, but only in low numbers. The species is most common on arable land in eastern England. The brown hare's long, black-tipped ears and large eyes mean it can sense danger early in the open countryside.

Reptiles

Common Lizard
(Zootoca vivipara)

The common lizard occurs on many warm limestone grassland slopes, especially south-facing slopes where there is plenty of dead grass, or thatch, on which to bask and in which to hide. Common or viviparous lizards are usually dull brown in colour, perhaps with a tinge of red, yellow or green, with markings that usually include dark stripes along the back and sides.

Snakes

Grass snakes, slow worms and adders all occur locally, usually only occupying small parts of a limestone grassland site. You have to know exactly where to look for them, not least because they are all shy and retiring.

Left: The common lizard can fool predators by shedding its tail when frightened. It consumes insects, slugs, snails and earthworms and stuns prey by shaking it, before consuming it whole.

Below: The adder, a viper, is quite placid and does not bite unless threatened. The venom is toxic, but rarely fatal, although medical assistance should always be sought if bitten.

Grass snake
(Natrix natrix)

The grass snake is the UK's largest snake at up to 1.5m (5ft) long. It is greenish black in colour, with a pale ring around its neck and black bars along the sides.

Adder
(Vipera berus)

The adder is immediately recognisable by the dark zigzag markings along its back; the rest of the body is usually greyish in colour, and there is a v-shaped mark on the back of the head. The adder is widespread in the UK but is not found in large numbers.

Slow worm
(Anguis fragilis)

The slow worm is a legless lizard rather than a snake. It is yellow-brown in colour and grows up to 50cm (20in) long. Unlike a snake, the slow worm has eyelids and can close its eyes, and its tongue has no fork.

Invertebrates

Grasshoppers and crickets

In high summer the warmer limestone grassland slopes vibrate with the songs, or stridulation, of crickets and grasshoppers. A good site will harbour eight or more species, some of which sing loudly on warm summer days.

Stripe-winged grasshopper
(Stenobothrus lineatus)
A denizen of short, hot downland turf in the south and east of the UK, the greenish stripe-winged grasshopper is characterised by a white stripe along the edge of its forewing. The song is high-pitched and varies in volume.

Rufous grasshopper
(Gomphocerippus rufus)
A brown species with distinctive white-tipped antennae, the rufous grasshopper is found only in the south of England.

Great green bush cricket
(Tettigonia viridissima)
Bush crickets are characterised by their long, thin antennae and tend to be more active at night than grasshoppers. Found in the southern part of Britain, the great green bush cricket is the UK's largest species, reaching 4.5cm (1¾in) in length.

Above right: The dingy skipper boasts beautifully intricate and subtle markings. These butterflies fly low by day, bask in the sunshine on grasses, and roost overnight on flowerheads.

Right: Crickets rub their wings together to produce the noisy variety of high-pitched vibrating trills that can be heard in the summer.

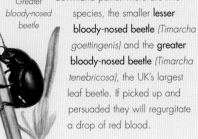

Bloody-nosed beetles

Bloody-nosed beetles are often to be found on downland paths. There are two species, the smaller **lesser bloody-nosed beetle** *(Timarcha goettingensis)* and the **greater bloody-nosed beetle** *(Timarcha tenebricosa)*, the UK's largest leaf beetle. If picked up and persuaded they will regurgitate a drop of red blood.

Greater bloody-nosed beetle

Butterflies and day-flying moths

Southern chalk and limestone grassland are the best habitats for butterflies in Britain and also support a rich fauna of other invertebrates. A good southern down may support well over 30 species of butterfly – more than half of those that occur in the UK. The south of England does

not have total dominance here, for the carboniferous limestone hills of the Morecambe Bay region are the stronghold of violet-feeding fritillary butterflies. One example is the high brown fritillary, which is in decline elsewhere, though it remains numerous in this area.

Silver-spotted skipper
(Hesperia comma)
The silver-spotted skipper is a small orange butterfly that flies low and at speed over short sheep's fescue turf. It is quite rare and is the most difficult of all our butterflies to follow. Sheep's fescue is the foodplant of the silver-spotted skipper, and if it is allowed to be choked by scrub species by a lack of grazing, the butterfly is unable to breed. This is what happened in its downland breeding grounds following the introduction of myxomatosis in the 1950s to control rabbit populations. However, in recent years the species has re-colonised many former sites as a result of careful nature conservation grazing regimes, and the recovery of rabbit populations.

Dingy skipper
(Erynnis tages)
When is a moth not a moth? The answer: when it is a dingy skipper butterfly. This is a small, dull brown butterfly that lives in loose colonies, primarily on southern limestone grassland. It behaves like a butterfly with a strong and direct flight. The males are highly belligerent.

Green hairstreak
(Callophrys rubi)
In early spring, the emerald green of the green hairstreak can be seen along warm, south-facing scrub edges. It is a small butterfly, whose colouration and patterning provides highly effective camouflage from predators, so spotting it is not easy. The males hold territories on bushes, and can be seen defending their air space.

Adonis blue
(Lysandra bellargus)

The adonis blue can be found in short downland turf where horseshoe vetch, its foodplant, grows. Like the silver-spotted skipper (see page 153), this species went into decline after the introduction of myxomatosis, when rabbit populations that kept their foodplant well-grazed were decimated. Recently, however, the Adonis blue has spectacularly recolonised the Cotswolds – after an absence of 40 years. This unexpected reappearance is probably due to the introduction of cattle grazing, coupled with milder winters and more hot summers.

Chalkhill blue
(Lysandra coridon)

In August, many southern downs shimmer with blue butterflies, as males search breeding grounds for emerging females. This phenomenon is best seen in early morning, and consists primarily of the male chalkhill blue (as well as the common blue and the male adonis blue).

Duke of Burgundy
(Hamearis lucina)

No one knows how this orange and black chequered butterfly got its name (it used to be called the Duke of Burgundy fritillary), but the males are fiercely territorial and behave appallingly – particularly to any female that might blunder into their territory. It is now quite a rare butterfly, restricted largely to a few rough downs in central southern England.

Dark green fritillary
(Argynnis aglaja)

A fast-flying species, the dark green fritillary emerges at the end of June and flies through until mid-August. The upper wings are orange spotted with dark brown; the underside of the hind wing has greenish scales. In hot weather, dark green fritillaries can cluster together on favoured nectar sources, such as clumps of greater knapweed and musk thistle.

Marbled white
(Melanargia galathea)

In late summer, the marbled white is abundant on many downs in the south and south east of England. This medium-sized, black-and-white chequered butterfly is easy to identify.

Meadow brown
(Maniola jurtina)

The humble meadow brown abounds on sheltered downs, from early June often through to early October. Both male and female have an eyespot on the forewing; the larger female also has an orange patch on the forewing that may or may not be present in the male.

Ringlet
(Aphantopus hyperantus)

This brownish-black butterfly has golden rings on its wing undersides, hence the name. It favours rough grassland and is widespread across the country, where it can be seen flying in June and July. Strangely it fares better in cool, wet summers.

Burnet and forester moths

There are a number of day-flying moths that occur on limestone grassland. Most notable are the burnet moths, of which there are several similar-looking species. On some downs you can see these red-and-black moths at any time from early June through

Above: The meadow brown is a common species. The markings on its velvety brown wings are exquisite. Males are a little paler than females.

Below: The male chalkhill blue has sky blue upper wings, while females are brown with white and red spots. Look for the white fringe, laced with black, that borders of the wings of both sexes.

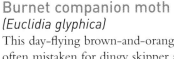

to mid-September. Forester moths have shiny metallic wings that range in colour from yellowish green to blue. Both forester and burnet moths are protected from predators by poisons – a fact advertised by their bright colours.

Six-spot burnet
(Zygaena filipendulae)
The forewings of the six-spot burnet are black with a metallic blue or green sheen and have six red spots. The antennae are thicker, or clubbed, at the ends. Found all over the country apart form highland areas, this moth can be seen flying between June and August.

Five-spot burnet
(Zygaena trifolii)
The five-spot burnet prefers damper grasslands to the six-spot. It can be seen between May and August, its five red spots visible on the greenish blue forewings.

Forester
(Adscita statices)
The shiny metallic wings of the forester whirr rapidly when in flight. This moth can be found from May to August in rough grassland throughout most of England.

Cistus forester
(Adscita geryon)
On some western downs, notably in the Cotswolds and on the Wiltshire downs, the delicate green cistus forester moth occurs in early summer.

Above: The six-spot burnet, a day-flying moth, has vivid metallic black wings punctured with red spots, which warn other predators away – their bodies contain cyanide and are poisonous.

Below: The hornet robberfly hunts from patches of bare ground. Its larvae are thought to be predators of subterranean dung-beetle larvae.

Right: The yellow meadow ant lives underground and is rarely seen except in July and August when young winged ants leave the nest.

Burnet companion moth
(Euclidia glyphica)
This day-flying brown-and-orange moth is often mistaken for dingy skipper and Duke of Burgundy butterflies in May. The orange hindwings are, however, quite distinctive.

Hornet robberfly
(Asilus crabroniformis)
Some special flies favour limestone grassland. The largest is the hornet robberfly, a huge, vicious-looking beast that mimics the hornet, and preys on grasshopper nymphs. It has no sting or bite and is quite rare.

Hornet-mimic hoverfly
(Volucella zonaria)
Limestone grassland is good for hoverflies, particularly along scrub and wood edges. The hornet-mimic hoverfly is a distinctive species that occurs in southern England in August. A giant of a fly, it mimics a queen wasp but is harmless and fond of flowers.

Yellow meadow ant
(Lasius flavus)
Short turf is the favourite habitat of the yellow meadow ant, which constructs huge, domed-shaped nests that become covered in flowers, such as wild thyme and common rockrose. Hot, south-facing downland slopes are especially important for this and other species of ant that require exceptionally hot microclimates.

Mining bees

Some of the south-facing downs of Hampshire, Dorset or the Isle of Wight, may well support over 100 species of bee, wasp and ant, including some that are strongly or even wholly associated with downland. A distinctive bee of western downland in spring is *Andrena cineraria*, a silver and black species of mining bee – so-called because most members of this family, Apidae, nest on the ground. Also worth noting is another local mining bee, *Andrena bucephala*, a plain bee that nests communally in old mouse and rabbit holes in spring.

Mountains and Moorlands

Mountain Building

The mountainous silhouette of the United Kingdom was formed between tens and thousands of million years ago by the drift of tectonic plates – the huge curved slabs of rock that make up the Earth's crust. As the plates collided, they forced layers of rock to bend and buckle into fold mountains, some of which have eroded over time into lower, more rounded hills. At the same time, molten lava from far underground spewed out through cracks between the plates to produce volcanic peaks, and where the plates pulled apart, or pushed together, vast cracks – faults and rifts – appeared, between which some blocks of land were squeezed up as others slipped downwards. In this way the great mountain building processes have raised the British landscape – and still fashion it today.

In the Cambrian period, some 500 million years ago, Britain was in two parts, separated by a vast ocean. Scotland lay near the Equator and was attached to what is now Greenland and North America.

England and Wales were attached to South America and Africa, nearer the South Pole. As the tectonic plates drifted, England and Wales came north and joined Scotland, roughly along the line of the present Solway Firth. Volcanic activity followed, resulting in the upwelling of magma, which then cooled and eroded to form the Cairngorm Mountains.

Sculpting the uplands

Scotland, the UK's most mountainous region, has an immense prehistory far beyond the Cambrian. Intermittent volcanic activity and uplift into highlands followed by erosion by rivers, plus cold periods of glaciations interspersed with natural global warming all contributed to its modern profile. Gneiss (pronounced 'nice') is

Below: The glacial landform of the Cairngorms in Scotland is a landscape shaped by ice and fine-tuned by subsequent weathering.

among the UK's oldest rock type, exposed where the roots of Scottish fold mountains have been exposed by erosion. It can be seen in the north west where the deposits are believed to be some 2,000 million years of age (almost half as old as the planet itself).

Moving diagonally from the north west across the British mainland, the rocks generally become younger, less mountainous and igneous, and more sedimentary in nature. Mighty granite batholiths appear in the far west – huge expanses of the igneous rock granite, formed by the cooling of magma following violent volcanic activity. These are seen on Dartmoor, Bodmin Moor and at Land's End. In the mid-west of the British mainland and Northern Ireland are cliffs, layers and intrusions of basalt, another igneous rock, formed by the cooling of lava, as at the Giant's Causeway.

Upland erosion

With extreme temperatures, ice and wind, rocky uplands are particularly prone to erosion. Rainwater and groundwater seep into cracks and crevices on rocky surfaces and expand as they freeze. This process of freeze-thaw gradually breaks up cliffs, escarpments and mountainsides, causing slivers and boulders to break off and tumble down the slopes, forming scree slopes. Few plants can gain a roothold in such a constantly eroding landscape. Streams, waterfalls and rivers cause further erosion to soft rock, such as sandstone or limestone, which can be eaten away to form deep ravines and gorges, seen especially in the Yorkshire Dales, Peak District and parts of Dartmoor and Exmoor.

The role of glaciers

Glacial action during the many ice ages of prehistory gouged massive scars across the British landscape. This created sharp mountain summits in Scotland and deep U-shaped valleys (as distinct from V-shaped valleys eroded by rivers) in the Lake District and Snowdonia. The grinding glaciers picked up and carried quantities of rocks many hundreds of kilometres, depositing their load as they melted. As temperatures rose after the last ice age, some 10,000 years ago, plants began to appear on the scraped-bare rocks. Lichens, then arctic willows, crowberries and bog myrtle were the early colonisers and still grow on the higher slopes today.

Top left: Tor formation, like the granite batholiths on Rough Tor, Bodmin Moor, is not fully understood, but the theories centre on weathering and erosion.

Above: Snowpatch lichen is a distinctive species confined to the highest ground in the Highlands, above 850m (2,790ft). Climate change and erosion due to human activities, such as skiing, pose a serious threat to many mountain lichens.

Britain's 'Himalaya'

There is no globally accepted definition as to what constitutes the difference between a mountain and a hill. In Britain a mountain is generally deemed to be an area that rises over 610m (2,000ft) above sea level. The Scottish mountains were certainly once higher, perhaps even as tall as the Himalaya. Compared to Mount Everest, at 8,850m (29,035ft), the tallest mountain in the UK is Scotland's Ben Nevis, reaching 1,344m (4,409ft). Indeed, the UK's ten highest mountains are all found in Scotland. The highest mountain in Wales is Snowdon, part of the Snowdonia Mountains, which reaches 1,085m (3,560ft). In England, Scafell Pike (see below) in the Cumbrian Mountains of the Lake District takes the record at 977m (3,205ft). In Northern Ireland, Slieve Donard in the Mourne Mountains is the tallest summit, at 852m (2,795ft).

Mountain Habitats

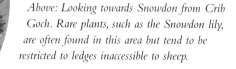

Upland habitats encompass far more than bare, rocky, windswept peaks. They include screes of jumbled rocks and coarse boulders on steeper slopes; cliffs and gorges; peat moors clad with heathers and other low shrubs, and tough grasses. In addition, woods and forests cloak higher slopes, conifers dominating as they best resist the low temperatures, wind and ice of high-altitude winters.

At the latitude of the UK, uplands higher than about 600m (2,000ft) have a montane zone – an area above the 'tree line' where trees cannot grow. More than nine-tenths of the UK's montane habitat is in Scotland. The exposed rocks, principally granite and quartzite, weather slowly and so soil formation is slow. Copious rain throughout the year, and snowmelt in spring, regularly wash away the soil. Although rainfall can be high, the steep slopes and lack of soil or plant roots mean that the water runs away fast, so there can be some drought conditions. Any soil that survives is leached of its nutrients by the rain, and dried out by the incessant winds.

Above: Looking towards Snowdon from Crib Goch. Rare plants, such as the Snowdon lily, are often found in this area but tend to be restricted to ledges inaccessible to sheep.

Left: Purple saxifrage flowers very early in the year. The flowers are, apparently, edible, though the plant is largely confined to nature reserves where such practices are inappropriate.

Life in the montane zone

Plants and animals of the montane zone face harsh conditions, with extremes of climate including snow and howling gales, and little in the way of shelter. None the less, these high-altitude habitats support many specialist species, particularly in summer. The rarest mountain flowers tend to be restricted to particular geological rock types, often limestone, on ledges and around crevices, out of the reach of hungry sheep. Good examples are the Snowdon lily, which is confined to crevices high up on Snowdon, and purple saxifrage, which inhabits inaccessible rocks in high places in the Brecon Beacons and some mountains in northern Britain.

Access versus conservation

Many of the UK's spectacular uplands are in the care of the National Trust, including large stretches of the Yorkshire Dales, the Peak District, the Lake District, Snowdonia, the Brecon Beacons, Dartmoor and Exmoor, all of which are national parks. Many parts of these treasured landscapes endure remarkably heavy vehicle and foot traffic – especially along the tracks to and from the best viewpoints. The Lake District National Park alone attracts over 20 million visitors per year, and the Peak District some 22 million visitors, so a careful balance must be struck between conservation and leisure activities to ensure that no permanent footprint is left on the landscape, primarily that caused by erosion. At Mam Tor, for example (shown right), in the High Peak Estate in Derbyshire, where spectacular views and prehistoric settlements attract large numbers of day visitors from the nearby urban areas of Sheffield and Manchester, the Trust has worked to preserve footpaths and slow the rate of erosion, installing surfaced paths including flagstones to protect any archaeology underneath.

The true mountain birds are mainly summer visitors, such as the wheatear, ring ouzel, whimbrel and golden plover. Raven and crow, the latter in the form of the hooded crow, represent the scavengers, while the peregrine falcon is the main predator. Mammals are few, other than the ubiquitous sheep and, locally, red deer and feral goats. The best-known example is the mountain hare that occurs in the Highlands and Southern Uplands of Scotland, and the High Peak area of the English Peak District. Insects are relatively few. Colonies of the mountain ringlet butterfly occur above 600m (2,000ft) in the Lake District and the Grampian Mountains, flying in late June and July. The only other butterfly seen that high up is the small heath, though some day-flying moths occur, notably the wood tiger moth. There is even a large diving beetle that inhabits stony tarns high on the mountains. Climate change is a major challenge for these montane species, which can retreat only a little further up the mountain as the climate warms the lower slopes. Eventually these montane species will disappear, having nowhere further to withdraw.

Working the land

The montane zones and the uplands below them have been intensively used since the Bronze Age, if not longer, chiefly for summer grazing of sheep and other livestock; from Roman times onwards the uplands have also been exploited for mining and quarrying. Historic land use is shown by the thousands of archaeological sites conserved in these regions, many of which have survived because they have not been damaged by ploughing.

More recently, human activities have had a damaging impact on plant life, the major problems being heavy grazing and erosion associated with human visitors. Sheep, in particular, have a lot to answer for; they nibble heathers and mountain wild flowers and, crucially, allow coarse grasses such as mat

Right: Some of the wildlife that occurs in mountain habitats when pressure from sheep grazing and the harsh weather conditions permit. The population of many of these species tends to be small, due to the challenging conditions.

grass *(Nardus stricta)* to dominate. Because they are loath to eat these nutritionally poor grasses, the sheep heavily graze the surrounding vegetation instead, so encouraging these thuggish grasses to spread. To exacerbate matters, EU farming subsidies during the 1970s through to the early 2000s encouraged high sheep numbers, much to the detriment of mountain and moorland vegetation and its associated wildlife. The good news, though, is that in most cases the vegetation recovers quickly after sheep numbers are reduced. At Cwm Idwal in northern Snowdonia, for example, after years of heavy grazing, sheep were precluded from this botanical haven in the late 1990s, since when flowers have almost bounced back.

Ring ouzel

Rowan

Northern eggar

Raven

Mountain hare

Mountain ringlet

Mountain avens

Bilberry

Bilberry bumblebee

Spring gentian

Moorlands

Below the mountain fringe, moorlands dominate the upland scenery. These specialised habitats develop in high rainfall areas where drainage is poor due to non-porous underlying rock. Water collects and plants grow, but their dead remains accumulate in the cold, oxygen-poor water and decompose slowly, forming acidic peat.

Moorlands are important wildlife habitats, although many moorland birds and animals occur only at low population densities. Heather is the feature plant of many moorlands; tough and resilient, it withstands wet and wind, though it is vulnerable to heavy sheep grazing. Other acid-loving plants such as cotton-grass, bilberry and crowberry may also thrive. Many of the specialist plants and animals found in moorlands, especially invertebrates, are restricted to particular features such as springs, pools, seepages and rills, often where calcareous water percolates through. Much, though, depends on the scale of the moor and the quality and variety of the habitat.

Carbon storage

Much of our moorland is covered in blanket bog – marshy vegetation that has developed over peat. This bog consists largely of heather and other acid-loving dwarf shrubs such as bilberry, along with purple moor grass, cotton-grasses and sphagnum mosses, all of which decompose naturally to form peat.

Below: On Marsden Moor in the high Pennines, the National Trust has reduced sheep numbers, blocked up drainage ditches and curtailed burning in order to conserve the peat fabric of the moor.

Watch for Wildlife

On moorland, look out for the waving white seed heads of **cotton-grass**, but do not get too close as its presence indicates boggy ground, as do the cushion-like clumps of spongy **sphagnum moss**. Dark purple **bilberries** can be spotted in July and, later in summer, tangy red **cowberries** appear in the same boggy ground. Beautiful and unusual birds can be seen in the broad skies. Birds of prey relish the environment, particularly the **brown buzzard** with its wide wings, or the smaller **peregrine falcon**, with its speckled underside and grey executioner's hood, as it drops like a stone on to its prey. Birds such as the **golden plover**, **wheatear** and **short-eared owl** breed here too, nesting in mature heather. In the Scottish Highlands you might spot a mighty **golden eagle** soaring high on a wingspan of 2m (6ft). Closer to the ground is the **red grouse**, with a red speckled back and red crest; it flies low on small wings with a distinctive whirring noise. Its close relative the **ptarmigan** turns white in winter for camouflage in snowy conditions, as does the **grey-brown mountain hare**.

Peregrine falcon

Bilberries

Red grouse

Above: A major conservation programme is running to restore Kinder Scout in the Pennines, where severe peat erosion was instigated by atmospheric pollution during the Industrial Revolution.

Above: Looking east along Hadrian's Wall in Northumberland towards Housesteads Fort, showing upland grazing land and a basin lake. The wall runs along the rocky Whin Sill Ridge.

Moors, in the Peak District in particular, are home to internationally important peat bogs, which can act as vital carbon stores. Each cubic metre of peat stores 100kg (220lb) of carbon, which is equivalent to the emissions from one car driving 3,000km (2,000 miles). Peat covers about three per cent of global land surface, yet the amount of carbon stored within it is enormous – equivalent to twice that of all the world's forests combined. Healthy peat is wet, covered in vegetation and protected from the air. But if the peat is eroded, drained, over grazed or dug up, causing it to come into contact with air, the carbon in the peat combines with oxygen in the air to form carbon dioxide (CO_2). This greenhouse gas is then released into the atmosphere where it contributes to global warming. A sustained programme is therefore essential to prevent further damage and erosion to the peat, thus avoiding an acceleration of carbon release.

Balancing land use

If anything, moorland has been more degraded by 20th-century land management than mountain habitats. The problems associated with heavy grazing by sheep have been compounded by excessive burning (usually associated with grouse moors) and damage caused by drainage. The latter is a major issue on peat, which erodes rapidly when drainage ditches are cut into upland moors; the equivalent of four millions bags of peat (and 38,000 tonnes of associated carbon) are washed off the gullied Peak District moors alone each year. Consequently, the National Trust has blocked up drainage ditches on most of its moors, notably on the Migneint in north Wales and around Kinder Scout in the Peak District. On Kinder, the Trust has also removed the sheep, channelled visitors along made-up stone paths and is now planting cotton-grass in order to encourage plant growth.

Wildlife of Mountains and Moorlands

Uplands are sought by many for the sense of space they offer as well as for their spectacular views. At higher altitudes the vegetation is dominated by lichens while further down the slopes the flora becomes more colourful and diverse. Moorland areas are characterised by heathers, grasses and gorse. Upland areas provide valuable breeding grounds for a wide range of birds. Some larger mammals, including the reindeer, have found a haven in the mountains but smaller mammals keep a low profile. Invertebrates are also less in evidence but specialists do exist.

Plants

Moss campion
(Silene acaulis)
Moss campion forms a cushion of pointed green leaves, dotted with rose-pink flowers that appear between June and August. It is common on Scottish mountains and also in north Wales and north-west England.

Cyphel
(Minuartia sedoides)
Another cushion-forming species, cyphel is a local species on Scottish mountains and some islands. The flowers are yellow-green rather than pink and often lack petals, and the leaves are stiff, pointed and fleshy.

European gorse
(Ulex europaeus)
Gorse, or furze, is a dense, hardy, prickly, evergreen shrub that thrives on the lower slopes of the uplands. In spring it is smothered with sweet-scented, bright yellow flowers that last from May to June. Gorse is a member of the pea family and the link can be clearly seen in the shape of the flowers and the seed pods, which break open when dry so that the seeds fly out at high speed. The crushed shoots of gorse were once used as animal feed.

Cloudberry
(Rubus chamaemorus)
The cloudberry is a montane plant that can withstand temperatures of -40°C (-40°F).

It is a low-growing relation of the bramble, with large, lobed, many-veined green leaves, and white flowers that appear between June and August. The red berries stand singly on erect stems and ripen to an amber colour. Moorland birds enjoy the berries and spread the seed in their droppings. Cloudberry usually grows on level ground on peaty moors and can be commonly seen in Scotland and occasionally in Ireland and northern England.

Mountain avens
(Dryas octopetala)
Mountain avens is a creeping plant with pretty flowers that look somewhat like the

Top: The cushioning growth of moss campion helps to protect it from cold and drying mountain winds. It is also found in the Alps and the Rocky Mountains.

Above: Mountain avens is a glacial remnant, which can survive in the most inhospitable environments. The seed heads are like beautiful fluffy feathers.

anemone. Each flower has eight white petals (hence '*octopetala*') and a cluster of yellow anthers at the centre. The oblong, toothed leaves are dark green above and white below, and form a mat. Mountain avens can be found in the north of England, north Wales and Scotland.

Starry saxifrage
(Saxifraga stellaris)

An upland species found in damp habitats in north Wales and the north of Britain, starry saxifrage has a rosette of unstalked leaves at its base, and five-petalled white flowers. Each petal has two yellow spots near the base, and the flowers themselves resemble a star, hence the name.

Heather
(Calluna vulgaris)

An evergreen undershrub, characteristic of upland moors, particularly in Scotland, heather or ling has small, narrow, grey-green leaves. The bell-shaped flowers are carried in groups on each stem, and vary in colour from lighter shades of pink, lilac, mauve and purple to deeper pinks and purples. The flowers can be seen between July and October. Cross-leaved heather *(Erica tetralix)* is also found on upland heaths and moors in wet areas.

Alpine lady's mantle
(Alchemilla alpina)

Alpine lady's mantle has silky, mid-green, palmate leaves covered in long hairs that lie flat against the surface. The clusters of small, greenish-yellow flowers, carried on stalks taller than the leaves, can be seen from June to September. Alpine lady's mantle is found in grassy places on mountains in the north.

Rowan
(Sorbus aucuparia)

Rowan or mountain ash can grow at higher altitudes than any other native tree. In May it is covered with masses of creamy white flowers, the petals of which float in the wind like confetti; by late summer or early autumn clusters of brilliant red berries mature. The bright green leaflets are carried in pairs and have serrated edges. The bark is smooth and silver grey. Rowan can be found all over the UK, but is most common in the north and west.

Purple saxifrage
(Saxifraga oppositifolia)

Purple saxifrage is a low-growing, mat-forming, evergreen alpine plant that grows close to the ground. It grows in harsh terrain in some of the most northerly locations. It has small, rounded, densely packed, blue-green leaves and pretty pink or pale purple cup-shaped flowers on short stalks. It is one of the first spring flowers to appear, but may continue to flower sporadically throughout summer. It will grow on damp mountain rocks or scree, and can also be found growing profusely at the foot of mountains, where seeds have been washed down by rain.

Cowberry
(Vaccinium vitis-idaea)

This evergreen shrub spreads by underground stems, and can be found on acidic soil on mountains, moorland and boggy woodland. It produces bell-shaped, white flowers in early summer and red fruit in late summer.

Crowberry
(Empetrum nigrum)

This is a low-growing, trailing, evergreen shrub that will form a dense mat given the opportunity. Crowberry resembles heather and is covered with small, pink and purple flowers in early summer. The fruit, initially green, appears during the summer and slowly ripens to black by autumn.

Net-leaved willow
(Salix reticulata)

This upland willow looks more like a herbaceous plant than an obvious member of the willow family. It throws out prostrate branches that often become buried and reach up to 15–30cm (6–12in) in length. It has rounded, heavily veined green leaves, and pinkish-red catkins that stand erect and appear from June to August. The net-leaved willow can be found in cold, remote mountainous areas and was one of the earlier plants to appear after the Ice Age.

Bilberry
(Vaccinium myrtillus)

Bilberries or whortleberries thrive in acidic soils and can be found on mountains and moorland across the UK and Ireland, including the uplands of the Weald, but are most common in the north and Scotland. This deciduous, spreading, low-growing shrub will reach around 60cm (2ft) in height. The leaves are thick, toothed ovals, and the bell-shaped flowers vary in colour from green to pink, and appear in April to June. The bilberry fruits in July, producing dark purple or black berries with a blue bloom.

Above: The cowberry is popular in central, northern and eastern Europe where it is commonly used as an accompaniment to meat.

Below: The crowberry, which thrives equally on acid rocky slopes and acid peat land, resembles the blueberry in appearance, but not in taste – it is edible, but rather bland.

Spring gentian
(Gentiana verna)

Spring gentian in full bloom is a glorious sight. This alpine plant throws up flat, starry, five-petalled purple or violet blue flowers, on short, solid stems, ringed with small, pointed lanceolate leaves. It grows on stony mountainsides, steep hillsides and rocky meadows with limestone soils. It can be

found in County Durham, Cumbria and the west of Ireland.

Common cotton-grass
(Eriophorum angustifolium)

This sedge species flourishes on the boggy moorland of the north and west, and in Ireland. Its stiff, brownish-green leaves surround a tall flower spike of around 60cm (2ft), which is topped by 5–7 yellow flowers. The seed is a distinctive, fluffy seed ball that waves in the breeze. A sea of these nodding white hairy heads can indicate potentially dangerous boggy ground.

Hare's-tail cotton-grass
(Eriphorum vaginatum)

Hare's-tail cotton-grass forms dense tussocks, in contrast to the rhizome-spreading habits of common cotton-grass. The flower spikes and seed heads are held on rather more erect stems, and it is most commonly found in the north and west of Britain.

Common sedge
(Carex nigra)

Sedges look like a grass but the stems are a different shape. Grass stems are principally hollow, rounded tubes, with swollen nodes or joints. Sedges have solid, three-sided stems that are triangular in cross section. The pointed green leaves range in height from 20–80cm (8–32in). The tall, brown, male flower spike has white stamens, and there are 2–4 shorter, female flower spikes, which are green and black. Common sedge is found on wet moorland, and its presence should alert you to boggy ground.

Purple moor grass
(Molinia caerulea)

Purple moor grass has suffered from loss of habitat through agricultural modification and reclamation. It is found on wet, peaty moorland in southern Scotland, south Wales and southern England. The plant forms tussocks of arching foliage, which dry and detach themselves in winter. The flower stems are tall, around 90cm (3ft), and are topped by tiny purple florets. The leaves of purple moor grass were once commonly used for thatching and weaving in Ireland.

Above: Hare's-tail cotton-grass can become dominant in drained peatland and blanket bogs as sphagnum moss disappears. It will colonise sites that have been burned, resulting in a haze of white seed heads.

Lichen

There are some 30,000 species of lichen in existence and they come in a glorious array of colours, from grey-browns to oranges, lime green and yellow. Some are extraordinarily beautiful when viewed through a microscope. They are highly sensitive to air pollution and can therefore act as an indicator of air quality. Lichen is not a single plant, but two partners, a fungus and a green alga, that live together symbiotically and function as one organism. The alga uses chlorophyll to produce essential nutrients that benefit the fungus, and the fungus creates a body, or thallus, in which the alga lives. Lichens grow extremely slowly, a colony extending by just 1–2mm a year, therefore a large area of lichen will easily be several hundreds of years old. Crustaceous species form a crust over boulders and headstones, whereas leafy (foliose) and shrubby (fruticose) species are found in wetter areas, where air quality is good, notably Scotland and the west coast of Wales. Lichens were used to make dyes in an extraordinary range of colours. Nowadays some are used in the production of antibiotics and sunscreen.

Lichen

Birds

Golden eagle
(Aquila chrysaetos)

The golden eagle can be seen gliding and soaring on air currents over Scottish mountains and moorland and in Cumbria. It is the second largest eagle in the UK, after the white-tailed eagle, and can measure up to 90cm (35in) in length with a wingspan of up to 2.1m (82in). It is dark brown with a golden brown head and a hooked beak. The golden eagle hunts close to the ground forcing frightened animals to run; it then swoops down on its prey and grabs it in its talons. It favours grouse, hare and carrion.

Red kite
(Milvus milvus)

The red kite is a beautiful sight in full flight as it glides on spread wings, hunting for prey. The body is red-brown, the wing tips dark, with dark, spread-fingertip feathers, the tail and armpits are red, and the undersides feature white patches. The red kite was close to extinction but, thanks to a breeding programme, numbers are increasing. It can be seen in parts of Scotland, northern England and central Wales. The red kite feeds on carrion, as well as rabbits, rodents and small birds.

Common buzzard
(Buteo buteo)

The buzzard is the most common bird of prey in the UK. It has phenomenal eyesight, eight times stronger than that of a human eye. Buzzards feed on small mammals such as rabbits and rodents, as well as taking some smaller game birds and carrion. The buzzard can reach 60cm (24in) in length and has a wingspan of up to 1.3m (51in). It is dark brown in colour and speckled with bars and streaks on its pale underside. It holds its wings in a shallow V-shape as it flies, showing off long, dark, feathered wing tips that look like elegant, outstretched fingers. It has a hooked beak and yellow feet. Buzzards

Right: The red kite has an impressive wing span of nearly 2m (6½ft) though its body is quite small in comparison, weighing somewhere around 1kg (2–3lb).

Reintroducing the golden eagle

The golden eagle (shown below) is one of the largest birds in the United Kingdom, but it has gradually declined over the last few decades. Around 420 breeding pairs existed in 2007, mainly in the Scottish highlands. They had previously been known to breed in the Lake District and are slowly returning, in particular to the RSPB's Haweswater reserve in Cumbria. A creature of habit, golden eagles often would nest in the same place for generations and soar and glide on air currents for hours over the same territory. This has meant that they are sensitive to human presence and may abandon their nests if disturbed.

are most common in Scotland, Wales, the Lake District and south-west England.

Peregrine falcon
(Falco peregrinus)

This falcon is about the size of a small crow, but it has a wingspan that can reach an impressive 1.2m (47in), and it can dive for prey at speeds of up to 322km per hour (200mph). It has a blue-grey back, speckled white undersides, a grey executioner's hood, and a vicious, hooked bill. Peregrines can be found on mountains, moorland, beside estuaries and around farmland, where they hunt for medium-sized birds, such as pigeons or waterfowl, at dawn and dusk.

Merlin
(Falco columbarius)

The merlin is the smallest bird of prey in the UK; it measures around 30cm (12in), and has a 60cm (24in) wingspan. The male has a grey-blue back, pale orange undersides with brown speckles, a black, tear-mark stripe running from its eye, and a square tail. It feeds on small birds, and flies close to the ground, where it will set up a chase. Breeding pairs hunt cooperatively, with one partner flushing out the prey, and the other pursuing it. The merlin can be found on moorland from the south-west of England through to the north of Scotland.

Red grouse
(Lagopus lagopus)

The red grouse is a game bird about the size of a chicken. It is red-brown in colour, with bright red eyebrows, a black tail and white-feathered legs. It lives on upland heather moors and flies with fast-beating wings when alarmed. It eats heather, insects, berries and seeds. The grouse shooting season starts traditionally on 12th August (commonly referred to as the 'Glorious Twelfth') and runs until 10th December.

Ptarmigan
(Lagopus muta)

The ptarmigan is the only British bird to turn white in winter; in summer it is grey, brown and black, with pale undersides and a red eye patch. It breeds high in the Scottish mountains and eats shoots, berries, insects and leaves.

Golden plover
(Pluvialis apricaria)

The golden plover is a wading bird that nests on moorland. It is gold, speckled with

Above: The ptarmigan's seasonal plumage acts as camouflage – it loses it's winter white feathers in spring. Males can easily be distinguished from females by the red wattles above their eyes.

Above left: Great flocks of golden plover can be seen in winter. They can adopt chevron formations in flight and will undertake spectacular aerial manoeuvres.

brown, and has a black face mask and breast, which turns to buff and white in winter. In summer, golden plovers can be seen in Scotland, the Western and Northern Isles, the Peak District, north Yorkshire, Wales and Devon. In winter, they move to lowland fields and live in flocks with lapwings, looking for worms, insects and seeds. Their plaintive call is associated with moorland.

Short-eared owl
(Asio flammeus)

Unlike other owls, the short-eared owl hunts by day and night for small mammals, birds and large insects. It breeds on Scottish and northern moorland and grassland, but moves south for the winter, favouring coastal marshes and wetlands, where its numbers are swelled by birds arriving to overwinter. The short-eared owl has dark brown and buff feathers flecked with white, a barred tail and

Above: There are an estimated 1,000–3,500 breeding pairs of short-eared owl in the UK, but in winter numbers are hugely swelled by visitors from Scandinavia, Russia and Iceland.

wings, and a silvery grey face with yellow eyes ringed in black. As the name implies the short feathered 'ear' tufts are barely visible. It will tease predators away from its nest by acting as though it has a wounded wing.

Meadow pipit
(Anthus pratensis)

A close cousin of the skylark, this plain little bird is found in lonely open places, where its distinctive call is part of the spirit of place. It

Below: The whinchat makes a rough and rasping 'chack' sound, typical of birds from the chat family, as well as a softer whistle.

has brown, streaked plumage with a paler belly. The meadow pipit is often found on moorland during the breeding season where it forms an important part of the diet of predators such as the merlin.

Wheatear
(Oenanthe oenanthe)

The wheatear spends the winter in the warmer climate of central Africa, returning to the west and north of the UK and Ireland in early summer to breed on mountains and moorland. It lives on insects and seeds and will often move to the warmer east coast in preparation for migration. The wheatear's plumage changes seasonally. In spring it has a blue-grey cap and shoulders, black back, wings and face mask, and a golden breast with white rump. By autumn the back will have faded to beige and the breast to a dull orange.

Whinchat
(Saxicola rubetra)

The whinchat also winters in Africa, and comes to the moorlands, heaths and conifer plantations of the north and west of Britain to breed, and feeds on insects and seeds. It resembles a robin in shape, but has a streaky brown back and face, white undersides, a white stripe above the eye, and pale orange breast.

Ring ouzel
(Turdus torquatus)

The ring ouzel is an unusual bird – it looks much like a blackbird but has a white bar across the breast and a grey panel on the wing. It is migratory, coming to the UK to breed in spring, and departing for warmer Mediterranean climates in October. It nests in hilly areas, low in bushes or among rocks. Numbers have declined by 60 per cent over the last ten years and this bird is being carefully monitored. It eats earthworms and berries and can be found in Scotland, northern England, West Wales and Dartmoor. When migrating in October and March, ring ouzels can be seen on south and east coasts.

northern England, northern Ireland and the Isle of Man. Winter visitors from Scandinavia can be seen outside its usual areas between October and March.

Raven
(Corvus corax)

The raven is the largest member of the crow family; it can measure 60cm (24in) in length, nearly twice the length of its relatives, and has a wingspan of up to 130cm (51in). It has iridescent black plumage from its large bill to its tail. It is a great opportunistic scavenger, consuming carrion, food waste, rodents, insects, berries, seeds and grain. The raven was once commonly seen on the streets of London, the last survivors of which can be seen at the Tower of London. The raven's natural home is the mountains, moorlands and cliffs of the north and the west and it can be seen in Scotland, the Lake District, the north Pennines, Wales and the south-west of England.

Above: The raven has an arched bill and a distinctive, diamond-shaped tail, which it reveals in flight. Birds typically live for 10–15 years in the wild, although ages of 40 years have been recorded.

Right: The twite is similar in appearance to the linnet and location is key to identifying species – twite favour moorland. It has an obvious yellow bill in winter and has a longer tail than the linnet.

Hooded crow
(Corvus cornix)

Unlike the rest of its relatives, which nest high in tall trees, the hooded crow sometimes nests among the heather on moorland, as well as in trees. It has distinctive, pale grey plumage, with just its head, throat, wings and tail being black. The hooded crow eats carrion, as well as stealing eggs from sea birds such as gulls, cormorants and puffins when the opportunity arises. It can be seen in north and west Scotland,

Twite
(Cardeulis flavirostris)

The twite is a small brown bird with a dark streaked back and wings, a warm brownish-pink chest striped with brown, and a white belly. The male's rump flushes pink in the spring. The twite breeds on moorlands in Scotland, northern England and north Wales, but moves to coastal areas for autumn and winter, where it hunts for seed. The bird is dependent on seed-rich sites on the edges of moorland for food. Its numbers have declined significantly and it is believed that this is due to loss of hay meadows and unmanaged sites.

Mammals

Pygmy shrew
(Sorex minutus)

The pygmy shrew is the smallest mammal found in the UK. It has toxic saliva, which, although it will merely cause a burning sensation on human skin, is strong enough to kill a mouse in a few minutes. Somewhat mouse-like, the pygmy shrew measures 15cm (6in) from nose to tail. Its back is grey-brown in colour, while its underside is white, and it has dense, velvety fur. It also has a distinctive, long, tapering snout, and razor-sharp needle-like teeth with orange-red tips. Shrews live on caterpillars, worms, beetles flies and woodlice as well as larger creatures, and will eat seeds. Shrews live for just one year, and are protected under the Wildlife and Countryside Act so may not be caught or trapped.

Field vole
(Microtus agrestis)

Although more readily associated with lowland grassy habitats, the field or short-tailed vole also occurs in upland areas. It has grey-brown fur with a yellow tinge, a blunt nose and short ears. Its body is about 10cm (4in) in length and the tail is 4cm (1½in) long. Field voles favour areas of dry, tussocky grass where they build nests and create pathways along which they range by day and night. Adults defend their territory aggressively and can be noisy.

Mountain hare
(Lepus timidus)

The mountain hare has a greyish black coat in summer, but in winter it is partially or completely white. It sheds its coat twice a year, in late autumn and spring, and in spring it has a bluish tinge. The ear tips are black. Mountain hares are solitary creatures, but in the depths of winter they can gather in large groups. In deep snow

Above: Pygmy shrews have a high metabolic rate and must eat their own body weight in food daily; they hunt for three hours and rest for three – if they stop eating they die.

Below left: The field vole is nocturnal, but in winter, when food is scarce, it will forage in the daylight.

Below: The mountain hare can reach speeds of around 60kmph (37mph) when in flight from a predator. It has broad feet that act like snowshoes.

they burrow for shelter, but the rest of the year home is a depression in the ground, close to the cover of rocky outcrops of heather, known as a form. The hare is most vulnerable to birds of prey while it feeds on heather, grasses and bilberry at twilight.

Red deer
(Cervus elaphus)
The largest species of deer, the red deer can reach 1.2m (47in) at the shoulder. It originated in woodland but has adapted to life on moor and mountain. As the name suggests, it has a red coat, though in winter the fur grows thicker and changes colour to brown. The undersides are paler and there is a buff patch on the rump. The males, or stags, have a shaggy fur mane at the neck. The antlers are shed at the end of winter and start to grow again in April. Red deer can be found in Scotland, Cumberland, and south-west England.

Reindeer
(Rangifer tarandus)
Reindeer are a native breed; they were hunted in Scotland in the 12th century but disappeared due to hunting and loss of habitat. They were reintroduced in 1952 and a controlled herd of 150 can now be found in the Cairngorms. Reindeer have dark grey shaggy coats with a white belly, rump, ruff and socks. Unusually both male and female reindeer carry large, flattened antlers.

Wild ponies

Ponies have roamed the moors and mountains of Britain for many hundreds of years. Archaeologists have uncovered remains that pre-date the Roman invasion in 43AD, and these show clear similarities with the ponies that can be seen today. A pony is a horse that measures less than 14.2 hands high, though ponies often have thicker coats and manes than horses, and are generally stocky and strong. These animals are not tame; the females live in herds and a stallion watches over them. They play an important role in maintaining habitats as they graze on saplings and stop trees from invading areas of moorland. The equestrian measurement of a 'hand' is used to define the height of a horse or pony; one hand equates to a measurement of 10cm (4in), the supposed width of the palm of the hand. When the measurement is cited as '.2', it indicates that an extra 5cm (2in) should be added to the total.

New Forest pony

One of the larger breeds, the New Forest pony can reach 12–14hh (hands high), and has lived in the Forest for over 1,000 years. Colours range from sand to chestnut, with darker coloured manes and tails, and paler legs. It frequently sports a white blaze on the forehead. An annual round-up takes place and some animals are sold on.

Exmoor pony

At around 12.2hh, the Exmoor pony has a thick, dark brown coat, a dark mane and tail, and paler legs, muzzle and belly. It is believed to be a descendant of the ponies that migrated across the prehistoric land bridge from North America.

Dartmoor pony

Also around 12.2hh, the Dartmoor pony is strong, and was once put to work in the tin mines. It has a mid-brown, dark brown or black coat, and a shaggy dark mane and tail.

Dale pony

A strong and stocky pony, the Dale pony has great stamina and endurance. It stands approximately 14.2hh and has a dark coat and a light mane.

Fell pony

The Fell pony can have a black, brown, bay or grey coat, and a pale mane and tail. It is around 13.2hh and is very strong and fast. It was once used to carry lead and coal.

Highland pony

Once used to carry goods across mountainous terrain by crofters, the Highland pony has a tough coat, and appears in a range of pale dun colours.

Shetland pony

A tiny but tough breed that is so small it is not measured in hands, the Shetland pony stands around 1m (3¼ft) tall, and can be almost any colour. It is very strong and can pull twice its own weight.

Welsh mountain pony

The Welsh mountain pony stands up to 12hh and is very strong. It was once put to work down in the mines.

Below: In cold, wet winters the Exmoor pony grows an extra thick coat. The undercoat is soft and woolly while the outer coat is longer, oily and more water repellent.

Invertebrates

Scotch argus
(Erebia aethiops)

The scotch argus, like the large heath, belongs to the brown butterfly family. It has mole-brown wings; both fore- and hindwings are decorated with a bright orange band, and are spotted with black-and-white eyes. Scotch argus butterflies can be seen from the end of July to early September in Scotland and northern England. Their foodplants are blue and purple moor grass.

Mountain ringlet
(Erebia epiphron)

Smaller than the Scotch argus, the mountain ringlet is a delicate butterfly with a dark brown upper side that features a variable orange band dotted with black spots. The markings are less distinct than those of the Scotch argus. The mountain ringlet is very local to the Lake District and the central Highlands of Scotland.

Large heath
(Coenonympha tullia)

The large heath butterfly can be seen on northern mountains where it feeds on hare's-tail and common cotton-grass. It is also found on damp moorland or boggy heathland; numbers have declined dramatically in recent years. Large heaths can be seen in June and July sitting with their wings folded closed. The forewing is an orangey brown, the hindwing dull beige; both are decorated with black eyespots. The tips of the wings are ringed with grey.

Northern eggar
(Lasiocampa quercus)

The northern eggar moth can be seen on heaths and moorland between May and August. The male is red-brown in colour, with a yellow band on the wings, a small white spot on the forewing, and long, curling, feathery antennae. The males fly by day.

Above: The Scotch argus is found in damp grassland in montane regions of Scotland up to 500m (1,640ft) above sea level. It is often seen at the edges of bogs and woodland clearings.

Below: The northern, or oak eggar, consumes heather, bramble and bilberry. Its common name comes from the acorn shape of its cocoon.

Bilberry bumblebee
(Bombus monticola)

The bilberry bumblebee is one of the fastest declining bumblebee species in the UK due to loss of flower-rich moorland habitats. It is a small bee with a distinctive red, heart-shaped abdomen and a black waist. A colony lasts for just one season and all members die in the autumn except for the young queens, which hibernate for the winter before forming a new colony in the spring. The bilberry bumblebee can be found in Scotland, Wales and the north and west of England.

Biting midges

There are around 4,000 species of biting midge, but in the UK only five of these will feed on humans. Midges favour boggy, acid ground and remain in one area, although the wind can blow them 1km (⅔ mile) or more in gentle breezes. They are most active at dawn and dusk and are less in evidence on sunny days. Midges feed on nectar, sap and rotting vegetation, but not blood. However, after copulation, females need to drink blood in order for their eggs to develop fully. They find their targets by the carbon dioxide they emit – mammals such as cattle and deer are typical targets. The female will ideally feed for around four minutes; when satiated she will release a pheromone to alert other females, which can trigger mass attacks at the height of the season in July and August.

Highland midge
(Culicoides impunctatus)

This is the species most likely to bite and is deemed responsible for 90 per cent of human bites in Scotland. Eggs are laid in moist soil in batches of 30–100 on water, five days after fertilisation, and hatch after just one day. In some parts of Scotland it is estimated that a single hectare can hold 50 million midge larvae. Each larva has four growth stages; it passes the winter in the final stage and pupates between mid-May and July. Each adult has a lifespan of around 20–30 days.

Lowland Heathlands

Heathland Habitats

Few of our landscapes are as breathtakingly beautiful as a heath in summer, covered in a purple haze of bell heather, and dotted with the yellow of gorse in flower. However, heathland is essentially a broad-brush range of vegetation types that occur on acidic mineral or shallow peat soils with low fertility. It by no means always consists of heather and gorse, for it may also contain areas of birch and Scots pine trees, bracken, long and short grasses, lichens, mosses and bare ground. Heathers may be absent altogether. Heathland habitats often occur as intimate mosaics, where many different types of heathland vegetation occur in juxtaposition, usually due to variation in soils, hydrology or topography.

The crucial factor is acidity, both in the soil and, usually, in the underlying geology. Heathland soils are hugely complex, but in the simplest terms they are either of shallow peat, or acidic clays, or pebble, flint or sandy mineral soils that are heavily depleted of nutrients and soluble minerals. Locally, they can also be brown earths that are regularly inundated by acidic streams. Many heathland soils are leached; for example, soluble minerals,

Above right: A typical view of the heather, gorse and invading birches on modern lowland dry heath at Rochford Common in the New Forest. The bare path near Rodeus Bottom is important for invertebrates.

Below: Early morning mist over wet heath and mire on the Purbeck heaths in Dorset, the haunt of myriad insects including some 20 types of dragonfly.

most notably calcium, have been washed away or deposited low down in the profile, where there is often a rich rusty-brown layer.

A human touch

The other primary point about nearly all forms of heathland is that they are essentially the product of grazing by farm animals. This grazing is backed up by that of wild grazing animals tolerated by humans, in conjunction with the cutting of trees, scrub, gorse and bracken, the burning of heather, gorse, scrub and bracken, and often the paring or stripping of turf and soil. Lowland heath itself is generally found below 300m (984ft) in the UK, though in northern latitudes the altitudinal limit is often lower. Above that vague limit, upland heath or moorland occurs.

Types of lowland heathland

Lowland heathland can be wet or dry, in between, or even both. At the wettest end of the spectrum there are mires, excessively boggy land found in saturated valleys. These usually merge into wet heath, which is permanently wet and often grades into tussock heath, which is grassy and fairly wet, and/or humid heath, which is wet only in wet weather. Then there is dry heath, which can consist of varying amounts of two species of heather, gorse, bracken, dry grass heath and acid grassland, and bare ground. These permutations depend on soil type and hydrology.

In the UK, heathland also has the habit of turning up unexpectedly. For example, it can occur in sand dunes, though only where the dunes are derived from acidic rocks. Such dunes can be isolated from other heaths, not least because of agricultural practices on the surrounding land. Good examples of dune heath on National Trust land include Murlough Dunes in Northern Ireland, which are backed by farmland

Coastal heathland

Some of the richest areas of lowland heath can be found in coastal regions. The heathland that lies behind Studland Beach (shown below), which stretches for 5km (3 miles) from South Haven Point to the chalk cliffs of Handfast Point and Old Harry Rocks, is a haven for many rare birds and native wildlife, and is a designated National Nature Reserve. Studland is the richest 1,000ha (2,400 acres) for wild flowers in Britain, and the heath is just one highlight of the 3,200ha (8,000 acre) Purbeck Estate, cared for by the National Trust.

Right: Some of the species strongly associated with lowland heathland, which is a rare haven for wildlife as it is grazed less than grassland.

and have the spectacular Mountains of Mourne as a backdrop, and Studland Dunes on the Purbeck Estate in Dorset.

More curiously, heathland can also occur on calcareous geology where the soil is so free-draining that it is prone to leaching and the minerals have been washed away. So you can encounter heathland plants on carboniferous limestone, where leaching has occurred patchily, or where acidic soils have drifted into cracks or shallow depressions. This is a feature of the carboniferous limestone hills of the Mendips and Morecambe Bay. There is also the phenomenon of chalk heath, which is all the more remarkable as chalk is the purest form of limestone occurring in the British Isles. Yet, in a few discrete places one sees heathers and other acid-loving, lime-hating plants growing close to lime-loving plants. A good example of chalk heath on National Trust land is Belle Tout, the chalk hill capped by a lighthouse immediately east of Birling Gap on the East Sussex coast.

Dartford warbler

Gorse

Potter wasp

Grayling

Bell heather

Mottled grasshopper

Sheep sorrel

Gold-ringed dragonfly

Marsh gentian

Silver studded blue

Nightjar

Stonechat

Sand lizard

Adder

Green tiger beetle

Heathland Past and Present

Lowland heathland started to come into being about 5,000 years ago, when hunter-gatherers developed into farmers, clearing woodland, herding animals and growing crops, especially grain. The thin, light soils on which today's heaths are situated were easily won for cultivation. However, clearance of woodland for cultivation produced irreversible changes to soil structure and to the ecological and chemical processes of the soil. These led rapidly to a loss of soil fertility, and crop yields declined. After a period the soil became exhausted of nutrients, and the farmers were forced to seek new ground for cultivation. But the woodland did not return, prevented from doing so by the grazing of cattle, sheep and ponies, alongside wild animals such as deer.

With the drive towards intensive food production following the Second World War, despite the inherently poor soils and unsuitable conditions for farming, many heaths were reclaimed for agricultural production. To sustain crops or productive pastures, regular ploughing,

Left: Silver birch and gorse invasion at Hale Purlieu in the north-west of the New Forest.

Below: Traditional breeds of pony and cattle, such as this Highland cow, help in maintaining and restoring open heathland. They are well adapted to the conditions and can thrive on a low-quality heathland diet.

re-seeding and constant additions of large quantities of nitrogen and phosphorus are necessary, a form of farming which is not sustainable. Much of our precious heathland was lost in this way. Because of this, many of the best tracts of surviving heathland are located on commons, where shared rights meant there was no immediate benefit from agricultural intensification. Military training grounds, such as the one on the Isle of Purbeck in east Dorset, are also surprising sanctuaries for heathland today.

Another factor to cause a decline in heathland resources occurred when the pastoral activities on which lowland heathland habitats depended – such as grazing – suddenly ceased, so that trees and forests started to develop instead. Some of these forests were planted, usually with non-native conifers, but the majority tend to be natural reversions, although they often include a number of invasive non-native trees or shrubs such as holm oak and the rhododendron. Many of these reverted woods are actually quite rich in wildlife, such as the National Trust's West Runton Heath near Cromer in Norfolk: here, within 50 years, an open heathery heath has been replaced by oak woodland that already contains a number of scarce woodland species. Both habitats are valuable for nature conservation, landscape and access, although woodland is more sustainable than heathland here.

Today, lowland heathland is being increasingly valued as an historic landscape rich in specialist plants and animals, of increasing significance for recreation, and of high aesthetic appeal, but otherwise without great economic benefit to human beings. Because it is a cultural landscape, created by now-defunct pastoralism, it requires new cultural processes if it is to be recognisably sustained. Research on the potential of heathland vegetation, notably bracken, for locking up carbon is developing fast, and the importance of peat as a carbon store is already well understood.

Conserving heathlands

At present, the National Trust and other conservation organisations are seeking to conserve and enhance heathland habitats wherever possible, not least because a high percentage of all the lowland heathland in Europe occurs within the UK, and because of the extent of heathland loss and fragmentation. Huge successes have recently been gained: the UK's Biodiversity Action Plan (which aims to protect Britain's precious biodiversity) has lead to 20,000ha (49,500 acres) of lowland heathland being restored in the UK since the mid-1990s, mainly from conifer plantation and scrub woodland, but also from arable land. The National Trust, which owns some 27,000ha (67,000 acres) of heathland, has been at the forefront of this restoration work, alongside other major landowners such as the Forestry Commission, the Ministry of Defence and the RSPB.

Above: Bracken-invaded heathland at Elterwater Common in the Great Langdale Valley, Cumbria. The future of such heathland tracts is by no means certain, as agricultural use of the land may decline. Access, recreation, carbon storage and clean drinking-water production may begin to dominate the way the land is used.

There is, however, a dilemma at the core of heathland conservation. If neglected, lowland heath can readily revert to broad-leaved or conifer woodland of value for landscape, access and recreation. With a reasonable amount of conservation management, such woodland can become rich in valued wildlife, while still supporting heathy elements. Over time, it may well be that practicalities and resources will help to resolve this dilemma.

Looking towards the future

Because the pastoral practices that maintained lowland heath are economically and culturally defunct, and the spectre of woodland reversion looms ominously overhead, the habitats, species and landscapes associated with heathlands are heavily dependent on conservation practice, which in turn needs a massive amount of public support and resource investment.

Even then, the impact of climate change on hydrology and vegetation dynamics suggest that traditional heathland cannot readily be maintained. The drying up of the wetter forms of heath is a very real threat, especially with increased demand for water extraction by a rising human population. In addition, and rightly so, modern attitudes to animal welfare mean that cattle, sheep and ponies cannot and will not be pushed as hard as in the past in order to preserve these areas. Certainly, the future of lowland heathland in the UK is far from secure.

Hindhead Commons

Covering 647.5ha (1,600 acres) in central southern England, Hindhead Commons (shown below) comprise some of the UK's most extensive areas of lowland heath in an Area of Outstanding Natural Beauty (AONB), and are important for their large expanses of undeveloped countryside. Grazing of the heathland by commoners ended around the mid-1900s, which allowed the spread of birch, pine and bracken over the heather. A programme of active reclamation, however, is now reversing this encroachment, with Exmoor ponies and Highland cattle helping to restore and maintain this highly scenic area.

Wildlife of Lowland Heathlands

One of Europe's most threatened habitats, lowland heathland survives in isolated pockets across England, Wales and Northern Ireland, with notable examples in the south of England and south Wales. As its name suggests, heathland is characterised by different species of heather, as well as swathes of gorse and bracken. It is also an important habitat for lichens. Many birds breed on heathland and the rich insect life, particularly dragonflies, grasshoppers, bees, wasps, moths, beetles and butterflies, provides their necessary food. Reptiles, too, thrive on heathland and some sites support all six of the UK's native species.

Plants

Wild flowers

The three richest lowland heathland habitats for wild plants are mires, wet heaths and old established grassy areas close to streams – such as the New Forest's streamside 'lawns', as they are termed. These habitats are a botanist's paradise, especially when they occur in juxtaposition. Botanising in the mires and wet heaths is, though, rather dangerous. The problem with botanising in areas such as the New Forest 'lawns', is that everything is so well-grazed that few of the plants actually flower, and one is reduced to identifying non-flowering plants. This is known as vegetative botanising.

European Gorse
(Ulex europaeus)

Gorse abounds on most heaths and moors, and also occurs in many other dry, acidic situations. Its foliage used to be valued as a winter fodder, and thick stems were used for fuel, as they produce a remarkably strong heat. Today, European gorse is advancing on almost all fronts, partly due to the decline of grazing on many heaths, but perhaps mainly due to today's mild winters, as it does not survive prolonged cold weather. It may also be benefiting from nitrogen deposition, and is certainly good at fixing nitrogen into the soil by itself. The two other British gorse species are low-growing in behaviour and local in their range: western gorse (Ulex gallii) occurs on heaths in the west, and dwarf gorse (Ulex minor) in central southern and eastern England.

Tormentil
(Potentilla erecta)

Tormentil is a common, yellow-flowered, creeping plant of rides through heathland woods. Its stems are thread-like and never root. The leaves comprise three toothed leaflets but appear to have five lobes as there are two leaf-like stipules at the base. The flowers have four petals and are carried on long, slender stems from May onwards.

Left: Gorse is a member of the pea family and the link can be clearly seen in both flowers and seedpod – the latter tears open when dry and seeds fly out at high speed.

Violets

The most common violet on heathland is the **common dog violet** (Viola riviniana), which grows among bracken. It has heart-shaped leaves and blue-violet flowers that appear between March and May. There are also two heathland specialists. The first is **heath dog violet** (Viola canina), a plant of sandy heaths. It has bluer flowers than the common dog violet, and its flowers appear later, between April and June. The **pale dog violet** (Viola lactea) has long leaves and deep lilac flowers. Both species are generally scarce, but where present can occur in profusion. The heath dog violet is widespread, but the pale heath violet is mainly found in the south west.

Common dog violet

Sundews

The sticky leaves of the three native sundews are effectively carnivorous, attracting flies and other small insects. All are found in acidic wet heaths and bogs. The **common sundew** (*Drosera rotundifolia*) has a rosette of red leaves, covered with long, sticky hairs that curve inwards to trap insects, and a white flower spike that rises from the centre of the rosette. The **great sundew** (*Drosera anglica*) is taller than the common sundew and has narrow leaves. It is common in wet bogs in Scotland and local in these habitats in the west of the country. The **oblong-leaved sundew** (*Drosera intermedia*) looks similar to the common sundew with a rosette of reddish, oblong leaves and a white flower spike. A local species of wet heaths and moors, it is more common in the south than the great sundew.

Great sundew

Above: Hampshire purslane is a rare plant, which is largely confined to the county of its common name. It is an easy plant to spot, with glossy red leaves and stems.

Below: The lovely smelling bog myrtle has been much used for centuries, as flavouring for beer and to keep the midges away. It is currently under development as an essential oil.

Hampshire purslane
(Ludwigia palustris)
The pride of the New Forest swamps, Hampshire purslane is a small plant of wet mud at the edges of pools. It has reddish stems and glossy, red-veined leaves, with an insignificant purple flower that appears in June and July.

Sheep's sorrel
(Rumex acetosella)
A plant of well-drained, acid soils, sheep's sorrel has arrow-shaped leaves, and reddish flower spikes that appear between May and August. It can be found on heaths and other grassy places throughout the country.

Bog myrtle
(Myrica gale)
Bog myrtle is a shrub that grows up to 1m (3¼ft) high in bogs, fens and wet heaths. It has oval grey-green leaves with a distinctive smell that explains another of its common names,

'sweet gale'. The male catkins are long and orange, and are carried on separate plants to the female catkins, which are short and red.

Bogbean
(Menyanthes trifoliata)
Bogbean is a large-leaved plant with large, fringed, white-pink flower spikes that appear in early summer. This plant can cover entire ponds, as many a gardener has discovered. It is a widespread species of peaty soils found in marshes, bogs and pools. The name 'bogbean' comes from the resemblance of its leaves to those of the broad bean.

Lousewort
(Pedicularis sylvatica)
A curious plant of early spring in boggy places, the flowers of lousewort are pink and snapdragon-like, and the foliage is distinctly feathery. It is a low, spreading plant with many stems, and the toothed leaves are carried in pairs.

Heather

There are three main species of heather, two of which grow in dry situations: **ling** or **common** heather *(Calluna vulgaris)*, which can form vast expanses, and the deeper pink and more exquisite **bell heather** *(Erica cinerea)*, which tends to grow in tussocks and is rarely seen in extensive drifts. Of these, ling is far more palatable to grazing animals, to the extent that it can be grazed out altogether, and be replaced by grasses. Grazing animals are loathe to eat bell heather – we do not know why – but it is a less vigorous shrub than ling and only occasionally occurs prolifically. On wet ground, these two heathers are replaced by the light pink **cross-leaved heath** *(Erica tetralix)*, which often grows in abundance, but usually among other vegetation. There are also two heathers that occur very locally: **Cornish heath** *(Erica vagans)* occurs only on the Lizard Peninsula, and **Dorset heath** *(Erica ciliaris)* on Purbeck.

Common butterwort
(Pinguicula vulgaris)

Butterworts are small but intricate and fascinating insectivorous plants, with violet or mauve flowers, that grow in bare, wet mud on wet heaths. They have distinctive, flattened rosettes of sticky, bright yellow-green, tongue-like leaves, which roll up over insects. Common butterwort is quite common in bogs in the north west, but is scarce elsewhere. The flowers appear in May and June. The pale butterwort *(Pinguicula lusitanica)* has pale lilac flowers and can be found on bogs in the west. The giant butterwort *(Pinguicula gigantea)* has large flowers, and is a rare plant in the UK, occurring only in the south west.

Greater bladderwort
(Utricularia vulgaris)

Found in still waters, greater bladderwort has bushy, feathery leaves that are carried below the water, and yellow, two-lipped flowers that appear above the water.

The leaves have small bladders that catch insects and fill with water. Greater bladderwort is uncommon but widespread; it is most common in the east of England. Even rarer, small bladderwort *(Utricularia minor)*, occurs in the shallower water of bog pools.

Pennyroyal
(Mentha pulegium)

A creeping plant of damp, grassy heathland with lilac flowers, pennyroyal is virtually confined to the New Forest 'lawns' where it survives because it is unpalatable to ponies. The flowers are carried in whorls along stems that are up to 23cm (9in) high.

Heath bedstraw
(Galium saxatile)

One of the classic herbs associated with the drier heaths and acid grasslands, heath bedstraw carries a myriad of white flowers. The flowers appear in opposite clusters along the stem. The leaves are short and pointed and form whorls around the stem. Heath bedstraw is widespread and often common.

Bog asphodel
(Narthecium ossifragum)

The mires support rare semi-aquatic and aquatic plants, such as the needle-like bog asphodel, which has to be one of the loveliest plants in Britain, not least because it grows in colonies: in summer its yellow flower spikes astound, while its orange-red dead stems bring colour to the depth of winter.

Wild gladiolus
(Gladiolus illyricus)

Wild gladiolus grows in some of the bracken beds in the National Trust's holdings on the western edge of the New Forest, though it is unpredictable in appearance, and extremely hard to find. It has reddish-purple flowers with pointed petals and narrow leaves. It can grow up to 30cm (12in) high.

Left: The herb pennyroyal is a member of the mint family and it has strong fragrance. The herb is toxic and must only be used with great care.

Orchids

Various species of orchid grow on the wet heaths. The reddish-purple **southern marsh orchid** (Dactylorhiza praetermissa) favours wet habitats, and can be found in water meadows, fens, marshes, swamps and dune slacks, as well as heaths. A tall orchid, up to 70cm (27in), it has glossy, dark green leaves and dense flower spikes that appear in May and June. The smaller **heath spotted orchid** (Dactylorhiza maculata) occurs only on the damp, acid soils of heaths and moors. The tall leaves have dark spots and the pale pink flowers also feature dark streaks and spots.

Southern marsh orchid

Bracken
(Pteridium aquilinum agg.)

Bracken is burgeoning on our lowland heaths and marching uphill on to our moors. As long as its canopy is not too dense or too tall, other plants are able to exist beneath it, but vigorous bracken casts heavy shade and produces so much dead litter that little else survives underneath. Formerly, bracken was cut for animal bedding; indeed, in late Victorian times train-loads of harvested bracken were sent up to London from as far away as the New Forest, mainly for bedding for hansom cab horses. When it is less dense, bracken stands support quite a rich flora of spring flowers, including flushes of violets and yellow tormentil. There are even a few rare plants associated with bracken, notably the wild gladiolus.

Lichen and mosses

The real botanical gems of the wet heaths are actually the 'lower plants' – the lichens and mosses. Many of these grow on lightly vegetated or bare ground, and require growth of the more vigorous 'higher plants' to be checked by grazing. Some lichens, though, grow on old heathers and other woody growth. On drier ground, many special mosses and lichens occur that as yet do not have English names.

Below: Bracken, the bedding of choice of Enid Blyton's Famous Five, is believed to be the oldest fern. Fossils of it have been found dating back 55 million years. It is toxic to animals and humans.

Peat moss
(Sphagnum spp.)

Sphagnum mosses act as a living, dying and decaying sponge, which decay to form peat. They are vital to wet heath systems. There are many species of sphagnum that are difficult to tell apart, but a typical example is *Sphagnum recurvum*, a fresh green, spongy moss that favours wetter areas of heathland, mainly in the north and west.

Heathland fungi

It would not be appropriate to cover heathland vegetation without mentioning the importance of heathland for fungi, together with the fact that many plants and vegetation systems are associated with the extensive underground root systems of fungi, called mycorrhiza. Many orchids, for a start, depend on specific mycorrhizal associations, which are mutually symbiotic between plant and fungi. One notable species is the endangered **nail fungus** (Poronia punctata), which grows mainly on pony dung, and is now found mainly in the New Forest.

Nail fungus

Birds

Lowland heathland supports a number of iconic birds, so much so that many of our larger tracts of heathland are designated as Special Protection Areas (SPAs) to protect rare birds. A good example is the National Trust's Frensham Little Pond in Surrey, which is run closely with adjoining land managed by the RSPB. The site and the surrounding heathland are of great importance for the nightjar, stonechat and woodlark.

Hen harrier
(Circus cyaneus)

The hen harrier breeds mainly on upland moorland, but many birds winter on the lowland heaths, sometimes roosting communally in pine trees. Watching them coming in to roost on a winter's sunset over an expanse of heath is one of the very best birding experiences. The female has the mottled brown plumage, typical of many birds of prey, but the smaller male is grey and white with black wing tips, giving it an almost gull-like appearance.

Hobby
(Falco subbuteo)

The slate-grey and black hobby is one of the most breathtaking of all predators to watch, but hobbies just visit in summer, and can be found on heaths and woodland edges in central, eastern and southern England, south Wales, and as far north as the south of Scotland. They are fast and agile enough to take birds on the wing. In late summer they can hunt over villages, picking off young swallows and martins, though they are more often seen taking high-flying dragonflies.

Long-eared owl
(Asio otus)

The elusive long-eared owl roosts in loose groups on heaths in winter, occasionally with hen harriers. It is a medium-sized owl, and has a brown body with darker streaks, long feathery 'ear' tufts and orange eyes. The long-eared owl is resident mainly in the north and west of the country; birds from Scotland and Europe migrate south for the winter.

Nightjar
(Caprimulgus europaeus)

The most notable heathland bird has to be the nightjar, though to encounter it you have to venture out at dusk in the summer, or be lucky enough to disturb one at roost on the ground during the day. The nightjar has superbly camouflaged plumage, and when resting among ground debris, looks just like a broken piece of lichen-encrusted wood. This nocturnal summer migrant is appropriately known in the New Forest as the 'fern owl', as it is primarily a creature of open bracken heaths and, increasingly, areas where woodland has been felled on former heathland sites. On warm, still evenings listen out for their monotonous, churring call. In flight, they appear semi-luminous and fly erratically, changing direction for

Above: The impact of the hen harrier on grouse numbers led to it being targeted by gamekeepers. It has been illegal to kill a bird of prey for over 50 years.

Left: The ears of the long-eared owl are not ears at all, but a tuft of feathers which only stand to attention when the bird is frightened.

no obvious reason – apparently in pursuit of moths and other nocturnal delicacies.

Woodlark
(Lullula arborea)

Heathland is also renowned for its song birds, the sweetest of which is the woodlark, a summer visitor to heavily grazed open heaths. Its song almost rivals that of the skylark. The woodlark usually sings from dead trees or the wires of electricity pylons. Mainly brown above with darker streaks, the woodlark is paler below with a pale eye stripe, and a short tail.

Stonechat
(Saxicola rubicola)

The male stonechat is boldly marked with a black head, a streaked brown back and an orange-red breast. Stonechats resent having their territories invaded and will sit on top of a gorse clump and chide strongly. The females are less strongly marked and lack the black head. Stonechats are residents in the west of the country on heaths, conifer forests and along coasts. They feed on insects, seeds and fruit.

Dartford warbler
(Sylvia undata)

Like the stonechat, the male Dartford warbler is capable of irate scolding, though his true song is quite delightful. Dartford warblers also favour the gorse-ridden heaths beloved by the stonechat and have benefited hugely from milder winters. The bird almost suffered extinction after the severe winter of 1962–63 but hung on in Purbeck in Dorset

Above: The woodlark, as its Latin name indicates, has a heartbreakingly sweet song. It spirals up and down in flight. Numbers have been hit by the decrease in lowland heath over the last 50 years, but are now slowly rising due to conservation efforts.

and the New Forest, and is now increasing its range, colonising heathlands as far away as Norfolk and the east Midlands, Devon and south Wales.

Heathland mammals

No mammals of particular note haunt the heaths, though the importance of ponies, cattle, sheep and rabbits in managing the ecology of heaths through their grazing activities cannot be understated: without them, woodland would develop. **Voles** and **shrews** are not uncommon among the ranker and grassier vegetation. The **fox** *(Vulpes vulpes)* tends to occur at low population density while the **badger** *(Meles meles)* is restricted to the slightly heavier soils that support its cavernous setts. **Deer**, both native and naturalised, occur at different levels on different heaths. No fewer than five species live on the Purbeck heaths in Dorset – **red deer** *(Cervus elaphus)*, **roe deer** *(Capreolus capreolus)*, **fallow deer** *(Dama dama)*, **sika** *(Cervus nippon)* and **Chinese water deer** *(Hydropotes inermis)*. Heaths provide feeding grounds for **bats**; several species hunt over heaths at night from nearby buildings or woods.

Fallow deer

Reptiles and amphibians

Natterjack toad
(Bufo calamita)

The obscurely named natterjack toad is a rare native of the soft sand and shallow pools of the coastal dunes of northern England and Scotland, notably on the sand dunes along the Merseyside coast, the coast of Cumbria and on the Scottish Solway. It was once quite common on the heaths of Surrey and Hampshire, and around the coast of East Anglia, but now only a few colonies survive. In the 20th century the natterjack population suffered a 70 per cent decline in the UK. It suffered the greatest losses in eastern and southern England due to reductions in its habitat. The natterjack spends the winter buried deep in moist sand, from which it emerges in spring to spawn in

pools of water that need to have a PH balance of between 5 and 7. This is challenging as most heathland pools contain acidic water. Another problem it faces is that the shallow pools it favours are heavily drought-prone, which means that entire annual crops of spawn and toadlets regularly perish.

Sand lizard
(Lacerta agilis)

Our scarcest lizard, the sand lizard, is exclusive to the heaths of central southern England. Sand lizards are difficult to see as they spend much time seeking food in dense cover. These cold-blooded reptiles favour open sandy patches among dense vegetation, requiring the options of warmth and shade in close proximity.

Common lizard
(Zootoca vivipara)

The most common heathland reptile is the common lizard. It feeds mainly on insects, spiders and worms, sucking the contents of worms and caterpillars dry. It is much duller in colour than the sand lizard.

Above: The smooth snake moves slowly and will often freeze if approached – it can emit a vile smelling liquid if handled.

Left: The natterjack toad has a loud mating call and a distinctive yellow stripe on its back; it can lighten or darken its skin as camouflage.

Grass snake
(Natrix natrix)

The grass snake can also be found on heathland, favouring damper areas and the edges of ponds, where its favoured food, the common frog, occurs. It will readily take to water and swim across a pond if disturbed on a bank. Its distinctive yellow collar separates it from other snakes.

Smooth snake
(Coronella austriaca)

The UK's rarest snake, the smooth snake, is exclusively a creature of the heaths of central southern England. This dull and evenly coloured snake is difficult to see, as it hunts chiefly at dusk, feeding largely on voles, mice and shrews, which it crushes to death. It is most readily seen hiding under sheets of corrugated tin strategically placed as reptile hideaways.

Adder
(Vipera berus)

The adder occurs in colonies on heaths and has special wintering sites called hibernacula. Adders have two basic colour forms: bronze or grey, though always with the distinctive zigzag black markings. Like all snakes and lizards, adders bask in warm places in late winter and early spring, and can at times be quite torpid. Thus the unwary wanderer of heaths can suddenly find themselves among a group of curled-up adders. There are two choices: panic and run, or admire these splendid creatures before slowly picking a respectful retreat.

Invertebrates

Dragonflies and damselflies

Heathland dragonflies and damselflies are one of the most interesting elements of our insect fauna. The pools, streams and mires are home to many UK species, which largely favour acidic water. For example, a heath with ponds, streams and seepages, may support over 20 species.

Small red damselfly
(Ceriagrion tenellum)

Heathlands support several of our rarest damselflies, including this species, which breeds in highly acidic pools in the south of England and west Wales. The male has a red abdomen and red legs; the female also has red legs but the abdomen is a mixture of black and red.

Red-eyed damselfly
(Erythromma najas)

The red-eyed damselfly congregates on lily pads and the leaves of pondweeds in high summer in the south and east of England. Unsurprisingly it is named for its large red eyes, and the male is black and blue, with a bright blue patch at the tip of the abdomen, while the female is black with a yellow collar.

Scarce blue-tailed damselfly
(Ischnura pumilio)

The scarce blue-tailed damselfly is a creature of boggy places on southern heaths, again in the south of England and west Wales. The abdomen of the male is mainly black with light blue patches, while the female never has a blue tail.

Right: The red-eyed damselfly can often be seen on floating vegetation in the water. The males will defend their lily-leaf territory aggressively.

Below: The gold-ringed dragonfly has an impressive wingspan, which can reach up to around 9–10cm (3½–4in). Its black-and-yellow colouring, which is the same for both males and females, is unique to this dragonfly species.

Gold-ringed dragonfly
(Cordulegaster boltonii)

The giant gold-ringed dragonfly breeds in heathland streams with gravel bottoms, and hunts everywhere, terrorising smaller winged insects. It has a dark body with distinctive gold bands on its abdomen and the wings are black. It occurs in the north and west of the country and can be seen flying between May and September.

Emperor dragonfly
(Anax imperator)

The emperor dragonfly rules over the ponds and their hinterlands. Indeed the scientific name of the emperor, *Anax imperator*, is derived from the Greek and Latin names for king and ruler respectively. The male has a striking bright blue abdomen while the female is green and brown. It occurs in the southern part of the country near open water.

Keeled skimmer
(Orthetrum coerulescens)

The keeled skimmer is a dragonfly of peat bogs, primarily in the south west of England and west Wales, and flies between June and September. The male has a slim, blue abdomen and the female is brown.

Black darter
(Sympetrum danae)

The black darter favours boggy pools and areas throughout the country. The male is black when viewed from above, and the female is yellow with black legs, and has a triangle marking on its back.

Butterflies and moths

The heathland invertebrate fauna is rich and diverse, containing a large number of butterflies and moths that are strongly or largely associated with heathland habitats. Both wet and dry heaths support a number of specialists.

Green hairstreak
(Callophrys rubi)
The green hairstreak breeds on gorse buds and flowers, but is hard to spot as the undersides of their emerald-green wings match the gorse perfectly. Green hairstreaks are most often seen in spiralling pairs, along gorse edges, because the territorial males are so belligerent that they frequently indulge in intense spiralling fights.

Small copper
(Lycaena phlaeas)
A pugnacious butterfly, the small copper, behaves like a fiery little dart. It occurs commonly on heaths, breeding on sheep's sorrel. The females only lay their eggs, though, on plants situated beside bare ground in the hottest of possible situations, such as along south-facing heather edges.

Silver-studded blue
(Plebejus argus)
The heathland race or subspecies of the silver-studded blue only occurs on heaths. It is found on the southern and south-western heaths, with outposts in East Anglia, North Wales, Shropshire, and there is an introduced colony on National Trust land on the Wirral. This tiny blue butterfly occurs in colonies, on low heathery heaths. Its larvae favour young growths of heather and gorse, though there is also a curious symbiotic association with black ants, which feed on a sugary fluid secreted by the larvae. More surprisingly, silver-studded blue pupae can quite readily be found in ant-nest tunnels, beneath flat stones or logs. The adults take nectar from bell heather and cross-leaved heath flowers, in particular, and roost communally on sheltered heather tussocks.

Green tiger beetle
(Cicindela campestris)
A metallic green beetle with light spots, that flies freely along sandy paths by day in spring, the green tiger beetle can be seen from May to August throughout the country. The larvae dig burrows in the sand.

Wood tiger beetle
(Cicindela sylvatica)
A rarer, darker species than its close relative the green tiger beetle, the wood tiger beetle is found on open heathland in the south of England. The body is black with a metallic purple tinge and there are wavy white markings and two pale spots at the rear.

Violet ground beetle
(Carabus violaceus)
At night, large ground beetles (Carabidae) scurry over ground with light vegetation, hunting and scavenging. Unlike the tiger

Above: Violet ground beetles hunts for small insects by night. By day they can be found concealed under leaf litter, stones and logs.

Opposite: The small copper butterfly is a fierce soul – males will defend their territory vigorously, even challenging other insects.

beetles, many species are flightless. A common example is the violet ground beetle that has a smooth black body with a purple tinge. Like other ground and tiger beetles, it is an active predator, and hunts invertebrates such as slugs.

Ron's diving beetle
(Hydroporus necopinatus roni)
Heathland pools and boggy places are great for water beetles. There is even a specialist of puddles on the Dorset heaths called Ron's diving beetle, named after a water beetle devotee called Ron!

Crickets and grasshoppers

large marsh grasshopper

A number of crickets and grasshoppers are heathland specialists, though the rarest are restricted to Purbeck in Dorset, and the western New Forest. Foremost among these is the **large marsh grasshopper** (Stethophyma grossum), which lives in quaking bogs, and makes a loud and distinctive popping sound, followed by a series of bubbles exploding. The most elusive of the heathland grasshoppers, though, is the **heath grasshopper** (Chorthippus vagans), a creature of the pebble heaths of the New Forest and Purbeck, whose song is likened to the quacking of a very quiet duck (too quiet, probably, for most ears). The most widespread of the heathland specialists are the **bog bush cricket** (Metrioptera brachyptera), which occurs in wet heaths almost throughout England and Wales, and the **mottled grasshopper** (Myrmeleotettix maculatus), which occurs on dry heaths with lichens.

Grayling
(Hipparchia semele)

The grayling is another classic heathland butterfly, though it also occurs in other habitats that contain bare ground, especially along the coast. On heaths it is confined to dry, sandy or stony areas, where its larvae feed on isolated tussocks of fine grasses, often along path edges. The butterflies are patterned in such a way that they imitate the bare ground on which they settle. The trick is simple: they settle only with their camouflaged wings closed, and edge-on to the sun so that no obvious shadow is cast.

Gatekeeper
(Pyronia tithonus)

Compared to many species, the gatekeeper is a passive, well-behaved butterfly. It can abound along bramble and scrub edges in August. It is smaller and brighter than the ubiquitous meadow brown.

Fox moth
(Macrothylacia rubi)

Not all heathland moths have curious names, and some fly readily by day. Most notable of these is the fox moth, a brown and orange giant that flies erratically by day, with little sense of direction.

Speckled footman
(Coscinia cribraria)

Heathland is a great habitat for moths, harbouring a number of rare specialists. A good example is the speckled footman,

which occurs only on the heaths of Purbeck and the New Forest. The location of its original discovery is now a housing estate, which at least bears its name.

Clouded buff
(Diacrisia sannio)

The yellow-orange males of this species of moth feed on heather by day. They fly in straight lines before landing once again. The wings of the male are edged in pink; the females are more orange in colour and they have heavy black marking on the hindwings.

True lover's knot
(Lycophotia porphyrea)

The most gloriously named heathland moth is the true lover's knot, an attractive and distinctive common species that breeds on heather. It wings are mottled in pink and browns, and are curiously folded back over the body.

Above: The characteristic eyespots on the gatekeeper's wing are believed to divert birds, directing attacks toward the wing instead of the body.

Below: The male clouded buff moth is active by day and night, but the females are nocturnal. The wings of the female are coloured orange with darker veins while males are yellow with pink veins.

Bees, wasps and ants

Over 100 species of solitary bees, wasps and ants occur on the larger heaths of southern England, including many that are restricted to this habitat. Many nest in areas with hot, bare sand, such as mini cliffs, where sandy banks have collapsed. South-facing sand martin cliffs are especially good for them. The **bee wolf** (*Philanthus triangulum*) looks a bit like a common wasp but is a solitary species, nesting in bare ground and preying on bees. The **potter wasp** (*Eumenes coarctatus*) constructs miniature clay pots on heather, and is a specialist of heaths on acidic clay soil. A problem for all these insects is the increased erosion of the heathland paths in which a great many species breed. Too much heathland is too heavily vegetated and there simply is not enough bare ground. Aerial photographs of modern heaths show that bare ground is restricted to well-used paths, which are often too heavily trampled for heathland bees, wasps and their wingless cousins, the ants. In some areas, conservation programmes are helping to protect species at risk. For example, Purbeck has its own **mason wasp** (*Pseudepipona herrichii*) and, in order to encourage breeding, special scrapes and mini cliffs are being created off the heathland paths, with spectacular results.

Potter wasp

Antlion
(Euroleon nostras)
At Dunwich Heath in Suffolk, a miniature sand cliff has been deliberately created for the aptly-named antlion, a species which was only discovered in the UK in the mid-1990s. The antlion is a type of lacewing, whose larvae lurk in the bottom of homemade pits where they prey on passing ants.

Horse flies
(Tabanus spp.)
Heathland fly fauna is distinctly exciting, not least the biting flies of the wetter heaths. These biting flies come in all sizes, from giant to miniscule, but all are adept at piercing the skin of the unwary or unprotected. Knowing that only the females

Heathland dollies

Look in high summer at the surface of any heathland pool, even a boggy impression in a path, and you will see tiny metallic blue-green flies; these are members of the (vast) family Dolichopodidae and are known among Dipterists (fly-hunters) as 'dollies'.

Above: Adult antlions are nocturnal. Females lay their eggs in warm sand and retreat back to the trees. Sometimes adults are caught and eaten by young predatory antlion larvae.

Left: The female deer fly does not have a needle-like device for puncturing the skin to obtain mammal blood; instead she rips flesh with serrated, curved mandibles, leaving a triangular hole.

bite provides little comfort, as the sexes are almost impossible to tell apart, but the males leave us alone. They turn to humans when they run out of ponies or deer. There are several species of large horse fly, especially in the southern heaths. Most are dark, and some have luminous bright green eyes.

Deer flies
(Chrysops spp.)
These flies are triangular-shaped when at rest, and have multicoloured, iridescent eyes. The females behave like mosquitoes and feed on blood. They will buzz round your head for several minutes before seeking to land, and are therefore eminently swottable. Do not let them bite, as they favour the eyelids, and are capable of closing an eye for a week. The common deer fly *(Chrysops caecutiens)* is found most often, but a rare

all-black species *(Chrysops sepulcralis)* abounds on the Purbeck heaths in July.

Mottled bee-fly
(Thyridanthrax fenestratus)
Many of the flies that occur on the drier heaths are harmless, at least to humans. Of interest are the bee flies and robber flies that live on sandy heaths, such as the mottled bee-fly, whose larvae are parasites of the large sand wasp *Ammophila pubescens*. This fly has wings that are half black and half clear. It flies low and fast over bare sand in July and August.

Deer tick
(Ixodes scapularis)
Far more dangerous to humans than the biting flies is the deer tick, another beneficiary of mild winters, that now abounds on lowland heaths, especially in bracken. It acts as the vector for Lyme Disease, which can be fatal to humans. Acute awareness of these creatures is imperative as they are spreading phenomenally.

Swamp spider
(Dolomedes fimbriatus)
A large and striking spider with a body up to 25mm (1in) long, the swamp spider has brown legs and a brown body with a yellow line around the edge. A heathland species, it is found mainly in the south of England, and will sit at the edge of pools with its front legs touching the water.

Rivers, Lakes
and Waterways

Forming Rivers and Lakes

Like so much else in our landscape, rivers, streams and lakes are largely visible reminders of our glacial past, with their origins in the last ice age, about 20,000 years ago. As the ice melted over thousands of years ago, great torrents of fresh water from the melting glaciers surged through the countryside, gouging out new channels, creating waterfalls the size of Niagara, and turning low-lying land into swamps and lakes. The torrents also swept along huge chunks of melting ice and glacial boulders that further eroded the land. Many such mighty boulders, known as 'erratics', are to be found high and dry in a landscape to which they have no geological connection. As the melt subsided, the rushing torrents that had carved deep V-shaped valleys were reduced to smaller trickling streams, now dubbed 'misfits'.

During the height of the Ice Age, glaciers had carved out U-shaped valleys and bowl-like hollows in the landscape. The ice was thickest in the north of Britain and so this area was the most affected. The lochs of Scotland and the lakes of the Lake District were created at this time, mainly under ice. The great thaw filled these hollows, trenches and depressions with meltwater. For example, deep, round bodies of water, known as kettle-hole lakes, were created when a glacier deposited a large chunk of ice, which then sank into the boggy ground, leaving a huge hole that filled with water as the ice thawed. Loch Leven in Kinross is the largest example of a kettle-hole in the UK.

Wetland formation

As the meltwaters and rain surged down from the mountains and uplands, they formed streams and rivers, which all headed for the coast via the most direct route. In lowland areas the waterways branched out into endless meandering creeks and snaking tributaries, which split and joined along their slow, gradually sloping journey to the sea. In the flattest parts of the country, water had even more trouble flowing away and the land became saturated. In some areas this created fens, which are wetlands fed mainly by groundwater and surface water (see page 206). In contrast, the wetlands known as bogs are fed mainly by rainwater.

Springs

Springs occur where groundwater emerges at the surface from a layer of permeable (water-bearing) rock. The flow of water can be intermittent or continuous, depending upon its source. Spring water contains minerals dissolved during its long passage through underground rock and may introduce carbon dioxide bubbles to

Above: The famous Aberdulais Falls near Neath in south Wales were first put to industrial use in 1584 for the production of copper, and then tin.

Above left: The bulk of the millstone grit has long been eroded away at Brimham Rocks in North Yorkshire. Today, it is vital to manage the surrounding moorland well to prevent soil erosion and ensure quality water supply.

Spa towns

The warm spring at Bath is one of the UK's best-known springs. It was used as a shrine by the Celts, as a bath by the Romans, and the spa town that built up around it became a popular resort in Georgian times, the Assembly Rooms (shown right) becoming the hub of fashionable society that flocked to Bath to 'take the waters'. The spring water here falls as rain on the Mendip Hills, where it percolates down to limestone aquifers (underground layers of water-bearing permeable rock) to depths of between 2,700 and 4,300m (8,800 and 14,100ft). At this level geothermal energy heats the water to 64°C–96°C (147–205°F). The hot water then passes along faults in the limestone to emerge in Bath itself. Other warm or hot spring spa towns include Harrogate, Matlock, Buxton and Royal Leamington Spa in England, Llandrindod Wells in Powys, Wales, and Strathpeffer in Ross and Cromarty, Scotland.

produce a natural sparkle. When water is geothermally heated within the earth's crust it emerges as a warm or hot spring. Heated water can hold more dissolved matter than cold water and therefore hot springs often have a high mineral content, once believed to have therapeutic effects.

Human influences

Many of our wetland features have been modified or even created by man. Sections of rivers have been straightened, deepened and embanked to reduce natural flooding. The whole ethos has been to get water off the land and out to sea as quickly as possible, although, today, thinking and practice are having to be realigned now that climate change is producing wetter winters and more extreme downpours. Canals have been built, and some sections of rivers canalised for navigation, such as the

River Wey Navigation in Surrey, which runs for 24km (15 miles) from Guildford to the Thames at Weybridge. The need for drinking water for farm animals has resulted in the creation of myriad field ponds, while many springheads were tapped and piped, both for farm stock and for human water supplies. More recently, numerous ponds have been created for fishing, and vast gravel-pit lakes created where gravel has been extracted.

Below: The River Wey Navigation in Surrey is an example of a canalised river, opened in 1653. Pleasure craft have long replaced the horse-drawn barges that formerly negotiated the 16 locks.

Lakes and Ponds

Bodies of still or hardly flowing fresh water range hugely in size, from large lakes and lochs to small pools and ponds. The character and nature of these aquatic habitats are dictated by their origins and the geological nature of the drainage basin. The water in upland glacial lakes is soft, has a low mineral content and tends to support less plant and animal life. Low-lying lakes are warmer, with greater nutrient levels brought by their feeder rivers, and so enjoy a wider range of wildlife. In addition to these natural freshwater bodies, for centuries people have created lakes and ponds by damming rivers and flooding valleys. The reasons are many, and have varied over time – from a pond where livestock could drink, to a lake excavated as part of a landscaped garden, as popularised by Lancelot 'Capability' Brown in the 18th century, to a reservoir behind a modern hydroelectric dam.

Ireland's Lough Neagh is easily the largest lake in the UK, measuring an impressive 392km^2 (151 square miles). Legend has it that the giant Finn McCool scooped out earth to throw at a rival in Scotland, so forming its hollow. Loch Lomond is the third largest UK lake and the biggest in Scotland, with an area of 71km^2 (27.46 square miles), although Loch Ness has a greater volume of water. Windermere is England's largest lake at 14.7km^2 (5.69 square miles), and Lake Vyrnwy is the largest in Wales, at 4.53km^2 (3.18 square miles). The latter 'lake' is

Below: Buttermere, in the north west of the Lake District, was created during the Ice Age. It is naturally low in nutrients and supports a variety of rare crustacea and fish, including char, a Celtic trout from the Ice Age that requires cold water.

in fact a Victorian reservoir, created by building a dam to flood the Vyrnwy Valley in 1881. The village of Llanwddyn was lost when the valley filled; its remains can still be seen in times of drought.

The lake ecosystem

Each lake supports its own ecosystem, with its waters split horizontally into layers or zones. In spring the temperature of the surface water begins to rise, creating a warm upper layer on top of a very cold deep layer. As temperatures continue to rise, a third intermediate layer forms as a gradation between the two. Thus temperature is stratified and falls rapidly from the warmest waters at the surface to the coldest, sometimes almost freezing water just above the lake bed.

For anything to survive in water, oxygen must be present. This can enter a freshwater body by diffusion through its surface or by plants growing in the water, producing oxygen by photosynthesis. As the surface layer warms in spring, phytoplankton (minute plants) start to grow, which in turn support zooplankton in the form of tiny floating animals and small crustaceans. These in turn feed bigger creatures like young fish, and so on along the food chains.

As the summer continues, the warm surface becomes depleted of nutrients and supports less plant growth and animal life. Meanwhile, the first flush of plankton has died and sunk to the bottom where it gradually decomposes. Thus the bottom waters are nutrient–rich but cold and low in oxygen – the reverse of the surface. Autumn winds can stir up the waters and encourage a brief recovery in phytoplankton. Then, as the surface layer cools in winter and temperature differentials reduce, the water layers circulate more easily, mixing oxygen from the top with nutrients from the bottom. By spring, the lake is once again ready for its annual cycle of productivity.

Above: Much of the nation's water supply comes from upland valleys, from both natural lakes and reservoirs created by dams, such as the Angram Reservoir in Nidderdale, Yorkshire.

Right: The grey heron is at the pinnacle of the aquatic food chain. It waits for fish at the water's edge, standing motionless for long periods – the fish are swallowed head first, to avoid problems with spiky fins. It is the largest European heron and inhabits wetland marshes, lakes, rivers, estuaries and reservoirs.

Watch for Wildlife

Most plant and animal life is found in the shallow waters at the edges or margins of lakes and ponds, where light can penetrate. Here, **reedmace**, **bur-reed** and **yellow flag iris** can be found, perhaps fringed by pink clouds of **ragged robin**. In deeper water, look for **water lilies**, **grassy pondweed** and **water horsetail**. The water lily is one of the UK's largest wild flowers. Its leaves and flowers float on the surface, but the fruit sinks and ripens under the water.

Mallard

The plants provide food and shelter for small worms, insects and crustaceans, which in turn feed larger fish and birds, especially ducks and geese. The **mallard** is one of our most distinctive and ubiquitous ducks. It can often be seen 'dabbling' for food in shallower water, assuming a head-down, tail-up pose while searching for anything edible, from seeds to young fish. Mallards often hybridise with domesticated ducks. Grebes dive for food and can stay under water for long periods, popping up like a cork. The **great crested grebe**, a handsome brown and silver-white bird of large lakes and rivers, puts on a spectacular courtship display in spring, including the male offering nesting material; later, the chicks hitch lifts on their mother's back.

Great reedmace

Pollution

Common causes of pollution, as at Lyveden New Bield, Northamptonshire, (shown below) vary from fertilisers leached from agricultural land to accidental discharge from factories, industrial plants or sewage outflows when normal water treatment fails. Pollution is exacerbated by the droppings of water birds, especially from large numbers of Canada or feral geese, and of numerous bottom-feeding fish, notably carp, which are so popular with anglers today. These pollutants expand the growth of unnaturally thick algal blooms that choke other life. Particulate sediments washed from fields by heavy rain or from building projects also smother the usual wildlife. Since the 1960s water treatment standards have risen, and industrial, agricultural and sewage effluents have been reduced. Legislation has also been tightened along the principle of 'polluter pays' for the clean up, but climate change now presents a new set of challenges, with algal blooms flourishing in warm weather. Lakes, ponds and other still freshwater bodies need continual monitoring and vigilance, since they take much longer to recover from pollution incidents than flowing waters.

Pond life

There is little technical difference between a pond and a lake apart from surface area – a pond generally being below 2ha (5 acres), a lake above. The plant and animal life within an individual pond depends on the pond's situation and condition. Woodland ponds are heavily shaded and accumulate fallen leaves that reduce the oxygen levels, which lowers the opportunities for aquatic plants and invertebrates. They are often suitable only for mosquitoes and midges, and can be covered in duckweed that thrives where air circulation is poor.

Ponds in more open situations receiving more light and less wind-blown dead plant material usually support a more varied array of plants and animals. Tiny leaves of duckweed and large round leaves of water lilies spread across the surface. Canadian pondweed *(Elodea canadensis)*, frogbit and water crowfoot may spread fast in warm, bright weather. Around the fringes are rushes, reeds, meadowsweet, forget-me-not, flag iris and kingcups that form the zone of emergent vegetation that is essential to pond and wetland ecosystems.

Below: Ponds are immensely rich in wildlife, as illustrated here, including plants and animals that spend only part of the time submerged. The aquatic food chain is particularly sophisticated in ponds.

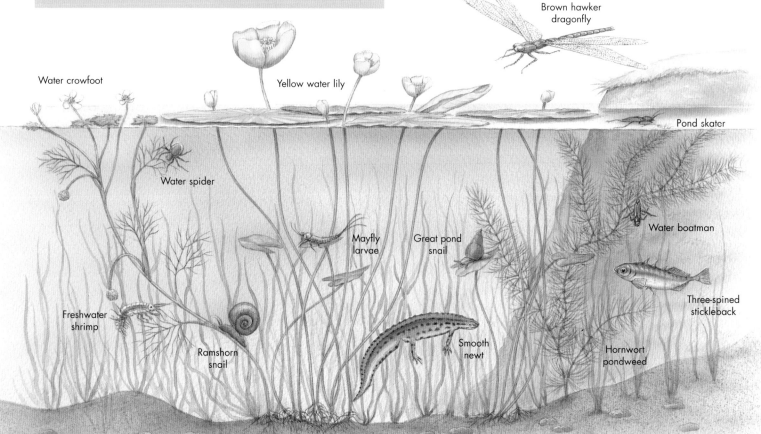

Brown hawker dragonfly

Water crowfoot

Yellow water lily

Pond skater

Water spider

Water boatman

Mayfly larvae

Great pond snail

Three-spined stickleback

Freshwater shrimp

Ramshorn snail

Smooth newt

Hornwort pondweed

Restoring a masterpiece

Lying just south of Worcester, Croome Park was Lancelot 'Capability' Brown's first masterpiece, the key design feature being a long, serpentine mirror lake fed by piped spring water (shown below). But the 20th century saw a railway line, a wartime airfield, a motorway, a sewage treatment plant and a satellite tracking station all inflicted on the designed landscape. In addition, most of the grassland fields were ploughed up for cereal crops, which meant that much of the sandy soil ended up in the serpentine lake. The National Trust has subtly restored the lake over a ten-year period, and improved water quality, putting the fields back to permanent grassland, forming artificial wetlands to help clean up the water running off the motorway, and creating a large wetland nature reserve to compensate for the reedbed habitat that was lost when the lake was cleared of vegetation.

These larger plants, along with microscopic algae, are the basis of food chains involving pond snails, the young tadpoles of both frogs and toads, and pea mussels. Larger creatures, such as adult amphibians and fish, are also to be found, although fish are limited in smaller ponds. High numbers of bottom-feeding fish, such as carp and tench, cause considerable damage by clouding the water with silt particles and eating out their food supply, while their bodily wastes build up and reduce water quality. Newts, frogs and toads arrive at shallow ponds to breed in spring, but then gradually disperse to live away from the water for the rest of the year – although they remain in damp, shady places such as ditches, mossy banks and undergrowth.

Small ponds are liable to freeze over when temperatures plummet in winter, overflow in spring and autumn, and dry up in summer. Their inhabitants must be adaptable to a broad range of conditions, or have the ability to migrate to more stable waters nearby when conditions become unsuitable. Several kinds of water bugs and beetles, including the great diving beetle – often the biggest predator in the small pond ecosystem – are able fliers.

Ornamental ponds

During the 18th century, many lakes, ponds and serpentine rivers were created as works of landscape art, primarily by Lancelot 'Capability' Brown and his followers. These works include a large number of mirror ponds, designed to reflect the landscape, buildings or simply the sky, and which therefore need to be void of vegetation. This, however, is ecologically unsound, for algal blooms and duckweeds thrive in the absence of oxygenating aquatic vegetation. Furthermore, Brown undoubtedly had better water quality to work with than is generally available today thanks to current farming practices – the sustainability of mirror ponds is therefore a massive challenge, with no easy solutions. In addition, many of these designed ponds are on-line, meaning that the feeder stream or river runs through them. This turns them into giant silt traps, where silt and topsoil eroded from upstream gathers. In theory, such lakes need to be dredged frequently, at huge cost. The National Trust, however, which owns many ornamental lakes and ponds, has adopted more sustainable solutions, such as cutting a stream by-pass with a feeder and outlet system and, in particular, removing inappropriate arable farming upstream.

Right: The origins of the lily pond on Brownsea Island, in Poole Harbour, are uncertain. The clean acidic water supports a rich flora and fauna and is in particularly good condition for dragonflies and water beetles.

Rivers, Streams and Estuaries

Rivers are havens for wildlife; they also provide us with fresh water for drinking, industry and agriculture, and are popular recreational centres for a host of leisure activities, from angling to sailing, rowing and cruising. Traditionally, they are also a means of transport exploited over the centuries by all manner of river traffic, from small rowing boats to huge barges. It is for good reason that most of our cities are sited along riverbanks, with some of the UK's major ports at or near estuaries.

The life of a river

The nature of a watercourse changes greatly from origin to destination, and a river must be viewed in terms of its whole catchment area. A stream begins high in the mountains, tumbling down waterfalls and rocky slopes, eroding V-shaped channels, and scouring its bed of smaller particles so that only gravel and pebbles remain. Only liverworts and mosses can grow in this fast-moving water. However, the swirling, rippling pace oxygenates the water and allows plenty of invertebrates to survive.

As the slope lessens, the river collects tributaries and its pace slows as it curves and meanders through the landscape, following the line of least resistance as gravity pulls it ever downwards. On the outside of a bend the water moves faster, scouring away the soil and rock, while on the inside the slower flow deposits mud, sand and other sediments. In this way the curve enlarges. Suddenly the water may break through into a neighbouring low area and forge a new course. The old channel is isolated as a curving ox-bow lake which may gradually, over time, fill with sediment and revert to dry land.

Eventually the river arrives at the sea via its widening mouth or estuary. Fresh water meets salty with a complex interaction of tidal ebbs and flows, shoreline currents and periodic floods from the river. There is also horizontal layering since fresh water tends to float away on the surface, while heavier salt water lies below. The water's speed slows to drop sediments of sand, silt and mud. These form banks and flats filled with nutrients and teeming with worms and molluscs, which in turn support large wading bird communities (see Saltmarshes and Mudflats, page 32).

River conservation

A river's wildlife changes greatly along its journey from source to sea; surprisingly few species occur along the whole length, apart from on short rivers occupying small catchments (such as along the north Cornwall coast). This means that rivers are truly biodiverse, and also

Below: A classic view of an upland stream, the River Wharfe high in the Yorkshire Dales. After rain, such rivers are raging torrents, hence the absence of aquatic plants, soil and small stones in this vista.

Naming rivers

Britain's ancient rivers often have names that can be traced back to Saxon or Celtic roots. For example, names featuring the words 'burn' or 'bourne', such as the Rivers Otterburn and Ashbourne, reveal Saxon origins. For the Celts in particular, waterways were worshipped and admired, and the names bestowed upon certain rivers and springs were often related to the deities they believed resided within the waters. The River Clyst in Devon can be traced back to the Celtic name *cloust*, which translates as 'cleansing one'. The River Kennet, which flows through Wiltshire and Berkshire, derives from the Celtic *cunetio*, meaning 'holy' or 'regal'.

Many of Britain's rivers have names unchanged for thousands of years, such as the Frome, Tees, Don, Lune and Severn. Several waterways throughout England have been given the name Avon. The Gloucestershire Avon rises at Tetbury and winds through Wiltshire and Bath to Bristol, where it passes along the Avon Gorge below the Clifton suspension bridge before finally emerging at Avonmouth. The Hampshire Avon meets the Dorset Stour at the town of Christchurch, previously known as Twynham, meaning 'where two waters meet'.

Far left: The mouth of the Cuckmere River at the western end of the Seven Sisters, East Sussex. The meanders are actually separated from the main river, which has been canalised, embanked and straightened (see middle distance).

Left: The mouth of the Afon Dwyryd in Snowdonia exhibits many of the features of British estuaries, including prominent shingle banks and sand banks.

that conservation needs may vary from section to section. The critical requirement is for clean water, free of pollutants emanating from agriculture, sewage and urban industry. Also, and more challenging, is the need for rivers to be allowed space, including the freedom to be able to cut new courses and actually flood.

There is also the challenge presented by non-native invasive species. Japanese knotweed and Himalayan balsam, for example, are highly invasive plants along watercourses, and there are other issues – diseases carried by the American signal crayfish are killing off our native crayfish. Dealing with such problems requires a whole catchment approach, involving all landowners and interested parties.

River records
The longest river in the UK is the River Severn at 354km (220 miles) long; it rises in west Wales and discharges itself into the Bristol Channel. It is just 8km (5 miles) longer than the River Thames, which at 346km (215 miles) is the longest river wholly within England. This rises in the Cotswold Hills just below Cirencester and runs down past Oxford, Reading, Windsor and London to the North Sea. The longest river within Wales is the Towy, 102km (64 miles), from the Cambrian Mountains in central Wales south-west to Carmarthen Bay. In Scotland the River Tay takes the prize at 188km (117 miles) long. It starts in the Highlands and runs down through Perth and past Dundee on the Firth of Tay into the North Sea.

Flooding
It is a basic function of rivers to drain land. Inevitably, when rainfall is high, or extended over a long period, flooding will occur. The water spreads out across generally flat, low-lying areas alongside the watercourse, known as flood plains. These areas have adapted over millennia to disperse, absorb and soak away the water, as part of the natural cycle of events.

The demand for new building areas, especially for housing, is greatly altering this natural cycle. Flood plains, being flat and easily accessed, are ripe for development. Much of the flooding experienced throughout Britain in recent years is in part due to extensive building on these plains. Proponents point to our ability to control the flow of water by deepening or straightening river channels and heightening flood defences, so the river does not overflow in the first place. In fact this often serves merely to shift the problem further downstream. The Environment Agency of England and Wales, which issues flood warnings, regularly raises concerns over housing developments on flood plains, which effectively remove a natural and effective flood-defence mechanism.

Climate change predictions suggest that our winters will become warmer and wetter, not only with increasing average rainfall, but also more extreme downpours to overwhelm the existing river drainage network. And the danger is not over when the storm abates and river levels begin to drop. Often the heavy rainfall has also occurred on local highlands, where the mountain streams turn into raging torrents as they surge down to meet rivers

Left: Climate change and flood-plain development are likely to combine to produce more vistas such as this postbox, submerged by floodwaters in Toll Bar Village, near Doncaster.

already bursting at the seams. Up to 24 hours later, the flood surge reaches the lowlands, and it is only then that the river bursts its banks and the real flood problems begin.

Water meadows

Water meadows are associated with a particular system of man-made drains and carrier channels designed to guide flood water on to flat land in spring, where the water

Watch for Wildlife

Lowland rivers are great places for birds, especially if fringed by reeds or other dense vegetation. Reedbeds come alive in summer with **reed warblers**, and provide shelter for many birds in winter, including the ubiquitous **coot** and **moorhen**. **Kingfishers** and **sand martins** nest in exposed high sandy banks, particularly on meander bends. Their holes are obvious, but can be confused with holes close to the water line that are used by the shy **water vole**. You often hear the shrill piping call of the kingfisher before it flashes past. In summer, **damselflies** bask on lily pads while their larger cousins, such as the **club-tailed dragonfly**, patrol their territories.

deposits fertile silt and creates warm soil conditions for early grass growth. After a few weeks the drains efficiently remove the excess water to allow grazing animals to move in or crops to grow. Examples of water meadows include the Backs in Cambridge, dating from the 17th century, as well as several sites along the Avon in Wiltshire, and in Sherborne, Gloucestershire, where the National Trust has restored a working water meadow on the River Windrush. This practice of controlled flooding and then draining

Below: Traditional riverside meadows, such as this on the Thames at Runnymede, are now decidedly rare due to huge agricultural changes and urban development. They are wildlife havens and important places for floodwater storage.

a site to increase farming productivity has disappeared over the past century. However, it would make sense for it to return, given the rising cost of artificial fertilisers and the high levels of nutrients in modern rivers.

Wildlife of running water

In the fast current of streams and young rivers, the larvae of mayflies, caddisflies, stoneflies and black flies flourish, along with molluscs such as river limpets, the river snail and the fountain bladder-snail. Brown trout, which enjoy small prey, such as worms and insect larvae, can be found laying their eggs in the clear, well-oxygenated gravel; dippers and grey wagtails also feed on these food items. Still farther downstream, fast-moving stretches of water are interspersed with deep, still pools where salmon, eel and trout lie up and rest. Grayling, chub and minnows are also found, feasting on insect larvae, worms and small molluscs.

As the river reaches the lowlands, its pace slows, allowing more bankside and shallow-water vegetation to take root. Trees such as alder and willow stabilise the riverbanks, while reeds, watercress, yellow flag iris, meadowsweet and speedwell line the muddy banks. Bream, roach and perch are all found in the slow-moving waters.

An estuary has a very specialised flora and fauna that can cope with the swings in salinity, as salty water surges up at each high tide, then the river's fresh water takes over as the tide retreats. Lugworms and molluscs, such as spireshells, burrow in the mud. Shore crabs, three-spined sticklebacks, flounders, gobies, shrimps and prawns have lives ruled by the tides. Salmon and sea trout swim through the estuary on their way upstream to spawn, while eels do the reverse, swimming downstream and out to sea to breed.

Wetlands

Wetlands constitute the richest wildlife habitat in Britain, but are at threat from increasing water pollution as sea levels rise, and from declining groundwater as climate change raises temperatures and decreases rainfall. Wetland wildlife often needs large areas of wetland to survive and often human intervention is necessary to ensure the habitats do not shrink or become less biodiverse. Over the last 400 years, Britain's wetlands have shrunk beyond recognition. Since the Fens first began to be drained for agriculture in the 17th century, there is now very little fen left. Unlike a bog, which is acidic and fed mainly by rainwater, fens are fed by surface and/or groundwater and are mainly neutral or alkaline in nature. The continued existence of both fens and bogs depend on a regular supply of fresh water, to avoid peat drying out and shrinking. Most of fenland East Anglia only remains above sea level because of a complex system of drainage canals and flood defences. Indeed, the National Trust's Wicken Fen in Cambridgeshire is now the last 0.1% of fenland left in Britain. There are ambitious plans to expand the fen tenfold and restore this lost landscape, populated by reeds, rushes, sedges and water-tolerant trees such as willow and alder.

The Norfolk Broads are an area of navigable rivers and lakes formed by the flooding of peat excavations, but are mainly freshwater. Some areas are surrounded by fenland as the water provides a continuous source of hydration for the surrounding peat. Both fenland and broads are known for their abundant wildfowl, flora and fauna, which are also a characteristic of bogs and marshes. Like fenland, bogs are composed of peat formed by decomposed mosses, but are not necessarily low-lying and are acidic, rather than alkaline. Unlike bogs and fenland, marshes do not need continuous hydration, but must be frequently flooded to preserve the grasses, rushes, reeds and other herbaceous plants. They may be acidic, in the case of saltmarsh on the coastline, or neutral in the case of many marshy areas around freshwater.

Wetlands should not just be restricted to bogs, fenland and marshes; it is vital that small wetland features like ponds and wet flushes in the countryside are maintained, to ensure breeding grounds for birds and other wildlife.

Above: The swallowtail, our largest butterfly, is today confined to the Norfolk Broads, where it breeds on rare wetland plants such as milk parsley. The butterflies range over huge areas of reedbed and wetland.

Left: Wicken Fen, north of Cambridge, is the country's oldest nature reserve. The original acquisition was to preserve a renowned collecting ground for Lepidoptera such as the swallowtail butterfly. Today, water quality and quantity are vital for the habitat, and the National Trust is working hard to make the reserver better — and wetter.

Industrial Waterways

The growth in trade during the Industrial Revolution presented major transportation problems. Horse-drawn vehicles simply could not move goods around in sufficient quantities and the road system could not handle the increased traffic. The solution was to build a canal network across the country. The Romans first introduced the concept of canals, which they used for irrigation as well as transport. Foss Dyke, built around the 2nd century AD, is a prime example. The next era of canal building began in 1755 when a 20-km (12-mile) waterway was cut between St Helen's in Lancashire and Winsford in Cheshire. This was followed by the famous Bridgewater Canal, built in 1761 by James Brindley to carry coal from the Duke of Bridgewater's mines to Manchester. It reduced transportation costs so much that the price of coal fell by three-quarters. Over the following century an impressive 6,000km (almost 4,000 miles) of navigable waterways were constructed (later to be replaced by railways, after which they fell into decline).

Most canals are not especially rich in wildlife. They were created by human endeavour and are unnatural features in their landscape. Left to their own devices, they slowly 'terrestrialise'. Reeds and other plants spread, choke the open water and build up vegetable matter and silt. Gradually the water disappears as alders, willows and brambles take over and the canal disappears.

Below: The Royal Military Canal, near Appledore in Kent, was constructed as a defence against possible Napoleonic invasion.

Watermills

Another invention that made industrial use of water was the watermill, also introduced to Britain by the Romans. Its use was fully implemented by the Saxons to drive millstones for grinding flour, threshing devices and other heavy-duty mechanical work. Later, water power was important to the burgeoning cotton industry, which was so significant to the prosperity of some English regions. Quarry Bank Mill in Cheshire, an astonishing industrial heritage site in the care of the National Trust, is home to the most powerful working water wheel in Europe. The factory was founded in 1784 for the spinning of cotton and was the largest such business in the UK; it ceased commercial production as recently as 1959.

Left: Quarry Bank Mill, which was powered by water drawn from the river Bollin south of Manchester, is today run as a demonstration cotton mill.

Wildlife of Rivers, Lakes and Waterways

The changing face of the British landscape always has one constant: water. Whether it is in the form of running water, such as streams or rivers, standing water like lochs, tarns or pools, or even man-made bodies of water, including canals, reservoirs, gravel pits and ponds, water is never far away. Although changes in land use have reduced the number of wetlands in the UK, their variety and diversity remain. Rivers and streams are a dynamic habitat, surrounded by lush vegetation and populated by a huge number of fish, insects, mammals and birds. Lake and ponds have a peaceful and serene character; the tall grasses and rushes that surround them provide a safe refuge for rare amphibians and breeding birds.

Plants

Black poplar
(Populus nigra)

A member of the willow family, the black poplar enjoys damp and marshy situations, where it can grow to heights of 30m (100ft). It occurs locally in the lowland zone of central England and famously featured in John Constable's *The Hay Wain* (1821). Leaves resemble serrated, rounded triangles, and the tree has a spreading crown with massive drooping branches, and grey cracked bark.

Willows

There are around 400 species of willow from the genus Salix. They take many different forms, but all have a watery sap and bark that is full of salicylic acid, a compound similar to the active ingredient of aspirin. The bark develops square fissures as it ages. The wood is tough and light – white willow *(Salix alba)* is famously the source of wood for cricket

Above: The branches of the crack willow break off easily and float downstream where they will take root and colonise a new area.

Left: Fresh seed from the grey willow can only germinate within a fortnight of being released, which explains why large colonies form in a limited area, although the hair on the seed assists wind dispersal.

bats. Supple young willow wands are light and tough and used for basket weaving or hurdle or wattle fencing.

Crack willow
(Salix fragilis)

The tallest species of willow, reaching heights of 90m (295ft), the crack willow is a common sight on the riverbank. The name comes from the brittle nature of the twigs that snap off easily at the joints. The leaves are long and narrow, green on top and grey and hairy beneath. Male catkins are yellow fluffy tassels, while female catkins are green and spiky. They appear on separate trees and are pollinated by bees.

Grey willow
(Salix cinerea)

A common small tree or shrub found in wet lowlands reaching 4–6m (13–20ft). The oval

ovals, and female catkins are dangling, spiky, green cylinders.

Common alder
(Alnus glutinosa)
Alder is a fast-growing deciduous tree that can be seen alongside riverbanks, streams and wetlands, reaching heights of 22m (72ft). It is the most common waterside tree and is easily recognisable with black, cracked bark and rounded green, heavily veined leaves with downy undersides. It produces catkins early in the year, providing important nectar for bees when other sources are scarce. Male catkins are brownish and dangle, scattering pollen onto the green, cone-like female flowers. The alder has long roots that help to stabilise the banks of streams and rivers.

Marsh marigold
(Caltha palustris)
The flower of the marsh marigold, or kingcup, looks much like that of the glossy buttercup. It has large, green, shiny, kidney-shaped leaves and bright yellow, five-petalled flowers on tall stems that appear early in spring and which are popular with pollinating insects. It grows in shallow water alongside streams and in marshes and bogs. Once common, plant numbers have suffered along with hundreds of other wetland species, due to land drainage.

or lance-shaped leaves are green and hairy on their upper side and shiny blue-green underneath. The egg-shaped shrub produces flowers in early spring that appear before the leaves. Male catkins are fluffy yellow balls and the female flowers are green.

Above: The alder utilises nitrogen from the atmosphere via bacteria around its roots, thus building up the soil fertility of the surrounding area.

Below: Water crowfoot has pretty papery white flowers, it provides valuable shelter for many forms of aquatic wildlife and the fruit is eaten by some waterfowl.

Osier
(Salix viminalis)
The osier is a shrubby multi-stemmed willow and its slender, pliable twigs are used extensively for basket making. 'Osier' is also the term used to describe a person who used willows for fencing and basketwork. The shrub can grow to 3–6m (10–20ft). Leaves are long and slender, green on the upper side and silvery grey underneath. Male flowers are yellow

Water crowfoot
(Ranunculus aquatilis)
There are seven species of water crowfoot and all are very similar. Water crowfoot is a member of the buttercup family, but has white flowers with a yellow eye, that appear in May and June. A critical point of identification is the foliage: thread-like leaves, typical of aquatic plants are submerged, while larger, toothed leaves float on the surface of the water. It offers cover for many insects, including the larvae of dragonflies and damselflies. It is found in still or slow-moving water and is a distinguishing feature of healthy, well-oxygenated streams.

Watercress
(Rorippa nasturtium-aquaticum)

Watercress is one of the earliest leaf vegetables eaten by man. It has a tangy, peppery flavour and contains significant amounts of iron, folic acid and calcium as well as vitamins A and C. Usually 10–30cm (4–12in) in height, the plants have dark green, oval leaves. Clusters of four-petalled white flowers appear between May and October and develop into long green seed pods. The plant spreads both by seed and by creeping rhizomes.

Ragged robin
(Lychnis flos-cuculi)

Ragged robin is a member of the carnation and pink family, with characteristic opposite pairs of leaves, and swollen nodes on the stem. The pretty pink flowers have deeply-divided, four-lobed petals that give the flowers a delicate, spidery appearance. It has narrow, grass-like leaves and grows to heights of 60cm (2ft). The Latin name *flos-cuculi* means 'cuckoo flower', and refers to the fact that the flower blooms in May

Water lily

There are two species of water lily that can be found growing wild: the familiar white water lily *(Nymphaea alba)*, and the less well-known yellow water lily *(Nuphar lutea)*. The plants root themselves in soil in ponds, lakes or slow-moving rivers. They have long stems that grow up from their roots, and the leaves and flowers, which bloom only during the day, float on the surface of the water. The **white water lily** has the largest flower of any native wild flower in the UK; it can measure up to 20cm (8in), and has 25 or more white petals with a yellow centre. The leaves are large, green, notched circles and can measure 30cm (12in). It is most common in the north and west of the country, but its natural distribution is entirely obscured by introductions. The **yellow water lily** looks rather like a giant buttercup. It blooms from June to September and can be found in water up to depths of 3m (10ft). Unlike the white water lily its flowers do not float on the surface of the water, but are held up on strong stalks. The floating summer leaves, which reach 40cm (16in), are heart shaped. The submerged leaves seen during winter and spring are lurid green, crumpled and spinach-like.

White water lily

and June, traditionally the months when the cuckoo can be heard calling.

Himalayan balsam
(Impatiens glandulifera)

Himalayan balsam is not a native plant; its home was the western Himalayas but it was introduced to Britain in 1839, whereupon it promptly escaped the confines of gardens and colonised riverbanks, suppressing native plants and leaving banks vulnerable to erosion. Reputed to be the tallest annual plant growing in the UK, it can reach 3m (10ft) in height. It has tall, hollow stems and spear-shaped, shiny, dark green leaves with serrated edges. The helmet-shaped flowers range in colour from pink to purple or white and appear from July to October.

Meadowsweet
(Filipendula ulmaria)

Meadowsweet is a sweetly scented plant found in damp environments by rivers, swamps, marshes and fenland where the vegetation is infrequently cut or grazed. It is a tall, hardy perennial that can reach 60–120cm (2–4ft) with aromatic foliage. The oval leaves are a strong dark green and have finely serrated edges. It produces clusters of creamy-white blooms throughout the summer.

Purple loosestrife
(Lythrum salicaria)

Purple loosestrife is a tall herbaceous perennial that will easily reach heights of 1m (3¼ft). It has red-brown stems; the green downy leaves are elongated ovals, arranged in whorls of three around the stalk. They turn red late in summer. The tiny pink flowers are clustered together in tall flower spikes and appear from June to September. A single mature plant can produce 2–3 million tiny seeds in a year that remain viable for two years. Purple loosestrife grows in boggy ground or shallow water.

Great willowherb
(Epilobium hirsutum)

This giant perennial will rapidly spread around riverbanks and pond edges. It can reach the impressive heights of 1.8m (6ft) and has green, willow-like, toothed leaves covered in downy hair. Small pink flowers are borne in July and August around the top of the stem. The flower stem develops into the seed pod, which splits open to reveal downy, dandelion-type seeds that are carried away by the wind.

Mare's tail
(Hippuris vulgaris)

Mare's tail grows in still and slow moving water and mud. It grows in two forms, a submerged aquatic, and an emergent plant. The former has crowded, long and linear leaves which are flaccid and pale, giving the plant its name. The emergent plant has erect, reddish stems that are ringed by whorls of narrow, short, up-curling leaves. Insignificant green flowers appear in June and July at leaf and stem joints. It looks very similar to the herb field horsetail (Equisetum arvense), a species found in damp, grassy places.

Above: Mare's tail will usually grow upright in stagnant water, but in running water it will tend to bend with the current. It is a relative of the herb horsetail and the plant goosegrass.

Above left: The seed of the bogbean floats and will remain floating for as long as 15 months before its seed case ruptures, releasing its many seeds. The plant is also able to spread by means of floating rhizomes.

Bogbean
(Menyanthes trifoliata)

The bogbean grows in shallow, still water or in waterlogged bogs, often in upland, acid water. The leaves are grey-green and trifoliate and appear to float on the surface of the water. It has pretty pale pink or white fringed flowers that appear in clusters in May and June. These are pollinated by bees and butterflies but their fetid smell also attracts beetles and flies. The shiny yellow seeds are held in a capsule. The leaves were once used as flavouring in the making of beer, prior to the use of hops.

Water forget-me-not

There are ten species of forget-me-not that can be seen in the British Isles. The flowers of the **water forget-me-not** (*Myosotis scorpioides*) look much like those of the garden variety, although its blue petals are blunter and notched in the centre. The eye of the flower is a bright yellow and the buds are pink. The flowers open sequentially along the stalk, which curls up to resemble a scorpion's tail – hence the Latin name. The rest of the plant is bushier with long, green, hairy, oval leaves and stems that root readily wherever they lie, so that it quickly forms a large mat. It can be seen in shaded, wet places and thrives along the edges of streams and ponds. **Creeping water forget-me-knot** (*Myosotis secunda*) also favours damp places but the flowers of the water forget-me-not are larger.

Water forget-me-not

Comfrey
(Symphytum officinale)

For centuries comfrey was an important medicinal herb, used to treat wounds, cuts, ulcers, bruises and sprains. It enjoys moist situations and thrives in damp ground near water. Comfrey is a tall, spreading perennial that grows to 1m (3¼ft). It has large, coarse, spear-shaped leaves, and spikes of cream or blue flowers from May to July, that bees adore.

Water mint
(Mentha aquatica)

Water mint can be found on the banks of streams, rivers and lakes and in marshes. This perennial herb grows from 15–90cm (6–35in) and spreads readily by creeping rhizomes. It has reddish stems, toothed oval leaves and mauve flowers born in whorls at the top of the stems from July to October.

Guelder rose
(Viburnum opulus)

The guelder rose is known by many common names, including swamp elder, because its fruit resembles those of the elder in shape. This deciduous shrub grows in a variety of base-rich soils from chalk downland to woodland and fens. It can reach 4–5m (13–16ft) in height. It has green, three to five lobed leaves, shaped rather like those of the maple. Its white flowers are actually sterile and are designed to attract pollinating insects, while the real flowers resemble a circle of unopened buds in the centre. Its bright red berries are held on thin stalks in clusters and, like elderberries, hang down when they are fully ripe. Bullfinches and mistle thrushes enjoy this treat and disperse the seed in their droppings.

Left: The nectar from the fragrant guelder rose is very attractive to hoverflies and other insects. The bright red juicy berries, which turn purple later in the year, attract plenty of birds, and are particularly favoured by birds such as bull finches and mistle thrushes.

Broad-leaved pondweed
(Potamogeton natans)

Broad-leaved pondweed is found mainly in sunshine in slow flowing water up to depths of around 1.5m (5ft). It sends up leaf and flower stalks from rhizomes that are buried in mud. The underwater foliage is long and linear, but on the surface it flattens into neat oval leaves that look as though they have just fallen onto the surface of the water. The flowers are yellow-green, inconspicuous and catkin-like, growing at a sharp right angle to the stem. The leaves can clog streams and cause flooding.

Yellow flag iris
(Iris pseudacorus)

This is a beautiful herbaceous perennial with glorious, yellow flowers, which consist of three large down-turned petals, with three smaller up-tilted petals in the centre. The leaves are tall green spears that stand upright or occasionally flop at the top. The brown seeds appear in large green pods. The yellow flag iris grows in wet, boggy soils and spreads by means of rhizomes and seed. It can take up metals that are polluting the water as a result of acid rain, industrial effluents and lead in petrol, and therefore acts as a filter system, improving water quality.

Southern marsh orchid
(Dactylorhiza praetermissa)

The southern marsh orchid is one of 54 native species. The glossy leaves are dark green and sword-shaped. The flower spike carries 20–30 pinkish-purple flowers up to 70cm (28in). The petals have a broad, three-lobed lip and are marked with darker spots and streaks. It is found in fens, marshes, swamps, and wet meadows in the south, and is replaced with northern marsh orchid (D. purpurella) in the north of the country.

Left: The powdered root of the yellow flag iris was used as an ingredient in snuff and American and Australian settlers took the plant with them.

Below: Many colonies of the southern marsh orchid have been destroyed by land being drained for agricultural purposes, though the root is remarkably sturdy and can withstand many years of drought.

Bulrushes

Great reedmace *(Typha latifolia)* acquired the name 'bulrush' after Sir Lawrence Alma-Tadema painted the Biblical scene of Moses in the bulrushes in his *The Finding of Moses* (1904) featuring this species. It is a tall waterside plant with stems that reach 3m (10ft). It has long, strap-like leaves, its brown spikes are a mass of chocolate-brown female flowers, and above them is the tall yellow spike of the male flower. Both appear in June and July. The developing seeds are contained within the brown spikes that burst open over the winter to release thousands of downy seeds that are dispersed by the wind. In winter the dead leaf sheaths provide shelter for several species of bug and beetle. The **lesser bulrush** *(Typha angustifolia)* is less common and is found in English lowlands. It is taller, growing to 2.7m (9ft), and the seed head is divided into two parts with a gap of 5cm (2in) in its middle. The plants are very useful; in the past leaves and roots were eaten and the seed heads were used to make bedding.

Lesser bulrush

Duckweed
(Lemna minor)
Duckweed is a remarkable plant, which consists of two simple, plate-like structures that resemble leaves that float on, or just below, the surface of the water and has a single trailing rootlet. The plant grows rapidly to form colonies and these absorb excess mineral nutrients, notably nitrogen and phosphates, from the water and this provides nutritious vegetation for ducks and swans. It is something of a mixed blessing, for while it filters the water and feeds birds, it can also become a suffocating green blanket that blocks out the light and kills off oxygenating water plants which, in turn, kills off fish.

Common clubrush
(Schoenoplectus lacustris)
Common clubrush is a tall, rush-like plant that will reach heights of 3m (10ft). It grows on the edges of lakes, ponds or slow-moving rivers. The plant has long, glossy, tubular leaves and produces egg-shaped clusters of brownish flowers on slender round stems in June and July.

Common reed
(Phragmites australis)
The common reed is the tallest native grass to be found in the UK: it can reach heights of 1.5–3m (5–10ft). It grows in the shallow waters of rivers, lakes and ponds and spreads by means of underground stems that help to stabilise banks and prevent erosion. The roots also absorb nitrates that leach into the water and the reed can be used in artificial reed beds for sewage treatment. It can tolerate brackish water and is also often found near estuaries. The stems and the broad, grassy leaves, which can grow to 50cm (20in), persist through winter; new growth comes through to replace it in the spring. The purple flower plumes appear between August and October. The common reed is the main species of reed used for thatching.

Left: Duckweed is an important food source for waterfowl and provides shelter for amphibians. It can absorb contaminants from water as it grows, restoring it to its natural condition.

Below: The stems of the common reed bleach in winter and the seed heads turn to a shimmering silver.

Birds

Grebes

Grebes are diving birds with large feet placed far back on their bodies that make them somewhat clumsy on land. They are excellent swimmers, but poor fliers, and when alarmed will dive rather than take to the wing. They can move their feathers to adjust buoyancy.

Little grebe
(Tachybaptus ruficollis)

A dumpy diving bird commonly seen on ponds and small lakes and on slow-moving rivers and canals, where there is plenty of cover, right across the British Isles. The little grebe is shy and will dive for long periods, hunting for fish and aquatic invertebrates, only to pop up to the surface some distance away. It has a dark brown head and back, warm brown cheeks and neck and a dappled brown underside. It has a prominent 'powder-puff' tail.

Great crested grebe
(Podiceps cristatus)

Hunted to virtual extinction in the 19th century for its magnificent courting foliage that was used to decorate hats, the great crested grebe has a white face, neck and chest, a dark brown back and red-brown undersides. In spring and summer the breeding plumage is an impressive tippet of red and black. It can be seen on lakes and ponds across the British Isles, though it is not seen in the north of Scotland nor the south west of England.

Grey heron
(Ardea cinerea)

The grey heron is the largest European heron, standing 1m (3¼ft) tall, with an impressive 1.6m (5¼ft) wingspan. It is a solitary bird that can be seen stalking through freshwater habitats and standing

Above: The great crested grebe carry their young on their back, extending a foot onto the surface of the water to enable their zebra-striped babies to hop aboard.

Right: The bittern is a conservation priority: the RSPB estimates that there are just 51 breeding males in the whole of the UK.

motionless in shallow water for long periods while it scans for food to spear. The grey heron has a white face and neck and a grey body with black stripes on its neck and wing. It has a drooping black crest on its head, a long yellow bill and yellow legs. It can be seen anywhere from garden ponds to rivers and estuaries.

Bittern
(Botaurus stellaris)

A very rare bird with a distinctive cry, like a low note on an oboe. A member of the heron family, it resembles a heron, but has a shorter neck and is patterned all over in cream and buff and speckled and striped in brown. These markings serve as camouflage as it wades through the water. It is a shy bird that conceals itself among the reeds; if frightened it freezes with its neck held tall in an attempt to disappear into the undergrowth. Land drainage and persecution led to the extinction of the bittern in the UK in the late 19th century. The species reappeared in Norfolk in the early 20th century, but numbers have remained small, although reed-bed conservation will help to encourage breeding.

Swans

Three species of swan can be seen in Britain. All have the characteristic S-shaped neck and webbed feet. One is the native mute swan, the other two species, the whooper swan and Bewick's swan, are winter visitors known collectively as wild swans. It is hard to tell the species apart as this relies on having a close view of the bill. Swans are one of the heaviest flying birds in the world and weigh 9–18kg (20–40lb). Swans generally mate for life, though if breeding problems occur pairs can separate. The earliest pens – quills – were made from swan feathers.

Mute swan
(Cygnus olor)

As its name suggests, the mute swan is a quiet bird, and can be seen on lakes and slow-moving rivers across the country. Populations suffered in the past as birds consumed lead weights (used by anglers) while hunting for insects, water plants and snails. The use of lead weights has been banned and numbers are now increasing. The bill of the mute swan is orange-topped and tipped with black. The largest bird in the British Isles it has an impressive 2.2m (7ft) wingspan. Mute swans can be aggressive and the male bird, or cob, in particular will be defensive of its nest and its young.

Bewick's swan
(Cygnus columbianus)

Named after the engraver Thomas Bewick, who was a specialist in bird and animal illustrations, Bewick's swan comes to the UK in mid-October, and departs in March. It is the smallest swan seen in the UK and looks rather goose-like. The beak is mostly black with a yellow patch at the top. It eats leaves and roots. Numbers are threatened by loss of habitat.

Above: The Bewick's swan breeds in Siberia and flies to Britain to spend the winter in a warmer climate. Around 8,000 birds arrive in the UK each year and are commonly seen in Lancashire, the Severn Estuary, Cambridgeshire and Gloucestershire.

Below: The whooper swan breeds in Iceland, passing the winter in northern England, East Anglia, Scotland and Northern Ireland. Birds depart again in mid-March.

Whooper swan
(Cygnus cygnus)

The wedge-shaped beak of the whooper swan is largely yellow with a black tip. Unlike the mute swan, it is loud and noisy and makes a hoarse, whooping sound. It has a wingspan of up to 1.5m (5ft). It spends much of its time in the water as its legs cannot bear the weight of its body for long. The whooper swan can be seen in winter in Ireland, Scotland and northern England.

Geese

Geese are sociable creatures and communicate with honks on land and in flight. They have large bodies, long necks and webbed feet and like ducks they fly in a V-shape, called a skein, to obtain a group aerodynamic lift. They have a chiefly vegetarian diet, and can be a nuisance in large groups, stripping grass bare and damaging crops. Like swans, they tend to mate for life, though pairs can part on occasion.

Greylag goose
(Anser anser)

The ancestor of all domestic geese, the greylag goose is a large grey bird, with a wingspan of around 1.5m (5ft). It is dappled with brown and white all over save for its white tail. Legs and feet are pink and the beak orange-pink with a pale tip. Once common, numbers have declined, in part due to hunting. The species was reintroduced, but has hybridised with the Canada goose *(Branta canadensis)*, the result being a feral flock that is semi-tame. Greylags can be seen on lakes and grassy fields in lowland areas all over the country. True wild greylags from Iceland visit in winter, gathering in northern Scotland.

Bean goose
(Anser fabalis)

Dappled all over in grey-brown and white, the head and wings of the bean goose are darker, the legs are orange and the beak is black with an orange stripe. Visitors from Scandinavia spend the winter in Norfolk and southern Scotland, but it is the rarest winter goose to visit.

Pink-footed goose
(Anser brachyrhynchus)

Only seen in winter in the UK, the pink-footed goose breeds in Spitsbergen, Greenland and Iceland, and visits in large numbers between October and April. Birds gather on large estuaries with surrounding farmland, most commonly on the east coast, where they feed during the day on grass, cereal and potatoes. This goose has a brown and grey body and a white rump. As its name suggests its legs and feet are pink and its beak has a pink stripe across it.

White-fronted goose
(Anser albifrons)

This goose has a small white patch right at the top of its beak and on its rump, while the rest of its body is a mass of intricate brown, grey, black and white bars. The head is brown, the feet are orange and the beak a dull orange. It eats grain, grass, clover and potatoes. White-fronted geese are commonly seen in the south east of England and the north west of Ireland.

Left: The numbers of pink-footed geese spending winter in the UK has risen tenfold in the last 50 years, a change attributed to shooting restrictions.

Below: The Romans were said to regard greylag geese as sacred after they warned them of an impending attack on Rome, after which Caesar decreed they could not be eaten.

Ducks

Twenty species of duck can be seen in the UK; 15 breed here, five are winter visitors. There are four distinct groups: sea ducks; surface-feeding ducks, which obtain their food from the surface of the water; diving ducks, which dive down into the water for food; and sawbills, a group of ducks with serrated beaks that allow them to grab hold of slippery fish. Ducks have solid bodies, long necks and pointed wings. They fly with necks stretched forwards, flapping their wings firmly; they only glide as they land. When trying to differentiate between species, look at the males, which have the most distinctive plumage, notably prior to breeding when plumage is used to attract females. After breeding, many males moult and have a duller eclipse plumage. Female ducks, particularly among the surface feeders, are hard to identify as they all have the same mottled-brown plumage. Ducks fly in a V-formation so that they each give their

Above: The male mallard is the duck that most people can confidently identify. The birds live in large flocks, but males without a mate can become a nuisance and will threaten both male and female birds.

Below: The Mandarin duck is not native to the UK – birds have escaped from collections and feral flocks can be seen in Wales, Scotland and Northern Ireland.

neighbour an up-current that requires less lifting power; flying in a straight line would not give an equal energy saving advantage to every bird. Those flying in the centre of the 'V' enjoy twice the advantage of those at the tips.

Mandarin duck
(Aix galericulata)

Belonging to a group known as the perching ducks, the Mandarin duck was introduced to the UK from China and has established itself in south, central and eastern England following escapes from captivity. The male has the most exotic plumage of all ducks, with an orange 'beard' and a down-turned, white eye patch; his breast is purple and his back green. The beak is red and the legs are yellow. Wings are mostly orange with black and white accents and are turned up like the sails of a boat.

Mallard
(Anas platyrhynchos)

The first of the surface-feeders, the mallard is both common and distinctive. The drake's head and neck is a dark forest green, it has a purple-brown breast, and a grey body. It has a white stripe around its neck and has a bright yellow broad and flat bill. Mallards eat seeds, berries, plants, acorns, shellfish and insects. They are very sociable and will gather in large flocks in winter.

Gadwall
(Anas strepera)

A grey speckled and barred duck with a white patch on its wing and a black patch on its rear end. The bill is black in the centre and orange-yellow at the sides. It can be found in reservoirs, lakes and gravel pits in the summer, but is more readily seen in winter on coastal wetlands when numbers are swelled by migrants. The male has a whistling call, the female quacks like the mallard. Gadwalls live principally on vegetation and seeds, supplemented by shellfish when breeding.

Pintail
(Anas acuta)

A little larger than the mallard, the pintail is a beautifully marked duck with a pointed tail. The head is a dark chocolate brown, the neck and breast are white, the back and beak grey, the tail black, the rump a dull yellow and the wings are striped with black, white

and brown. Its long neck enables it to feed from water up to 30cm (1ft) deep. Only 50 pairs actually breed in the UK – most pintails are wintering migrants.

Teal
(Anas crecca)

A small, short-necked duck, the teal is the smallest dabbling bird. It has a reddish brown head with green patches on the eyes. The chest is buff-coloured and spotted, the back grey and the tail yellow, edged with black. A flash of green can be seen under the wings in flight. It breeds inland on northern moorland, marshes and bogs over the summer, laying around ten cream eggs in nests close to water. The rest of the year it can be seen in estuaries, lakes, ponds and reservoirs all around the country.

Garganey
(Anas querquedula)

Most commonly seen in central and southern England, the garganey is an elusive bird, that likes to hide in tall vegetation. It visits in the summer to breed, and non-breeding birds can be seen on migration in October and March. The plumage, although not strikingly coloured, is ornate; the head and breast is brown and there is a loose white crescent shape over the eye. The rest of the plumage is patterned in shades of grey, although the forewings are blue and the underwings patterned in black and white.

Shoveler
(Anas clypeata)

This duck has a wide, distinctive, spoon-shaped bill, about 6.5cm (2½in) long, with fine projections along the edges for straining food. Males have a green head, chestnut belly and flanks, white breast and a stripe of pale blue feathers on the forewing. Shovelers favour marshes and wetlands in

Above: Teal are migratory and spend their winters in Africa and southern Asia, or less exotically in the south and west of the UK if they fly in from Siberia and the Baltic.

Below: The male pochard has a distinctive, dark red head and puffed-out cheeks like a child with mumps. Pochards feed at night, so can often be seen dozing by day.

central England and Ireland, moving further south for winter, but a large number of winter visitors then take the place of the breeding birds. As well as sieving water through its bill in search of vegetation, it also eats invertebrates and molluscs.

Pochard
(Aythya ferina)

The first of the diving ducks, the pochard is smaller than a mallard and has a red-brown head, a black breast and tail and a pale grey body. The bill is dark with a central grey band. It can be seen bobbing asleep in the water. Most birds are winter visitors that breed in central Russia and northern and eastern Europe. Native birds breed in eastern England, lowland Scotland and Northern Ireland. They feed mostly at night, eating aquatic plants, invertebrates, molluscs and small fish.

Tufted duck
(Aythya fuligula)

A common, medium-sized duck, the male has a black head, neck, back and breast, and white on its sides. It has a small black crest on the back of its head, the eyes are yellow and the grey beak is tipped with black. It is very common in lowland Scotland, England and Ireland, but is less common in Wales. In winter, numbers are swelled by visitors from Iceland and northern Europe. Tufted ducks eat selected vegetation, invertebrates and molluscs.

Smew
(Mergus albellus)

A member of the group of diving ducks known as sawbills, the smew is an uncommon bird. It is most likely to be seen in winter in the south east of England. The male is white with a dashing black crest, eye patch and back. The female has a brown head and grey body with black-and-white wings. The smew eats fish and insect larvae.

Goosander
(Mergus merganser)

Introduced to the UK in 1871, the goosander can be seen in Scotland, northern England and Wales, where it forms large flocks. The males have a dark, bottle-green head and neck, a white body with a central black panel, and a grey tail. The red beak is long, narrow and drooping. Females have a chestnut brown head and a chestnut mane.

Above: The female goosander has a distinctive rusty brown head. She will eat fish, favouring salmon and trout, which she clasps in her serrated-edged beak to the disgust of fishermen.

Left: The red-breasted merganser sports a splendid tufted crest like a sparse mohican. Red-breasted mergansers are happy in both salt and fresh water.

Opposite: The osprey can vary the angle of entry into the water according to whether it is catching fish that swim quickly near the surface, or slower, deeper swimming fish. As soon as it emerges from the water it turns the fish so that it hangs head down, which helps it to fly smoothly.

Red-breasted merganser
(Mergus serrator)

A distinctive duck with a tufted crest, male red-breasted mergansers have dark green heads, and a white stripe around the neck. The chest is speckled brown, the back black, and the underparts white. Wings are brown, white and black, and the long beak is orange. The female's head is a warm, chestnut brown. Resident birds move to the north west of Scotland, England and Wales in March to breed. They move south in July when breeding is over and congregate around the coast, where they are joined in October by winter visitors from northern Europe.

Ruddy duck
(Oxyura jamaicensis)

Another feral escapee from wildfowl collections, which was introduced to the UK from North America, the ruddy duck commonly hybridises with the white-headed duck. Male birds have a chestnut-brown body and a white face and neck with a black stripe running over the top of the head. The black and white tail is held upright and the bill is blue. Able to submerge itself without diving, the ruddy duck can be seen in southern Scotland, Anglesey, the west Midlands and northern England.

Osprey
(Pandion haliaetus)

The osprey is a rare bird of prey with a dazzling hunting technique: it hovers up to 40m (130ft) above the water then falls, feet first, into the water to grab the fish. Its neck, back, wings, tail and eye mask are all dark brown in colour, but its head, throat, undersides and legs are all white. It is around 60cm (2ft) in length and has a 1.8m (6ft) wingspan. Pairs usually mate for life. The birds migrate to Africa in August and September for the winter and return in April. The best place to see the osprey is on the shores of Bassenthwaite Lake in Cumbria and at special sites in Scotland.

Marsh harrier
(Circus aeruginosus)

The largest of all the harriers, the marsh harrier flies close to the ground, criss-crossing its territory hunting for prey – frogs, grass snakes, birds, from songbirds to ducks, waders and coots and small mammals. Its body is streaked with brown, the wings and the long, narrow, rounded tail is grey, as are the wings, though the finger-like feather tips are black and are held in a distinctive narrow V-shape in flight. Head colour can vary from dull yellow to a creamy yellow. Numbers declined seriously in the 19th and 20th centuries due to persecution, pollution and loss of habitat, but the bird is now protected in the UK and numbers have increased slightly.

Crakes, rails and waders

Crakes and rails are waterside birds with long, partially webbed toes that allow them to move on water-logged ground. They have little flight power and the tendency to run, rather than fly, from danger. Waders inhabit wetlands and estuaries, often only in winter.

Water rail
(Rallus aquaticus)

A shy bird, the water rail is rarely seen but it can be heard making the most extraordinary noise, rather like a squealing pig, as it walks through the reeds. It is smaller and slimmer than the moorhen, has a grey face and breast, a dappled, warm-brown back, brown flanks barred with white, and a long, pointed, curved, orange and black beak. The tail is an upward-curving tuft of brown, black and white plumage. The water rail is most likely to be seen in marshland on the east and south coasts; numbers increase in winter when birds fly in from Europe.

Above: When alarmed, the water rail will freeze in position. It can be seen in marshland on the east and south coast. Numbers increase in winter when birds fly in from Europe.

Right: When frightened, the moorhen will sink into the water until just its beak is left above. It eats aquatic plants, grasses, seeds, worms and snails, snatching up food as it swims along.

Coot
(Fulica atra)

A common and familiar water bird that scurries on thin legs, the coot is black all over, and has a white bill and a white shield on its face. Its feet are huge and look like they belong to another bird altogether. When taking off it appears to run noisily over the water. It eats vegetation, snails and insect larvae. It can be seen rivers, lakes and reservoirs all around the country; in hard

winters when freshwater is frozen it may move to the coast until conditions improve.

Moorhen
(Gallinula chloropus)

Smaller than the coot, the moorhen appears to be black all over from the distance, but seen close up its back and wings are a dark chocolate brown, while its head and undersides are dark grey and its rump white. It has a distinctive red flash on the forehead and a red beak, tipped with yellow. It is seen on and near shallow water across the UK in lowland areas and is therefore less common in Scotland.

Common sandpiper
(Actitis hypoleucos)

The common sandpiper is a wading bird with a speckled brown cap, back, wings and tail, buff legs and white face and undersides. It wears a brown eye mask and grubs around

Snipe

The members of this group of waders fly in an aerial zigzag, low across the ground and are beautifully camouflaged to blend in with the reeds. Their hunters, tagged 'snipers', had to be very adept to shoot them – with the term later being adopted by the army and passing into general usage. Snipes undertake spectacular aeronautical displays when breeding, indulging in dramatic dives to impress females.

Common snipe
(Gallinago gallinago)

This bird can be seen wading through soft mud, hunting for insects and plant material. The body is mottled in brown tones with dark streaks on the chest and pale underparts. The bill is yellow, long and pointed. Snipe breed on moorlands and wet grassland, and spend the winter on wetlands; their numbers are swelled in Devon and Cornwall by migratory birds. The snipe population has declined, possibly because of the drainage of wetlands.

Jack snipe
(Lymnocryptes minimus)

A winter visitor, arriving in September and October and leaving in February, the jack snipe can be found in wetlands, fens and marshes or on riverbanks. Similar to the common snipe, it is smaller and has a shorter beak. It creeps through the undergrowth and only flies into the air when disturbed.

in the mud and in shallow water with its long beak hunting for invertebrates. It migrates to Africa in the winter and can be seen en route across the country. A few birds pass the winter on the south coast.

Green sandpiper
(Tringa ochropus)

Rounder and plumper than the common sandpiper, the green sandpiper's cap, back, wings and tail are black, speckled with grey, and the undersides are white. It is quite unusual and is only seen near freshwater in southern England and south-west Ireland during winter, or in migration between northern Europe and Africa.

Wood sandpiper
(Tringa glareola)

Also seen on migration, the wood sandpiper looks much like the common and green sandpiper, but has white eyebrows and longer yellow legs.

Above: The common sandpiper breeds alongside rivers, lakes, lochs in Scotland, Ireland, Wales and the north of England, laying four blotchy green eggs in a nest close to water.

Below: The common snipe shares its parental duties equally: both male and female birds care for half of the chicks for two weeks until they learn to fly.

Kingfisher
(Alcedo atthis)

If you catch a flash of blue and orange beside slow-moving water you have been lucky enough to see a kingfisher. The plumage on its head and back is green-blue, while the undersides, feet and cheeks are a rusty orange. It has a white stripe on each side of its throat. The bill is long, pointed and sharp; males have a black beak while the lower part of the female's beak is orange. The kingfisher is able to catch aquatic insects and fish that can measure as much as half of its body length. The kingfisher population was affected badly by the severe winter of 1963 but numbers have since slowly recovered; it is also susceptible to pollution and changes to habitat.

Sand martin
(Riparia riparia)

The head, back, wings and forked tail of the sand martin are dark brown, and the chest white. In flight its resemblance to its relative the swallow can be clearly seen. It flies very fast over water catching insects. Sand martins can be seen between March and October. They are sociable birds and nest in colonies.

Grey wagtail
(Motacilla cinerea)

The grey wagtail has the longest tail of the wagtails seen in the UK – around 10cm (4in) long. The head and back are slate grey, but the breast and underparts are bright yellow, right down to the start of the tail. The tail and wings are black and white, the throat is black, and there are two white stripes on the face. Grey wagtails can be found near fast-flowing rivers all over the UK and Ireland, though they are unusual in the north west.

Dipper
(Cinclus cinclus)

It is wonderful to watch a dipper hunting for food. Although they are land birds, they will walk into the water or dive off stones, using their wings to swim under water, looking for insect larvae and invertebrates. The adult has a chocolate-brown head and belly, a white breast and a black back. It is a very busy bird and will bob about hunting for food and whizz through the air. It is most commonly seen in the north and west along fast-flowing rivers and streams.

Grasshopper warbler
(Locustella naevia)

This warbler has the uncanny knack of apparently being able to throw its voice, for it never seems to be where its sound is coming from. Its brown colouring helps to provide camouflage; it creeps quietly through the undergrowth close to water where it hunts for insects. The grasshopper warbler can be found in small numbers all over the UK near to reed beds and gravel pits between mid-April and September. It sings at dawn and dusk and sometimes all through the night.

Cetti's warbler
(Cettia cetti)

A recent arrival from the Mediterranean, cetti's warbler is believed to have nested in the UK for the first time in 1973, and remains here throughout the year in the extreme south and east. It has a pale grey face and breast with a brown hood, back, wings and tail and a dark stripe over its eye.

Above: The grey wagtail nests on banks or in walls and, as its name suggests, it constantly wags its tail. The species suffers badly in harsh winters.

Left: The grasshopper warbler passes the winter south of the Sahara in West Africa, returning to the UK in mid-April. The bird has high conservation priority yet numbers are still declining rapidly.

Sedge warbler
(Acrocephalus schoenobaenus)

A plump little bird, the sedge warbler has a brown and black-streaked back, a cream throat, breast and belly and a white flash above the eye. It passes the winter in Africa and comes to the UK to breed.

Reed warbler
(Acrocephalus scirpaceus)

A small bird, brown above and buff below. It passes the summer in reed beds in central and southern England and Wales and can be seen, if you're lucky, hiding among the reeds from mid-April to September, hunting for insects and berries. It lays four blotchy white eggs.

Bearded tit
(Panurus biarmicus)

The bearded tit has a dove-grey face and chest and a dark orange back, tail and sides. The wings are orange, black and white striped. The male's most distinctive feature is a flamboyant black handlebar moustache. It can be seen darting around reed beds hunting for insects and seeds. Highly localised, you may be lucky enough to see one in Suffolk, East Anglia or Norfolk. Numbers are variable as the bearded tit is vulnerable to cold weather.

Reed bunting
(Emberiza schoeniclus)

The reed bunting looks rather like a sparrow with a black hood thrown over its head, a black bib on its chest and a white wrap encircling its throat. Traditionally its home is marshy wetlands where males can be found perched on top of reeds singing loudly to attract a mate, but it is beginning to colonise town gardens. Reed buntings eat seeds and insects. Numbers have seriously declined in recent years.

Right: The sedge warbler is an enthusiastic song bird, though his tune is very varied and can be both sweet and grating – he is known occasionally to impersonate the song of other birds.

Below: Only the male bearded tit sports a moustache – he also has a longer tail than the female; research has shown that females are attracted to males with the longest tails.

Mammals

Water shrew
(Neomys fodiens)

The water shrew favours clear, slow-moving streams where it makes a burrow with a tiny entrance that helps force water out of its fur as it squeezes its way through. It dives for fish, tadpoles, worms and frogs and like other shrews has toxic saliva which helps to quieten its prey. It has a pointed nose, small ears and eyes and dense, velvety black fur, tipped with white around the ears and eyes. The teeth are alarmingly tipped with red. Its predators are owls, foxes, large fish such as pike, and kestrels.

Water vole
(Arvicola terrestris)

The water vole, immortalised as 'Ratty' by Kenneth Graham in *The Wind in the Willows* (1908), is in decline, in part due to the introduction of American mink, which is their main predator, and in part through loss of habitat. They are good swimmers and plop audibly into the water from the bank. Do not confuse them with brown rats,

Above: The water shrew is preyed on by kestrels, owls, foxes and large fish such as pike. It is not a long-lived species; adults die after breeding at around 18 months of age.

Below: The water vole resembles a small rat, with a fat body, a round, flat face and a long, fur-covered tail. These voles make grass-lined burrows on the river bank in which they produce up to five litters of six young per year.

Otter

Following a significant decline in the UK population between the 1950s and 1970s, due to the pollution of watercourses, the otter (*Lutra lutra*) practically disappeared from central and south-east England. Populations remain in Wales, south-west England and Scotland. Signs indicate that the decline has now halted. Otters live on the banks of freshwater rivers and lakes, building a burrow – holt – usually with an underwater entrance, where they hide by day. They have a long, streamlined body covered with short brown under fur and an outer layer of long guard fur; this combination traps air, helping to keep them warm and dry under water. However, the coat alone is not sufficient; they have a high metabolic rate and must eat 15 per cent of their body weight per day to survive. Their limbs are short and their paws are webbed, the tail is long and muscular and acts like a rudder under the water. They eat eels, fish, shellfish, frogs, insects, small birds and mammals.

Otter

which also often live on the riverbank; distinguishing characteristics are silky fur, a blunt nose and small hidden ears, where rats have long, pink hairless tails, big ears, a pointed nose and grey-brown fur.

Mink
(Mustela vison)

The mink is not a native, but has escaped into the wild from fur farms. It is a semi-aquatic predator, which causes considerable damage in the UK, as it has no natural predators itself, and is a threat to native species such as the water vole. It will eat fish, eels, shellfish, small mammals and the eggs of waterside birds. It looks much like a ferret and has a long, dark brown body covered in super soft, slightly shaggy brown fur. The eyes are beady, the ears small and the tail short.

Daubenton's bat
(Myotis daubentoni)

Daubenton's bat is small, around 9cm (3½in) in length, with a wingspan of 24cm (9½in). It

has a pink face, dark grey-brown fur on its back and silvery grey undersides. Daubenton's bat hunts from twilight over water, preferring tree-lined watercourses, taking small aquatic insects such as midges, mosquito and mayflies. During the summer it roosts in stonework and hollow trees close to water. It hibernates between September and April, sometimes in large numbers, in caves, tunnels and cellars.

Chinese water deer
(Hydropotes inermis)

The Chinese water deer is the only deer found in the UK that does not have antlers. Instead, males have tusks, which protrude downwards from their jaw, somewhat like those of a walrus. It is small, measuring just

Above: The diminutive Chinese water deer commonly produces two to three young after a six or seven month gestation period, but have been known to give birth to as many as seven fawns at one time.

Left: Daubenton's bat has large furry feet, which it uses to grasp prey from the top of the water, a practice known as trawling, and then consumes the prey while in flight.

48cm (19in) at the shoulder, and is a red-brown in summer and a dark grey-brown in winter. The eyes and nose are black and the ears are large and round. The deer was introduced from China to parkland, but escapees and releases have resulted in wild herds in Bedfordshire, the Cambridgeshire fens and the Norfolk Broads. It can be heard making a distinctive barking noise.

Reptiles and amphibians

Grass snake
(Natrix natrix)

The grass snake, Britain's largest snake, can grow to lengths of 1.2m (4ft) and is found in England and Wales, but it is absent from Ireland and much of Scotland. It is brown or green in colour, and has two yellow or orange stripes at the back of the head, and small black dashes along its sides. The undersides are somewhat paler. It lives close to water and is a strong swimmer. It feeds almost entirely on amphibians, notably frogs, newts and toads, though it will also take fish, small mammals and eggs. It hibernates in leaf litter, holes in the ground or under logs, emerging in April and May. Grass snakes have no venom, however they will emit a vile-smelling substance from their anal glands to deter predators.

Above: The female grass snake lays around 30 white eggs in piles of rotting vegetation and compost, which hatch after ten weeks. The young are independent at birth and measure around 18cm (7in).

Right: Young newts, known as eft, leave the water when their legs and lungs have developed and do not return until fully mature and ready to breed two or three years later. Their sideways gait coined the expression 'drunk as a newt'.

Newts

Three species of newt occur in the UK. Their skin is smooth and the male is more highly coloured than the female. Two of the three species spend most of their time on land, returning to the water to breed in spring. This is the time of year when it is easiest to tell the differences between the sexes, as the males develop a crest along their back and tail, and they become more brightly coloured. Newts pass their time in damp places, feeding at night, on land. On land they will eat slugs, worms and insects, in the water they will consume water snails, insect larvae, shrimps and tadpoles. Newts can regenerate lost limbs and eyeballs. They hibernate in winter under stones or wood.

Common newt
(Triturus vulgaris)

Also known as the smooth newt, this species is the most widespread. It is brown to dull green in colour and speckled with dark spots and grows to around 10cm (4in) in length. Its undersides are shaded from yellow to pink with a central red belly stripe that is spotted with black.

Palmate newt
(Triturus helveticus)

Smaller than the common newt, reaching just 7.5cm (3in) in length, the palmate newt favours the acid soils the common newt dislikes, and is found on mountains and moorland. It is very similar in appearance to the common newt, but the male develops a flat crest along its back and black webbed back feet in spring. The undersides are coloured from white to orange.

Great crested newt
(Triturus cristatus)

Larger than its relatives, measuring an impressive 16cm (6¼in) in length, the great crested newt is able to stay in water all year round, unlike the common and palmate newts. Apart from its size, the great crested newt can be identified by its jagged crest and warty skin, which emits a distasteful sticky fluid designed to discourage would-be predators. Its back is brown and undersides yellow to orange; both are covered in black spots. The tail has a silver stripe running along its side. This is a protected species under the Wildlife and Countryside Act and you are not allowed to handle it without a licence.

Common frog
(Rana temporaria)

The UK's only native frog, the common frog has smooth skin, the colour of which is variable as it slowly changes hue to correspond with its surroundings. It can therefore be seen with a yellow, green, brown or orange back. This is decorated with irregular black spots and blotches, there is a distinct black mask over the eyes and ears. Undersides are white or yellow. It measures around 10cm (4in) in length, the female being slightly larger than the male. A frog's powerful legs enable it to leap a distance of 45cm (18in) in a single hop.

Marsh frog
(Rana ridibunda)

Introduced to the UK in 1935 via a garden pond near Romney Marsh, the marsh frog

Above: The eggs of the common frog are fertilised by the male as the female lays them in batches of around 4,000 at a time. The eggs sink initially, but rise as their protective coating swell; they hatch into tadpoles around the end of May.

Below: The numbers of the great crested newt have declined in recent years due to the destruction and pollution of their habitats through development and land drainage.

has since spread across the county and into neighbouring Sussex. It is light or dark brown with irregular black spots on its green-tinged back. It is larger than the common frog with females reaching lengths of 13cm (5in).

Fish

Just under 40 species of freshwater fish are native to the UK and, anglers aside, we generally know less about them than we do about the plants, birds, mammals and insects that are found on and around our rivers and waterways. This is a curious oversight as fish are integral to the overall health of a stretch of water, providing a vital source of food for a wide variety of creatures, and helping to keep insect populations under control. Fish are both relatively long-lived and mobile – but they keep their lives secret and we have to work hard to observe them. Anglers are the experts and considerate anglers make an important contribution toward the preservation of waterways and are welcome at a range of National Trust sites. The Trust promotes the development of wild fish stocks without resorting to artificial stocking, and the removal of coarse fish and grayling from National Trust rivers is discouraged.

Above: The European eel is an endangered species; the numbers of young (glass eels) entering rivers all over Europe dropped to ten per cent of former levels 20 years ago, and today stands at just one per cent, though no single cause has yet been identified.

Below: The pike has a justifiably mean reputation and can grow to impressive lengths and weights over its life.

European eel
(Anguilla anguilla)

The eel is a thin, brown, snake-like fish. Eels have pointed heads, and the lower jaw extends beyond the upper jaw, containing an impressive number of sharp teeth. All eels spawn in the Sargasso Sea, and larvae migrate towards northern Europe over a three-year period, where they enter estuaries proceeding upstream into freshwater, where they spend most of their lives. In freshwater the belly becomes yellow. Eels can live out of the water for short periods and can move over wet ground, grass or sand. They can reach lengths of 1.5m (5ft), but most eels are smaller than this, and feed off crustaceans, worms, fish, frogs and invertebrates, and usefully eat decaying meat.

Pike
(Esox lucius)

The pike has a long head and a green-brown body that is spotted and striped with pale gold for camouflage. The mouth curves slightly upward, and the teeth curve backwards to prevent prey from escaping.

As youngsters they eat larvae and fish fry, but when mature their diet exclusively comprises fish, although the remains of birds and mammals have been found in the stomachs of large fish. They are cannibalistic and will eat young pike and have been known to bite swimmers. Pike can live for 25 years, reaching 1m (3¼ft) in length, and can weigh in at around 14kg (31lb).

Salmon
(Salmo salar)
The salmon is an extraordinary fish; although much of its life is spent at sea, it makes a long annual journey upstream in freshwater, sometimes travelling thousands of miles to return to its birthplace to spawn. Initially salmon have dark blotches along their sides, but as they mature they turn silver. In the sea, salmon is a silvery green colour but in freshwater it becomes green or brown and is flecked with red or orange spots. It can grow as long as 1.5m (5ft) in length. Salmon is a valuable food source that is now farmed extensively, but wild salmon can still be found in rivers in Scotland, Wales, Northern Ireland and south-west England.

Brown trout
(Salmo trutta)
The trout is a member of the salmon family. It is a long, slim, green to brown fish, dotted

Above: The brown trout hunts for food both day and night, consuming small fish, invertebrates, larvae and frogs. Like salmon it migrates from lakes into rivers and streams to spawn.

Right: The common carp lays many thousands of eggs. Incubation is related to water temperature and constant temperatures are required over a one to two week period to spawn successfully.

with orange spots, with a silvery or white belly. Having been a popular fish exploited by man for centuries, the distribution of the brown trout has been much affected by the introduction of bred fish. It is now found in any well-oxygenated clean water in rivers and gravel-bottomed lakes across the UK, and favours sites that offer plenty of cover, such as submerged banks or overhanging vegetation. It can grow to reach 9kg (20lb) in weight, but a 1kg (2lb) fish is more common.

Grayling
(Thymallus thymallus)
The grayling is related to both salmon and trout. It is a slender fish with a silvery green back dotted with small bluish spots and pale

undersides. Its distinguishing feature is a long, high, pinkish dorsal fin on its back. This fish favours clean, fast, deep running water with rocky or gravel floors. Grayling consume invertebrates, notably insect larvae or any drowning insect. The flesh is reputed to be thyme-scented – hence the Latin name. It is found in rivers across the UK.

Common carp
(Cyprinus carpio)
Carp can live for up to 40 years in captivity, but 15 years in the wild is more realistic. It resembles the goldfish (to which it is related) in shape, but its colour varies from greenish brown to silver. The mouth has four barbels – two whiskers on each side. Most fish are around 25cm (10in) long but can reach 1m (3¼ft). The carp is not native to the UK, but is believed to have been introduced by the Romans. Carp live in silty ponds and lakes, often devoid of vegetation, in groups of at least six. They eat weed, crustaceans and insects. Although popular with anglers, carp are unpopular with conservationists as, unless in low numbers, they cause major ecological damage.

Tench
(Tinca tinca)

The tench favours slow-moving water with a clay or silt bottom, and can survive in poorly oxygenated water in conditions that few other fish can tolerate. Here it will hunt for invertebrates and algae, rooting around the muddy floor for delicacies at night. It is a solid fish that grows rapidly and can reach 70cm (27½in) in length. It is dark in colour ranging from green to brown; the belly is sometimes golden and its small eyes are orange. It has two barbels on each side of its mouth.

Gudgeon
(Gobio gobio)

The gudgeon is found in shoals in still water where it hunts for food, fish eggs and small invertebrates on the floor. Its back is green to brown while its sides are yellowish silver, decorated with 6–12 dark spots. A pair of fleshy barbels hangs down from each side of the mouth. It grows on average to around 10–12cm (4–5in) but larger fish are found.

Roach
(Rutilus rutilus)

A plentiful fish, roach are commonly found in rivers and lakes all across the UK, except in northern Scotland. The roach is a small, streamlined fish, commonly reaching 35cm (14in) in length. Generally silver in colour, it has a dark blue back and orange-red fins on its belly. The iris of the eye is red. Roach feed on algae, larvae, worms and drowning insects. They can easily be confused with rudd with which they often interbreed.

Rudd
(Scardinius erythrophthalmus)

Rudd are very similar to roach, but can be differentiated from it in three ways: mouths are turned upwards; the iris of the eye is yellow or orange; and the dorsal fin is set further back – though this last feature is only helpful if you really know your fish. Rudd lives in still water and is found in canals, lakes, ponds, gravel pits and slow rivers, where it lives on aquatic plants, insect larvae and crustaceans.

Dace
(Leuciscus leuciscus)

The dace is found in clean, fast-flowing water across England. It is a small fish, with a blue-green head and back, and silver sides. It lives near the surface of the water in summer and swims in large shoals. Dace consume invertebrates and small crustaceans.

Minnow
(Phoxinus phoxinus)

The minnow is a small fish that haunts fast-flowing freshwater and well-oxygenated ponds and lakes. It grows to around 8–10cm

Above: The minnow is a common British freshwater fish. Females can lay up to around 1000 eggs at a time and these hatch out after just six to ten days.

Left: The largest rudd to be caught in UK waters according to official records weighed 2.09kg (4lb 10oz) and was caught in 2001 in Northern Ireland.

Three-spined stickleback
(Gasterosteus aculeatus)

One of the best-known fish in the UK, the stickleback swims in shoals in ponds, lakes, rivers and even ditches, and is readily caught in nets. It is silvery-blue or green in colour with pale undersides, though the throat and belly of the male fish is orange or red when spawning. It is a small fish, measuring just 6–10cm (2½–4in). On its back, in front of the dorsal fin, are two or three distinct spines. The stickleback feeds on tiny fish and fish eggs, but is in turn a food source for a wide variety of wildlife such as perch, pike, otters and kingfishers.

Bullhead
(Cottus gobio)

The bullhead favours clean running water with stony or gravel beds, but it is also found in lakes and streams across most of the UK. It is hard to spot for it is an expert at concealing itself among the rocks and weed. It has a mottled greenish-brown body and a gloriously ugly, flattened, lugubrious face with down-turned mouth and prominent eyes. It can reach a little over 15cm (6in) in length. Males turn black when spawning.

(3–4in) in length, and is olive green in colour, with a dark line along its sides. During the breeding season males have golden sides and a red belly. Minnows are gregarious fish that live in large shoals. They are an important food source for waterside birds, such as the heron and kingfisher, as well as for larger fish.

Above: The stone loach makes a nest from weed or stones in which around 10,000 eggs are laid and guarded by the male.

Below: Perch spawn in April and May, laying many thousands of eggs in long strings around water plants.

Stone loach
(Nemacheilus barbatulus)

True to its name the stone loach conceals itself under stones where it feeds on insect larvae and pupae at night. It is brown or grey-green in colour with dark blotches; the belly is pale. There are six barbels around the mouth, with the ones at the corners being the longest. It reaches an average length of around 10cm (4in). It is found in clean rivers and favours stone or gravel bottoms.

Perch
(Perca fluviatilis)

The perch is a large, common fish, immediately familiar to anglers, which can reach 30cm (12in) in length. Its base colour is a silvery green, the belly is yellow and it is hooped with broad dark stripes. It carries two large dorsal fins, the first being spiny with a distinctive spot at the rear and the second one soft. The lower fins are a distinctive orange-red. It feeds on crustaceans when small, moving on to insect larvae and small fish as it increases in size. Young fish stay in shoals and hunt as a group, whereas older fish prefer a more solitary existence.

Invertebrates

Mayfly
(Ephemera danica)

Mayflies are aquatic insects, which like the dragonfly, spend the bulk of their lives in an immature or nymph stage. Buried in the silt and sand on the bottom of rivers and lakes, they undergo several moults, or instars. When fully grown they come out of the water and emerge from their nymphal skin before moulting once again into the adult. The primary function of this final stage is reproduction. This species has a 4cm (1½in) wingspan and long antennae emerging from the head. The body is semi-translucent and has a long tail curling out from the rear; the wings are a beautiful silvery patchwork of veins and spots. The mayfly is an important food source for fish at all stages of its development.

Pond skater
(Gerris lacustris)

A predatory creature, the hairs on the legs and body of the pond skater sense vibrations on the water, enabling it to detect dying or struggling insects trapped in the water. They also allow it to walk on water, with a rowing motion, using surface tension. It has thin, brownish grey body and a small head with large eyes. Eggs are laid on vegetation, the pond skater then moves through four nymph stages from hatching to maturity in just two or three weeks, and goes on to produce four to six broods per year. The last brood will hibernate overwinter before reaching sexual maturity the following spring.

Water boatman
(Notonecta glauca)

The water boatman is one of the most recognisable and commonly known aquatic insects. It has a long, flat, green or brown body that measures around 1.5cm (⅜in) and the eyes are bright red. It has four legs; the long thin back legs are used much like oars to move through the water – it swims upside-down. It rests on the surface of the water using its legs to detect vibrations and will dive to catch tadpoles, insect larvae and fish fry.

Water scorpion
(Nepa cinerea)

The water scorpion is a brown insect with three pairs of legs and two pairs of wings. It creeps around slowly, using its front legs like pincers (hence the common name), to catch prey such as tadpoles, insects and small fish. The water scorpion lurks, head down, often just under the surface, looking much like a leaf. It uses its tail, which is actually a breathing tube, to access oxygen. It will emerge at intervals to top up its air supply.

Whirligig beetle
(Gyrinus substriatus)

This species clusters together on the surface of the water to avoid predators and whirls around – hence its common name. It has remarkable divided eyes that allow it

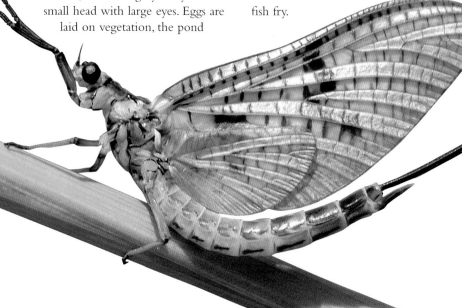

Above: Water boatmen can deliver a nasty nip and have toxic saliva, which they use to catch tadpoles and fish fry, though some species live off algae and aquatic plants.

Left: Masses of mayfly can be seen dancing over the water on early summer evenings. Eggs are dropped into the surface of the water by females – some dip in or even submerge themselves to lay.

to see both above and below the water at the same time. It is black in colour with six legs. It consumes organisms on the water surface and usefully enjoys mosquito larvae.

Great diving beetle
(Dytiscus marginalis)

A mighty creature – the yellow-brown larvae alone measure around 5cm (2in) in length and take a year to develop. The adult beetle is 3.5cm (1½in) long. It is dark brown to black in colour with a yellow border around the wing cases and has an almond-shaped body. Both adult and larvae are aggressively carnivorous. The male has smooth wing cases, while the female's are grooved. Both adults and larvae will snack on aquatic insects, small fish and tadpoles, and favour lakes and ponds with plenty of vegetation.

Swallowtail butterfly
(Papilio machaon)

The swallowtail is the largest and one of our most beautiful native butterflies. It can reach 10cm (4in) in length. It is yellow with black markings, has a long black tail at the rear, and false red and blue 'eyes' on the hindwings. The swallowtail favours wetlands, where milk parsley thrives, but is now only found in the Norfolk Broads after so much of its habitat was lost to land drainage. It is protected under the Wildlife and Countryside Act.

Above: The great diving beetle can create air bubbles in their abdomen which provide a supply of air when underwater.

Left: The caterpillar of the swallowtail butterfly starts black and white but matures to pale green, ringed with black stripes and orange dashes. It has a fancy pair of retractable horns, which emit a smell like overripe pineapple.

Dragonflies and damselflies

Dragonflies are the fastest and largest insects in the world and there are over 6,000 species worldwide. The insect order dragonflies (Odonata) has three sub orders, one of which is dragonflies (Anisoptera) and one is damselflies (Zygoptera), the third order containing dragonflies is found only in Nepal and China.

There are numerous varieties of both dragonfly and damselfly but there are distinct differences between them. The first clue is size: in general dragonflies are larger than damselflies. However, comparisons are often impossible to make, and so the wings provide a second clue. The hindwing of a dragonfly is wider at the base and has a larger surface area than the forewing – Anisoptera means 'unequal wings' and Zygoptera means 'equal wings'. This is best seen when the dragonfly is still with its wings stretched out. In contrast the fore- and hindwings of a damselfly are almost identical in size, the insect holding them together above the body when at rest. The eyes of a dragonfly are large, and occupy much of the face, whereas those of the damselfly are set apart. In addition damselflies fly more slowly and quietly than dragonflies.

The larvae are very different too: damselflies have long 'tails' while dragonflies have short, stubby protuberances. The life cycle is truly amazing: eggs are laid on the stalk of aquatic plants, and sometimes the female dips into, or even under, the water to lay. The males

Above: An emperor dragonfly emerges from its moult. Its full colour will take a few days to develop. Some species of dragonflies change colour as they age; mature females can take on the colouring of a male.

provide a lifeline if required and guard the female carefully during this process. When the eggs hatch the larvae live in the water, hunting for other insect larvae, tadpoles and fish fry. This stage can last from a couple of months to five years depending on the size of the species, for unlike the butterfly, dragonflies and damselflies do not build a cocoon in which to transform themselves but undergo 9–16 instars, or moults. When fully grown they move out of the water, first thing in the morning, to moult for the last time. They break out of the larval case and emerge after several hours as a fully grown nymph. Colouring is quite pale initially but darkens within a few days.

Adult dragonflies and damselflies can survive anything from a few weeks to four months, depending on the species. They hunt for midges, mosquitoes and small flies and can fly at around the same speed as birds.

Emperor dragonfly
(Anax imperator)

The largest and most colourful of the UK dragonflies, the wingspan and body length of the emperor dragonfly can be as much as 10cm (4in). The head and thorax is emerald green. Males have a turquoise-blue abdomen, while females have an emerald-green abdomen. Both sexes have a black stripe along the back. The emperor dragonfly can be seen between May and October and is most common in the south east of England.

Common hawker dragonfly
(Aeshna juncea)

This fast-flying species is common throughout the UK. It is about 7cm (2¾in) long, with blue eyes and blue markings on its abdomen, and narrow yellow lines across its thorax. It can be seen in flight from June to October.

Above: Common blue damselflies join together when mating to make a 'wheel' shape and fly together. The male will stay attached to the female while she lays her eggs.

Brown hawker dragonfly
(Aeshna grandis)

The brown hawker dragonfly is a common species. As the name indicates, the body is brown, and the wings are amber and patterned with a network of fine brown veins. This species measures 7.4cm (3in) in length, and flies from July to September.

Common darter
(Sympetrum striolatum)

This small dragonfly is one of commonest species, frequently seen resting on the ground. It has a narrow body measuring 3.6cm (1½in), and the male has a deep red abdomen; the female's abdomen is orange-brown. Common darters fly from June to early November.

Blue-tailed damselfly
(Ischnura elegans)

This common and widespread damselfly has a mainly black body with the eighth segment of the abdomen a distinctive sky blue. It has a body length of 3.3cm (1¼in) and flies from May to August.

Common blue damselfly
(Enallagma cyathigerum)

The common blue damselfly has a wingspan of around 4cm (1½in) and a slightly smaller body length. The abdomen is bright blue. It can be seen on sunny days between April and August.

Large red damselfly
(Pyrrhosoma nymphula)

The large red damselfly has a distinctive orange-red body with brown stripes on the thorax and black legs. It has a 5cm (2in) wingspan and a body length of 3cm (1¼in) and can be seen between April and August.

Left: An emperor dragonfly displays the complex Anisoptera wing structure which consists of a network of variously sized hollow veins linked by a membrane. The wings appear flat, but actually have a three dimensional relief which allows them to hover and fly in many directions.

insects as large as dragonflies and has been known to take very small fish and tadpoles. It is dark in colour with a distinctive yellow or cream stripe on each side of its body. Its favoured habitat is swampy areas in southern heathlands.

Great pond snail
(Lymnaea stagnalis)

Found in slow-moving, stagnant or brackish water, the great pond snail feeds on rotting organic matter and algae. It floats upside down on surface water to take in air, and can also absorb oxygen from the water, which means the snail can stay under water for several months at a time. It buries itself in soft mud and seals up its shell before hibernating for the winter. The shell is a light brownish grey and can grow to 5cm (2in) in length.

Above: The water spider lays its eggs under water in its bell-shaped retreat where the eggs hatch. While young, the spiders live in discarded snail shells, which they fill with air.

Below: The great pond snail lays eggs cocooned in long strings off jelly that are attached to water plants or stones.

Water spider
(Argyroneta aquatica)

The water spider lives under the water, where it builds itself a domed web, which it fills with air collected from hairs on its abdomen. It remains here by day, venturing out at night to catch prey – invertebrates and baby fish – that it takes back to its web. The water spider sheds its skin regularly on dry land, thus increasing its size. On land the spider is dark grey but in the water it resembles a blob of silver moving through the water.

Swamp spider
(Dolomedes fimbriatus)

The largest British spider, the body of the swamp spider alone can measure 2.5cm (1in). It is semi-aquatic and either sits at the edge of the water, or floats on vegetation on the surface of the water, dabbling its front legs to detect vibrations from insects and larvae. When it senses prey it runs across the surface of the water to catch it. It can catch

disease, known as crayfish plague. The white-clawed crayfish is olive brown in colour and the claws have paler undersides. By day it conceals itself among stones and rocks, emerging only at night to hunt for aquatic invertebrates and tadpoles, it also eats vegetable matter.

Freshwater shrimp
(Gammarus pulex)
The freshwater shrimp is a shrimp-like crustacean and is a different creature to the saltwater shrimp. It typically measures in at a little over 1cm (½in) in length, though males can grow larger, and has a curved yellow-brown body. It is found in ponds and streams where it consumes decaying organic matter and is eaten by fishes and water insects.

Ramshorn snail
(Planorbis planorbis)
Less commonly seen than the great pond snail, the ramshorn can be found in ponds, lakes and slow-moving water. Its flattened, brown to black shell is shaped like a coil of rope or a ram's horn and grows to 2.5cm (1in) in diameter. The snail inside may be brown or red. This species feeds on algae from rocks and water plants.

White-clawed crayfish
(Austropotamobius pallipes)
Crayfish are the largest freshwater crustaceans in the UK and resemble small lobster. The white-clawed crayfish, our native species, is found only in clean running water up to 1m (3¼ft) deep in England, eastern Wales and Northern Ireland. It is threatened by the non-native American signal crayfish that was introduced for farming purposes in the 1970s and escaped into the wild. Not only does this species compete effectively against native crayfish, it also carries a fungal

Above: The freshwater shrimp can only survive in very clean, unpolluted water where it helps maintain a pristine habitat.

Right: The native white-clawed crayfish is threatened; numbers have diminished alarmingly through loss of habitat, pollution and disease carried by the non-native species now breeding in the wild.

Part Two
Places to Visit

South West England

The Lizard Peninsula

The Lizard Peninsula has some of the most beautiful scenery in the UK and is an Area of Outstanding Natural Beauty (AONB). The Peninsula is a rugged outcrop of rock with sea on two sides and the Helford River to the north. Lizard Point marks the most southerly tip of the UK. The Lizard has an extraordinarily mild climate, which has led to the growth of some sub-tropical vegetation. It is regarded as being an area of international botanical importance, and is home to 15 of the UK's rarest plants, including some that occur only in this area. The coast is dotted with tiny fishing villages tucked into small coves that are accessible by narrow roads that dip between tall banks of wild flowers; primroses can be seen before Christmas, daffodils often appear in January, and tree ferns and palms can be seen along the banks of the Helford River. On the cliff top, green-winged orchid, fringed rupturewort, campion and thrift can all be found.

The air is clean, the sea is clear, cold and blue, and the coastline is littered with treacherous rocks – the cause of many shipwrecks. A lighthouse has been situated at the tip of Lizard Point since 1751; Tennyson described its twin towers as 'the southern eyes of England'. It has a 46km (29 mile) beam to alert passing shipping to danger.

The peninsula is geologically significant for it is the UK's only example of an ophiolite, an igneous rock sequence which indicates that the oceanic crust and upper mantle material was forced up to

The return of the chough

The coast between Lizard Point and Kynance Cove is home to one of the UK's rarest breeding birds – the Cornish chough, which features on the Cornish coat of arms. Legend has it that the soul of King Arthur departed in a chough, its red beak and legs signifying his bloody end. The chough is a member of the crow family, and has the characteristic black plumage, offset by bright red legs and a striking curved red beak. Key to its reappearance in Cornwall has been the reintroduction of cliff-top grazing to maintain the desired habitat. In 2002 a nesting pair bred successfully for the first time in 50 years and the population has been increasing ever since.

Left: A rare adult chough shows off its striking, livid-red legs and beak.

Below: The Lizard Peninsula produces some of the most spectacular coastal scenery in the United Kingdom, such as this a view across Housel Bay to the lighthouse.

the earth's surface by the action of the oceanic tectonic plates millions of years ago. It is composed of a metamorphic rock called serpentine, which is dark green, veined with red and white. Most of the Lizard's rare plants occur on this serpentine rock.

The Lizard has deep wooded valleys, sheltered inlets and expanses of plateau heathland, which contain a unique mix of flora producing a devastating array of wild flowers, notably in May and June. There are numerous varieties of clover, chives grow in the wild, and harebell and bloody cranesbill flower profusely.

The Lizard

This walk around Lizard Peninsula, the southerly tip of mainland Britain, takes in dramatic cliff scenery, rare wild flowers and an interesting coastal history. Kynance Cove has a sandy beach and islands of serpentine stone. The bay attracted visitors in Victorian times and still captivates people today.

Getting there and facilities:
Lizard village is 18km (11 miles) from Helston on the A3083. There is a regular bus service throughout the year. WCs at Kynance and the Lizard car parks. Refreshments available from the eco café on Kynance beach and at Lizard Point.

Start point:
Kynance cove – OS Landranger 203 map, or GR SW703125.

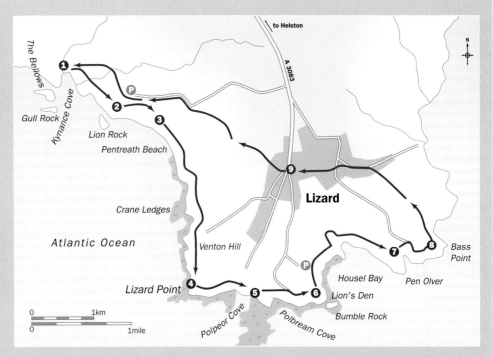

Distance, terrain and accessibility:
A 7km (4½ mile) route along sandy beaches and stony cliff-top paths. Some slopes and steps: height gain of 220m (720ft). At the beach, beware of strong currents. Swimming is not advised at low tide and do not use inflatables.

Route and directions:
1 Set out from Kynance Cove heading towards Lizard Point. Look out for the Devil's Letterbox on the north side of Asparagus Island – a cave crack with powerful suction caused by the pull of air from the waves below.

2 Steps lead to a headland from the eastern end of Kynance beach. Walk through the car park and rejoin the cliff path.

3 Follow the cliff path, passing above Pentreath Beach. Seals and basking sharks are commonly spotted on this route. Basking sharks can be up to 9m (30ft) long but cruise these warm waters feeding on nothing more than tiny plankton.

4 Look down towards the disused Victorian lifeboat station at Polpeor Cove.

5 The Lizard Lighthouse is just round the headland from Lizard Point. An electric foghorn kicks in when humidity levels rise above a certain point. Make sure you cover your ears! The blast is so thunderous (about 30 times louder than a pneumatic drill) you will feel the vibrations if passing close by.

6 Lion's Den is a 12m (40ft) hole in the cliff created when a cave collapsed one night in the mid 1800s.

7 With stunning views, Pen Olver is the perfect spot for a picnic but don't forget to take your rubbish home.

8 Continue on the coastal path beyond the old coastguard lookout and some houses and then turn inland on to a farm track.

9 Pass the village green, taking a path towards Kynance Cove.

The National Trust looks after land from Kynance Cove to the tip of the Lizard Peninsula, allowing visitors to enjoy the staggering beauty of a cliff-top walk. Here you can see serpentine stone in the cliffs and islands; look for seals and basking sharks in the sea, and for seabirds such as gannet, shearwater and guillemot offshore. In summer the coastal scenery is smothered with a breathtaking array of the most beautiful and fragrant wild flowers.

Above left: The water around the Lizard Peninsula is cold and clear. This is an early morning view of the sparkling water at Kynance Cove.

Above: The water around Loe Bar has strong currents and powerful waves, making it hazardous for bathing, especially at low tide.

Left: The towering, rocky cliff tops on the Lizard Peninsula are decorated with swathes of glorious wild flowers.

Two black huts stand on the headland of Pen Olver. It was here that Guglielmo Marconi made his first pioneering wireless experiments. In January 1901 he received a message that had travelled 302.5km (188 miles) from the Isle of Wight, and on 12 December 1901 he made the first transatlantic wireless transmission to Newfoundland. The huts have been restored and are open to the public. In the centre of the peninsula, the white dishes of the Goonhilly Satellite Earth Station represent a modern means of communication.

Loe Pool and Bar

Close to the Lizard lies the Penrose Estate, at the heart of which is Loe Pool, Cornwall's largest freshwater lake, which meets the sea at the shingle bank of Loe Bar. Legend has it that this is the place where Sir Bedivere cast away the sword Excalibur as King Arthur

lay dying. Some people believe that Tennyson was thinking of Loe Pool when he wrote *Morte d'Arthur* (1842): 'On one side lay the ocean and on one lay a great water'.

Loe Bar is a huge, low pebble dam that separates the lake from the sea, and this habitat supports its own moth sub-species, the Cornish sandhill rustic. Both the Bar and the moth are threatened by rising sea levels, which would turn its freshwater into saltmarsh. Wildlife is in abundance here, including many birds and mammals such as otters. Hides allow you to watch widgeon, shoveller, pochard, tufted duck, coot and otters. Cormorants roost in the enormous trees at the water's edge. Surrounding the lake is a mix of rich farmland and woodland through which there are many paths, including the 8km (5 mile) circuit of Loe Pool.

Dartmoor

Dartmoor is the largest area of open country in the south of England, covering an area just short of 1,000km² (368 square miles). It was established as a National Park in 1951 and 40 locations within it are designated Sites of Special Scientific Interest (SSSIs). Dartmoor contains a rich diversity of wildlife and flora as well as over 1,000 scheduled ancient monuments and 2,500 listed buildings. It is largely common land – unfenced open land on which local farmers hold rights to graze cattle, ponies and sheep. Dartmoor has its own breed of pony, a hardy creature well able to cope with the extremes of the open moor. The open Dartmoor landscape we know today is the product of grazing by commoners' stock, though much of the moor, particularly the western side, has been very heavily grazed in recent times, to the extent that the heather cover has been grazed out and replaced with tough grasses.

The geology of Dartmoor

A large area of Dartmoor – around 65 per cent – is made up of a piece of granite that is around 280 million years old. The process began with molten rock or magma that was pushed up through both the Earth's crust and a prehistoric ocean. As it slowly solidified, the magma nearest to the surface formed granite, which crystallised, giving the rock its hardness. The cooling process also caused the rock to contract, creating fractures. Over time the area developed into sub-tropical forest and then later still it became a frozen wasteland. This freeze-thaw effect saw water permeate the rock, freeze and expand, creating further cracks within the structure. When the last ice age ended, the rock fragmented, leaving piles of boulders and chippings, which slid downhill with the passage of the water, leaving the distinctive profile we see today. Sedimentary rocks, such as limestone, sandstone and shale, surround Dartmoor's granite core.

It is perhaps the tors for which Dartmoor is best known; these granite hilltops are tall, but then over half of the park is 300m (984ft) above sea level. In short it is a mountain range, the highest land south of Snowdon and Cader Idris in Wales. There are over 160 tors on Dartmoor, the tallest of which is High Willhays, which stands at 621m (2,039ft), followed by Yes Tor at 619m (2,030ft).

Below: The upper reaches of the River Dart, seen here near the ancient, lichen-encrusted Wistman's Wood, runs fast and furious and is popular with canoeists.

Settlements on Dartmoor

Despite the weather conditions and the hostile environment, Dartmoor is littered with evidence of human activity, from the Neolithic chambered tombs of 3500BC, to standing stones and stone circles dating from around 2000BC, and stone huts and field boundaries from 1500BC. The soil is acidic and no organic remains have survived, however the strength and durability of the local granite means that buildings and monuments have remained, including numerous menhirs (isolated upright stones), stone circles, stone rows and cairns (artificial piles of stones). The area contains the highest concentration of Bronze Age remains found in north-west

Europe; there are around 5,000 hut circles (remnants of houses), and good examples can be found at Grimspound, near Postridge.

After this period it is believed that cold weather kept Dartmoor free from habitation until medieval times, since when the land has been farmed and worked continuously. As well as farming, lead, tin, copper and silver were mined on Dartmoor. Tin mining, which started in the 12th century, had all but disappeared by the 20th century and the last working mine, which produced micaceous hematite, closed in 1969. The practice of peat cutting ceased in the 1970s – but all these activities left their individual scars on the landscape, now slowly fading.

Woods and meadows

The Forestry Commission owns swathes of land on Dartmoor, growing plantations of Sitka and Norway spruce, which attract

Above: Megaliths – large stones used to create a monument or structure such as stone circles or stone rows – litter Dartmoor, evidence of prehistoric life in this wild area. There are more megaliths found here than anywhere else in the UK.

The climate of Dartmoor

Dartmoor is generally wetter, warmer and windier than much of the UK, with the prevailing wind coming from the south west or west, laden with moisture from the mid-Atlantic drift that flows around the UK coast – hence the local saying: 'Nine months winter and three months bad weather.' The height of the tors and the exposed landscape often produce extremes of weather. Rainfall sends water pouring off the tors into many of the county's rivers, which rise on Dartmoor as well as in to the eight reservoirs that lie within the National Park.

Watch for Wildlife

Dartmoor encompasses a series of significant habitats: here you can find blanket bog on the highest northern and southern plateaus, ringed by heathland and grassland. Blanket bogs see an accumulation of plant matter, which does not rot because of the acidic conditions. **Sphagnum moss** proliferates. This species absorbs water, helping to create waterlogged conditions and discouraging plant breakdown. **Hare's-tail cotton-grass, bog grass, deer grass, bog asphodel** and **cross-leaved heath** all thrive, and **golden plover** and **dunlin** nest in these conditions. As water pours down from higher ground into areas with peat valley bottoms, known as valley mires, it tends to create waterlogged, boggy conditions. As well as the usual grasses and mosses, moorland **water crowfoot, bog pimpernel, pale butterwort, bogbean** and the **bog orchid** thrive, providing perfect conditions for **lapwings, damselflies** and **dragonflies.** The steeper and better-drained slopes form areas of moorland where heather, bilberry and western gorse produce a cold mix of purple and yellow in August. Beehives, particularly those from the Benedictine community at Buckfast Abbey, are brought here so that the bees can feed on the sweet perfumed nectar. **Buzzards** circle overhead, and **skylarks** and **meadow pipits** are easy to spot. **Wheatear** and **ring ouzel** can also be seen, along with **Dartmoor ponies.** The rocky outcrops provide nesting sites for **peregrine falcon** and **raven.**

Dartmoor pony

birds such as goldcrest, siskin and coal tit. Valley woodlands attract all three species of British woodpecker, tree-creepers, nuthatches and tits. Migrants include the redstart, wood warbler and tree pipit. In spring the floor is carpeted with wild flowers, notably bluebell and aromatic wild garlic. Lydford Gorge, the deepest gorge in the south west of England, passes through oak woods, where walkers can enjoy a woodland trail that takes in the 30m (98ft) White Lady Waterfall, and the Devil's Cauldron whirlpool.

Running along the flat valley floors are wet pastures and ancient hay meadows where wild flowers such as the heath spotted orchid, ivy-leaved bellflower, ox-eye daisy and yellow rattle can be seen attracting rare insects such as the marsh fritillary butterfly. Alongside the rivers and streams, birds such as the kingfisher, grey heron and dipper can be seen, with reservoirs attracting cormorants and flocks of wild ducks. In autumn salmon swim upriver from the sea to breed.

Ancient woodland

Wistman's Wood, at 427m (1,400ft), is situated higher than any other oak wood in the country. The trees are stunted ancients, no more than 4.5m (15ft) in height, the branches are twisted and tangled, and their density has created an extraordinary microclimate. Hembury and Holne Woods are similar fine examples of ancient woodland, mainly oak, which run along the banks and rise to high above the River Dart, giving fine views of the surrounding area. In addition to being a SSSI, the summit of Hembury is crowned by the grassland of Hembury Castle, an Iron Age hill fort, complete with the motte and bailey earthworks of Dane's Castle. The trees are covered with moss and lichens and decorated with a mass of epiphytic ferns, which, like those in the rain forest, survive on rain water and nutrients derived from fallen leaves, while wood sorrel grows up from their roots. Flowers include bluebells, primroses, ramsons, wild daffodil and wood anemone, while royal ferns can be seen mainly on the river banks. These diverse species support a rich variety of invertebrates.

Above: The ancient trees at Wistman's Wood are draped and adorned with mosses and lichens and surrounded by moorland and granite tors.

Left: The thunderous White Lady Waterfall drops some 30m (100ft) in the wooded ravine at Lydford Gorge and is most impressive after heavy rain.

Lundy

Lundy is a tiny island situated in the Bristol Channel about 19km (12 miles) off the Devon coast. Bought by the National Trust in 1969, this granite outcrop measures just 6km (3¾ miles) from north to south and is 1.6km (1 mile) wide. It was the UK's first Marine Nature Reserve and has been designated a SSSI.

Huge cliffs dominate the north, south and west sides of the island, standing 122m (400ft) tall, and offer glorious views across the sea to England and Wales. The only sheltered landing site is on the south-east corner of the island, where boats run from Bideford between April and October; in the winter months a helicopter service operates. A steep, winding path leads up from the jetty through the cliffs to the flat central plateau. Working lighthouses mark the north and south

corners. The number of residents varies slightly, but is under 30; most are employees of the Landmark Trust who manage the island for the National Trust.

The name Lundy is possibly derived from Old Norse for 'puffin', and puffins have certainly lived here for centuries. In 1939 there were some 3,500 breeding pairs on the island, but by the year 2000 this number had fallen to ten pairs. Puffins are very susceptible to predators, and it was believed that the decline in numbers was due to the loss of eggs to the black rat, which had become abundant on Lundy (see page 26).

Left: The mile-long 'Main Road' in Lundy leads from the landing beach to the village and was originally constructed in the first half of the 19th century.

Below: Lundy is a dramatic granite outcrop that rises 122m (400ft) above sea level, a veritable paradise for bird watchers, divers and rock climbers.

A turbulent past

For a small rocky island, Lundy has attracted notorious bands of ruffians, and was a popular haven for smugglers and pirates. The earliest settlements are believed to be Neolithic or Bronze Age. Early Christians arrived in the Dark Ages (leaving memorial stones in the Old Cemetery on the island, shown below) and the Vikings and the Normans both invaded the island. The Knights Templar owned Lundy for much of the 12th and 13th centuries; on the east side of the island is a rock in the shape of a head known as the Knights Templar Rock. The de Marisco family built a castle on Lundy and thrived on raiding passing ships and the north Devon coast, until William de Marisco organised an ill-fated assassination attempt on Henry III, for which he was executed in 1242. Despite Henry's attempt to fortify Lundy, pirates and smugglers of various nationalities continually overran the island, all threatening local ships and promising raids on England. The island was staunchly Royalist during the Civil War and was the very last part of the UK to surrender to Oliver Cromwell.

Birdlife

Lundy is home to an interesting array of wildlife. There is a spectacular range of marine life, and the island is home to many birds, as well as attracting migrating birds and vagrants. **Fulmar, puffin, shag, oystercatcher, guillemot, black-legged kittiwake** and **razorbill** all breed on the island, as does the **linnet**, the **meadow pipit**, the **raven** and the **peregrine falcon**. Migrating birds such as **short-eared owls, ring ouzels, merlins** and **black redstarts** appear regularly.

Several species of vagrant bird have made their first UK appearance on Lundy: the **bimaculated lark**, the **American robin** and the **ancient murrelet** – which usually resides on the north Pacific coast – have all dropped by. Other rare visiting birds already on the British list include the **gyrfalcon**, the **glossy ibis**, the **laughing gull** and the **yellow-billed cuckoo**.

Merlin

Below: Soay sheep and domestic sheep are found on Lundy. Soay sheep, an endangered breed originating from St Kilda in Western Scotland, are allowed to roam free on the island.

Lundy supports many – perhaps too many – grazing animals, both wild and domesticated, including its own breed of pony. The tough and hardy Lundy pony runs wild on the island, and Sika deer, feral goats, soay sheep (a primitive domestic breed) and rabbits are all found here. The rabbit population was decimated by myxomatosis in 2006 but should recover. On the east side of the island, the deer live among the rhododendrons. These imported plants have become invasive and efforts are being made to control their spread. Arachnophobes will be alarmed to hear that the island is home to the purse web spider – the only UK member of the family of bird-eating spiders. Bracken, grass and heather are the principle vegetation; thrift can be seen turning the cliff tops and ledges pink in spring, and the unique Lundy cabbage, a primitive form of Brassica, attracts the unusual bronze Lundy cabbage flea beetle.

Lundy was declared a Marine Nature Reserve in 1986, one of only three in the UK. It has a range of underwater habitats, ranging from rocks to sand and gravel; these, allied with a combination of warm waters from the Mediterranean, cooler Atlantic currents, and the strong tidal stream, produce an attractive underwater habitat. The water is so clear that the coastline provides a spectacular trail for scuba divers to follow. A glorious array of coloured seaweed can be seen, including six different types of kelp, along with branching sponges, sea fans, compass jellyfish and cup corals – indeed, all five species of native British coral can be found here. Grey seals can be seen in the water or on rocks; they should not be disturbed during breeding from September to November. A fishing No Take Zone (NTZ) has been enforced on the eastern side of Lundy to try to improve fish stocks and ensure the continuity of the food chain.

The Jurassic Coast

The Jurassic Coast covers 152km (95 miles) of breathtaking coastline, with rocks that showcase 185 million years of evolution. The area, one third of which is owned by the National Trust, extends from Exmouth in Devon to Swanage in Dorset, and offers an extraordinary view of the earth sciences, spanning the Triassic, Jurassic and Cretaceous periods. It is England's only natural World Heritage Site and is ranked alongside the Grand Canyon and the Great Barrier Reef.

The age of the rocks on show is staggering; the Triassic period dates from 250–200 million years ago, when dinosaurs and flying reptiles emerged, and is characterised by red sandstone and mud that can be seen at Ladram Bay and Sidmouth. The Jurassic period dates from 200–140 million years ago and features clays, sandstone and limestone. During this period, dinosaurs such as *Brachiosaurus* and *Diplodocus* proliferated on land and ichthyosaurs and pliosaurs swam in the sea. Fossils from Lyme Regis and Charmouth are rich in material from this era; many are uncovered by winter storms. The Cretaceous Period, between 140 and 65 million years ago, was characterised by pure white chalk formed by the skeletons of warm-water algae. It witnessed the birth of flowering plants and the evolution and extinction of dinosaurs such as *Tyrannosaurus rex*, *Velociraptor* and *Triceratops*. Dinosaur footprints are found among the limestone coves at Purbeck and the Isle of Portland.

Mary Anning, from Lyme Regis, who followed in her father's footsteps collecting and selling fossils to supplement the family income, highlighted the fascinating geology

Above: The Salcombe Hill Cliff at Sidmouth in Devon is formed of sandstone and mudstone, which gives a rippling red profile.

Below: A mile to the east of Lulworth Cove, a fossil forest can be seen on the cliff edge, showing that coniferous trees once towered over a entirely different environment.

of the area. A year after her father's death, aged 12, she uncovered the first ever complete skeleton of an ichthyosaur and later, among many extraordinary finds, she uncovered the first plesiosaur. Her contribution to the burgeoning field of palaeontology was immense. The Jurassic Coast continues to yield a steady stream of dinosaur remains, including previously unknown species, and is also famous for both Portland and Purbeck stone.

Coastal features

The coastline offers many examples of landforms, including the natural arch at Durdle Door, the cove and limestone folding at Lulworth Cove, a tombolo (a deposition landform, such as a bar or spit, attached to the mainland by a narrow piece of land), such as the one connecting the Isle of Portland to the mainland at Abbotsbury, and storm beaches (affected by particularly fierce waves) such as Chesil Beach. In addition, there are stretches of concordant and discordant coastlines. A concordant coastline reveals bands of different types of rock that run parallel to the coast, Lulworth Cove being a prime example; here the sea has broken through the outer barrier of Portland limestone, eroded the soft clay behind it, and cut into the chalk. More recently the sea has broken through to the west at Stair Hole. A discordant coastline features bands of different rocks which run perpendicular to the coast, leading to the formation of headlands and bays, as seen at Durlston Head. The highest point of the Jurassic Coast is Golden Cap where you can enjoy fantastic views and a centuries-old landscape of meadows and hedgerows.

The South West Coast Path runs 1,008km (630 miles) from Minehead on the edge of Exmoor, all around the west coast, to Poole Harbour in Dorset, and includes the entire length of the Jurassic Coast. The coastline is a constantly shifting and dynamic environment; cliff falls and landslips can close sections of the path temporarily and there are sometimes inland diversions, so it is worth checking local websites for up-to-date information. In spring 2008, a 400m (1,312ft) section of the coastline fell into the sea in a landslip that was described as the worst in 100 years. The area is an AONB, and contains 14 SSSIs, a National Natural Reserve (NNR) in the Axmouth to Lyme Regis Undercliffs, and many inland sites that are home to protected flora and fauna. The greatest threat to the area is through coastal defences and inappropriate fossil collecting.

Below: The rocks of the Golden Cap beach turn gold in autumn sunlight. Magnificent views can be seen from the top of the towering cliffs.

Golden Cap

With its summit 191m (627ft) above sea level, Golden Cap (shown below), to the east of Lyme Regis, is the highest sea cliff on the south coast of England. The name of the cliff comes from the golden yellow rock covering its summit – a rich, yellow sandstone. The steeply rolling countryside, with its cliffs, deeply incised valleys, small fields, ponds and heaths, is perhaps the epitome of the English landscape. The cliffs are rich in fossils. Erosion is rapid, and cliff falls are frequent. The terraces formed by these falls have a very diverse plant and animal life. Some areas are covered in willow scrub, while others have grass, heather or reeds that grow around small pools. Hay meadows are rich with green-winged orchid, corky-fruited water dropwort, pepper saxifrage and adder's tongue fern. The tangled scrub of the undercliff is a haven for migratory birds. A number of rare insects can be seen here, notably solitary bees and wasps, rare beetles and the grey bush-cricket.

Dorset Heaths and the Studland Peninsula

Thomas Hardy immortalised the beautiful Dorset Heaths with the fictional Wessex location Egdon Heath, which features in *The Return of the Native*, *The Withered Arm* and *The Mayor of Casterbridge*. Heathland once stretched from Dorchester in the west, to the Avon Valley in the east, covering over 50,000ha (123,550 acres). Today, just 7,000ha (17,300 acres) remain, heavily fragmented and crisscrossed by roads, and threatened by urban sprawl. Of this, over 96 per cent has been designated as a SSSIs, and in each location the habitat supports a great variety of flora and fauna.

The Isle of Purbeck

A large expanse of Dorset heath can be found on the Isle of Purbeck, which is home to many rare plants and creatures. All of the heathland is designated as SSSI and as such is carefully managed to maintain its natural biodiversity and to protect the heath for future generations. The lichen communities found here are important for dragonflies, grasshoppers, crickets, moths, beetles and butterflies. The scarce blue-tailed damselfly can often be seen in August and September. In addition, all six British reptiles can be found here, including the sand lizard and smooth snake, and it is one of the most important breeding sites for heathland birds in the country.

Brownsea Island

In the middle of Poole Harbour lies Brownsea Island, owned by the National Trust. The island, which offers spectacular views across the harbour, contains beautiful heathland, some invasive rhododendron thickets, and glorious mixed woodland where the rare red squirrel still thrives in the absence of the highly competitive, larger grey squirrel. Almost half the island is a nature reserve, run by the Dorset Trust for Nature Conservation. There are regular guided walks, and a public hide gives views over the lagoon and its small gravel islets, which have been specially created as nesting sites for terns. Other seabirds breeding on Brownsea include the great and lesser black-backed gulls, herring gull and shelduck. Many waders can be seen on and around the island, including the

Left: The male sand lizard can be identified by his green sides, which become brighter still during the breeding season.

Below: Rock falls and landslips from the tall Salcombe Hill Cliffs are commonplace. High tide reaches a good length up the cliff face and walkers must take care not to be cut off.

Arne Nature Reserve

Arne is situated on the northern edge of the Isle of Purbeck, next to Poole Harbour. The area around Arne is a RSPB nature reserve and is popular with walkers and bird watchers. The Arne reserve comprises a large spread of dry lowland heath, saltmarsh, mixed woodland and valley bogs. The heathland attracts birds that like to nest on, or near to, the ground, such as the nightjar, whose males make a distinctive clapping sound with their wings to attract females, and the Dartford warbler. The latter, often seen perched on common gorse, was almost wiped out by the brutal winter of 1961, but numbers are increasing dramatically due largely to mild winters and the spread of its beloved gorse. Stonechats, linnets and hen harriers can be seen, and you may even see a hobby pursuing insects such as the rare downy emerald dragonfly. Many unusual species of butterfly occur, including the heathland race of the silver-studded blue. Sand lizards, known as 'little dragons', are uncommon across much of the UK with 80 per cent of the national population found on Dorset heathland. Smooth snakes prey on this colourful local character, and slow worms, grass snakes and common snakes can also be seen at Arne.

curlew, oystercatcher, dunlin, greenshank, bar-tailed and black-tailed godwit, common and spotted redshank, and avocet. The largest little egret colony in the UK is found here along with an impressive heronry. The National Trust is working to increase the area of heathland where butterflies such as the small copper, the green hairstreak and the silver-studded blue can be seen.

The Studland Peninsula

The Studland Peninsula sits on the south side of the entrance to Poole Harbour. The National Trust owns around 607ha (1,500 acres) here, and the land comprises a variety of habitats: woodland, heathland, sandy beaches, sand dunes, bogs and saltmarsh. From South Haven Point to the chalk cliffs of Handfast Point and Old Harry Rocks at the eastern end of the Jurassic Coast World Heritage site, is a beautiful 5km (3 mile) long beach, behind which lies heathland believed to be the richest 1,000ha (2,471 acres) site for wild flowers and lichens in the UK. This extensive nature reserve is one of the National Trust's finest wildlife properties. Its complex mix of habitats can best be appreciated from high ground, on the road that runs between Corfe Castle and Studland. From here, the great sweep of open heathland, with its drainage lines and bogs, falls away dramatically to the distant dunes. Many interesting plants can be seen in the wetter areas, such as oblong-leaved sundew, bog myrtle, marsh club-moss, meadow thistle, marsh gentian and royal fern. The area's birdlife is very varied, with gulls and waterfowl, as well as the stonechat, nightjar and Dartford warbler. Common lizards, sand lizards, adders and slow worms all thrive in the sunny climate and sandy soil. Insects abound, including rare bees and wasps, such as the Purbeck mason wasp, and butterflies such as the grayling and silver-studded blue.

The South West Coast Path, which runs all the way along the Dorset, Devon and Cornish coasts to Minehead in Somerset, begins at Studland Bay and there are beautiful walks here through what was once part of the Kingston Lacy and Corfe Castle estates. In spring and summer the areas around the paths are filled with wild flowers and butterflies such as the painted lady, a migrant from north Africa, and the clouded yellow, a migrant from southern Europe.

Left: The Pinnacles are a series of chalk sea stacks standing off Swanage in Dorset and are a feature of the Jurassic Coast UNESCO World Heritage Site.

Right: The red-eyed dartford warbler perches on its favoured gorse bushes to sing. Its numbers are decimated in severe winters.

Wiltshire's Prehistoric Landscapes

Littered around the UK countryside are many man-made structures that serve as a reminder that this island has been inhabited since prehistoric times. Henges and stone circles are considered to be unique to the UK, the most famous being the internationally renowned Stonehenge. Their precise function is unknown, though it is believed that they were used for rituals, religion and for astronomical observation – all are engineering marvels of their day. In addition, a range of other ancient structures can be found, from burial mounds to white horses carved into chalk hills. The Wiltshire countryside offers an extraordinarily rich variety of prehistoric sites for those eager to explore our distant past.

Avebury

Avebury, in Wiltshire, is a designated World Heritage Site and home to one of Europe's largest stone circles, as well as a henge, or boundary earthwork. The Neolithic monument is estimated to be around 5,000 years old. The outer circle is around 335m (1,099ft) in diameter and originally comprised 98 standing stones

Below: The standing stones at Avebury, Wiltshire, have been dated to between 3000–2000BC and form part of the largest known stone circle in pre-history.

3.6–4.2m (12–14ft) in height; the inner ring was 108m (354ft) in diameter, though little of this now remains. Part of the village of Avebury is enclosed within the monument. A 5.5m (18ft) monolith stands in the centre and avenues of stones lead in and out of the circle. Many of the original stones were destroyed and some were re-erected in the 1930s. Unlike Stonehenge, it is still possible to walk freely around the area. Nearby, the gentle rise of Windmill Hill, once the site of an important Neolithic settlement, has several well-preserved Bronze Age burial mounds and boasts commanding views.

Stonehenge

Stonehenge on Salisbury Plain, also a World Heritage Site, is just 3.2km (2 miles) west of Avebury and consists of earthworks surrounding large standing stones. The stone circle is estimated to date between 3000 and 1600BC and originally featured 80 stones in total. The lintels that rest on the top of the stones make Stonehenge unique. The bluestones, the smaller inner stones, were transported from the Preseli Hills in West Wales some 257km (160 miles) away; they turn blue only when wet. The central monolith, known as the Altar Stone, weighs 6 tonnes and is made from Welsh sandstone.

The landscape of Stonehenge

The land around Stonehenge includes not only the world-famous stones, but also monuments and landscape features including Stonehenge Down, King Barrow Ridge, Woodhenge, Normanton Down, Durrington Walls and Winterbourne Stoke Long Barrows. Home to skylark and brown hare, Stonehenge Down is an open landscape with fine views of the famous stone circle. From here it is possible to explore Bronze Age barrow cemeteries and prehistoric monuments, such as the Stonehenge Avenue and the mysterious Cursus. The former is a grand-scale earthwork monument sweeping 3km (1.8 miles) from the River Avon to the north-eastern entrance of Stonehenge, dating from between 2600 and 1700BC and contemporary to the construction of the stone circle; the latter is a long, rectangular earthwork that runs for about 3km (1.8 miles) on an east-west alignment. On King Barrow Ridge lie Bronze Age burial mounds among impressive beech trees, with views of Stonehenge and the downs. Hazel coppice provides shelter for wildlife along the ridge, while in summer downland flora attracts butterflies such as the marbled white. Normanton Down with its fascinating burial mounds offers one of the best approaches to Stonehenge, and is home to farmland birds such as corn bunting and stonechat. In 2005, Durrington Walls was revealed to be the site of a rare Neolithic village, with evidence of shrines and feasting. Some of the banks of this circular earthwork can still be seen, the largest complete henge in Europe.

Below: Stonehenge is perhaps the best-known prehistoric site in the world. The site was sold at auction in 1915 and was given to the nation by the purchaser, Cecil Chubb, in 1918.

Woodhenge

A few miles to the north east of Stonehenge, Woodhenge is a Neolithic henge and timber circle monument, with very little remaining of the original structure. Around 168 wooden posts have been marked with concrete posts to show the circular layout of the henge, although it is believed that some standing stones also formed part of the earthworks and burial ground.

Hill figures

At one time there are believed to have been around 24 hill figures in Britain, 13 of which were cut into the chalk downs of Wiltshire. They include both animal and human forms, although the reason for their creation is unknown. Hill figures are carved on chalk by removing the poor topsoil – some are estimated to be 3,000 years old, but most are just 300 years old. The figures require regular maintenance if the landmarks are to be preserved.

Burial mounds

Ancient burial mounds or long barrows formed part of a Neolithic burial process and date from the last part of the Stone Age. There are 300 of them in England and Scotland. Wooden chambers were constructed as a final resting place and these contained as many as 50 bodies at a time

Left: The Cerne Giant stands an impressive 55m (180ft) tall. According to local legend, this sheep-eating Danish giant was slain by locals who then cut around his outline to warn off other giants.

including men, women and children. Some bodies were buried *en masse*, others apparently over a period of time. The remains appear to have had all flesh removed before interment. The wooden structures were then covered with stones and the earth barrow constructed over the top. This was often much larger than the burial chamber beneath; some measure as much as 107m (350ft). Barrows were generally oriented with the larger end facing the east and the tapering end pointing west. Long Barrows can be seen at Stonehenge, King Barrow Ridge and Durrington Walls. The round barrow cemetery of Normanton Down dates from 2600–1600BC and is one of the most remarkable groups of burial mounds in the Stonehenge landscape. At Winterbourne Stoke Barrows stands another fascinating example of a prehistoric cemetery. The wide range of barrow shapes found here show that this site was used over a long period of time for burials of people of high status.

Cherhill Down and Calstone Coombes

The prominent chalk ridge of Cherhill Down in north Wiltshire, with its monument and white horse cut into the turf, is crested by a hill fort and flanked by steep slopes and dry coombes. The southern slope and adjacent land at the western end is the best place for wild flowers, which include the lesser butterfly orchid. Cherhill Down has large numbers of adonis blue butterflies, as well as the brown argus, marbled white and dingy skipper. Skylarks, meadow pipits and partridges can usually be seen. Below to the south lies Calstone Coombes, the most extensive chalkland valley system in the UK, and a fantastic site for wild flowers such as bastard toadflax and insects such as the rare wart-biter bush cricket and marsh fritillary butterfly.

Above: The Cherhill white horse was created by Doctor Christopher Alsop in 1780. It was reputed to have had a distinctive glass eye, formed from the base of an upturned bottle, but this was repeatedly stolen.

Right: Only the male chalkhill blue is a beautiful blue colour – females are chocolate brown. Males will gather together in large numbers in bright sunshine, searching for a mate.

Cley Hill

The site of an Iron Age hill fort capped by Bronze Age burial mounds, this isolated chalk hill 3.2km (2 miles) from Warminster is a landmark for miles around. It was once well known for its adonis and chalkhill blue butterflies, but both disappeared in the 1970s. Happily, the adonis blue is now back in some numbers, and the chalkhill blue has also returned. The hill's butterflies also include the marbled white and brown argus. Cley Hill's 'unimproved' grassland has a profusion of chalk-loving flowers, including early gentians.

Figsbury Ring

Figsbury Ring's Iron Age earthworks overlook Porton Down in the south of Wiltshire, and provide warm, south-facing slopes that suit many downland plants. Orchids are common here, with pyramidal, fragrant, bee, common spotted and frog orchids growing in the turf, which is regularly grazed by sheep. This is a particularly good site for butterflies, especially the chalkhill and small blues, and for the rare hornet robberfly, a large hornet-mimic that preys on grasshopper nymphs.

Stonehenge

This walk explores chalk downland at the heart of the Stonehenge World Heritage Site. From Bronze Age burial mounds to ancient ceremonial pathways, the landscape surrounding Britain's most famous prehistoric monument is full of intriguing archaeology. There's also a fantastic array of wildlife to look out for.

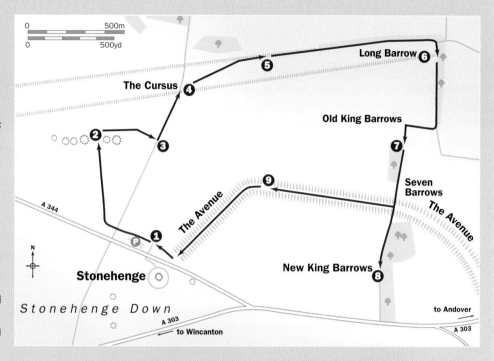

Getting there and facilities:

A regular bus service runs from Salisbury station 14km (9 miles) to Stonehenge. Stonehenge can be reached from Salisbury or Avebury on Sustrans route 45. If driving, the walk begins 3.2km (2 miles) west of Amesbury, near the junction of the A303 and A344. Toilets, refreshments and visitor centre at the Stonehenge car park (English Heritage) Leaflets are available.

Start point:

Stonehenge car park – GR SU120420, OS Landranger 184, or Explorer 130 maps.

Distance, terrain and accessibility:

This 5.6km (3 mile) circular trail follows hard tracks and gently sloping meadows. Take care as the surfaces can be uneven, with potholes or long tussocky grass. This route includes four stiles, but there are alternative routes which only use accessible gates.

Route and directions:

1   From the car park cross the bridleway and climb over the nearby stile into a grass meadow. Head right and walk towards a pair of barrow mounds on the horizon.

2   Once at the barrows you will find an information panel behind them. Turn right and walk towards the small road again, on to the next information panel.

3   At the panel, go through a gate and follow the road left, away from Stonehenge. Remember to look back at the stones as they disappear from view in the distance.

4   When you reach the next information panel, pass through a gate on the right-hand side of the road and continue along the route of the Cursus.

5   Cross both the stiles at the valley bottom and head uphill towards some trees.

6   At the end of the field, cross another stile and walk towards an information panel. Continue to a junction and take the right fork, heading behind a row of trees.

7   At the next junction turn right through a gate and follow the path ahead. Pass two more information panels and head for a third among the beech trees at New King Barrows for a fine view of Stonehenge and its surroundings.

8   Return to the previous information panel and enter the field. Now follow the course of the Avenue back in the direction of the Cursus Barrows. In the valley, pass through the gate and walk towards the next information panel.

9   From here, stay left of the panel and head in the direction of Stonehenge. As you ascend the slope you will be able to see the ditches of the avenue leading toward the Stones. Return to the car park on your right.

Other Sites in South West England

Cornwall

Cape Cornwall,
north Cornwall coast
Maritime cliff, rocky shore, heath
Cape Cornwall's rocky patch of coastline is perfect for the common seal. These animals are often seen in the water, or hauling themselves on to the rocks for a rest. A climb up the Cape headland offers panoramic views of Land's End, Sennen Cove, Brisons Rocks and the Isles of Scilly.

Chapel Carn Brea,
north Cornwall coast
Heath, grassland, granite outcrops, scattered boulders
Chapel Carn Brea's exposed position, granite outcrops and steep slopes have a marked effect on its plant life. The main vegetation here is heath, which is dominated by four plants – ling, bell heather, western gorse and bristle-leaved bent grass. Purple moor grass and cross-leaved heath also grow in damper places, while heath milkwort, heath bedstraw and bluebells can also be seen. Many insects and other invertebrate animals thrive in the shelter of crevices and hollows under the boulders.

Chapel Porth,
north Cornwall coast
Heath, grassland, marsh, maritime cliff and slope, old mining spoil
Chapel Porth is a flat coastal plateau about 85m (279ft) above sea level. Wind has had a profound influence on the natural history of this site. Ling and bell heather grow in wave-like clumps where they are most exposed, and in places the soil's fertility is increased by blown sand. This has created a very rich plant life, with 16 nationally rare plants and a further six that are only found in a few localities, including the early gentian. These plants include the hairy green-weed, black bog-rush, pale heath violet, bloody cranesbill, burnet rose, Dorset heath and salad burnet. The majestic royal fern thrives in damp places near the cliff tops. Chapel Porth is a good place to see both reptiles and sea birds. The common lizard, slow worm, adder and grass snake have all been recorded here. Among the seabirds, razorbills breed on the cliffs nearer the northern end, and guillemots, kittiwakes and shags feed in the water offshore.

Fowey Estuary to Pencarrow
Head, south-east Cornwall coast
Scrub, grassland with bracken, cliffs, pools, shingle beaches
Breathtaking natural beauty and a spectacular coastline, combined with

Left: Rocks have been eroded by the sea at Porth Nanven, Cape Cornwall, the point at which the Atlantic currents divide, either going south up the English channel or north up the Bristol Channel.

the pride and vitality of a working Cornish port, lends this area its unique character and charm. Visible from land and sea, Gribbin Head is Fowey's sentinel. It is a striking landmark due to its red-and-white daymark tower. The daymark has sat upon the Gribbin since 1832, providing a navigational aid to mariners. From Fowey Harbour, the coast path leads east for just over 3.2km (2 miles) to Pencarrow Head. A mix of rock, plant life, insects and birds, together with far-reaching views and the unspoilt sands of Great Lantic Beach, make Pencarrow Head a wonderful place to linger. Alongside Ethy Creek in the upper reaches of the Fowey estuary, lichens grow in abundance on ancient trees and the wooded slopes are covered with mosses, ferns, heather and ivy.

Right: A view from the cliffs of Chapel Porth in the evening sun looking towards the ruined tin mines of Wheal Coates and the engine house Towanroath.

The north Cornwall coast

The National Trust owns large parts of the north coast of Cornwall, from Cape Cornwall to the west and Boscastle to the east. The coastline from Godrevy to Navax Point is a sweep of high cliffs and sheltered coves with sandy beaches. The coves here were once the haunt of smugglers. You can walk for miles along the coast path looking out for wildlife, including seals. Further north along the coast lies Pentire Point, where the superb views are as extensive as anywhere in north Cornwall. To the south and west are the expanse of Padstow Bay and the mouth of the River Camel and its tributaries. This stretch of coastline is rich in wildlife, particularly for wild flowers such as autumn squill and meadow clary, and for insects such as the dark green and small pearl-bordered fritillary butterflies. The National Trust farm at West Pentire (shown below) is of national importance for arable weeds (see page 115), and is run by the Trust for their conservation. Over 60 species of arable weed occur, including rarities such as shepherd's needle, Venus's looking-glass and smooth and rough poppy.

Godolphin Estate and the Cornish mines, south-west Cornwall
Heathland, garden, parkland

Cornwall's mines and engine houses are dramatic reminders of the time when the county was a powerhouse of tin, copper and china clay mining. No other industry has moved into Cornwall to replace mining and the physical remains of a great industrial boom still form a significant part of the landscape. The ancient Godolphin Estate, including its former mining sites, offers extensive walks with fine views. You can see over much of west Cornwall from the top of Godolphin Hill. More than 400 archaeological features have been recorded within this historic landscape, including Bronze Age enclosures. The Estate is home to a variety of wildlife. Estate buildings are important for lesser horseshoe bats, which require careful conservation. Many of the trees drip with 'epiphytic' lichens and ferns, and Godolphin Hill supports populations of dark green and small pearl-bordered fritillary butterflies.

Lanhydrock, central Cornwall
Parkland, woodland, gardens, river
Lanhydrock is a magnificent late-Victorian country house with extensive servants' quarters, gardens and wooded estate. Forestry work here has enabled wildlife to thrive. The trees in the park and avenue are home to more than 100 species of lichen and at least nine of the 17 species of British bat can be found on the estate. The elusive dormouse has also recently been recorded breeding in the woods for the first time. Beyond the house and garden there are numerous paths through woods and parkland leading down to the banks of the River Fowey, haunt of otters and kingfishers. The woods are important for ferns, including royal fern and hay-scented buckler fern, along with pied flycatcher, redstart, wood warbler and the spectacular silver-washed fritillary butterfly.

Lantic and Lantivet Bays, south Cornwall coast
Scrub, grassland with bracken, cliffs, pools, shingle beaches
Located between Polperro and Polruan to the east of Fowey, Lantic and Lantivet Bays are a collection of small but perfectly formed coves, of which Palace Cove is the most stunning. The cliff-slopes behind these coves were once used for farming, but have become largely covered with bracken and scrub, though the National Trust is now re-establishing grazing where feasible. Scrub woodland at the western end shows a later stage as nature takes over farmland. Here, ash and sycamore grow among blackthorn, hawthorn and elder. Although small and scattered, the numerous different habitats, including cliff-slopes, pools, rocky platforms, and a shingle beach at Lantic Bay, create great natural diversity. The parasitic ivy broomrape and the maidenhair fern, a rarity in the wild, both grow here, while the mown verges to the footpaths create a habitat for plants that cannot compete with the bracken. These less-vigorous plants include the rare slender bird's-foot trefoil and also the hairy bird's-foot trefoil, a very local plant of low turf.

Rough Tor, north-east Cornwall
Moorland, grassland, rocky outcrops
Reaching over 365m (1,200ft), this isolated and rugged granite tor is Cornwall's second highest point. Rough Tor rises out of an extensive sweep of Bodmin Moor. Its grassland and peaty soils support plants typical of high, acid conditions. They include heathers, common bent, sheep's fescue, and in damper places, purple moor grass and bog asphodel. Bilberry, ling and bell heather are scattered thinly among them. Despite the apparently harsh conditions, insects can be abundant. Rough Tor's birds include wheatears, ring ouzels, meadow pipits, kestrels and buzzards.

Below: The granite outcrops of Rough Tor combine to make one of the most famous landmarks of Bodmin Moor. The tor forms the north-west point of the moor, above Camelford, though it is smaller than its neighbour, Brown Willy, the highest point.

St Anthony's Head, south Cornwall coast
Scrub, grassland, cliffs, saltmarsh, mudflats

At the southernmost tip of the Roseland peninsula, opposite Falmouth, St Anthony's Head overlooks the spectacular entrance to one of the world's largest natural harbours, a deep tidal basin opening into Falmouth Bay, fed by numerous rivers and creeks. The Head bears recently revealed remains of a century of defensive fortifications and consists mainly of unimproved grassland and some woodland-grassland transitional habitat. The Fal estuary includes saltmarsh and mudflats that are rare in the south west and which are important for wintering birds such as avocet and ruff.

Trelissick Garden, south Cornwall coast
Gardens, woodland

Trelissick is a tranquil maritime garden in an extraordinary position on a wooded peninsula at the head of the Fal estuary. It houses a superb collection of tender and exotic plants. The 12ha (30 acre) garden is rich in wildlife, including orchids, ferns and all three species of woodpecker.

Devon

Arlington Court, north Devon
Woodland, parkland, river

Hidden in a wooded valley on the edge of Exmoor, the Arlington Estate houses numerous extraordinary collections, inside and out. The last owner, Miss Rosalie Chichester, developed a deer park and encouraged wildlife on her 1,125ha (2,700 acre) estate, which includes an ancient heronry. Today Arlington is recognised as one of the top spots in Devon for wildlife and is particularly famed for its rare lichens, as well as for bats, dormice, hares, otters and owls. The colony of lesser horseshoe bats roosting in the roof of the house can be observed using the

Above: The grounds in Arlington Court are famous for rare lichens and tree mosses, which thrive because the air is so moist and clean.

Right: In July and August, Ashclyst Forest is teeming with butterflies; white admirals, silver-washed fritillaries and purple hairstreak can all be seen. Here, an earlier visitor, a small pearl-bordered fritillary, settles on a bluebell.

interactive 'bat-cam'. Brown hares can often be seen on open grassland in March, especially near arable land. Marsh, silver-washed and small pearl-bordered fritillary butterflies also occur.

Ashclyst Forest, Killerton Estate, south Devon
Woodland

Ashclyst Forest, part of the National Trust's Killerton Estate, lies just to the east of Killerton House. In the past, parts of this large forest were open heathland, but the majority was wood pasture before the whole area was turned into plantation woodland. The National Trust has restored an area of grazed wood pasture, which is

developing a rich ground flora, and will be removing the conifer plantations over time. Ashclyst is an important place for woodland butterflies, notably a population of the declining pearl-bordered fritillary and colonies of the similar small pearl-bordered fritillary. In July silver-washed fritillary and white admiral abound, and can be seen feeding on the abundant bramble flowers. The birdlife is also interesting, with hobby and nightjar regularly breeding. The spring flora is rich and varied, offering attractive vistas of bluebells mixed with yellow archangel, early purple orchid and primrose.

Branscombe and Salcombe Regis, south Devon coast

Chalk grassland, scrubby cliff slope, woodland, streams, shingle beach

This coastal property is divided into two main sections, both situated at the westernmost point at which chalk is found in southern England. The chalk gives rise to a small but rich area of grassland along the cliffs. As well as many common plants and animals, a number of local species are found, such as Nottingham catchfly, blue gromwell, yellow-wort, horseshoe vetch and wood vetch. The mixed undercliff scrub attracts many migrating warblers, including the willow warbler, blackcap and chiffchaff. Larger birds, including buzzards, peregrines and ravens, can usually be seen in the vicinity of the bare rocky outcrops, along with a scattering of herring gulls. Lichens are rich on the pasture woodland trees, including the protected species golden-hair lichen and purple gromwell. Wood white butterflies breed in the more sheltered flowery places.

Clovelly, north Devon coast

Woodland, grassland, heath, scrub

Several detached sections make up this property on the Hartland Heritage Coast, including land in the vicinity of Brownsham, where one of the easier points of access is situated. In the area from Beckland to Fatacott, low, wind-trimmed shrubs cover much of the undercliff. Here blackthorn, hawthorn and brambles are abundant. Where there is more shelter, rowans, sycamores and oaks also grow. Mixed woodland occurs in the relatively undisturbed Beckland Wood and at Brownsham. Old 'unimproved' damp 'culm' grassland still survives in a few scattered locations, for example on Brownsham Moors.

Glenthorne, north Devon coast

Woodland, heath, grassland, ravines, streams

Glenthorne has a long, wild and beautiful coastal frontage on the Exmoor Heritage Coast, with steep slopes, landslips and ravines running to the sea. Much of the woodland is old coppiced oak, but there are also areas of ash, beech and sycamore. The open slopes are covered with bracken, grass, ling and bell heather, and at least two rare varieties of whitebeam grow among the rocks. Insects and snails thrive in the undisturbed dead wood, while abundant mosses and lichens show that this stretch of coast has largely escaped man's influence.

Heddon Valley, north Devon coast

Woodland, heath, grassland, cliffs, streams, beach

Along this stretch of Exmoor coast, wooded valleys converge and run into the sea. Included within the boundary of this site is an area of heathland, Trentishoe Down, and a long stretch of coastline with rugged cliffs and a small shingle beach. The woodland, mainly sessile oak and ash, is the haunt of the redstart, pied flycatcher, wood warbler, lesser spotted woodpecker, buzzard and sparrowhawk. Red deer also pass through it. Butterflies, too, are abundant. Heddon Valley's steep slopes support strong colonies of high brown, dark-green and silver-washed fritillary. The dipper, grey wagtail and heron can be seen along the streams, and the yellowhammer, linnet, stonechat, whinchat, tree pipit and wheatear live in the heathland. A variety of cliff-nesting birds, including fulmars and razorbills, help to make this a prime site for birdwatchers.

Plym Bridge Valley, south Devon coast

Ancient woodland, quarries, river

The River Plym, which rises on Dartmoor, flows down to the sea through Plym Bridge Woods. It is a favourite green space for the people of Plymouth. During the Industrial Revolution, the area was quarried, and tram and railway lines brought granite from Dartmoor and local slate through the woods to Plymouth. Cann Viaduct still stands and is a good place to view peregrine falcons. Spring flowers abound, particularly wood anemone, wild garlic, primrose and bluebells. Several old quarries with interesting industrial archaeological remains now support an abundance of ferns, mosses and lichens. The site is home to many animals, including a herd of fallow deer, and a wide range of birds. Kingfishers and dippers can be seen along the river, and lesser spotted woodpecker and tree pipit are found within the woods. The site supports many damselflies and butterflies, such as the speckled wood.

Above: A view over the Salcombe Estuary from the coastal garden at Overbeck's. Despite the name, it is not an estuary but a ria – a tidal inlet with no fresh water running into it. Dolphins and basking sharks visit and herons and cormorants can also be seen.

and rocky outcrops are clothed in bloody cranesbill, spring and autumn squills, rock samphire and thrift. Sheltered spots are good places to see butterflies, including the silver-studded blue. Ants, grasshoppers and bush crickets are also well represented in grass and heathland.

Watersmeet Estate, north Devon coast
Woodland, heath, grassland, cliffs, streams

The tranquillity of the west Exmoor coast provides a haven for coastal and woodland birds, and includes several types of landscape, from spectacular towering cliffs and ancient woodland to remote heather coastal moorland. The National Trust's land around Lynmouth, part of the Watersmeet Estate, comprises a mixture of both exposed and sheltered ground. Wooded areas provide breeding cover for buzzards, redstarts, pied flycatchers and wood warblers, while dippers feed in the fast-flowing streams of the East and West Lyn rivers, and otters have recently returned to parts of the river. While the woodland is mostly oak, it also contains ash, birch, rowan and three rare local species of whitebeam. Woodland butterflies are prominent. The dark green fritillary flies over bracken-covered slopes in June, and a little later in July, the larger silver-washed fritillary feeds on bramble flowers along valley pathways. The coastal areas play host to breeding grey seals and many nesting sea birds such as Manx shearwater, puffin, razorbill and guillemot. There are spectacular views over the Bristol Channel to be found along the coastline from the South West Coast Path, which runs along Glenthorne Cliffs towards Devon's most northerly outcrop, Foreland Point.

Salcombe, south Devon coast
Cliffs, woodland, heath, grassland

The extensive section of coastline that lies to east and west of Salcombe, including Bolt Head, Portlemouth Down, Prawle Point and Gammon Head, is a magnificent destination for the birdwatcher. The scrub and rough ground attracts stonechats, whinchats, yellowhammers, cirl bunting, linnets and many species of warbler. Along the steeper rocks and cliffs there are ravens, kestrels, rock pipits and wheatears, with a scattering of herring gulls, fulmars and kittiwakes nesting in more inaccessible sites. The seaward slopes

Above: A view of coastal heath in late summer on the cliff top of Highveer Point above Heddon's Mouth, a rocky cove famed for smuggling, on the north Devon Coast.

Above right: Beautiful woodland walks can be taken through the Lyn Valley and the Watersmeet Estate. Here, sunlight filters through the trees on to the East Lyn river highlighting its lichen-covered boulders.

Wembury Bay and Yealm Estuary, south Devon coast
Cliffs, woodland, beach, mudflats

The National Trust owns 2.5km (1½ miles) of coastline from Wembury to Warren Point, Wembury Woods and land on either side of the scenic Yealm estuary. Wembury Bay, at the mouth of Plymouth Sound, is notable for its marine conservation area, which was established in 1981. It has many rock pools, and is an ideal place for exploring the plant and animal life of the lower shore. Wembury Point is an important staging point for waders and migratory birds. Great Mewstone, a platform of rock 3.2km (2 miles) off the coast, was recently acquired from the Ministry of Defence, and is a breeding site for black-backed and herring gulls, cormorants, shags and buzzards. After storms, wagtails and turnstones can be seen hunting for insects along the shores of Wembury Bay, which they find among the mounds of seaweed flung up on the beach. Stonechats, whinchats, wheatears and cirl buntings breed inland.

Whiddon Deer Park, south Devon
Parkland, ancient woodland

Whiddon is an internationally important site for lichens and beetles associated with ancient oak and ash trees. Designated a

Below: The rocky coast at Wembury, Devon, is a wave-cut platform that extends right out into the sea to the Great Mewstone, which sits at the mouth of Plymouth Sound.

SSSI, it comprises pasture woodland with an exceptionally diverse lichen flora, and a rich invertebrate fauna with many nationally rare species. Lying on the north-eastern edge of Dartmoor, the park occupies the floor and steep west-facing slope of a valley above a stream that feeds into the nearby River Teign. The underlying rock is granite, which outcrops frequently, and has led to the formation of acid soils. Derived from and still retaining much of the original character of a medieval deer park, the site has many exceptionally large and old oak, ash and beech trees interspersed, unusually so for ancient pasture woodland, with many younger trees, mainly oak, but also birch, holly, willow and hawthorn. The park is now grazed by cattle and sheep. Over 235 lichen species have been recorded in the park,

Above: The National Trust purchased 9.6km (6 miles) of land on the West Exmoor Coast in 1965 with Enterprise Neptune funds. It incorporates towering cliffs, secluded coves such as Woody Bay, seen here, wooded river valleys and heather moorland.

mainly on ancient trees and granite rocks. Unusually for pasture woodland, there is an interesting moss flora, primarily associated with old ash trees. The old trees support a rich community of invertebrates, particularly some rare beetles, mainly associated with their dead wood.

Woody Bay, north Devon coast
Woodland, grassland, cliffs

Woody Bay is a quiet cove to the east of the Heddon Valley, with views over the Bristol Channel. In places, the oaks that surround it extend to the very edge of the precipitous cliffs. Yew trees are common here, and are believed to be native, one of the few places in Devon and Cornwall where this is so. Rare species of whitebeam, including the

Devon whitebeam, perch precariously at the edge of rocky cliff overhangs. The seabirds that breed on the secluded rock stack and in the general region of Wringapeak are mainly herring gulls, kittiwakes, razorbills and guillemots. Fulmars, ravens and peregrines are all resident along the cliffs.

Dorset

Ballard Down, south-east Dorset coast
Chalk grassland and gorse scrub
This dramatic chalk ridge rises to over 150m (500ft) to the south of Studland Bay. The steep, south-facing slope is a fine example of 'unimproved' chalk grassland that was once so common in this area. Although no great rarities grow on Ballard Down, horseshoe vetch, kidney vetch, bee orchid and autumn lady's tresses make exploring its slopes in spring and summer an enjoyable experience. Many insects thrive in the warm climate of the Dorset coast. A total of 21 species of butterfly breed here, including the adonis blue, small blue and Lulworth skipper. The gorse provides cover and perches for whitethroats and stonechats.

Cerne Abbas Giant, north-west Dorset
Chalk-hill figure
The largest chalk-hill figure in Britain, the Cerne Abbas Giant is a huge outline of a naked man holding a club, sculpted into the chalk hillside above the village of Cerne Abbas to the north of Dorchester. The figure has conventionally been viewed as a great symbol of ancient spirituality. A mound below the giant's left hand may be the sculpted remnant of a severed head, which the figure once clutched – a grisly, if common, ancient Celtic religious symbol. Alternatively, the Roman hero Hercules was often depicted naked with a club in his right hand, and a lion skin draped over his left shoulder. Scientific tests have suggested that there might once have been something draped over the giant's left side but this has long since grassed over. Despite an abundant archive of local medieval documents, there is no written reference to the giant before 1694. In 1774 the Reverend John Hutchins claimed he was told that the giant was 'a modern thing' cut by Lord Holles, who owned Giant Hill in the 17th century, and who was a fierce critic of Oliver Cromwell. Could the Cerne Abbas Giant seek to satirise Cromwell's stern puritanical rule? Giant Hill is superb for chalk grassland flowers and butterflies, including a large colony of the rare marsh fritillary butterfly.

Fontmell Down, north-east Dorset
Chalk grassland, scrub, flint scree
Fontmell Down's steep grassy slopes have never felt the effect of the plough, and have never been treated with fertilisers or herbicides. As a result, the plant and animal life remains much as it has done for hundreds of years. The turf abounds

Above: Fontmell Down, near Shaftesbury, has botanically rich chalk grassland that is smothered in wild flowers in summer and home to nine species of orchid, the rare early gentian, a mass of butterflies and the skylark.

with squinancywort, horseshoe vetch, quaking grass, the rare moss species *Rhodobryum roseum* and other chalk-loving plants. Over 55 bird species have been recorded, including nightingales, grasshopper warblers, sparrowhawks, kestrels, buzzards and hen harriers. The sheltered combes and the south-facing slopes are good places to find chalkland butterflies, including the adonis blue and the elusive silver-spotted skipper.

Hod Hill, north-east Dorset
Chalk grassland, scrub
Rising steeply above the River Stour, and crowned by the ramparts and ditches of a hill fort, Hod Hill is one of the richest sites for chalkland wildlife in England. Thirty-five species of butterfly have been recorded here, although some of them – for example, the silver-spotted skipper and white-letter hairstreak – may have become extinct in recent times. In summer, the chalkhill blue, common blue, small blue and brown argus can all be seen on the hill, and another scarce species, the marsh fritillary, is common here. Over 200 species of flowering plant have been recorded, including horseshoe vetch, bastard toadflax, squinancywort, field fleawort, and an abundance of the scarce dwarf sedge.

Kingston Lacy Estate, east Dorset
Woodland, scrub, parkland, chalk grassland, meadows, marsh, river

This largely agricultural estate has several areas that are interesting for their wildlife, the most notable being Badbury Rings and the banks of the River Stour. The plant life of Badbury Rings includes the greater butterfly orchid, frog orchid and bee orchid. Bastard toadflax, adder's tongue fern and knapweed broomrape can also be found on this part of the estate. The River Stour attracts many birds, including sedge and reed warblers, kingfishers, mute swans and little grebes. A large black poplar – rare in Britain – grows near White Mill Bridge, and young trees are being propagated from it.

Gloucestershire

Crickley Hill, mid-Gloucestershire
Limestone grassland, woodland

This impressive site, with its abundant flowers and insects, gives sweeping views over the Severn Valley and the city of Gloucester. Its north-west slopes are covered in limestone grassland, which contains a range of different grasses, as well as plants such as devil's-bit scabious, salad burnet, bird's-foot trefoil and squinancywort. Mosses and liverworts can be found in the damper areas. A hill fort stands on the western end of the limestone promontory, and wild thyme and clustered bellflower can be seen in the drier grasslands around it. Butterflies, such as the marbled white, abound.

Dover's Hill, north Gloucestershire
Woodland, grassland, ponds

Dover's Hill lies on the edge of the Cotswold escarpment where the limestone hills drop steeply towards the Vale of Evesham. The grassland contains a local speciality – meadow saxifrage – and large numbers of snails live in some areas. The scrub mainly comprises hawthorn, ash and sallow, and its tangled cover provides an excellent habitat for nesting birds, such as the whitethroat, garden warbler and turtle dove. The tawny owl, great spotted woodpecker and blackcap nest in the woodland. The large old pollards of ash, oak and field maple are home to many insects.

Littleworth Wood, north Gloucestershire
Woodland, scrub

With its stands of field maple, oak and hazel, the ancient, semi-natural Littleworth Wood, near Snowshill, south east of Evesham, is partly managed as a coppice. Beneath the trees, a dense shrub layer consists of hazel, spindle, wayfaring tree, whitebeam and hawthorn. These diverse trees and shrubs harbour a great range of insects, attracting birds such as blackcap, goldcrest and green woodpecker. Deer and badgers also live in the wood. Littleworth contains a number of unusual plants, such as herb paris, meadow saffron, four species of orchid, and the adder's tongue and hard shield ferns.

May Hill, west Gloucestershire
Grassland, heath, ponds

The steep climb to the top of this isolated hill, 275m (900ft) high, and mid-way between Gloucester and Ross-on-Wye, is rewarded with spectacular views. The hill's vegetation consists mainly of acid grassland. Cutting now controls spreading gorse and bracken. The hill's butterflies include the small copper and wood white, and the ponds and marshy ground are the haunt of pondskaters, damselflies and newts. The plant life of these wet areas includes marsh pennywort, bog stitchwort, round-leaved crowfoot and bog pimpernel. The whinchat is a regular summer visitor, nesting among tussocks of grass. The adjacent May Hill Common is still largely covered by bracken.

Rodborough and Minchinhampton Commons, mid-Gloucestershire
Limestone grassland, Beech woodland, scrub

This extensive area of limestone grassland lies on the plateau of the Cotswolds and the steep escarpment that forms the abrupt western flank of the hill overlooking Stroud. The commons, which are edged with scrub and furrowed by ancient earthworks, are still grazed by cattle owned by local people exercising their rights as 'commoners'. Abundant wild flowers, including the pasque flower, meadow saffron and 11 species of orchid, help to create a carpet of colour in spring and summer. Local wildlife includes the greater horseshoe bat, and butterflies such as the chalkhill and small blue, Duke of Burgundy and dark green fritillary.

Westridge Wood, south Gloucestershire
Woodland

This small wood is characteristic of the many beautiful woods and copses that cling to the steep Cotswold escarpment. Beech is the most abundant tree, but ash, oak, whitebeam and field maple also grow well on the limestone slopes. Holly, spindle and wayfaring tree form a broken shrub layer. Springtime sees the woods carpeted in bluebells and dog's mercury, while patches of wood anemone, sweet woodruff and yellow archangel add further colour. The rare angular Solomon's seal also grows on the woodland floor. The animal life of the wood includes the striking scarlet tiger moth, many birds and the diminutive dormouse.

Woodchester Park, mid-Gloucestershire
River valley, woodland, parkland, lakes, coppice

Woodchester Park is a beautiful secluded valley to the south-west of Stroud. The valley contains the remains of an 18th- and 19th-century landscaped park, a mansion and a chain of five lakes fringed by woodland and pasture. The historic landscape is partially hidden under conifer and mixed woodlands planted in the mid-20th century. The upper valley slopes consist of deciduous woodland (beech, ash and hazel), and the remainder comprises conifers and mixed plantation, both planted and naturally regenerated. A sweep of permanent pasture adjoining the unfinished Victorian gothic mansion contains a scattering of magnificent old parkland trees, including oaks, sweet chestnut, sycamore, cedars and monkey puzzle. The entire valley is designated as

Right: White rockrose, a rare limestone plant, is abundant at Brean Down, Somerset.

Below: A frosty view across 'The Park', Minchinhampton Common, towards the church. In summer the common is grazed by the local commoners' cattle.

a SSSI. Buzzards, owls and woodpeckers breed in the woodland and the lakes are home to coots, moorhens, mallard and Mandarin ducks. The lime-rich soils encourage colourful wild flowers such as primroses and columbine, as well as less common ones such as orchids, Solomon's seal and lily-of-the-valley. Greater horseshoe bats have breeding roosts in the mansion, and lesser horseshoe, pipistrelle, Daubenton's and long-eared bats are also found in the valley. Woodchester has one of the largest concentrations of badger setts in Britain.

Somerset

Brean Down, Somerset coast
Cliff, coastal grassland, scrub

This wild, narrow promontory jutting into the Bristol Channel is of great botanical and archaeological interest. The steep, south-facing slopes are home to a mix of plants that is found nowhere else in Britain, including the white rockrose, Somerset hairgrass and the dwarf sedge. The area also teems with insect life, including the chalkhill blue and dark green fritillary butterflies. In the spring and autumn, the scrub provides cover for migrating birds such as the wheatear, ring ouzel, whinchat, warblers and finches.

Collard Hill, east Somerset
Grassland

Collard Hill stands above the Somerset levels where the narrow ridge of the Polden Hills turns at right angles to head south. It offers wonderful views over the levels and the southern Poldens. The National Trust has dedicated Collard Hill to the conservation of the large blue butterfly, and to people's engagement with this rare and special insect. It is the only place in Britain where people can see the large blue, the English race of which became extinct in 1979. The butterfly was reintroduced here in 2000, using stock from Sweden. Despite the odd set-back, the butterfly has thrived here, and is now quite easy to spot on sunny days in mid-June. Grazing is the key to this success, as the large blue caterpillars feed on the grubs of a single species of red ant that requires short, hot turf. Other wildlife also benefits from the grazing required by the ant and butterfly, including the rare nit grass, bee orchids and several scarce species of ant, bee and beetle.

Dolebury Warren, north Somerset
Limestone grassland, heath, scrub, woodland

Dolebury Warren's steep limestone ridge is crowned with a large and impressive Iron

Above: Ancient stunted sessile oak trees, swathed in internationally important lichen flora, can be found on Leg Hill in Horner Wood, on the Holnicote Estate.

Age hill fort with massive banks and ditches. The ridge rises to 180m (600ft) and is an outstanding site for butterflies. Over 30 species have been recorded here, among them the grizzled skipper and small blue. The flanks of the ridge are covered by grass, hawthorn scrub and also woodland, which is dominated by ash trees. In spring and summer, the grassland is studded with the flowers of common rockrose, salad burnet, kidney vetch, wild thyme and yellow rattle. Heath has developed on the hilltop.

Holnicote Estate, west Somerset
Moorland, bogs, grassland, ancient woodland, rivers, cliffs, saltmarsh, shingle beach

This varied estate covers about 50km² (20 square miles) of west Somerset. The high, windswept moorland – home of the estate's red deer – is dominated by heather, with patches of bilberry, bell heather and gorse. Lower down, Horner Wood is home to ancient oak and ash trees that are covered with epiphytic lichens, wood-rotting fungi, mosses, liverworts and ferns. The ancient trees

are also havens for many species of bat. These steep, wooded valleys are inhabited by buzzards, sparrowhawks, green and lesser spotted woodpeckers, as well as pied flycatchers, wood warblers and redstarts. The fast-flowing Horner Water is home to dipper and grey wagtail, while the coastal heath and cliffs provide a habitat for whinchats, stonechats, wheatears and nightjars. Throughout the estate, insects are abundant and include beetles and deadwood flies. Large colonies of the rare heath fritillary butterfly inhabit some of the moorland combes, notably Bin Combe and Halse Combe.

Leigh Woods, north Somerset
Woodland, scrub, grassland, cliffs

These verdant woods cling to the limestone of the Avon Gorge, just a short distance from the centre of Bristol. They are in part ancient and in part woodland that once contained areas of pasture. A wide range of trees grows here, including oak, ash, small-leaved lime, wild cherry, and also a type of whitebeam that is unique to the Avon Gorge. The plant life of Leigh Woods is exceptionally rich. Ivy and bluebells grow on the woodland floor, together with more unusual plants, such as lily-of-the-valley and ivy broomrape. Ferns, which appreciate the damp conditions, are also abundant.

Mendip Hills and Cheddar Gorge, north-east Somerset
Gorges, ancient woodland, grassland, limestone cliffs

South of Bath and Bristol lie the dramatic gorges, distinctive peaks and ancient woodland of the Mendips that rise above the Somerset Levels. The National Trust owns the north side of Britain's largest gorge at Cheddar. This great, deep fissure cutting through the Mendips began forming about one million years ago during the last ice age, carved by the waters of melting glaciers. Look out for rare flowers such as the Cheddar pink, orchids and rock stonecrop on the limestone cliffs. Spot peregrine, raven, soay sheep and feral goats here, too. From Wavering Down's summit savour the extensive views of the Bristol Channel and Welsh Hills. It is then a short walk to the prominent limestone hill of Crook Peak. Surrounded by ancient woodland and open grassland, this is a haven for butterflies like dark green and small pearl-bordered fritillary. The rocky summit offers great views towards Cheddar Reservoir and Brean Down. Ebbor Gorge is a dramatic limestone gorge managed by Natural England with interesting caves, some of which were home to prehistoric humans. Its ancient woodlands are rich in wildlife. There are some steep scrambles on the way to the top, but once you emerge from the trees you are rewarded with spectacular views.

Middle Hope and Sand Point, Somerset coast
Limestone grassland, scrub, rock, saltmarsh

This very varied site is dominated by a limestone ridge 30m (100ft) high that juts out into the Bristol Channel, giving views across to Wales and inland to the Mendips. The ridge becomes craggier towards its western tip, while at its eastern end it grades into saltmarsh. Rock samphire and thrift grow on the rocks, while the rabbit-grazed turf is rich in lime-loving flowers, such as yellow-wort, common centaury, salad burnet, common rockrose, wild thyme, dwarf thistle, bee orchid and green-winged orchid.

Quantock Hills, west Somerset
Woodland, heathland, grassland, streams

The National Trust owns several properties on this small but fascinating range of hills. At Fyne Court, the Somerset Wildlife Trust runs several nature trails, providing a useful introduction to the region's natural history. The open hills contain large areas of heather, but in places this has reverted to grassland

Below: A view of the sunlit Cheddar Cliffs and Cheddar Gorge. It is the largest gorge – a deep valley between cliffs – to be found in the UK. The cliffs on the north side are owned by the National Trust.

and bracken. A variety of birds can be found on the heathland, including the meadow pipit, stonechat, whinchat and nightjar. Red deer, introduced in the 1860s, can be seen on the high ground together with ponies and sheep.

Wiltshire

Pepperbox Hill, south-east Wiltshire
Scrub, chalk grassland

The name Pepperbox Hill comes from the 17th-century folly that sits on the hilltop. The hill is home to many old juniper bushes and there are also some good specimens of whitebeam, dogwood, hawthorn, wayfaring tree, guelder rose and wild privet. Seven species of orchid bloom on the hill, and other plants include the greater knapweed, dropwort and chalk milkwort. A total of 80 species of butterfly and moth have been recorded on the hillside.

White Sheet Hill, west Wiltshire
Chalk, grassland, old quarry

White Sheet Hill adjoins the National Trust's Stourhead Estate, and contains one of the richest prehistoric sites in Wiltshire. Some 12 Bronze Age barrows dating from around 1800BC are scattered over White Sheet Hill, along with the remains of a Neolithic causeway camp and an Iron Age hill fort. Like any area of 'unimproved' chalk grassland, the downs are a haven for butterflies, including the chalkhill and small blues, marsh fritillary, marbled white, and, in early summer, good numbers of grizzled and dingy skippers. Coltsfoot, cowslips and primroses grow in the old quarry, and bird's-foot trefoil, harebell, salad burnet, yellow rattle, wild thyme and lady's bedstraw flower here in summer. Several species of orchid grow on the hill, and rockrose flowers in profusion in summer, creating a carpet of yellow that contrasts with the late summer 'blue period' when the devil's-bit scabious comes into flower.

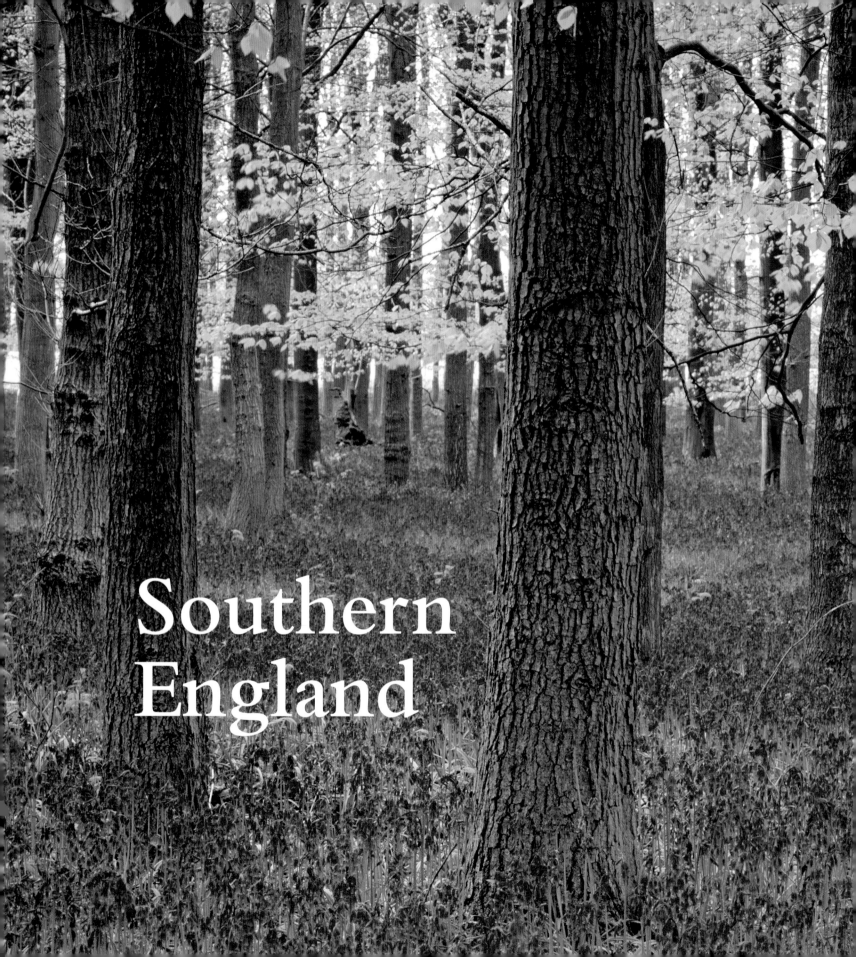

Southern
England

The South Downs

The South Downs are a long, narrow range of chalk hills, covering some 1,374km² (530 square miles), that run from Beachy Head in East Sussex westwards to Winchester in central Hampshire. They consist of a steep, north-facing scarp slope and a gentle, southward-running dip slope. The downs run from Eastbourne on the East Sussex coast, past Brighton and Hove, to join with the central Hampshire chalklands. Two areas within the Downs are designated Areas of Outstanding Natural Beauty (AONBs), East Hampshire AONB and Sussex Downs AONB. The South Downs are home to 670 scheduled ancient monuments and attract an estimated 32 million visitors per year.

The South Downs are the southern remaining section of the former Wealden Dome, and consist of a layer of Lower Cretaceous rocks topped by sandstone, clay and chalky deposits laid down under the sea. Later, movements in the earth's crust pushed up the sea bed into a dome, or anticline, leaving a sequence of rock layers with the oldest at the centre. Erosion and weathering caused the less-resistant rocks to erode faster, producing sandstone ridges and

clay valleys. The undulating Seven Sisters cliffs, that run east from Seaford towards Eastbourne, reveal the remnants of dry valleys that are being eroded by the cliffs. The rocks contain flint and are rich in fossils.

The South Downs are characterised by rolling chalk downs, deep, dry valleys or combes, and a steep escarpment that offers views over the wooded farmland of the Sussex Weald. They cover around 112km (70 miles) from west to east, and are just 11km (7 miles) across. Four river valleys cut through the downs en route to the English Channel. Beneath the downs lies a chalk aquifer (underground layer of water-bearing rock). A shallow layer of clay and flint covers much of the tops of the downs. It is thought

Left: The South Downs are renowned for their wild flowers but vast areas were ploughed up for agriculture. Here, ox-eye daisies flourish in land now being put back to downland flowers.

Below: The Seven Sisters cliffs distinctive, undulating profile marks the southernmost point of the South Downs. Fossil hunters come to collect echinoid, brachiopods, bivalves and crinoids from the foreshore.

Insects on the South Downs

Several of the country's top butterfly sites occur on the South Downs, such as Newtimber Hill, Cissbury Ring and Old Winchester Hill National Nature Reserve. On sunny days much of the downs is alive with butterflies. In spring, **green hairstreak**, **dingy skipper** and the rare **Duke of Burgundy** can be found. These are replaced in high summer by the distinctive **marbled white** and bold **dark green fritillary**. But the downs are at their best for insects in August, when the short turf can shimmer with the brilliant blue wings of the **chalkhill** and **adonis blue** butterflies, and the keen sighted can spot the swift, low flight of the **silver-spotted skipper**. Day-flying moths also abound, notably the **burnet companion** in May and red and black **burnet** moths in high summer. The downs are also good for hoverflies and solitary bees, while on warm summer days, they pulsate with the songs of crickets and grasshoppers.

Dingy skipper

Above: The Southdown sheep became an important recognised breed some 200 years ago. It was exported across the world and had an impact on the development of the popular New Zealand Canterbury Lamb. Today it is recognised as an 'at risk' breed.

that man effectively cleared the woodland on the downs around 2,500 years ago, and that grazing by sheep and cattle produced the open chalk landscape we see today. The area even has its own breed of sheep, the Southdown.

The downs are renowned for their wild flowers and butterflies. The flowers are at their most beautiful from late spring through to late summer. In spring and early summer, yellows predominate, with cowslip, bird's-foot trefoil, horseshoe vetch and buttercups. In June, pink is the main colour, with patches of wild thyme showing strongly alongside fragrant, pyramidal and common spotted orchids. In July, the blues and purples of the scabious and knapweed flowers dominate. These include the round-headed rampion, an exquisite deep blue scabious that is all but restricted to this area, and is known as the Pride of Sussex. Although the birdlife is far less diverse than that described by W.H. Hudson, skylarks are still locally common, red kites have been reintroduced to the area, buzzards circle overhead and flocks of goldfinches appear in autumn, when they feed on thistledown. Wheatears can be seen in early spring and autumn, and lapwings in winter.

Some 20 per cent of the South Downs is comprised of woodland, of which half is ancient woodland. Some

Below: The round-headed rampion produces the most exquisite violet-blue flower heads between June and August and is only found on the South Downs.

consists of mixed broad-leaved species, notably oak and ash, which can cope with the thin, chalky soil. Hanging beech woods on a dry valley scarp can be seen at the National Trust's Slindon Estate near Arundel. At the Drovers Estate near Singleton there are large stands of woodland, including gnarled beech trees that were planted to commemorate the Battle of Trafalgar in 1805. Near Chichester, at the Kingley Vale Nature Reserve, is one of the finest yew forests in western Europe, spreading over just under 81ha (200 acres). Some of the trees here are estimated to be 500–800 years old and are twisted and tangled by time.

The South Downs meet the sea west of Beachy Head, where the downland becomes a coastal habitat. Along this stretch, coarse tor grass is dominant, and requires careful grazing to allow the more delicate plants to grow. In effect, there are major differences between the exposed eastern downs and the more sheltered downs of West Sussex, both in landform and vegetation.

Above: The South Downs escarpment above the village of Poynings, behind Devil's Dyke, showing steep slope chalk grassland and looking out into the Sussex Weald.

Left: The low tide exposes the chalk flats at Birling Gap. The eroding cliffs are said to provide the best cross-section of a dry valley in the UK.

Birling Gap

Birling Gap nestles in some of the most spectacular coastal scenery on the Sussex coast, where high chalk cliffs form a vertical rampart, which is being constantly eroded by the sea. A ladder allows access to the shingle beach. At high tide, only a narrow strip of shingle remains above the water, but low tide exposes chalk flats capped with flints that have been sculpted and hollowed by the sea. The chalk provides a foothold for seaweeds, and also for small animals such as limpets, mussels and sea anemones. Gulls, fulmars and jackdaws patrol the cliffs, making use of the strong updraught created by the onshore wind. Belle Tout, directly to the east, is an interesting area of chalk heath, scrub and chalk grassland.

Devil's Dyke

Legend has it that the Devil created this valley to drown the parishioners of the Weald. Scientists, on the other hand, believe the largest 'dry' valley in Britain was formed during the last ice age. This huge feature carves its way through ridges of rolling chalk grassland and gives stunning views north to the Weald and south to the

English Channel. It is home to butterflies, such as adonis blue and silver-spotted skipper, that thrive on the plants supported by the chalk grassland habitat. The ramparts or walls of an Iron Age hill fort can be seen as you walk around the hill. As grazing declined through the 20th century, scrub began to invade the grassland. Careful management by grazing animals has helped to maintain the grassland.

Cissbury Ring

Set on a chalk promontory on the South Downs, this Iron Age hill fort with its ditch and ramparts is the second largest in England. Also a Site of Special Scientific Interest (SSSI), the chalk grassland covering the earthworks supports a wide range of downland plants such as horseshoe vetch, cowslip, stemless thistle and several species of orchid (including pyramid and common spotted). Butterflies include the chalkhill blue and dark green fritillary. A dry combe or steep-sided valley cuts into the chalk plateau, and is also rich in lime-loving flowers and grasses such as rockrose, horseshoe vetch, quaking grass and ploughman's spikenard.

Harting Downs

One of the largest areas of ancient chalk downland in National Trust care, Harting Down in West Sussex is a renowned nature reserve and Site of Special Scientific Interest. Sheep grazing helps to conserve this grassland environment where rare wildlife thrives. This walk offers panoramic views over the Weald to the North Downs, before descending into secluded valleys of natural and historical interest.

Getting there and facilities:

Easily accessible by cycle, there is a traffic-free route under 1.6km (1 mile) away. There is a bus stop in South Harting, 1.6km (1 mile) away, reached on the 54 from Petersfield to Chichester, and Petersfield train station is 7.5km (5 miles) away. There is a car park (free to National Trust members), picnic areas, refreshments and toilets at nearby Uppark (National Trust house and garden) or South Harting village. A self-guided walk pack, 'Stroll the South Downs' is also available.

Start point:

The start point is 8.8km (5½ miles) south east of Petersfield and 1.6km (1 mile) south of South Harting, off the B2141. OS Landranger 197 – SU791180

Distance, terrain and accessibility:

The walk is 3km (2 miles) on grassy paths with several hills and rather steep ascents and descents. It can be muddy in places after wet weather and in winter. Shorter walks are listed in a walks pack.

Route and directions:

1   Start in Harting Down National Trust car park, with a fantastic view across the flat plain of the Weald towards Hog's Back ridge and North Downs. Walk through a gate and cross Harting Hill.

2   Go over the undulating 'cross-ridge dykes'. These parallel mounds date back to the Iron Age, and may have been boundary markers or a 'checkpoint' across the ridgeway.

3   Follow the right-hand track up Round Down hill, keeping a hedge on your left. You'll see a huge variety of plants here all year round.

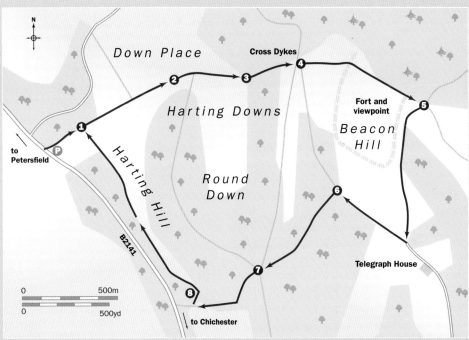

Just over the top of the hill, turn left and go through a gate, before walking down into the next valley. After another gate at the bottom, walk across to the base of Beacon Hill. Catch a whiff of the berries that grow on the female juniper bush and in springtime, enjoy a buttery-yellow carpet of cowslips, often used to make a potent local wine.

4   Here is the ridge of an Iron Age Hill Fort, probably created as an animal enclosure and a symbol of status, rather than a defensive stronghold. Either climb to the summit of Beacon Hill or turn right and skirt across its lower slopes.

5   If you do walk over the top, turn right at a crossroads of paths on the other side and skirt back round the lower slopes of Beacon Hill until you meet the short-cut again.

6   At a signpost turn away from Beacon Hill on a path down to a dew pond and a little hill, 'Granny's Bottom', on your right.

7   Pass the pond and cross into a yew wood, known as 'the darkest place on the downs'. It's cold in here, even on a hot day! Yew trees are home to birds like wren, thrush and finch.

8   Climb up through the shade back on to Harting Hill. Follow the path until you emerge through an opening (not gate) on the right. Stay on the grassy path back to the car park.

Cuckmere Estuary

The Cuckmere Valley is an iconic landscape of significant national importance and is a SSSI, an AONB and a Heritage Coast (HC). Through it the Cuckmere River flows from the downland villages of East Sussex to the sea via Cuckmere Haven. Today, the valley estuary, with its celebrated relict meanders and shingle beach, is still a heavily managed landscape, with the Victorian cut channel surrounded by reclaimed farmland of limited biodiversity. The meanders sit in isolation to the rest of the river and are silting up. The flood-plain grassland has been agriculturally improved, but there is a rich area of saltmarsh, and a series of ponds and tidal creeks. This is an important area for wintering birds, especially lapwing, teal, wigeon and mute swan. Waders are less numerous, due to the shortage of bare mud, which is restricted to the tidal creek edges. The saltmarsh is dominated by sea purslane, and supports some uncommon invertebrates. The ponds hold rare water beetles.

Fulking Escarpment and Newtimber Hill

Following its South Downs Appeal, the National Trust has acquired large areas of this steep chalkland escarpment. Orchids are common in the short turf. Chalkland butterflies abound here, and they include several different species of blue. Carder bees and cardinal beetles live on the slopes, and a number of rare species of grasshopper can be found in the grass. The downland birds include the nightingale, as well as the occasional hoopoe that flies in from across the English Channel.

Harting Down and Beacon Hill

One of the largest areas of ancient chalk downland owned by the National Trust, Harting Down is a SSSI, which is managed through careful grazing and scrub removal in association with the local people. Scrub is a serious problem here, and its management has to be robust and ongoing. The sward on the steep slopes is dominated by upright brome grass so that short-turf rarities, such as chalk milkwort and musk orchid, are restricted to the skeletal soil areas. There is a small area of chalk heath and a large juniper stand. Two large areas have been taken out of arable farming and are reverting spectacularly to rich chalk grassland. Invertebrates include Duke of Burgundy, dark green fritillary and grizzled skipper butterflies, the blue carpenter bee and the rare cheese snail.

Slindon Woods

The remains of the woods at Slindon are a testament to the power of the great storm that swept across southern England in 1987. Although a large proportion of the woods on this estate were destroyed, some plants have benefited from the increased light, as have the birds that feed among them. In the coming years Slindon Woods will be a fascinating case history of woodland reasserting itself.

Below: From Fulking Escarpment at Devil's Dyke you can see the rolling hills of the South Downs descend to the plain below.

Isle of Wight

The Isle of Wight is separated from the British mainland by a sea channel called the Solent, although the stretch of water between the entrance to Portsmouth Harbour, and 1.6km (1 mile) north of Ryde and Bembridge on the island, is historically known as Spithead. Measuring just 37km (23 miles) by 21km (13 miles), the Isle of Wight is much more than a beautiful seaside holiday location, because it contains a remarkable diversity of landscapes within a small area, including wooded valleys, chalk grasslands, all manner of coastline, and the marshy basin of the River Yar. This unusual variation emanates from the island's acutely varied geology, which has parallels with the Weald and the New Forest. Over half of the island is a designated AONB.

The island has been inhabited since it was possible to walk the 5–8km (3–5 miles) to mainland England without getting your feet wet. The chalk hills were cleared of timber and there is much evidence of Bronze Age life here from burial mounds. There is a strong agricultural heritage; sheep, dairy and arable farming are practised here, and crops such as lavender and garlic thrive in the warmer environment. Fishing was an important industry, and in the 17th century, fishermen were required to take it in turns to operate a form of ferry service to Portsmouth. Queen Victoria's fondness for the island is well documented and it was during this time that it began the transition from fishing villages to coastal resorts.

The island has always been regarded as an important defensive stronghold; it was occupied by the Romans, and the Vikings invaded repeatedly for 100 years from around 897. It was a target for the marauding French during the Hundred Years War, necessitating the establishment of a permanent naval base. Spain threatened the Isle of Wight during the time of Elizabeth I, and Charles I made the mistake of fleeing there in 1647 – he was imprisoned, leading eventually to his trial and execution.

The Isle of Wight is shaped roughly like a diamond with an area of 380km² (147½ square miles) and 92km (57 miles) of coastline. The oldest rocks on the island, the ones that contain the dinosaur fossils that the island is famous for, were formed around 110 million years ago when much of southern England and the English Channel was part of a large river valley, later flooded by the sea. Sand, clay and microscopic algae that would eventually form limestone were laid down, and consequently all the rocks in the island are sedimentary.

Left: The view from Compton Chine across to Tennyson Down, where Alfred Lord Tennyson famously walked. Black-and-white Friesian cattle graze in the foreground.

Above: Chalk stacks of The Needles from Scratchells Bay, off the western side of the island. The lighthouse at the western end was built in 1859, replacing earlier constructions.

Thirty million years ago, the earth's crust lifted and the rock folded, and the island began to take on its present shape. A prominent chalk ridge outcrop runs through the centre of the island from The Needles in the west to Culver Cliff in the east. The ridge used to be part of the Purbeck chalk ridge to the west and South Downs to the east. The Needles are three chalk stacks that rise out of the sea beyond the western tip of the island. The group takes its name from

Above: Wild flowers flourish on top of Freshwater Cliffs, looking towards Compton Bay, a mile-long stretch of sand. The water here is clean and the bay is popular with surfers.

Right: Dinosaur footprints can sometimes be seen imprinted on the rocks at low tide at Compton Bay. The two visible rocky lines mark the edges of the sedimentary rock that underlies the beach. The view beyond is to Tennyson Down and Afton Down.

a fourth, needle-shaped pillar, known as Lot's wife, which collapsed in a storm in 1764. Just beyond the Needles is a 5km (3 miles) shifting shoal of pebbles, known as The Shingles, on which many boats have foundered. The Isle of Wight Coast Path is a good way to get a flavour of the island; it follows the coast for 107km (67 miles) and takes in many of the island's attractions, including the stunning chalk geography to the south and west.

The island's position, just a little further south than the mainland, ensures that it is just that little bit warmer; the southern end of the island is renowned for an almost sub-tropical climate, allowing an extraordinary array of flowers to flourish. Rarities such as field cow wheat, which looks like a small purple feather duster, autumn squill, a tiny upturned bluebell, the stunning pyramidal orchid, which relies on the presence of a specific fungus in the soil, and the pink

or purple green-winged orchid, are a delight to behold. Wall lizards, a denizen of southern Europe, breed in Ventnor Botanic Garden.

Plants thrive on the soft cliff ledges, including sweet-scented hoary stock on the south-facing cliffs. At Headon Warren there is a large area of heathland that tumbles down into the sea at Totland Bay. At Tennyson Down, named after the poet who lived and walked there, is grassland rich in flowers, and the cliffs are home to many nesting seabirds, such as guillemot, fulmar, shag and razorbill. Just to the east, runs the continuous raised ground of Afton, Compton and Brook downs, which is arguably the richest chalk downland in England. Culver Cliff is a prime nesting site for gulls, cormorants, shags, guillemot and razorbill. Compton Bay is perfect for bathing, and often, at low tide, fossilised dinosaur footprints and tree stumps are evident. Here, the cliffs regularly subside, exposing new fossils and dinosaur casts. Steep narrow gorges, known as 'chines', run down to the sea and these are cut by streams and filled with luxuriant vegetation.

Most of the significant woodland is found on clay soils on the northern side of the island; in Firestone Copse, you can see the wild service tree with its white summer flowers and glorious autumn colour, jostling for space with oak and grand fir. Butterflies such as silver-washed fritillaries and white admirals flutter in the clearings. Here, in early spring, you will find the rare narrow-leaved lungwort with its purple and blue, funnel-shaped flowers.

Wroxall and Rew copses are ancient woodland containing many veteran trees. These woods are vitally important for the red squirrel, which is still well established on the island, due to the absence of the dominant, competitive grey. The Isle of Wight is also believed to be an area of international importance for bats – ten different species, including two of Europe's rarest bats, Bechstein's and barbastelle, are found here.

The National Trust owns around ten per cent of the total area of the Isle of Wight with 27km (17 miles) of unspoilt coastline, mainly between The Needles and St Catherine's Point – the most southerly point of the island. The Trust also owns the downs east of Freshwater (Afton, Compton and Brook), St Boniface Down and the adjoining Luccombe Down at Ventnor, the Bembridge chalk cliffs, The Duver at St Helens, and the estuary and ancient meadows around Newtown in the north of the island.

Afton, Compton and Brook Downs

From the top of this bold chalk ridge there are views over land and sea in every direction. The chalk grassland on the south-facing slope is extremely rich in plants and insects. This slope is hot and dry in the summer and exposed to gales in the winter. Most of this land is grazed by a herd of Galloway cattle. The characteristic plants of chalk grassland, such as the horseshoe vetch, dwarf thistle, rockrose and kidney vetch, are common. Orchids grow here in abundance. Where the vegetation is sparse, the exposed chalk rubble is clad with lichens. Snails are plentiful and butterflies, notably the chalkhill, adonis and small blue, can be readily found in favoured sheltered spots. The flamboyant yellow-horned poppy grows on the exposed cliff edge to the south of the road.

Compton to Shippards Chine Cliff

These unstable sandy cliffs, above a superb family beach, are always changing as the sea eats away at their feet. The consequent slumping creates ideal conditions for a wide range of plants and animals, notably the Glanville fritillary butterfly, whose caterpillars feed on ribwort plantain. The sea fern grass and burrowing clover also do well, here. The loose, warm sand encourages mining bees and wasps, which can be seen in late spring excavating and stocking their burrows.

Headon Warren

The cliffs of Headon Warren comprise sandy deposits, similar to those at nearby Alum Bay, and are very different to the chalk of The Needles to the west. They support one of the few remaining heathlands on the Isle of Wight. The main dwarf shrubs

Above right: The male Dartford Warbler has a rose chest spotted with white and a bright red eye. It can be found in heathland near the coast. This species suffered terribly in the harsh winter of 1962 and only a very few pairs were known to have survived – it still has amber status with the RSPB.

Right: The view from The Needles Old Battery over the sheer chalk cliffs into Scratchwell Bay. This coastal defence was built in 1862 against the threat of French invasion.

are heather, which is closely grazed by rabbits, and bell heather, with smaller amounts of gorse. The mottled grasshopper, grayling butterfly and common lizard are among the heath's inhabitants, alongside Dartford warbler and stonechat.

The Needles to Tennyson Down

This impressive chalk ridge, with vertical chalk cliffs on its southern edge, is topped with grassland, and the nature of this grassland varies with the level and type of grazing. Tennyson Down's wild flowers include clustered bellflower, autumn gentian, tufted centaury and frog orchid. West High Down is grazed by sheep and has fewer plants, while the ungrazed section near The Needles is covered with rough grass. Even in this exposed location chalkland butterflies are common. Cormorants, kittiwakes, guillemots and shags regularly nest on the cliffs, while peregrines breed occasionally.

Newtown Estuary

The National Trust owns much of this unspoiled estuary, three-quarters of which is covered by the high tide. In winter, up to 10,000 waders and waterfowl feed out on the mud. Birds that are seen regularly here in winter include the golden plover, curlew, black-tailed godwit, brent goose, wigeon and pintail. Shelduck also breed here, along with the oystercatcher, redshank, ringed plover and two species of gull. Typical saltmarsh plants border the edges of the estuary. The woodland comprises oak, ash, hazel and field maple. It is particularly important for mammals because it harbours both red squirrels and dormice. The silver-washed fritillary, white admiral and purple hairstreak butterfly, and the wood cricket also live within it. Newtown meadows are a superb example of unimproved meadowland with drifts of devil's bit scabious and dyer's greenweed.

Ventnor

The National Trust's holdings at Ventnor include St. Boniface Down, which at 233m (764ft) is the highest point of the Isle of Wight. In early summer, horseshoe vetch produces beautiful sheets of yellow flowers in the grassland areas. Rockrose, autumn gentian and woolly thistle are common, and slender centaury, common broomrape and bee orchid also grow here. This is also the only place on the Isle of Wight where the stripe-winged grasshopper is found, and in summer, chalkhill blue, adonis blue and brown argus butterflies are a common sight.

Above: A mass of bluebells in spring on Ventnor Downs as seen from the north-west side of Benchurch Down looking north towards Shanklin Down.

Below: Newton Estuary, a National Nature Reserve, is a flat landscape of salt marshes, mudflats, ancient woodland and meadows. It is a wintering ground for wildfowl and waders and attracts significant numbers of brent goose, black-tailed godwit, teal and wigeon.

Borthwood Copse

Located on the eastern side of the Isle of Wight, this walk takes you through beautiful ancient oak woodland, which is a good site for red squirrels throughout the year. In spring, the woodland floor is carpeted with bluebells.

Getting there and facilities:

By car, take Alverstone Road, Apse Heath, off the A3056 Newport–Sandown road. The parish council car park is labelled P on the map. There is a bus stop on Alverstone Road that is opposite the entrance to Borthwood Copse and marks the beginning of the walk. The nearest railway stations are Lake and Shanklin. There are various options on foot as the area is well served by public rights of way. Facilities are available in nearby Sandown.

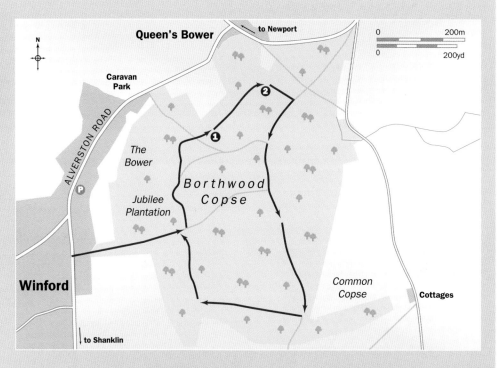

Start point:

OS Landranger 196 gr 570 844 or Explorer OL29.

Distance, terrain and accessibility:

The walk is 1.6km (1 mile) long, with some slopes. Paths can be muddy following rain. The footpath is accessed via a squeeze stile or kissing gate.

Route and directions:

1   Start the walk at the bus stop on Alverston Road – the entrance to Borthwood Copse and the start of the walk is directly opposite the bus stop. During the walk look out for the carpets of bluebells that can be seen throughout the woods during late spring. This area is also a good site for spotting red squirrels throughout the year – however, it is easiest to spot them following a leaf fall.

2   Continue your walk around the woodland paths until you reach the starting point. Scattered stands of old beech can be found in the north half of the wood and this is also a good area to spot red squirrels – although there is plenty of other wildlife in the area too. Keep your eyes open for woodland butterflies along rides and glades, such as brimstone, speckled wood and white admiral. Interesting woodland flora in the area includes wood anemone, common cowwheat, foxgloves, primroses and wood sorrel and there are various woodland birds, such as green and great spotted woodpecker, blackcaps and chiffchaffs. Dormice are also common, though rarely seen.

The New Forest

The New Forest is the largest area of wild uncultivated land in lowland Britain, with 20,000ha (49,400 acres) of open, unfenced heathland and woodland. The forest consists of 12,500ha (31,000 acres) of dry heathland, 3,000ha (7,500 acres) of mire, 20,000ha (49,400 acres) of ancient pasture woodland open to grazing animals, and nearly 1,000ha (2,500 acres) of enclosed plantation woodland, much of which lies on ancient woodland sites. All but the plantations are open to the cattle and ponies that graze the New Forest. The forest is home to an outstanding array of wildlife. It lies between the Avon Valley in the west and Southampton Water in the east, and runs from the southern edge of the Wiltshire Downs to the Solent in the south. It became a National Park in 2005, the first to be created in nearly 50 years, though as open access land it has effectively been regarded as such since late Victorian times. Topographically, the New Forest lies on a series of flat terraces, with the highest in the north, and is dissected by river valleys. The underlying rocks are soft sedimentary clays and tertiary sands; the sands and most of the clays are acidic.

It is perhaps the human history of this space that makes it so special, and has moulded its wildlife. Stone Age and Bronze Age people cleared areas of the forest for cultivation and the subsequent leaching of nutrients left the soil impoverished and infertile. Some 150 scheduled ancient monuments and 250 round barrow burial grounds bear testament to the lives of these early settlers. William the Conqueror made the area a royal forest in 1079, recorded as *Nova Foresta* in the Domesday Book in 1086. Here the beasts of the chase – namely deer and wild boar – were protected for the exclusive pleasure of the monarch and thus it has stayed; anyone breaking the law was harshly dealt with. A system of rights was established that allowed commoners to graze their animals, cut peat and wood for fuel, and turn out their pigs to forage on the commons at specified times of the year.

Above: The New Forest is a particular delight to visit in autumn. As well as the glorious autumn colours, it is the perfect time to look for interesting fungi, nuts and berries.

Right: The view from Stagbury Hill, the highest point in the New Forest, looking south over Furzley Common and Cadnam Common. The hill was used as a rabbit warren, a practice that disturbed the Bronze Age barrows that also sit on the knoll of the hill.

Hunting became less significant over the centuries and the monarchy effectively lost interest in the place. Instead, timber became a precious resource, notably for ship building. Ironically in the absence of hunting, the deer population spiralled out of control and began to damage trees, thus threatening the timber supply. Control measures were put in place, culminating in the New Forest Deer Removal Act of 1851, which all but removed deer from the entire New Forest area. Careful regulation of the deer population is still required today. During the First World War a large number of broad-leaved trees were felled. Immediately after the war, the newly formed Forestry Commission took over from the old Office of Woods, which had managed the forest on behalf of the Crown. The Forestry Commission was established for the purpose of making the nation self-sufficient in timber, using fast-growing, non-native conifers. Old broad-leaved woodland was rapidly replaced with conifer plantations, but today the process is being reversed, with broad-leaved trees being planted instead of conifers, and areas of plantation woodland being returned to heathland. The forest still produces around 50,000 tonnes of timber each year.

The New Forest has around 15,000ha (37,000 acres) of broad-leaved pasture woodland that is open to grazing by commoners' stock. Oak and beech predominate in these ancient woodlands, which have been called Ancient and Ornamental since the New Forest Act of 1877. The most famous tree is the Knightwood Oak, a classic pollard that

Above: A New Forest lawn of wild chamomile at Cadnam Green. The forest lawns only cover a small area of the New Forest but provide important grazing for the commoners' stock.

Left: Honey or bootlace fungus is a parasitic fungus that lives on trees and shrubs; it can be seen from June to November.

appeared on an ordnance survey map back in 1870. It is reputed to be the largest oak in the forest, with a girth in excess of 7.5m (25ft) and is around 600 years old. There are some 40 other ancient pollards with girths in excess of 5m (16½ft). There are also beech and holly trees that are around 300 years old.

The open areas of the New Forest are so heavily grazed that few of the plants present manage to flower in any given year. However, this grazing pressure is essential to prevent the heathland reverting to dense woodland. A large number of rarities occur nonetheless, notably the flame-red wild gladiolus that occurs among bracken, and Hampshire purslane. Most of the rare plants are found in the mires or around the edges of the ponds, though the heavily grazed grassland areas, known as the New Forest lawns, are also incredibly rich. Wild chamomile, for example, is common in the damper parts of these lawns. In addition, mosses, lichens and liverworts thrive in both the heath and woodland environments, and there are around 2,700 species of fungi, including the amethyst deceiver, razor strop

(or birch bracket), the toxic red-capped sickener, orange birch bolete, fly agaric, stinkhorn, oyster mushroom, penny bun, chanterelle and the horn of plenty.

Five species of deer occur, only two of which are native; red, fallow, roe deer, sika and muntjac can be seen grazing in small herds. Bats come out at dusk, and 13 of the UK species are found here, including the very rare barbastelle and Bechstein's bat, which are creatures of ancient woodland. The woodland is home to some 10,000 invertebrate species; impressive stag beetles can be seen flying at dusk in midsummer – the males have large antlers – and the large emerald-green rose chafer is commonly seen during June. Until recently butterfly and moth collectors flocked to the forest, but populations have been greatly reduced by soft wood forestry. However, silver-washed fritillaries occur in most woods, and in some areas there are populations of white admiral and both species of pearl-bordered fritillary.

Many birds can be seen in the New Forest including the sparrowhawk, kestrel, common buzzard, tawny owl, hobby and the rare honey buzzard. All three woodpeckers are present. The birdlife of pasture woodland is varied, with nightjars, linnets, stonechats, yellowhammers, lapwings, redshanks and curlews. Woodland birds are also here in numbers, including all three British woodpeckers, nuthatch, treecreeper, marsh tit, redstart, wood warbler and hawfinch. If you are fortunate, firecrest, goldcrest and crossbill can be seen among the conifers. Stonechats and Dartford warblers breed in the gorse thickets, and woodlarks can be frequent in the heavily grazed areas. The main summer speciality is the nightjar, or fern owl, as it is locally known. In winter, hen harriers and long-eared owls roost in discrete places.

The New Forest heathland is the largest piece of continuous lowland heath in Europe; it accounts for two-thirds of the forest area. These heaths are maintained by grazing cattle and ponies, and by careful burning of gorse that would otherwise take over. Three species of heather occur: ordinary heather or ling is frequent in the drier areas, alongside bright pink bell heather, while the less-conspicuous cross-leaved heath dominates the areas of damp heathland. Insects flourish, including large colonies of the tiny silver-studded blue butterfly. Adders, smooth snakes and sand lizards like the dry, sandy soil, and can sometimes be seen basking in the sun.

Wild flower species found in wet areas include bog asphodel, bog orchid, butterwort, marsh gentian, pennyroyal, small fleabane, marsh St John's wort and the extraordinary sundew, which traps small insects for food. Look out for the rare plant coral necklace, which grows on the edges of shallow ponds – it bears beautiful clusters of white flowers on red stems. Three species of newt, the common frog and the common toad enjoy this habitat. Curiously though, it seems that the natterjack toad, a denizen of warm, shallow acidic pools, has never been recorded in the New Forest. Dragonflies abound, including the southern damselfly and scarce blue-tailed damselfly. The rare fairy shrimp occurs in seasonal pools.

The National Trust owns three large parts of the New Forest and is actually the second biggest landowner after the Crown. These three areas are along the northern and western edges. At Bramshaw, in the north of the forest, the Trust owns 715ha (1,767 acres) of open heath and pasture woodland, which includes the richest stretch of wet woodland in the New Forest, and some of the richest heaths and lawns. The heathland area is being extended by the removal of plantation conifers from Foxbury Plantation, which was acquired for this purpose in 2006. In the north-west corner of the forest lies the Trust's Hale Purlieu holding, some 207ha (512 acres) of wet and dry heath. In 1999 the Trust acquired a large tract along the forest's western fringe, Rockford and Ibsley Commons, which total 565ha (1,396 acres) are one of the most beautiful, wildlife-rich and loneliest parts of the forest.

Left: All three woodpecker species are present in the New Forest, including the green woodpecker, which is the largest of the UK's breeding woodpeckers. They climb up tree trunks and branches and are somewhat shy, hiding away from prying eyes by moving around the trunk to keep out of sight. Here an adult male is seen at his nest hole.

Bramshaw Commons

Bramshaw Commons, 16km (10 miles) west of Southampton, are owned by the National Trust and comprise over 715ha (1,767 acres) of manorial wastes and commons. Manorial waste comprises land that has little agricultural value, often consisting of wide strips of roadside verge, hedgerow or scrub which, along with common land, does not produce income for the manor. This land was used by commoners as a source of timber and fuel. Cadnam Common is the best area of mire, bog and wet woodland. The well-grazed dry heathland of Plaitford Common is important for lichens and mosses, and other species of rare lichen occur on trees in the blocks of grazed pasture woodland. Insects of all variety thrive; the wet areas support the scarce blue-tailed damselfly, bog bush cricket and numerous rare flies, and the dry heaths are important for bees, wasps and butterflies such as the grayling and silver-studded blue. The dry heathland provides an important habitat for birds such as the Dartford warbler. Listen out for the exquisite fluting song of the woodlark, which, despite its name, relishes lowland heath habitat, and is quite numerous here, especially on Half Moon Common.

Hale Purlieu

With its open ground and dense thickets, Hale Purlieu is a good example of the mix of habitats that is common throughout the New Forest area. 'Ling' heather, bell heather, cross-leaved heath, dwarf gorse and purple moor grass grow in the well-drained, higher areas. Heather and purple moor grass also grow on the wetter low-lying ground, alongside oblong-leaved sundew, cotton-grass and meadow thistle. The New Forest is famous for its birdlife, and Hale Purlieu is no exception. Nightjars nest on the heath, and can be seen on the wing at dusk in summer. The silver-studded blue butterfly is common here.

Below: The area of heathland at Hale Purlieu was once part of the historic royal hunting ground of the New Forest and it is still grazed under traditional commoners' rights.

New Forest ponies

About 3,000 ponies wander freely across heaths, woodland, roads and often into villages. Most are of the New Forest breed (shown below), which is unique and has changed very little over the Forest's 900-year history. There are other breeds, such as Shetland ponies, in smaller numbers; you may see these near Stoney Cross. The ponies are owned by around 400 'commoners' who have the right to allow their animals to graze on forest land. Grazing is very important to the forest conservation and there are byelaws that make it an offence to feed a pony or any other forest animal. Ponies tend to remember where they were fed and will come back expecting more food, rather than wandering off to graze. If feeding were allowed to continue this could upset the balance of the forest. The New Forest pony is one of the larger breeds of wild pony in the UK and can reach 12–14 hands high (hh). Colours range from sand to chestnut with darker coloured manes and tails and paler legs; they frequently have a white blaze or wide stripe down the middle of their faces.

The Chiltern Hills

The Chilterns, an area of rolling chalk hills and quiet valleys, contain some of the most beautiful tracts of woodland in the UK, as well as flower-strewn grasslands and sweet clear streams. It is a designated AONB covering some 833 km² (322 square miles).

The hills lie to the north west of London, and stretch from the Thames Valley in Oxfordshire, north east through Buckingham and Bedfordshire, up to Hitchin in Hertfordshire on a 121km (75 mile)

Below: It is said that some of the best honey-making areas are on plains overlying chalk, with plenty of clover and sainfoin, in the south and east of England. Here a hive sits in an idyllic spot on a wild flower meadow on an organic farm in the Chilterns.

diagonal. The boundary is clearly defined on the north-west side by the scarp slope, the southernmost extent of the ice sheet during the last ice age. It subsides to the south east, and naturally dips through sloping countryside, merging with the landscape. The hills are part of the southern England chalk formation, which spreads southwards to the South Downs, Salisbury and the Isle of Wight, and was laid down during the Upper Cretaceous period.

The highest point is Haddington Hill in Wendover Woods in Buckinghamshire, which reaches 267m (876ft). Coombe Hill near Princess Risborough comes a close second at 260m (852ft). Ivinghoe Beacon marks the start of both the Icknield Way, one of the oldest roads in the UK, which existed before the Romans came

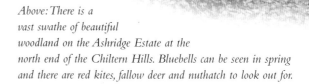

to Britain, and the Ridgeway Long Distance Path, which follows the line of the Chilterns to the west. On top of Ivinghoe Beacon is a Bronze Age hill fort, around which lie Bronze Age burial chambers or barrows. On the low ground the chalk can be seen gleaming through the soil, but higher on the hills it is often covered by clay dotted with flints.

Chalk streams are fed from groundwater held in the chalk, known as aquifers. Since groundwater levels in the chalk are variable, the streams are necessarily intermittent. Only a few permanent streams run through the valleys; many of the streams are fed by springs and dry up in the summer – these are known as winterbournes. Watercress, water crowsfoot and yellow flag iris can be seen alongside the streams, and fish such as the brown trout attract heron and kingfisher, and occasionally the little egret. The brown rat, water vole and mink live along the banks, and waterfowl such as moorhen, little grebe and water rail dabble in the water.

The Chiltern Hills are famous for their beautiful beech woods. Stunning in spring when their new leaves make a lively contrast to the carpets of bluebells, and in autumn they glow with colour. Over

Above: There is a vast swathe of beautiful woodland on the Ashridge Estate at the north end of the Chiltern Hills. Bluebells can be seen in spring and there are red kites, fallow deer and nuthatch to look out for.

The red kite in the Chilterns

Red kites (shown below), driven to extinction in England and Scotland by human persecution at the end of the 19th century, have been successfully reintroduced to the area, and have become a self-supporting population with over 300 breeding pairs, which are widespread over the southern and central Chilterns. They can frequently be seen both over open land and towns, and from the M40 that cuts through the Chilterns near High Wycombe.

half the woods are ancient and have been in existence for at least the last 400 years. Coppiced beeches, scarred and multi-stemmed, indicate that the wood was repeatedly cut down, almost to its base, to produce firewood, charcoal and hurdles. Some of the beech forests were planted in the 18th century when the wood was grown to support the burgeoning furniture industry. Oak, ash, yew, holly and cherry can also be found in the woodlands and these species are more valuable for wildlife – the seldom-seen dormouse still flourishes in these woods. Rare plants such as coralroot, yellow bird's nest and a number of orchids, can be seen along with primroses and foxglove. Fungi flourish on the rotting wood.

Scattered between the woods and the dry valley sides are small areas of grassland and over 200 commons, both large and small. These are carpeted with a wonderful array of wild flowers. The white-flowered heath bedstraw, yellow cat's ear, pale blue harebell, and the small red flowers of the herb salad burnet attract the brown ringlet butterfly, the common blue and the flamboyantly coloured burnet moth. Certain types of grazing animal are being introduced to some areas of grassland to allow plant species such as the rare Chiltern gentian and the dark pink pasque flower to flourish.

village, provide an impressive backdrop to the sloping village green. A network of paths through the estate provides easy access for walkers to explore the delightful surrounding countryside. Bradenham Woods, an extensive area of ancient beech wood, is considered among the best in the Chilterns. The woodland floor is covered in flowers with dog's mercury, primrose, sweet woodruff, wood anemone and bluebell often visible. The ash-black slug, a scarce species of ancient forests, occurs on the woodland floor. There are some small but extremely valuable pockets of chalk grassland along the south-facing slope below the woodland edge. Some scarce plants grow here, including juniper and fragrant bee and fly orchids. There is a rich butterfly fauna, notably small blue and Duke of Burgundy. To the south, there is a stunning area of downland and yew woodland at Watlington Hill, famed for its flowering candytuft, Chiltern gentian and silver-spotted skipper butterflies.

Dunstable and Whipsnade Downs are ancient grasslands, the result of centuries of grazing sheep. The downs form the second-largest area of chalk grassland in Bedfordshire, and, despite agricultural improvement of some of the original downland and the encroachment of hawthorn scrub, the steep slopes are rich in flowers and grasses with associated flora and fauna. The areas of ancient grassland are fenced off for grazing to maintain their conservation interest, and common rights still exist on a large part of Whipsnade Green.

Sheep's fescue, quaking grass, crested dog's tail, dwarf thistle, orchids, rockrose, horseshoe vetch, thyme, harebell and bird's-foot trefoil, are some of the many flowers and grasses found here, with some local downland butterflies including chalkhill blue and Duke of Burgundy.

Commanding grand views of West Wycombe Park, the River Wye and the surrounding countryside, West Wycombe Hill is crowned with a great golden ball on the top of the church tower of St Lawrence. There is a huge hexagonal mausoleum next to the church, as well as the remains of an Iron Age hill fort. Nearby is the delightful village of West Wycombe, which contains buildings of interest from medieval to Victorian times, many of which are owned by the National Trust. Chalk grassland, ancient woodland, scrub, old hazel coppice and mature trees, planted as part of the grander landscape design of West Wycombe Park, add to the significance of this historic landscape. The grassland supports many wild flowers and herbs, with lady's bedstraw, bird's-foot trefoil, common rockrose, wild basil, stemless thistle and hairy violet. Yew, blackthorn, juniper, whitebeam and wayfaring tree scrub merge into oak, ash and beech woods.

Above: Ivinghoe Beacon on the Ashridge Estate stands 250m (820ft) above sea level and offers exceptional views over Buckinghamshire and Hertfordshire from the summit. The chalk grassland is an important habitat for butterflies and orchids in summer.

Above right: The Chiltern gentian is a nationally scarce species of chalk downland that flowers from August to October. Its decline is thought to result from habitat loss due to the cessation of grazing. The National Trust is looking at clearing scrub and reintroducing grazing where appropriate.

The National Trust owns a number of special areas of countryside in the Chilterns. At the north end lie Sharpenhoe Clappers and Moleskin Hill, an area of steep-slope scrub and chalk grassland. Dunstable Downs, a little to the south, is an area well used for recreation and offers great views. The Ashridge Estate, situated between Aylesbury and Hemel Hempstead, includes extensive areas of woodland and open grass common land, and Ivinghoe Beacon, which is renowned for its flowers and butterflies, including a large population of the rare Duke of Burgundy. Towards Princess Risborough, the Trust owns Coombe Hill, another famous chalk downland viewpoint, the woodland and grassland of Pulpit Hill, and several areas of open woodland and downland at Bradenham. At the Bradenham Estate just outside High Wycombe, the church and 17th-century manor house, in a mainly National Trust-owned

Ashridge Estate

On the main ridge of the magnificent Chiltern Hills, there are over 2,000ha (4,942 acres) of open countryside, chalk downland and woodland to explore at Ashridge. This range of habitats means that there's plenty of wildlife (the estate is renowned for butterflies and wild flowers). Bluebell displays in spring are superb and you can find lots of grassland flowers like orchids. Autumn is a great time to watch deer rut and enjoy the golden hues of the surrounding countryside.

Getting there and facilities:

There is a traffic-free and signed cycle route to within 1.6km (1 mile) of the estate. By road, the estate is between Berkhamsted and Northchurch, and Ringshall and Dagnall, just off the B4506. Tring railway station is 2.8km (1¾ miles) from Monument, and Cheddington station 5.6km (3½ miles) from Beacon. If you are travelling to the property by bus, for Monument take 30/31 from Tring railway station, which stops within 0.8km (½ mile) of the estate. For Beacon, take 61 Aylesbury–Luton, which passes close to Aylesbury and Luton. Alternatively, the Chiltern Rambler 327 from Tring to Monument or Beacon (Sundays, May–September). There is free parking 50m (165ft) away, a visitor centre, tea room, National Trust gift shop, WC (not always available), baby-changing facilities and a short cycle path, 14.5km (9 miles) on a bridleway. Self-guided walks are available.

Start point:

OS Explorer 181: SP970130 (Ashridge Visitor Centre)

Distance, terrain and accessibility:

The walk is a 3km (2 mile) signposted route, perfect for families. The walk is linear, so you can return at any point. Level surfaces are good for pushchairs and wheelchairs. Maps of accessible routes available.

Route and directions:

1 Start at Ashridge Visitor Centre, near the Bridgewater Monument. Cross the green, taking the path leading off the main track (it has studposts at the entrance).

2 Enter the ancient woodland. In the late summer, note that lots of the sycamores along the path have tar spot fungus (black marks) – a good indicator of unpolluted air. Also look for butterflies in sunny openings and any signs of badgers or their tracks.

3 Go over a bridge and you are now on an ancient drover's path, which was worn away into a ditch by villagers taking their animals to graze on Pitstone Common. Continue to Moneybrook Hill, so-called because of the buried coins found here.

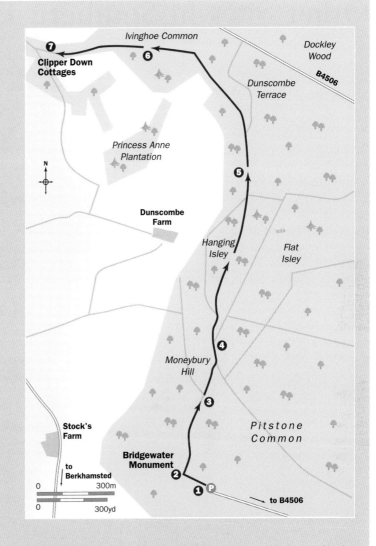

4 Pass the left-hand mound, called the Bell Barrow (due to its shape). It is thought to be a Bronze Age burial mound. The wooden lodge on the left is a copy of a Victorian shooting lodge that burned down in 1989.

5 On the right is a huge giant's bench with lovely views of Pitsone Hill and Aldbury Nowers. Continuing along, note the hazel trees that have been coppiced (cut at the ground, then left to grow) to provide a wildlife habitat. The fallen cedar is still alive and growing. As you walk through the pine woodland between here and point 6, enjoy the smell of the conifers.

6 Emerge from the pine trees on to the Clipper Down.

7 Either turn around (this is also the turning point for mobility vehicles) and return by the same route, or continue for another mile to Ivinghoe Beacon for more wonderful views.

Other Sites in Southern England

Berkshire

Basildon Park, mid-Berkshire
Parkland, woodland, chalk grassland
The park surrounding the imposing Basildon House has a rich natural history. It covers an area of 164ha (406 acres), and comprises open grassland with scattered trees and woods. Much of the woodland is recent, but some areas are semi-natural, and are dominated by ash and yew. Some of the old yews are particularly fine specimens. Box also grows well here. The park boasts four species of helleborine – the violet, white, green and narrow-lipped – and a small area of chalk grassland contains stemless thistle, cowslip, purging flax and bee orchid.

Sparrowhawk, kestrel, little owl and tawny owl, can often be seen, along with the white admiral butterfly.

Cliveden, east Berkshire
Formal gardens
Not only is Cliveden known for its involvement in political scandal, it also has a stunning series of formal gardens and Italianate terraces. It made history again in 2008 when a small colony of an Italian snail, *Papillifera papillaris*, was discovered in Britain for the first time. This attractive snail, which has no English common name, has become

Below: Cattle grazing in the extensive parkland at Basildon Park. The estate had become very overgrown but has now been restored – much of the woodland is recent.

known as the Cliveden snail. It has a spindle-shaped shell that is only about 11mm (½in) long. It is common in the Mediterranean, where it is often found in old buildings. This new addition to the British fauna had managed to lie undiscovered since 1896 when a large balustrade, made of brick and marble, was shipped to the UK from the gardens of the grand Villa Borghese in Rome. There are several hundred Cliveden snails and they can be found in the crevices and deeply carved details in the marble balustrade.

Lardon Chase and Lough Down, mid-Berkshire
Chalk grassland, lowland beech and yew woodland
This is one of the largest remaining areas of chalk grassland in Berkshire. Its steep east- and south-facing chalk slopes give

good views of the Chilterns and the valley of the Thames. This is the richest butterfly site in Berkshire, with a variety of species, including chalkhill and adonis blue. Chalk milkwort, autumn gentian and clustered bellflower are among the site's many chalkland plants.

Buckinghamshire

Coombe Hill and Low Scrubs, mid-Buckinghamshire
Chalk grassland, scrub, dry acid grassland, woodland
At 260m (852ft), Coombe Hill is one of the highest viewpoints in the Chilterns. Nearby Low Scrubs is a fantasy world of strangely shaped trees. The steep slopes of Coombe Hill are rich in chalk grassland plants, including horseshoe vetch, kidney vetch and dropwort. The juniper that grows here brings with it a range of special insects and other animals. In wooded areas, oak predominates, and beech is common. The woodland is mainly of recent origin, but much of it was formerly coppiced, and some ancient pollards can still be identified.

Hampshire

Ludshott Common and Waggoner's Wells, east Hampshire
Lowland heath, scrub, woodland, ponds
Much of Ludshott Common is covered by lowland heath. Heather, which regenerated well after a severe fire in 1980, is common

Above: The summit of Coombe Hill is 260m (852ft) above sea level and is one of the highest viewpoints in the Chilterns.

Left: A wintry scene on Ludshott Common with silver birch in silhouette and frost-crusted grass in the foreground.

throughout the heath, as are gorse and bracken. The common's butterflies include the silver-studded blue, grayling and green hairstreak. Many different species of spider live in and near the heather. The woods near the old hammer ponds at Waggoner's Wells contain fine old beech trees and also sessile oaks, which are uncommon in Hampshire. These woods are believed to be a surviving fragment of ancient woodland. Redstarts and wood warblers nest in the trees, while nightjars, stonechats, linnets, redpolls and nightingales breed on the margins of the heath.

Selborne, east Hampshire
Woodland, scrub, acid grassland
Selborne is inseparably linked with the writings of the Reverend Gilbert White, the father of British natural history. The beech hangers adjoining the village – hallowed ground to the naturalist – still live up to the descriptions so faithfully recorded in *The Natural History of Selborne* (1789). The main hanger, along the chalk slope to the west of the village, is home to a rich array of wild flowers, including woodruff, yellow archangel, wood spurge and wood anemone as well as the bird's nest orchid. This is also one of the best places in Britain to see land snails, with dozens of species living in the woods. Above the hanger, on the plateau of Selborne Common, is an area of oak and ash with clearings bordered by shrubs. Over 30 species of butterfly have been found here, including the silver-washed fritillary, the brown, purple and green hairstreaks and the majestic purple emperor. Grazing has been reintroduced to this former area of pasture woodland with the support of the local community.

by gypsywort, meadowsweet, hairy willowherb, hemlock and water dropwort. Conifers attract goldcrests and crossbills, and several species of warbler, including blackcap, garden warbler, willow warbler, chiffchaff and wood warbler, are known to breed here.

Kent

Langdon Cliffs, east Kent
Cliffs, chalk grassland, scrub, woodland
Langdon Cliffs form part of the majestic wall of chalk for which the coast around Dover is so famous. Its rich grassland is full of chalk-loving plants. These include the pyramidal, bee and fragrant orchids, and also meadow clary and a rare species of parasitic broomrape. The small blue is among the many butterflies that can be seen here in warm, sunny weather. The shrubby thickets near the cliffs are important staging posts for migrating birds, especially warblers, and a number of small birds also breed there. Exmoor ponies graze the downland.

Sandwich Bay and Pegwell Bay, east Kent
Sand dunes, saltmarsh, shingle, beach, foreshore
Separated by the estuary of the River Great Stour, these two bays are both managed as nature reserves by the Kent Wildlife Trust. The reserves lie on a migration route for birds and butterflies. Over 150 species of bird have been recorded, and wildfowl and waders overwinter in large numbers on the estuary. The dunes and shingle provide a habitat for plants such as marram grass, sea bindweed, sea holly and sea sandwort.

St. Margaret's Bay, east Kent
Cliffs, farmland
The largest of the National Trust's holdings on the chalk cliffs north east of Dover is Bockhill Farm. It lies in a part of south-east England that is believed to have remained as grassland when the rest of Britain was covered in forest. It is a refuge for grassland

Above: One of England's most famous national landmarks where the rounded outlines of the North Downs meet the sea in the spectacular chalk cliffs that are the White Cliffs of Dover.

Left: The cliffs at St Margaret's-at-Cliffe are where the sun is reputed to first reach the UK each morning. This view looks over the fields to the Victorian South Foreland lighthouse.

Stockbridge Down, west Hampshire
Chalk grassland, scrub
This area of Hampshire chalkland is common land and, unusually for a common, it has a long history of being cut for hay. It has a distinctive mix of grasses and plants such as horseshoe vetch, knapweed broomrape and bee orchid. The wide range of butterflies includes the chalkhill blue and dark green fritillary, and the insect life of the area also features a native species of cockroach. The dry chalk suits some interesting shrubs, including juniper along with the more common yew, dogwood and blackthorn, and these provide cover for birds such as blackcap and linnet.

Woolton Hill, The Chase, north Hampshire
Woodland, grassland, stream, lake
The Chase is made up principally of woodland, through which a chalk stream winds, eventually flowing into a picturesque lake. The woodland contains oaks, beeches and conifers, while alders grow on the banks of the stream. The flowers of the wet ground are one of the attractions of this nature reserve, with golden saxifrage and marsh marigold flowering in early spring, followed

plants, some of which are only found in this locality. The cliffs shelter fulmars and kittiwakes and the peregrine falcon, which once bred here regularly, now appears to be returning.

Toy's Hill, north-west Kent
Woodland, heathland

Standing on the Greensand Ridge of the North Downs, Toy's Hill has superb views over the northern part of Kent. From early times, this area was part of the Brasted Chart Commons, and was used for firewood and for feeding pigs and cattle. The beech woods were cut for charcoal to fuel the Wealden iron trade, and also for local oasts (kilns) to dry hops. In places, old beeches and oaks still remain, but the great storm of 1987 felled nearly all the trees on the woodland plateau. The woods have, though, regenerated spectacularly. The slopes lower down the hill are covered with bluebells in the spring and many other woodland species flower throughout the summer.

London

Morden Hall Park, south London
Parkland, fen, river

Morden Hall Park is a rich oasis for wildlife in south London, with its riverbanks, fen and parkland trees. The River Wandle has many aquatic plants, including duckweed and curled pondweed, and dragonflies patrol the waterways in search of insects. Grey wagtails and kingfishers both nest along the river. The trees and shrubs harbour a range of woodland birds, including the nuthatch and great spotted woodpecker. Like many birds in towns and cities, those in the park are used to humans and therefore easy to watch. The Trust has created a new wetland here, rich in wildlife.

Left: Scord's Wood is part of the 80ha (200 acres) of glorious woodland at Toy's Hill. The area was damaged in the Great Storm of 1987 but has been left to regenerate naturally.

Selsdon Wood, south-east London
Woodland, grassland, pond

At one time, Selsdon Wood was in deepest countryside. Today, it lies on the very fringes of London, offering a welcome respite from the busy city. About three-quarters of its area comprises broad-leaved woodland, divided by wide rides, and the rest is rough meadows. In May, large tracts of ground are carpeted with bluebells, and herb paris is one of the more unusual woodland plants. Selsdon's birdlife contains no great rarities but it is abundant. The woodland butterflies include the comma and the less common white-letter and purple hairstreaks, with browns and skippers in the meadows.

Oxfordshire

Watlington Hill, south-east Oxfordshire
Chalk grassland, scrub, woodland

With its marvellous chalk grassland full of wild flowers, Watlington Hill is one of the biological highlights of the Chilterns.

Horseshoe vetch, kidney vetch, rockrose and squinancywort are all common, and the frog orchid, bee orchid, pyramidal orchid, candytuft, autumn gentian and Chiltern gentian can all be found here. The grassland is the home of about 30 species of butterfly, notably a large population of silver-spotted skipper. Other habitats of interest include areas of yew woodland and two kinds of scrub, one over the chalk with lime-loving shrubs such as wayfaring tree, dogwood, whitebeam, privet and juniper, and another quite different type on areas of acid soil, with gorse, hawthorn and blackthorn.

White Horse Hill, Uffington, west Oxfordshire
Chalk grassland

This chalk hill, with its earthworks and famous white horse, lies on the ridge of the Lambourn Downs. Much of the land around the ridge is now intensively farmed, but the hill still retains many tropical chalkland

Below: An aerial view of the Uffington White Horse, an ancient hill figure cut into the turf to reveal the chalk underneath. It measures 114m (374ft) in length.

flowers, such as bird's-foot trefoil and early gentian, and a variety of butterflies. The turf is heavily dominated by tor grass but the National Trust is working hard to control this invasive species.

Surrey

Bookham Commons, mid-Surrey
Grassland, ancient woodland, scrub, ponds, streams, marsh

The large expanse of wooded and open common land at Bookham is rich in animal life and contains over 500 species of flowering plant. The commons' grassland, grazed for centuries, fell into disuse after 1947 and now contains plants such as hogweed, rosebay willowherb and bracken. Grazing has now been reintroduced. The woodlands are largely of oak with many fine old trees and an understorey of holly and hawthorn. Wood pigeons, blackbirds, woodpeckers, tawny owls and woodcock all breed in the woods, while the streams are visited by kingfishers, herons and grey wagtails. In summer, warblers and

nightingales are common in the scrub. All three species of newt live in the ponds, and grass snakes are numerous. This is a renowned site for butterflies, notably the elusive purple emperor.

Box Hill and Headley Heath, mid-Surrey
Heathland, woodland, chalk grassland
On a prominent chalk scarp overlooking the River Mole, this important SSSI is cut by a number of dry combes that form the attractive 'karst' or limestone scenery, a rare feature in southern Britain. The hill is named for the box trees, native to the site, although the prolific yew is also distinctive. Much of the high beech wood was destroyed in the storms of 1987 and 1990, but natural regeneration and replanting has ensured the continuity and richness of the associated wildlife. The chalk grasslands contain over a dozen species of orchid and at least 400 species of other plants. Over two-thirds of Britain's butterflies are found on the hill, thriving on key plants such as horseshoe vetch, bird's-foot trefoil, hairy violet and cowslip. The box bushes harbour the rare box shield bug and juniper

attracts the juniper shield bug. Scrubby areas of dogwood, wayfaring tree, yew and spindle, among others, provide nesting sites for many smaller birds, which in turn attract many birds of prey. Kingfisher and grey wagtail can be seen near the river, while badger, roe deer, fox, yellow-necked mouse, weasel and rabbit make the woods their home.

Above left: Bookham Commons comprise three ancient commons: Great Bookham, Little Bookham and Banks Commons. All are part of the Saxon settlement of 'Bocham' – the village by the beeches. This path leads across a wooden bridge over to a lush grassy bank and on to mixed woodland at Bookham Commons.

Above right: A yew tree on a snowy Box Hill, one of the best known summits of the North Downs, measuring in at 193m (634ft) in height.

Left: The nightjar, a nocturnal bird with a shape similar to a cuckoo or a kestrel, hunts for moths and beetles at dawn and dusk and is found at Frensham Common.

Frensham Common, west Surrey
Heathland, woodland, scrub, bogs, reedbeds, lakes
This property, part of which is a country park, is a fine example of Surrey heathland. The dry areas of the heath contain bell heather, ling, gorse, bracken, birch and Scots pine, while mosses, sedges and sundews grow where the ground is wet. The ponds provide a habitat for the yellow iris, sweet flag, common reed and bulrush, and in summer the reedbeds are home to reed bunting, and reed and sedge warbler. Heathland birds include the elusive nightjar, as well as the Dartford warbler, woodlark, stonechat, whinchat, snipe and redshank.

Hindhead Common, south west Surrey
Lowland heath, woodland, farmland, stream
The National Trust's land at Hindhead Common includes Gibbet Hill and the great amphitheatre of the Devil's Punchbowl. Woodland of many types can be found here, some made up of Scots pine, while other woodlands are mixed, and include oak, beech, whitebeam and rowan. In some areas of open ground, repeated fires have inhibited the heather and allowed bracken to take over. Great spotted and green woodpeckers live in the woods, and where scrub has become established, it provides cover and a supply of insects for nightjars, woodlarks, blue tits, long-tailed tits, coal tits and goldcrests. Roe deer also live on the common, but are rarely seen. The heaths are grazed by hardy Exmoor ponies.

Leith Hill, south Surrey
Woodland, heathland, grassland

At 294m (965ft), Leith Hill is the highest point in south-east England, giving extensive views across the Surrey–Sussex border. Its well-wooded slopes are covered with a mix of broad-leaved trees such as oak and birch, and conifers such as Scots pine. The fine show of bluebells and the spring colours of the rhododendrons in Mosses Wood are a local highlight, as is the white admiral butterfly, which lives on the hill in some numbers. Woodland birds, including woodpeckers, nuthatches, treecreepers and wood warblers, find the dense tree cover to their liking.

Ranmore Common, mid-Surrey
Woodland, common, fields

This wooded common lies on the slopes of the North Downs. The woodland here is predominantly composed of beech, oak and ash with some yews interspersed among the taller trees. Columbines, white helleborines, bluebells, foxgloves and wood anemones can be seen on the woodland floor in spring. The common is the haunt of roe deer, as well as fox and rabbit. Woodland butterflies found here include the purple hairstreak, white admiral, and silver-washed fritillary. Sparrowhawks, wood warblers, woodcock and all three of our native woodpeckers live and breed in the woods.

Runnymede, west Surrey
Meadows, marsh, woods, hedges, ponds, riverbank

These historic meadows, where King John set his seal on the Magna Carta, are today a haven for wetland plants and animals. The ponds contain the fringed water lily, duckweeds, frogbit, water dropwort and flowering rush. The rich turf of nearby Cooper's Hill contains many species of flowering plants.

Witley and Milford Commons, south-west Surrey
Heathland, chalk downland, woodland

Until early this century, cattle and horses were grazed at Witley, and bracken was cut for pig litter. Today, after being occupied by the army during both World Wars, the character of the commons has changed. This is particularly noticeable where 'foreign' soil was brought in by the military. Bell heather and ling – two typical heathland plants – have been joined by chalk downland species such as stemless thistle and marjoram. The mixture of broad-leaved trees encourages a variety of birds. Siskins and redpolls feed on birch seeds, and wood pigeons and jays eat the plentiful acorns. A vast variety of insects feed on the trees and scrub. Common lizards and adders both live on the commons, as do roe deer and a small number of red deer.

Sussex

Black Down, north-west Sussex
Woodland, heath, old pasture

The sandstone plateau of Black Down is the highest point in west Sussex, standing 280m (918ft) above the well-wooded countryside of the Weald. Majestic beeches grow on the eastern slopes, and the top of the hill is clad with birch, scrub oak, Scots pine, gorse and

Above: Fungi perform an essential role in the ecosystem; they consume the tough lignum material (woody tissue) contained in dead wood, helping to decompose organic matter and playing a vital role in nutrient cycling and exchange. The fungi that we see are the fruiting bodies.

Top: The Sandy beaches at East Head, a sand dune spit, are a natural and dynamic coastal feature which is home to many over-wintering migrant birds.

heather. Oak and rhododendron also grow on the slopes, together with rowan and alder buckthorn. The damper areas are home to many moisture-loving plants such as whortleberry, sphagnum moss and sundew. Green and great spotted woodpeckers are common near tree cover, as are warblers, tree pipits, wrens and the occasional crossbill. Meadow pipits, linnets and yellowhammers can be seen over open ground. With the support of local people the National Trust is reintroducing grazing to restore the heathland habitats here.

East Head, west Sussex coast
Sand and shingle beach, sand dunes, saltmarsh, inter-tidal mudflats
East Head is a narrow spit of sand and shingle beach that juts out into Chichester Harbour. At the mercy of storms and high tides, its shape and position are constantly changing. Almost 100 species of flowering plant have been found on East Head, from glasswort, thrift and sea knotgrass and sea lavender to the rare sea heath, sea bindweed, golden samphire and evening primrose.

Chichester Harbour is, as might be expected, a haven for many seabirds, wildfowl and waders. Shelduck live here in their thousands. Brent geese, wigeon, pochard, teal, mallard, golden-eye and merganser, share the rich mudflats and inshore waters with redshank, curlew, grey plover, sanderling and bar-tailed and black-tailed godwits. Terns nest on the shingle. The dunes are important for solitary bees and wasps.

Petworth Park, mid-west Sussex
Parkland, woodland
Petworth Park, which was landscaped by 'Capability' Brown, contains one of the finest deer parks in Britain. Its many ancient trees include gnarled oaks and sweet chestnuts. The abundant insects living on the trees provide food for treecreepers, woodpeckers and nuthatches, while the acorns and chestnuts are eaten by grey squirrels and jays. The park's fallow deer are particularly impressive in early autumn, when the antlers of the bucks are fully grown and the rutting season begins. The grassland is a rich site for waxcap fungi.

East of England

The Fens

The Fens lie around the coast of the Wash, with a toe in Lincolnshire, Norfolk, Cambridgeshire and a tiny piece of Suffolk. The vast, flat landscape is a man-made habitat. It was once subject to regular seasonal flooding, with desolate islands of higher ground surrounded by reed swamp and marshland vegetation, and large areas were vulnerable to periodic tidal inundation.

As the last ice age ended and land-ice melted, sea and river levels rose, flooding low-lying areas to create salt-water and freshwater wetlands. Clay and silt soils were deposited in areas of salt-water floods, while peat developed in the freshwater marshes, composed of decaying plant material. It appears that water levels were at their highest in the Iron Age, for both Bronze Age and Neolithic settlements have been uncovered underneath peat deposits. Water levels retreated again in Roman times and settlements were viable on the rich and fertile silt soils. Artificial banks were built so that

Whittlesea Mere

Situated to the south east of Peterborough, Whittlesea Mere was a massive, shallow inland lake surrounded by wet fen, the haunt of bittern and swallowtail and the large copper butterfly. Dutch engineers drained the lake during the mid-19th century and, as a result, the spectacular large copper became extinct in Britain. Today, the area is a vast shallow bowl of intensively managed farmland, prone to dust-storm conditions as the dried-out peat blows about on desiccating east winds.

Below: Wicken Fen is reputed to be one of the most species-rich wetland nature reserves in the UK. Over 230 bird species visit in the course of the year and these can be observed from hides in the reserve. Birds such as the marsh harrier, bearded tit, reed bunting and cuckoo can be seen, according to the season.

coastal settlements were protected from fluctuating sea levels but peat continued to build up in the freshwater wetlands. The Romans recognised the potential of these fertile soils and made some attempts to drain the fens, and in medieval times the fenland monasteries also made early attempts to drain their land.

The communities that lived in the fens had a tough existence, hunting and gathering, using reeds and wattle to construct their houses and thatch their roofs. Many areas were deforested and grazing animals prevented scrub and trees encroaching and kept the landscape open. Real change came only when the Earl of Bedford invited Cornelius Vermuyden, a Dutch engineer, to try out Dutch reclamation methods in the fens whereby winding rivers were diverted to flow to the sea via the most direct route. The Old Bedford River was straightened and the New Bedford River was dug out just 1km (0.6 mile) away, to drain winter floodwater. The local fishermen and fowlers were hostile about the land reclamation scheme as their livelihoods were under threat; Oliver Cromwell made representations in parliament on behalf of the opponents of the drainage of the fens who stood to see little or no reward, while the king and the engineers of the scheme hoped to make handsome profits. In fact the area was flooded during the Civil War to prevent Royalist advances in the area, but slowly agricultural land took over from marshland.

Drainage and oxidisation caused the peat to shrink, the best example of this being seen at Holme where, in 1884, a metal gauge shaped like a lamp post was sunk into the newly drained peat as far as the clay below – its top now stands 4m (13ft) above the surface of the land. In many places the levels of farmland dropped substantially below that of the rivers. Isolated pockets of true fenland have remained, the Ouze washes being one of the best examples; the land is managed traditionally, it is grazed in summer and flooded in winter. More generally the National Trust, the RSPB, English Nature, the Environment Agency, the Wildlife Trust and the National Parks Agency are working to regenerate as much fenland as possible and working with farmers and commercial growers to minimise the damage caused by fertilisers and effluents and to encourage seasonal flooding.

There are still a few sites where fragments of the original undrained peat still exist with high levels of biodiversity. They are recognised nationally and internationally as important wildlife sites. The Great

Fen Project is a habitat restoration project aiming to create a huge expanse of wetland between Holme Fen and Woodwalton Fen, connecting the two sites and possibly also serving as a flood storage reservoir.

Wicken Fen, Cambridgeshire

Wicken Fen is one of the most important areas of wetland in Western Europe with a phenomenal 7,000 species of flora and fauna recorded. The first parcel of land, 0.8ha (2 acres) in all, was purchased for the National Trust in 1899; more portions of land were purchased over the years and the Trust now owns some 652ha (1,612 acres) and has plans to expand the site to become a 4,000ha

Left: Hoare frost bleaches the countryside near the windpump at Wicken Fen.

Below: One of the new ponds created in the landscape at The Mere, on Adventurer's Fen.

Many kinds of plant grow in the water and line the water's edge, such as **marsh pea**, **milk parsley**, **fen pondweed** and **fen orchid**. The water itself teems with life, from microscopic plants to water voles and fish. Just outside the original fen is a large artificial mere, created to attract water birds. This is the winter home of large numbers of **mallard** and **wigeon**. **Teal**, **pochard** and **tufted duck** can also be seen here, and in spring **great crested grebes** use it as an arena for their elaborate courtship displays. The mere is fringed with **reeds**, providing nesting sites for **reed warblers**, and an autumn roost for large numbers of **swallows** and **sand martins**. **Bearded tits** can sometimes be seen here, especially in winter. In other parts of the reserve, the fen vegetation is cut down every four years, keeping invading trees and shrubs at bay. Where the fen has been left unmown, woody plants have taken over. **Buckthorn**, **alder buckthorn** and **guelder rose** thrive in the damp ground, but eventually trees such as **birch**, **oak** and **alder** will oust the shrubs. The scrub and woodland is the haunt of **owls**, **woodcock** and **sparrowhawks**. Insects are particularly abundant, with thousands of species of moth, butterfly, beetle and fly, together with 20 dragonfly species. In addition there are 29 species of mammal including **otters**, **water voles** and semi-feral **konik ponies**.

Tufted duck

Fen orchid

Above: In spring the yellow flag iris blooms in profusion in the wetlands at Wicken Fen.

Left: The raft spider is the largest species of spider found in the UK and is semi-aquatic.

(10,000 acre) wetland reserve. Its flat, mysterious landscape is a reminder of what much of Cambridgeshire would have looked like before drainage became widespread. During the late 1990s and early 2000s the National Trust restored a vast area of open fen by clearing scrub.

Woodwalton Fen, Cambridgeshire

At Woodwalton Fen, north east of Huntingdon, there are 400 recorded species of plants including grasses, sedges, herbs and mosses. There are waving purple moor grass meadows, the rare fen violet and fen woodrush, as well as bog myrtle, lesser spearwort and marsh pea. The nectar from the carpet of flowers attracts a range of invertebrates such as the marsh carpet moth and unusual dragonflies such as the scarce chaser and the white-legged damselfly. Birds such as reed buntings and reed warblers breed in the reed beds, bitterns feed and nightingales and grasshopper warblers nest in the grass and scrub.

Holme Fen, Cambridgeshire

Holme Fen, south of Peterborough, contains the largest silver-birch woodland in lowland Britain and alder thrives in damp areas. The trees' seeds feed siskin and redpoll in winter, and nightingales, woodpeckers and blackcaps nest in the foliage. An impressive 450 species of fungi have been recorded at the site. The raised bog is home to sphagnum moss, bog myrtle and cross-leaved heath.

Redgrave and Lopham Fen, Suffolk

Redgrave and Lopham Fen boast a large colony of the UK's largest spider – the fen raft spider. At this site conservation efforts are focused on restoring the hydrology of the fen to ensure an adequate supply of water of a suitable quality, the removal of invading trees and shrubs, and the reintroduction of grazing.

Wicken Fen

This easy trail explores a fragment of the wilderness that once covered East Anglia. Only 0.1% of Britain's fenland remains undrained. Wicken Fen is the most accessible remnant of this habitat. It is the National Trust's oldest nature reserve and home to many plants and insects, plus rare birds like bittern, and mammals, like otter.

Getting there and facilities:

Wicken Fen is 27km (17 miles) north east of Cambridge and 5km (3 miles) west of Soham, just off the A1123. Ely rail station is 14.5km (9 miles) from Wicken Fen. If you are travelling by bus no.12, Cambridge–Ely, alight at Soham High Street, then 5km (3 miles) on footpaths to Wicken. Alternatively, National Cycle Network route 11 passes the reserve boundary.

There is a visitor centre, café, shop, picnic area, parking on Lode Lane (free for NT members) toilets, education room, children's quiz/trail. Trail guide leaflet available.

Start point:

Wicken Fen National Trust Visitor Centre – OS Landranger 154 – grid ref: TL563705

Distance, terrain and accessibility:

Adventurers' Trail: 4.5km (2¾ miles). A well-signed route along wide grassy paths (can be muddy). There are many other routes at Wicken Fen, including a Boardwalk Trail, accessible for wheelchairs, year round. See leaflet in visitor centre. Take care near the waterways and ponds.

Route and directions:

1   Take a look in the visitor centre to find out more about the wildlife and history of Wicken Fen. As you exit, Wicken Lode is on your right. Follow the path, keeping the water to your right. You will pass some ash trees and Wicken's Poor Fen on your left. This is common land – traditionally local villagers had the right to collect sedge and peat from here.

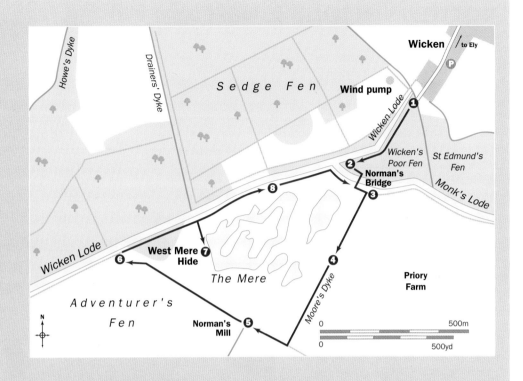

2   Cross Monk's Lode at Norman's Bridge. Look out for plants like arrowhead and water lilies. Turn after the bridge.

3   Walk along Monk's Lode, then turn right through the lower set of gates.

4   Note the two hides on your right. Look out for birds like wigeon, teal and shoveler in winter and lapwing and redshank in summer on the flooded fields; and for konik ponies and highland cattle.

5   Turn right along the next path and on your right is the site of Norman's Mill, originally used to drain the turf (peat) pits. The windpump is now restored on Sedge Fen. On your left, roe deer can often be spotted. This land was cultivated during the 'Dig for Victory' campaign of the Second World War, but is now being restored.

6   Note the reedbeds on your left and the many birds and insects inhabiting them. Turn right again to walk alongside Wicken Lode. There is a squeeze gap and path on the right leading to West Mere Hide, used to overlook the mere's west end and the island.

7   Continue on to a hide which has views across the whole mere.

8   Cross back over the Norman's Bridge and return towards the visitor centre.

North Norfolk Coast

The North Norfolk Coast is a designated Area of Outstanding Natural Beauty that extends over 450km² (174 square miles). The flat coastline sweeps around in a broad curve between the two ports of King's Lynn and Great Yarmouth. It stretches from the silt of the Wash, through the coastal marshes and soft cliffs of north Norfolk and embraces the dune system at Winterton in the east. There are great sweeps of intertidal sand, saltmarsh and mudflats, and shingle banks with the shifting sea beyond and the great expanse of sky overhead. The fields beyond the coast are dissected with channels and often lead to sand dunes that run down to the long beaches.

Large sections of the area are subject to marine erosion, and while the sea is calm in the summer, winter storms – North Sea tidal surges born out of spring tides – can be fearsome. In January 1953 catastrophic floods caused widespread devastation and more than 80 people died.

This is an internationally renowned area for birds, attracting birdwatchers from all over the UK and beyond. Wading birds throng here and migrating birds drop by to feed and rest. On the western coast towards the Wash is a huge area of tidal mudflat that attracts huge populations of wintering waders such as dunlin, knot and redshank. At the RSPB reserve at Snettisham visitors marvel at the twice-daily spectacle of thousands of birds flying from the mudflats to avoid the incoming tide. A little further around the coast, look out from the red, white and brown striped cliffs at Hunstanton and see curlew, dunlin and knot hunting for invertebrates in the mud. Seals can be seen on sand bars and brent geese land to look for eelgrass.

Much of the land between Cromer and Holme is wild and remote and dotted with nature reserves. The remains of a Bronze Age timber circle, known as Seahenge, were uncovered at Holme and hint at an emerging ancient landscape. Seahenge

Left: A group of seals bask in the sunshine on the sandbank at Blakeney Point, home to a colony of over 500 common and grey seals.

Below: Ladybirds dot the grasses at Brancaster Harbour, a designated Area of Outstanding Natural Beauty, following an immigration.

was removed by English Heritage for preservation. The National Trust looks after saltmarsh, intertidal mud and sand flats at Brancaster and some 200 species of bird can be seen here. The remains of a petrified forest appears at very low tide, but caution must be exercised when the tide is low, for the incoming tide can be very unpredictable. There is a private ferry service to the National Nature Reserve at Scolt Head Island, where little terns, arctic terns, roseate terns and sandwich terns can be found. There is also a Roman fort, Branodunum, which was built to protect the coast from marauding pirates.

There are many beautiful walks around the coast – the North Norfolk Coastal Path runs for 72km (45 miles) around the coast from Hunstanton to Cromer, and then links with the Weavers Way, which continues around the coast from Cromer to Great Yarmouth.

Holkham National Nature Reserve

The Holkham National Nature Reserve stretches from Burnham Norton to Blakeney. The Vikings were early visitors; they sailed through the saltmarshes and built a fort at Holkham, but the coastline is much changed and much of the land here has been reclaimed from the sea. Ringed plovers and sanderlings can be seen hunting for food on the tide line, while a little way out oystercatchers and curlew wade through the water looking for lugworms and cockles. Several thousand brent geese spend the winter here. Pines were planted to stabilise the dunes and redstarts and flycatchers drop in briefly on migration. Rarities such as the natterjack toad, and plants such as the marsh hellebore, can be found as well as masses of butterflies. A series of wet meadows sit inland from the pines, where dainty, striped pink-footed geese can be seen in winter. A beautiful walk along the Pinewoods/Holkham Gap track allows visitors to explore the area.

Blakeney National Nature Reserve

The Blakeney National Nature Reserve, owned by the National Trust, covers some 1,100ha (2,711 acres) and includes sand dune, saltmarsh and some scrub. Redshank and several species of tern both breed and visit, reed buntings can be seen and brent geese fly in from Russia and Greenland, arriving from October onwards. Rare vagrant birds such as bluethroat, firecrest, hoopoe, red-breasted flycatcher and barred warbler are seen every year. Blakeney Point is situated at the end of a long sand and shingle spit. The point is often a landfall for migrating birds, and one of the attractions of visiting Blakeney is that so many species can be seen on passage. Blakeney Point is one of Britain's most important breeding sites for terns. In May and June, thousands of sandwich, common and little terns throng the shingle spit, laying their camouflaged eggs directly on the pebbles. The sea itself is also worth watching, especially in autumn when seabirds move south, hugging the coast. Both common and grey seals lie up on the sand banks and can be seen from the special seal-watching boats run from the mainland quay.

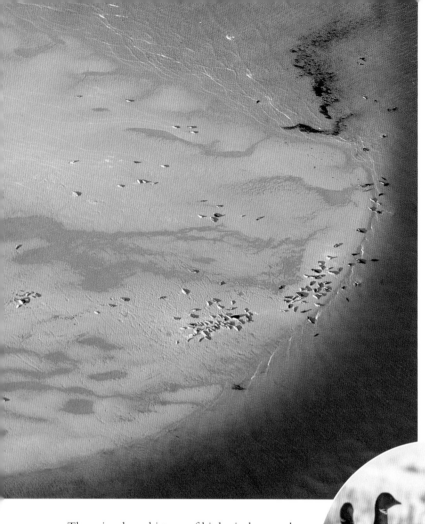

rare natterjack toad also lives here. In winter, large numbers of wildfowl and waders feed on the saltmarsh and mudflats. Scolt Head Island is also an exceptionally good place to see the plant life of dunes and saltmarshes.

Stiffkey Saltmarshes

Stiffkey saltmarshes abound with plants typical of this demanding habitat, especially sea lavender and sea aster, and a visit in late summer sees these in bloom. In spring and early summer, the shingle bank at the outer edge of the saltmarsh is an important breeding area for terns and shelduck. The saltmarsh is also worth visiting in winter, because at this time it is a feeding ground for migratory brent geese, wigeon, teal and other wildfowl.

Cley Marshes

Cley Marshes, looked after by the Norfolk Wildlife Trust, is an area with artificially created lagoons, reed beds and meadows where, with a little luck, you will see avocet, marsh harrier and garganey. This is a key site for the rare bittern. The area is under threat from the sea and it is possible that it may revert to saltmarsh in the future as sea levels rise.

Above left: Seals can be seen at Blakeney Point during their breeding season between June and August. The area is also an important breeding ground for migrant birds.

Left: Brent geese escape freezing artic temperatures in winter and migrate to the milder temperatures of the UK, seen here in the snow in Norfolk.

Below: Cley Marshes is a bird-watching site of international repute with stunning views across the reed beds to the North Sea in the distance.

There is a long history of biological research here, with the huts being used as a field studies centre. The path along the spit to the point, a 5km (3 mile) walk, is surrounded by swathes of the rare matted sea lavender, sea kale and the yellow horned poppy. Out in the mud, samphire grows readily.

Brancaster

This sweep of coastline, over 7km (4½ miles) long, is made up of a rich variety of habitats that is particularly attractive to birds. Large numbers of reed warblers and sedge warblers nest in the reed beds in summer, while the sand and mudflats are covered with algae, which provide winter food for flocks of brent geese. The dunes are held in place by marram grass. Cord grass grows in the lower saltmarsh, and above this are sea arrow grass, sea lavender and sea aster, the last two of which create a carpet of colour in late summer.

Scolt Head Island

This internationally important site for breeding seabirds is managed by Natural England as a National Nature Reserve. Common, sandwich and little terns breed on the shingle and dunes, and the

Coastal Walk

Blakeney to Stiffkey

Enjoy Norfolk's vast open landscape and big skies on this lovely walk along the coast path beside pristine saltmarsh. Remember to bring your binoculars, as there are lots of wildlife-spotting opportunities across the marshes and scrub. Several local families run ferries from Morston Quay out to the shingle split of Blakeney Point. The boat trip offers a great chance to get up close to common and grey seals. Visit the Old Lifeboat House, now a National Trust visitor centre, open at high tide during busy periods.

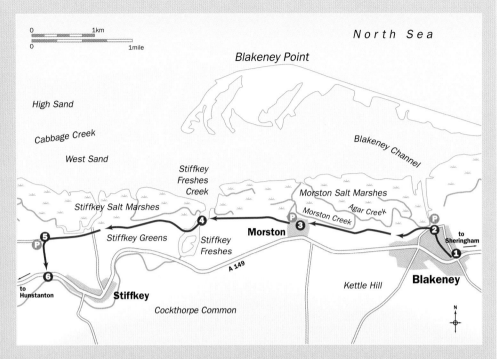

Getting there and facilities:

The Norfolk Coast Path runs 72km (45 miles) from Hunstanton to Cromer, passing Blakeney. Alternatively, the Norfolk Coast-hopper bus from Sheringham to Hunstanton can be taken for Blakeney, Morston and Stiffkey. If driving, take the A149 Sheringham to King's Lynn coast road for Blakeney, Morston and Stiffkey. Norfolk Coast Cycleway (National Cycle Network 30) runs along quiet lanes from King's Lynn to Cromer, it is an easy 1.5km (1 mile) detour to Blakeney.

There are WCs at Blakeney and Morston Quay and refreshments, pubs and car parks at Blakeney, Morston and Stiffkey. Dogs are welcome on the Coasthopper bus and ferries.

Start point:

Bus stop near Blakeney Church (grid ref: TG032436) or Blakeney Quay (TG028442) Landranger 132/133 and Explorer 251 on map.

Distance, terrain and accessibility:

A 7km (4 mile) walk along mostly level ground. Some uneven natural surfaces, may become muddy after wet weather. Some steps between Blakeney and Morston and Stiffkey Freshes, suitable for sturdier types of pushchairs. Once you have arrived at Stiffkey either return the way you came or take the Norfolk Coasthopper bus back to Blakeney.

Route and directions:

1   From the bus stop, head towards Blakeney village and turn right down the High Street. At the end of the High Street you will come out on to Blakeney Quay.

2   Turn left and follow the line of mooring posts. Join the Norfolk Coast Path that runs between the houses and the saltmarsh. Head away from the village, keeping the salt marsh on your right and fields and houses on your left.

3   At Morston Quay head past the National Trust visitor centre, along a track to its left. Pick up the coast path again (to the right of the building with 1922 on it). Continue walking beside the saltmarsh, but if you begin to cross a bridge on to the saltmarsh, you have gone too far north – head back to the visitor centre and turn right.

4   Stay on the coast path, passing Stiffkey Freshes Creek on your right and Stiffkey Freshes on your left.

5   Continue on the path, passing Stiffkey Greens, until you reach Stiffkey Greenway car park.

6   Turn left at the car park, heading inland. Walk up the Greenway Road until you reach the A149 coast road and the bus stop. Here you can catch the Norfolk Coasthopper bus back to Blakeney.

Other Sites in East of England

Bedfordshire

Sharpenhoe, south Bedfordshire
Chalk grassland, scrub, woodland
The steep, west-facing slope supports a rich chalk grassland that is heavily invaded by scrub. Efforts are being made to clear the scrub but this is difficult on such a steep slope. The grassland has a scattering of typical lime-loving plants, including wild thyme, horseshoe vetch, several species of orchid, clustered bellflower and autumn gentian. Nests of the yellow meadow ant are common, and mining bees, mining wasps and wolf spiders can all be seen here. Sharpenhoe Clappers has a rich butterfly community, including chalkhill blue and the dark green fritillary. The scrub, which is used by hedgerow birds, is made up mostly of hawthorn and elder. The areas of beech woodland have been planted; one is on the site of an Iron Age hill fort.

Essex

Danbury and Lingwood Commons, Essex
Neutral and acid grassland, acid heath, scrub, woodland, marsh, ponds
It is easy to get lost in this complex mosaic of habitats that has developed on hilltop gravel. In the past 100 years, much of the original heath has been invaded by scrub, birch and oak, and some areas have become covered with dense stands of gorse, broom and wild roses. However, heather does survive in a few areas, together with common milkwort and tormentil, and is spreading as the scrub is gradually cleared to recreate the heathland of days gone by. The common is rich in moths and birds, including a large number of nightingales. A small area of hornbeam is still regularly coppiced. Adders, great crested newt and the poplar leaf roller beetle are all typically found in the area.

Hatfield Forest, Essex
Woodland, parkland, grassland, scrub, marsh
This large area of pasture woodland and grassland is one of the most important relics of medieval forest in Britain. Its long history of exploitation, for timber, for coppice and pollard wood and for grazing, has created a wide variety of long-established habitats. In the coppiced areas the main trees are oak, hornbeam, ash, field maple and hazel. Altogether there are 36 native species of tree and shrub and 17 that have been introduced. Dog's mercury is the most common plant of the woodland floor. Over 500 species of fungi can be found in the woodland, and it is the only site in which all five bracket fungi *(Ganoderma)* can be found. The grassy rides have a wide range of plants that need damp conditions, including water figwort and common fleabane. The impressive pollard trees in the open grassy areas are home to many insects, including over 600 species of beetle. Nightingales, hawfinches, tree pipits and woodcock are among the birds of the coppiced areas. Great crested and little grebes can be seen on the lake, while cattle and wild fallow deer graze the pasture woodland.

Left: Bluebells abound for a short period in late April or May in the Great Wood of Blickling Hall, Norfolk.

Northey Island, Essex
Grassland, saltmarsh, mudflats
Northey Island's main attraction is its bird life. Between October and March, up to 2,000 dark-bellied brent geese can be seen feeding in the fields or on the saltmarshes. Other birds that regularly visit the island in winter include the short-eared owl and also many ducks and waders. In addition to its birds, Northey Island is renowned for its saltmarsh plants. Sea plantain, sea purslane, sea lavender and common scurvy grass all grow here. The dykes and sea walls are also rich in plants, while insects and other invertebrates live in the banks.

Norfolk

Blickling Estate, Norfolk
Meadows, heaths, hedgerows, woodlands, park, lakes, riverbank
Having escaped many of the 'improvements' of modern farming, Blickling's riverside meadows are a delight for all who appreciate wild flowers. In areas of open shallow water, the water whorl grass can be found – a common plant in Norfolk, but rarely seen elsewhere. Twayblade, climbing corydalis and lily-of-the-valley are among the less usual plants growing in the woodlands. The presence of the woods attracts breeding birds such as the hawfinch, redstart and lesser spotted woodpecker. Barn owls, wood warblers and nightjars also live on the estate. The lake is the home of the tufted duck, the great crested grebe and Egyptian and Canada geese, while the River Bure provides a habitat for kingfishers and water voles. Blickling is also a good place to see rabbits and hares.

Suffolk

Dunwich Heath, Suffolk
Acid heathland, soft cliffs, shingle beach
Dunwich Heath is a superb example of the heathland that was formerly so extensive on the sandy soil of this part of Suffolk. Near the sea, the heath is covered by wind-pruned bell heather, and clumps of gorse provide perches for stonechats, whinchats and warblers. Further inland, the heath has been overtaken by bracken, birch and pine, giving enough shelter to conceal roe deer. Nightjars nest in the clearings, and can be seen on the wing at dusk in summer. The slumping cliffs are a good demonstration of the erosive power of the sea. The cliff face is pockmarked with the nesting burrows of

Above: The shingle beach at Orford Ness combines an internationally important nature reserve with 20th-century military history. The pagodas were used in the research and development of the atomic bomb.

sand martins, which swoop through the air in pursuit of insects. Beneath them, the small pebbly beach harbours the yellow horned poppy, grayling butterflies, lesser marsh grasshopper, glow worms and the rare antlion, which was discovered here in 1996.

Orford Ness, Suffolk
Shingle spit, salt marsh, lagoon
This long 600ha (1,400 acre) shingle spit must be one of the most desolate and exposed places in Britain, yet it is of global significance for its shingle geomorphology and of at least national importance for its wildlife. For decades it was run as an experimental station by the Ministry of Defence, particularly for developing rocket-propelling systems for nuclear warheads during the Cold War. The old buildings, including hauntingly surreal nuclear bunkers, are being left to decay. The bird life is, of course, stunning, at all times of year. Rare or unusual species are of frequent occurrence, often as breeding species. The flora and invertebrate fauna is also exceptionally rich. A visit here is an essential experience for the British naturalist.

Central England

The Peak District

The Peak District is situated in central and northern England at the south end of the Pennine ridge, the upland range that forms the backbone of England, and runs for 240km (150 miles). The Pennine ridge was formed by a great upheaval, or anticline, of rocks, which had been laid down some 280 million years ago when the area was a vast river delta. Its underlying geology divides the area into three distinct landscapes; the limestone of the White Peak, the rugged Dark Peak, with its craggy outcrops and high moorland, and the lower hills and valleys of the South West Peak. This is a fragile and diverse landscape. Most of the area falls within the mighty Peak District National Park, which was the very first of England's National Parks, created in 1951. It covers 1,438km² (555 square miles). Despite the fact that the area is estimated to attract around 22 million visitors per year it is still famed for its remote beauty.

Perhaps more than any other National Park, the Peak District highlights the need for man to get back to nature – or at least to visit the countryside. It was created to give people living in nearby industrial cities access to the countryside, but it was not always so. Before 1951 much of the land belonged to wealthy landowners who preserved the moors for their exclusive use – notably grouse shooting – and clashes between gamekeepers and walkers were common. In April 1932 a mass trespass by ramblers working on the principle that where one trespasser could be turned back 500 could not, resulted in what is known as the Battle of Kinder Scout. It successfully highlighted the desire for freedom to walk on moor and mountain. It is estimated that half of the population lives within 96km (60 miles) of this National Park, and it is claimed that it is the second most visited National Park in the world, after Mount Fuji in Japan.

White Peak

The White Peak covers the area in the south and centre of the Peak District. It forms the much-eroded dome of the limestone plateau, which is cut by steep-sided valleys – or dales – and is crisscrossed by dry-stone walls that appear silver-white in the summer sun. These steep valleys are home to such rarities as the purple flowering Jacob's ladder, hutchinsia (a smaller version of wild mignonette), wheatears, pied flycatchers, glow worms and the northern brown argus butterfly. Green fields are grazed by cattle and sheep, and streams pour down the steep-sided dales. Joints and weaknesses in the limestone have been eroded by water, often

Right: A walker stands on a gritstone outcrop at the southern edge of Kinder Scout, much of which is 600m (1,968ft) above sea level, one of the most imposing areas of the Dark Peak.

Above: Jacob's Ladder, once one of the many packhorse routes that crossed the Dark Peak, winds its way through deep folding cloughs at the start of the Pennine Way.

Right: The blue flowers and ladder-shaped leaves of Jacob's ladder can be seen in the Peak District. It is the floral emblem of the county of Derbyshire.

through underground streams, to form stunning caves, notably around the Castleton area of Hope Valley, where the limestone meets the grit and shale of the Dark Peak. The Peak Cavern – or 'Devil's Arse' as it is sometimes known – is the largest natural cave entrance in the UK. Blue John and Treak Cliff caverns are the only source of semi-precious fluorite, a rare mineral known as blue John. The area has long been inhabited; the stone circle and henge of Arbor Low, near Youlgreave, has been dubbed the 'Stonehenge of the North'. The Romans are known to have mined lead, and the industry continued for centuries, leaving mounds in pastures as

reminders, and an estimated 10,000 miners are thought to have made their living in lead mines in the first half of the 18th century.

Dove Dale

The most famous dale in this area is Dove Dale, north of Ashbourne, which alone attracts an estimated two million visitors a year. The River Dove carved its way through the limestone plateau, creating a deep, spectacular gorge that is famous for its rock pinnacles, spires, arches and caves. Some of the best calcareous ash woods in the country grow here. In spring, when the willow warblers and blackcap arrive, it is carpeted with ramsons, dog's mercury and herb paris. Dovedale's south-facing grassland slopes are a fascinating habitat because they contain plants that are characteristic of northern or southern England, here growing side by side. These include the stemless thistle, Nottingham catchfly, dropwort, greater burnet saxifrage, Jacob's ladder and northern bedstraw. Glow worms, chalk carpet moth, and the northern brown argus butterfly also live on these

Above: A view of the 10m (33ft) high entrance to Thor's Cave, a natural cavern in a steep limestone crag in the Manifold Valley of the White Peak.

Below: The Peak District is home to many red grouse, which flourish in upland heather moors, feeding on the plant's shoots, seeds and flowers.

The National Trust at work

The National Trust has had a presence in the Peak District since 1906. It owns High Peak, a slice of wild and dramatic Pennine moorland that includes Mam Tor, the unspoilt valley of Snake Pass, and Kinder Scout where the mass trespass took place. At Longshaw Estate (shown below) moorland and woodland can be explored, including Padley Gorge with its ancient oaks. Ilam Park lies on both banks of the River Manifold and allows visitors to explore the limestone geography of the area. Visitors can also seek out Hinkley Wood and view 'boil holes', where rivers re-emerge after following underground courses. The National Trust is committed to conservation work in this area: it is relaying paths with stone to stop the erosion caused by ramblers, replanting woodland with more eco-friendly plants, and replanting eroded patches of moorland and bog.

slopes. Running parallel is Manifold Valley ('many fold'); the River Manifold disappears underground here, and there are caverns and potholes. Near the village of Whetton, some 80m (260ft) above the valley floor, is the natural cavern Thor's Cave. The entrance is a symmetrical arch measuring 10m (33ft) high by 7.5m (25ft) wide, and can easily be reached by the Manifold Way.

Dark Peak

The area of the Dark Peak almost surrounds the White Peak; it is made up principally of vast swathes of moorland dotted with blanket bog. The landscape was created thousands of years ago by humans, who cut down trees and used the land for grazing. Grouse shooting still takes place from 12th August each year and red grouse can be seen along with golden plover, curlew, peregrine falcon and hen harrier. The highest points of the Peak District are found in Dark Peak and include Kinder Scout, Bleaklow Plateau and Black Hill. This is a gritstone landscape with huge plateaus and deep valleys edged with millstone grit crags and scars that are enjoyed by serious rock climbers. Water pours from the heights and some 50 valleys have been flooded to form reservoirs, including the Upper Derwent Valley, which contains Ladybower, Derwent and Howden reservoirs, where sandpipers, goshawk and mergansers can be seen.

Peat bogs in the Peaks

Banks of peat stretch for miles, divided by drainage channels known as goughs. Peat bogs are first-class carbon sinks – they naturally store the gas carbon dioxide that contributes to the damaging effects of climate change, locking it up for many thousands of years and taking in 20 times more carbon than forestry. However, when the bogs are eroded by over-grazing, pollution or fire damage, they start leaking carbon dioxide instead of storing it. It is estimated that some 700m^2 (7,500ft^2) of southern Pennine Hills leaks as much carbon dioxide as a town of 50,000 people. Work is being undertaken to restore the peat bogs by reducing grazing pressure, blocking up drainage channels (grips), surfacing footpaths and even reseeding areas of exposed peat with heather, and planting cotton-grass.

South West Peak

The South West Peak features wild-heather moorland on the hilltops where grouse shooting takes place; some of the hilltops have gritstone ridges such as can be seen at Ramshaw Rocks or the Roaches. The area also contains valleys, filled with hay meadows and sweet pasture divided by gritstone walls.

Kinder Scout

This challenging and exhilarating walk takes you high up on the windswept Kinder plateau, one of the great upland areas of the gritstone Dark Peak. Enjoy the spectacular views across the Vale of Edale, explore mysterious rock formations and look out for a fantastic range of moorland wildlife.

Getting there and facilities:

Edale train station, on the scenic Sheffield–Manchester line, is 300m (1,000ft) from the start of the walk. There is car park, toilet, café, camp site and pubs in the village. The Peak District Park Moorland Centre in Edale has information on local wildlife, history and geology.

Start point:

Edale – OS Explorer map OL1 – grid ref SK 124856

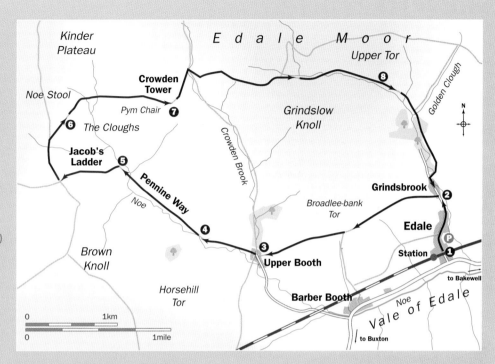

Distance, terrain and accessibility:

12km (7½ mile) circular route. The paths are generally good but rugged and there are some moderately challenging ascents and descents. Good fitness levels and hill-walking clothing are essential.

Route and directions:

1 Start off from Edale station and head up through the village, passing the Moorland Centre on your right.

2 Turn left on to the Pennine Way opposite the Nag's Head pub.

3 Follow the Pennine Way to Upper Booth Farm, which has won awards for its habitat restoration work.

4 As you walk alongside the River Noe, you pass some ancient clough woodland on your left. It is a remnant of far larger woods which used to cover these steep hillsides.

5 Climb Jacob's Ladder footpath. It was rebuilt recently by the National Trust using gritstone boulders, which were airlifted by helicopter. This section of the Pennine Way was once a packhorse route crossing the moors. Lead, coal, salt and wool were transported in this way from medieval times until the railways arrived. Turn right on to Kinder Plateau when you reach the top.

6 Come off the Pennine Way, taking a path to your right and skirt eastwards around Kinder Plateau. On the left, around the giant anvil-shaped rock known as Noe Stool, you will see heavily degraded areas of exposed peat.

7 The weathered gritstone rocks or 'tors' along the Kinder edges are some of the most spectacular sights in the Peak District. Continue past Crowden Tower then follow the footpath as it drops down into the Grindsbrook.

8 You will be treated to sweeping views of the Vale of Edale as you descend from the plateau. Notice the patterns of historic dry-stone walls and field boundaries. Follow the Grindsbrook footpath back to the Edale village.

Malvern Hills

The Malvern Hills, designated an Area of Outstanding Natural Beauty (AONB) in 1959, cover a distance of just 14.5km (9 miles), and run north–south, with a single bare ridge of peaks along the top. Although their range is small, they are an impressive sight as they rise some 425m (1,395ft) above the Severn Valley to their highest point, Worcestershire Beacon. The hills, situated in Worcestershire, Herefordshire and a small section of Gloucestershire, are famous for their mineral water and springs.

The Malvern Hills are made from igneous and metamorphic rocks from the Pre-Cambrian period, estimated to be around 700 million years old, and are some of the oldest rocks in England. The area to the north west is characterised by steep limestone topography. Sandstone and marls support the fertile plain to the south east and undulating hills of limestone and shale lie to the west. The area

Below: A view across the Malvern Hills from Herefordshire Beacon (British Camp) to the 292m (958ft) tall Broad Down.

forms part of the Abberley and Malvern Hills Geopark. Geopark status is a UNESCO-endorsed award that acknowledges the high quality of local geological heritage. Geoparks aim to promote geoconservation and sustainable geotourism. Much of the Malverns is also designated as a Site of Special Scientific Interest (SSSI), as much for its geology as biology.

The spine of the hills traditionally formed the county border between Herefordshire and Worcestershire and was an excellent defensive stronghold. Running along the summit is the Shire Dyke or Ditch; for many years it was believed that this was built in the 13th century by Gilbert de Clare, the Red Earl of Gloucester, after a boundary dispute with the Bishop of Hereford. However, a recent archaeological survey indicates that it may be 2,000 years older than thought, possibly late Bronze Age. At Midsummer Hill, the prehistoric hill fort is built on the top of the ditch, suggesting that it is even older. Experts now believe that the Red Duke strengthened and refurbished the ditch rather than building it from scratch.

The water of the Malvern Hills

The area has a rich history of human settlement, possibly because of the availability and purity of its water – certainly villages grew up close to the site of springs. Groundwater infiltrates the igneous rock of the hills via faults and fissures, working its way downwards until it reaches the less permeable sedimentary rocks, where it emerges as a spring. The first mention of the healing power of Malvern Water appears in Bannister's *Breviary of the Eyes* (1622); the water was bottled and sent around the country as early as the reign of James I. The first water-cure establishment opened in Great Malvern in 1842 and Charles Dickens and Charles Darwin both visited. There are over 100 springs and wells in the region, but only six still supply pure spring water.

Right: A lonely tree is silhouetted against the rising sun on Hangman's Hill in the Malvern Hills, which rises to 276m (906ft).

On the summit of the Herefordshire Beacon, or 'British Camp', are the remains of an Iron Age hill fort. In addition, a Norman motte fortification that crowns British Camp is visible for miles around, an imposing symbol of Norman lordship. Beacons have been lit on the spine of the hills since Norman times, as the fire could be seen many miles away on a clear night, and on most days it is possible to see the three cathedrals of Hereford, Worcester and Gloucester.

Malvern stone was quarried from the hills, sparking controversy between those with a living to make and the conservationists; George Bernard Shaw wrote a letter of complaint to *The Times*, highlighting the damage being done to the scenery. Much of the work was stopped after the Second World War, although quarrying continued at Gullet quarry until 1977.

The Malvern Hills contain a range of landscapes and habitats over a compact area, including open, flat, enclosed and unenclosed common, rolling pastures, ancient woodland, arable sandlands, farmland and hedgerows. Indeed, the area contains 15 SSSIs and one national nature reserve, and birdlife in particular is very rich. The soil at the top of the hills is highly acidic and supports heathers and bent grasses. The bracken-clad slopes support colonies of rare high brown fritillary. This butterfly abounded here during the 1980s but has been in steep decline since. At Hartlebury Common, an area of dry shrub heathland, sand-loving plants such as tower mustard and heath dog violet grow, and all three British newts live in this habitat. Nationally, dormice have disappeared from half of their historic range, however they occur in the woodland of the Malvern Hills, and local projects are underway to protect their habitats. The Colwall Tunnel at Wyche Cutting is an old railway tunnel 1,432m (4,700ft) long and is home to a colony of rare lesser horseshoe bats; pipistrelle, barbastelle and Bechstein's bats can also be seen in the wooded hills.

Watch for Wildlife

Birdlife in the Malvern Hills

It is the combination of habitats in the Malvern Hills that makes this region a paradise for birdwatchers, as many different species can be seen over a relatively small area. **Buzzards** are easy to spot, but **goshawk**, **hobby**, **red kites** and **peregrine falcons** can also be seen. The hilltops attract **meadow pipits** and **skylarks** as well as passing migrants such as **wheatear** and **ring ouzel**. The wooded hillsides attract the beautiful **pied flycatcher** and **redstart** in summer, as well as **chiffchaff** on the lower woodlands, and **willow warblers** higher up the hillsides. Both the **green** and the **great spotted woodpeckers** are found in a variety of habitats as well as **nuthatches** and **treecreepers**. Scrub and common land attracts **whitethroat**, **willow warbler**, **linnet** and **meadow pipit**, as well as waders including **snipe** and **jack snipe**. Assorted **ducks**, **moorhen**, **coots**, **herons** and **kingfishers** can all be seen near the water.

Skylark

Meadow pipit

Other Sites in Central England

Derbyshire

Calke Abbey, Derbyshire
Woodland, parkland, fields, hedges, grassland
Calke Abbey is hidden in rolling parkland of great interest for its natural history. Much of the parkland is a National Nature Reserve. Especially important for the park's wildlife are the many large, ancient oaks growing among bracken and grassland. The dead wood of these trees provides a home for wood-boring beetles found at very few locations in Britain. These stately trees are also an ideal habitat for green and great spotted woodpeckers, spotted flycatchers, nuthatches and treecreepers. The acid grassland contains plants such as heath bedstraw, sheep's sorrel, harebell and tormentil, as well as grasshoppers and meadow brown, common blue and small heath butterflies. In winter, large numbers of waterfowl congregate on the park's ponds.

Below: The Fishing Room on the lake at Kedleston Hall and Park was designed by Robert Adam and constructed between 1770 and 1772.

Kedleston Hall, Derbyshire
Grassland, parkland, lakes, woodland
Robert Adam's masterpiece of Palladian architecture that is Kedleston Hall is set in extensive grazed parkland, with a serpentine lake. Medieval oak groves survive from an old deer park and much of the invertebrate fauna that survives is associated with the ancient trees. The lakes are home to many breeding water birds, and although the huge flocks of Canada geese damage the quality of the habitat, they also enrich the lakeside grasslands. Great spotted woodpeckers and nuthatches can be seen in the woods.

Herefordshire and Worcestershire

Bradnor Hill, Herefordshire
Acid grassland, heath, bracken, scrub
This broad, rounded hill, part of which is managed as a golf course, has extensive views over the Welsh mountains to the west and the Wye Valley to the east. Its grasslands and grassy heaths contain bird's-foot trefoil and the uncommon upright chickweed, as well as many mosses and lichens. Hares live on these stretches of open ground, and meadow pipits, whinchats and wheatears can also be seen here. Yellowhammers, green woodpeckers, tree pipits and the tawny owl need more cover, and the hill's wooded northern slopes provide these birds with a suitable habitat. Dark green fritillary butterflies fly over the bracken-covered slopes.

Brockhampton Estate, Herefordshire
Dingle woodlands, parkland, old orchards, ponds, streams
Several nature walks have been laid out through this scenic country estate. The original woods consist mainly of old oaks, but redwoods and cedar of Lebanon were

later planted for ornament. More recently, beech has been planted to provide hardwood in the future. The veteran trees support wood-decay fauna, and the area holds the first British recorded location of the mistletoe weevil. The woodland plants include dog's mercury, yellow archangel and enchanter's nightshade. The younger plantations of larch and beech attract willow warblers and chiffchaffs, while tits, woodpeckers and redstarts prefer the older woodland.

Clent Hills, Worcestershire
Woodland, grassland, heath, pond, streams
The Clent Hills, which are managed as a country park, form a popular and heavily visited open space just a few miles from the centre of Birmingham. Most people visit the hill slopes above the village of Clent, but Walton Hill to the south east also falls within the park's boundary. The area's varied habitats, including patches of oak woodland, hawthorn scrub and grassland, guarantee a variety of plants and animals. The scarce bird cherry grows in the broad-leaved woodland, where many of the park's birds are found. These include redstarts, wood warblers, little and tawny owls as well as sparrowhawks. In more open areas, bilberry and western gorse grow in the remnants of shrubby heath. Over 20 species of butterfly have been recorded within the area, including green hairstreak and marbled white.

Above: A planted outcrop of trees on Adam's Hill, a slope that forms the south-west flank of Clent Hill, one of the tallest in the area.

Croft Castle, Herefordshire
Woodland, parkland, ponds, streams, common with acid grassland and bracken mosaic
The extensive and many-faceted Croft Castle estate lies on the gently rising slopes of a limestone ridge. Its parkland is notable for massive and ancient oaks, many of which have been pollarded, and for the abundant insect life that they harbour. White-clawed crayfish can be found in the waters. The scarce Natterer's bat lives in old buildings, while the woodland is the home of fallow deer and muntjac. Buzzards can often be seen soaring over the trees, and the pied flycatcher and lesser spotted woodpecker live among the woods. So, too, does the now scarce hawfinch, which feeds on the seeds of the hornbeam. Butterflies, including the silver-washed fritillary, are an important part of the estate's wildlife.

Poor's Acre, Herefordshire
Woodland
Although small in size, Poor's Acre is part of the ancient woodland of Haugh Wood, giving its plants and animals a special quality. The wild service tree occurs in unusual abundance, and spurge laurel, a plant usually confined to old woodlands, also grows here. The wood's wildlife is notable for its wealth of moths and butterflies, with over 650 species having been recorded in the locality. The pearl-bordered fritillary, wood white, white admiral and white-letter hairstreak all occur in the area.

Leicestershire

Charnwood Forest, Ulverscroft Nature Reserve, Leicestershire
Woodland, heath, grassland
Ulverscroft lies on a ridge of high ground, rising to 240m (800ft), with outcrops of syenite, an ancient volcanic rock. The oak woodland, with its scattered beech trees, is part of the ancient Charnwood Forest, and the old trees attract many woodland birds, including all three British woodpeckers, the nuthatch, redstart, treecreeper, tits and warblers. Small areas of heathland, now almost entirely covered by bracken, still contain some remnant patches of bilberry, a legacy of earlier days when the ground was more open. The bluebells in spring are particularly beautiful.

Nottinghamshire

Clumber Park, Nottinghamshire
Parkland, woodland, grassland, lakes, river
This great park on the edge of Sherwood Forest is, at 1,538ha (3,800 acres), large enough to absorb over one million visitors a year and yet still be a fascinating place for the naturalist. The extensive woodlands, together with heathland and grassland, are remnants from a time when vegetation like this covered much of the area. Like many parks, Clumber is a haven for insects that live in the wood of ancient oak and beech trees. The park's breeding birds include the nightingale, hawfinch, woodcock, lesser spotted woodpecker, redstart and long-eared owl. The large sweeps of acid grassland are dominated by wavy hair grass, and small-flowered

cranesbill can be found, as well as spring vetch and buckshorn plantain, which is usually a coastal species. The butterflies found here include the gatekeeper, small heath and small copper. The heathland, which is covered with heather, bell heather and gorse, provides a breeding area for nightjars, tree pipits, woodlarks and grasshopper warblers. The large lake is a magnet for wildfowl, the most notable being the gadwall, which breeds here.

Shropshire

Long Mynd, Carding Mill Valley and the Shropshire Hills, Shropshire
Moorland, acid grassland, heath, woodland, streams
The name Long Mynd is derived from the Welsh for 'long mountain'. From Carding Mill Valley the mountain reaches a height of 516m (1,693ft) and, on a clear day, gives breathtaking views as far as the Black Mountains to the south west and Cheshire to the north. The area is a biological and geological SSSI, as well as an AONB. Ravens, buzzards and curlews haunt the heather-clad upland plateau, while moorland birds such as

Below: Early morning mist over Long Mynd, or 'long mountain', and the undulating moorland of the Shropshire Hills at the head of Carding Mill Valley.

wheatear, stonechat, ring ouzel and red grouse are plentiful. Woodland birds include the tree pipit and pied flycatcher, while the dipper and grey wagtail patrol the streams for insects. On the high slopes, springs encourage moisture-loving plants such as butterwort and round-leaved sundew, bog pimpernel and sphagnum moss. The common spotted orchid grows on the moorland, and heath bedstraw on the grassy slopes. The National Trust has worked hard to reduce sheep grazing pressure here, with spectacular results. Freed from the attentions of sheep, heather has prospered, and the result is a vibrant late summer with plants blooming with an intensity not seen in years. Other species such as bilberry have recovered too, while grayling butterflies have made a comeback as their winter shelter in tussock grass is once again available.

Wenlock Edge, Shropshire
Woodland, limestone crags and grassland, scrub, marsh
This famous limestone escarpment provides superb views over the Shropshire plain. The National Trust's holdings on Wenlock Edge are mostly wooded areas. The trees include a mixture of conifers and broad-leaved species, with beech, oak, ash, hazel coppice, wild cherry and birch. Holly, rowan, spindle and guelder rose grow beneath them, and in spring bluebells and violets bloom in the clearings. Woodcock, woodpeckers, tits and warblers feed in the woods and copses, while

sparrowhawks, kestrels, tawny and little owls hunt in the woods or over open ground.

Attingham Estate, Shropshire
Deer park, grassland, river
The large, working estate outside the house is known for its deer park, landscaped by Humphry Repton, and is an area of great natural beauty as well as a SSSI. Set alongside the rivers Severn and Tern, the woodland, park and riverside support a rich variety of wildlife, from fallow deer to green woodpeckers, buzzards, house martins, and herons. It may be possible to spot the banded demoiselle damselfly by the river, along with otters.

Staffordshire

Hawksmoor and Mow Cop, Staffordshire
Woodland, pasture, farmland, river
Hawksmoor is a haven for wildlife just a short distance from the busy Potteries. Over 60 species of bird breed in its woods and open ground, and mammals found here include the fox, stoat, weasel, hare and badger. The broad-leaved woods comprise sessile oaks, American red oaks, field maple, beech, sycamore and glades of birch. The woodland birds include large numbers of warblers, and the older trees are ideal for woodpeckers as well as the treecreeper,

nuthatch and redstart. Conifers have been planted in some places, and here the tiny goldcrest and coal tit hunt for insects. Skylarks, curlews and lapwings all feed on the open pasture, and water birds include kingfishers, dippers, common sandpipers and yellow wagtails. Four trails lead through Hawksmoor, making delightful walking especially in spring, when the woodland floor is covered in bluebells, moschatel, wild garlic and wood anemones.

Kinver Edge, Staffordshire
Woodland, lowland heath, sand, scrub
This wooded escarpment and heath near Stourbridge is a surviving remnant of the vast forest that once covered this area. The woodlands that remain today are of oak, which was at one time coppiced for charcoal, and birch. The oak trees provide food for a great many different insect species, which in turn provide food for treecreepers, nightjar, tits and warblers. Adders, slow worms and lizards favour the sandy soil of the escarpment, and can often be seen on hot, dry days basking in the sun.

Warwickshire

Charlecote Park, Warwickshire
Parkland, pasture, riverbanks
A walk through Charlecote's historic deer park gives access to a lake and the banks of the River Avon, and leads past ancient trees that provide homes for birds, insects and bats. Black poplars, uncommon in Britain, grow beside the church, and pollarded willows are scattered in the meadows. Treecreepers, woodpeckers and nuthatches nest in holes in the older trees, and in summer the purple hairstreak butterfly can be seen on the wing. During the winter, regular flooding of the adjoining pastures attracts wildfowl.

Worcestershire

Croome Park, Worcestershire
Lake, grassland, parkland
This, Lancelot 'Capability' Brown's first complete landscaped park, was the work that made Brown's reputation and established a new style of garden design, which became universally adopted over the next 50 years. In 1996, the National Trust acquired the park and has since been restoring it, including removing some 50,000m^3 (1,766,000ft^3) of silt and vegetation when restoring the serpentine lake. During the process of restoration, a large reed bed was cleared, which was the home of reed warblers. However, the extensive new wetlands have been created on the edge of the park and are attracting large numbers of other birds.

Above: Cattle graze peacefully beside the river Croome in Croome Park, Worcestershire. This landscape was Lancelot 'Capability' Brown's first complete design.

Northern
England

The Lake District

The Lake District has some of the most breath-taking scenery in Europe, its deep, clear lakes and tall mountains have inspired poets, artists and writers since the mid-18th century. It is the largest National Park in England and covers an area of some 2,292 km² (885 square miles). The area holds many records: Scafell Peak is the tallest mountain in England, measuring 978m (3,209ft); Wastwater is the deepest lake, with depths of 79m (258ft); and Windermere is the longest lake, measuring 17km (10½ miles) in length.

The geology and topography of the Lakes

The rocks of the Lake District sit on a granite batholith (a large body of igneous rock formed by magma that has solidified beneath the Earth's surface), which underlies the whole area. The oldest rock was formed 500 million years ago in the Ordovician period, as mud on the seabed. Skiddaw slate, a metamorphosed sedimentary rock, occurs in this group and produces a landscape of smooth slopes and clear ridges, as seen at Skiddaw in the north. A period of intense volcanic activity produced the Borrowdale Volcanics, a mix of lava and ash flow, which was later lifted, folded and eroded producing the dramatic, rugged scenery seen in the centre of the Lake District. Further south again is rock from the Silurian period known as the Windermere group; it consists of sedimentary sandstone, siltstone and mudstone, and produces the gentle, undulating profile seen on the main tourist route into the Lake District.

The landscape of the Lake District has been created by glaciation; its deep U-shaped valleys were formed by glacial action and meltwater. In the highest peaks, glacial cirques – amphitheatre-like valleys – can be seen. These are often filled with tarns or small upland lakes. There are more than 14 lakes and tarns in the Lake District. The volcanic rock that underlies them does not allow the water to seep away, and the combination of high rainfall and deep glacial valleys, means that

Above: The smooth and graceful lines of Skiddaw, the fourth highest mountain in England, climb to an impressive 931m (3,054ft) above sea level. It is seen here from the eastern shore of Derwentwater.

large amounts of water are stored. The topography of the district is often likened to a wheel, with the hub just north of Grasmere at Dunmail Raise, and the valleys and lakes radiating outwards as spokes. The highest peaks are rocky and little grows there; lower down there are areas of open moorland and bog, and below the tree line there are deciduous woods and conifer plantations.

Settlements in the Lakes

The Lake District has been inhabited for over 10,000 years. There are over 6,000 known archaeological sites, including over 200 scheduled ancient monuments. There are a number of stone circles built during the Neolithic and Bronze Ages, and newly discovered examples of prehistoric rock art. Ordovician rock was hewn from high on the slopes of Great Langdale to be fashioned into axes. The Romans left roads and forts behind them, notably Hardknott Fort, built in the second century AD. Over the centuries, local inhabitants survived by farming, hunting and fishing. By the 13th century, the wool trade

Climate

The area has the dubious distinction of being the wettest part of England; the average annual rainfall is more than 2m (6½ft). There is, however, huge local variation. The driest months of the year are March to June while the wettest are October through to January. Its proximity to the sea ensures that much of the Lake District has milder winters and cooler summers than other parts of northern England, though much depends on altitude. Walking and climbing in the winter months can be dangerous, even with all the correct equipment, as hill fog is a common occurrence throughout the year.

Above: A misty view of Scafell Pike, the highest mountain in England at 978m (3,209ft), seen from the National Trust campsite at Wasdale Head. The summit is covered with shattered rock debris caused by weathering and frost action and known as a summit boulder field.

Below: The Castlerigg Stone Circle, near Keswick, comprises some 40 stones that are estimated to date back to 3,200BC. The stones are made of local metamorphic slate and are arranged in a rough circle measuring 32m (107ft) at its widest.

was becoming important and sheep farming became a thriving local industry. Trees were coppiced to supply the burgeoning charcoal industry. Later, minerals such as copper, iron, lead, silver and graphite were mined, and granite was quarried for kerbstones.

Tourism in the Lakes

The Lake District was effectively 'discovered' by the Picturesque movement of the mid-18th century. William Wordsworth lived in the area for 50 years until his death in 1850. His friend ST (he hated being called Samuel Taylor) Coleridge lived for some years at Keswick, alongside Robert Southey, who was Poet Laureate before Wordsworth. Together, their poems immortalised the area, and Wordsworth also published his *Guide through the District of the Lakes* in 1810. He strongly objected to the building of the railways in this beautiful landscape; however, the railways arrived in the 1840s, and for the first time it became easy for visitors to reach the Lake District. Guest houses and hotels began to spring up, marking the beginning of tourism here – it is now the area's primary source of income, with over 12 million visitors every year.

Although much of the woodland in the Lake District was cleared, small pieces of ancient woodland comprising oak and ash, can still be seen around the lakes and on hillsides. Grizedale Forest is the

largest in the Lake District, situated between Coniston Water and Windermere, and was decimated in the 18th century. The Forestry Commission has restored the oak, spruce, larch and pine woodland, and the area is dotted with giant wooden sculptures. The wooded ravine at Aira Force cuts through beautiful scenery and leads to the High Force waterfalls. There is also access to Brotherswater and Ullswater, the site of Wordsworth's famous daffodils.

Over 1,300 plant species have been recorded in the Lake District, not least a number of rare and fascinating lichens, notably in the north-western fells, and some impressive fungi in the woods. Sundew and butterwort, both carnivorous plants, attract flies to their sticky leaves and then close around them, dissolving them into a sort of nutritious soup. Both species can be found in soggy moss close to moorland bogs. High on the fells, arctic alpines thrive in pockets of rich soil, the highlight being the glowing pink flowers of the alpine catchfly.

Right: There are dramatic walks to be had in the vicinity of Aira Force waterfall. The area became renowned as a beauty spot during the reign of Queen Victoria.

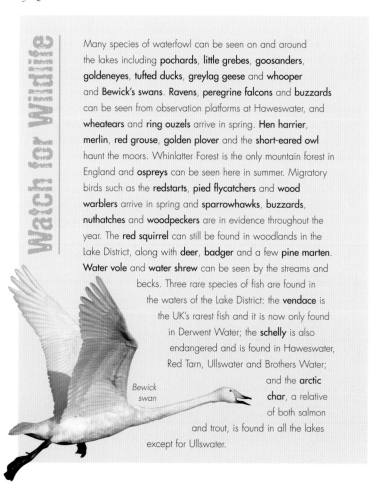

Watch for Wildlife

Many species of waterfowl can be seen on and around the lakes including **pochards**, **little grebes**, **goosanders**, **goldeneyes**, **tufted ducks**, **greylag geese** and **whooper** and **Bewick's swans**. **Ravens**, **peregrine falcons** and **buzzards** can be seen from observation platforms at Haweswater, and **wheatears** and **ring ouzels** arrive in spring. **Hen harrier**, **merlin**, **red grouse**, **golden plover** and the **short-eared owl** haunt the moors. Whinlatter Forest is the only mountain forest in England and **ospreys** can be seen here in summer. Migratory birds such as the **redstarts**, **pied flycatchers** and **wood warblers** arrive in spring and **sparrowhawks**, **buzzards**, **nuthatches** and **woodpeckers** are in evidence throughout the year. The **red squirrel** can still be found in woodlands in the Lake District, along with **deer**, **badger** and a few **pine marten**. **Water vole** and **water shrew** can be seen by the streams and becks. Three rare species of fish are found in the waters of the Lake District: the **vendace** is the UK's rarest fish and it is now only found in Derwent Water; the **schelly** is also endangered and is found in Haweswater, Red Tarn, Ullswater and Brothers Water; and the **arctic char**, a relative of both salmon and trout, is found in all the lakes except for Ullswater.

Bewick swan

Conservation in the Lakes

The National Trust manages a quarter of the land in the Lake District National Park including Scafell Pike and Wastwater, plus a large network of paths and tracks. The author Beatrix Potter left 1,618ha (4,000 acres) of land including 15 farms, to the care of the National Trust, a legacy that has gone some way to ensuring the survival of the stunning Lakeland landscape. Conservation in this beautiful district is crucial; the sheer number of tourists damages the terrain, flora and fauna, and often disturbs nesting birds. Grass is compacted by feet and worn away; in particular walkers are eroding and scarring the landscape each time they take shortcuts from marked paths. Locals are turning away from less traditional employment, such as sheep farming, in favour of the profitable tourist industry. The National Trust has purchased a large number of traditional farms to maintain the habitat and biodiversity, and works as a wool merchant in the area.

Borrowdale Woods

The woods owned by the National Trust in Borrowdale, account for over three-quarters of the woodland in this beautiful valley, which has more tree cover than almost any other in the Lake District. The predominant tree is the sessile oak, but ash and birch also find a place, along with cherry, rowan and alder. The composition of each wood is shaped by features such as the position, soil depth and rainfall. As a result, woods just a short distance apart can be quite different. All, however, are notable for their abundant growth of lichens, mosses and liverworts, which thrive in the damp air, covering trunks, branches and boulders alike. Red squirrels live in some of the woods, and the annual touch-me-not balsam thrives in the damp atmosphere. Pied flycatchers, redstarts, wood warblers and nuthatches feed on insects within them, while the woodcock probes the damp soil for its food.

Buttermere Valley

Framed by the peaks of Grasmoor, High Stile and Buttermere Fell, the Buttermere Valley is an area of classic Lakeland landscape. The main valley contains two lakes – Crummock Water and Buttermere itself – and at Ghyll Wood, Long How Wood and Nether How Wood, there are remnants of the sessile oak woodland that once covered many hillsides. A broad band of mixed woodland lies at nearby Loweswater, and this contains fine specimens of beech, oak, lime and sweet chestnut. With such a diversity of habitats, the valley's bird life is varied. Mergansers, great crested grebes, coots, mallards and goldeneyes live on the lakes, while common sandpipers nest on the shoreline. The birds of the woods and open ground include the pied flycatcher, barn owl, tawny owl, sparrowhawk, goldcrest and peregrine falcon. Buzzards soar overhead, announcing their presence with a distinctive mewing cry. Mountain ringlet butterflies fly on the high fell slopes; Fleetwith Pike is one notable site.

Left: The flora of the forest floor at Great Wood in Borrowdale, Keswick, is a beautiful sight at the height of spring. Borrowdale is the wettest place in the UK with an average rainfall of 469cm (185in) at Sprinkling Tarn.

Below: Buttermere Lake is set in the middle of a natural amphitheatre of mountains. The lake is relatively small at just 2.4km (1½ miles) long – it only takes between two and three hours to walk the perimeter.

Lakes. Great Gable, Pillar, Steeple, Haycock and Red Pike, some of the highest peaks in the area, rise above Ennerdale Forest, which dominates the valley to the east. Like Wastwater, the lake is interesting due to its purity and low nutrient levels, which provides an important habitat for char, crustacea and unusual plants. The poorly drained mire adjacent to the lake is rich in invertebrates and damp-loving plants. The broad-leaved woodlands, notably Side Wood, comprising sessile oak and upland birch, abound in mosses, lichens and ferns, and on the crags, in the gills and on the rock ledges, are mountain plant communities, which include saxifrages, alpine lady's mantle and heather.

Sandscale Haws

Sandscale Haws' large dunes, which give good views northwards into the Lake District and westwards into the Irish Sea, are noted for their plants and insects. The tall, chalk-rich dunes have an extensive covering of marram grass. The dune slacks, some of which flood in winter, have a rich plant life, including various species of orchid, such as coral-root and dune helleborine, and rarities such as the yellow vetch. Bloody cranesbill and sea kale also grow here. The area's insects include the uncommon coastal dart and shore wainscot moths, numerous dark green fritillaries, and a number of mining bees and wasps. The slacks between the dunes are also one of the few breeding sites of the natterjack toad and great crested newt.

Ullswater Valley, Glencoyne Wood and Gowbarrow Park

Seen against the backdrop of towering peaks, trees contribute greatly to Lakeland scenery. The trees around Ullswater include many that were planted in the 18th and 19th centuries for their visual appeal – copper beeches, wellingtonias, oaks, and a number of other species from all over the world. Now fully mature, they offer cover for birds and shelter for red deer. Glencoyne Wood, at the south end of the lake, contains many fine old oak trees. In spring, the ground is carpeted with daffodils, while autumn brings with it a large crop of many different species of fungi. Nearby in Gowbarrow Park, the spray generated by Aira Force, one of the most powerful waterfalls in the Lake District, bathes moisture-loving ferns, mosses and liverworts.

Wasdale and Wastwater

The reflection of Wasdale's screes – steep fans of unstable rocks and boulders – in the calm surface of Wastwater, is one of the most dramatic sights in the Lake District. The screes and the associated crags and gullies, are famous for their mountain plants, which include species such as the dwarf juniper, alpine lady's mantle, shrubby cinquefoil and purple saxifrage.

Left: The stately plumes of rosebay willowherb stand tall among the marram grasses of the vast dune systems at Sandscale Haws with the sand flats beside the estuary beyond.

Above right: Glencoyne wood in Ullswater valley is a riot of colour in autumn. The woods provide a stunning backdrop to Ullswater, the second largest lake in the Lake District.

Coniston and Tarn Hows

At the head of Coniston Water, north east of the village, lies Tarn Hows. It was landscaped to look like a Swiss lake in the 19th century. The shallow tarn contains some important habitat, including a boggy area rich in wetland plants, with marsh cinquefoil, bogbean, common spotted orchid, sweet gale and hare's-tail cotton-grass. The fells around are covered in the ubiquitous upland grassland fescues and bents, with juniper on the screes and some fellsides. Characteristic oak woodlands, some of which date back to the last ice age, are of great ecological importance and support a wide range of mosses, lichens and invertebrates. A scattering of oak, ash, rowan, hawthorn and Scots pine now covers the intake land of the fellsides, and fields in the valley bottom include some meadows rich in wild flowers.

Ennerdale

The difficult access to Ennerdale protects it from too many visitors and it remains one of the quieter and more secluded valleys in the

Townend and Troutbeck Valley

Uncover classic Lakeland scenery, farmland and architecture on this beautiful circular walk from Brockhole, near Lake Windermere, up into the Troutbeck Valley and to the charming and unique 17th-century farmhouse, Townend. On the way you will be rewarded with stunning views of the surrounding fells and Lake Windermere, diverse wildlife and some charming local architecture.

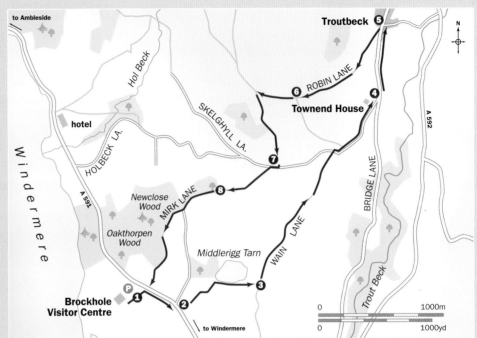

Getting there and facilities:
There are regular bus services from Windermere and Ambleside. Windermere train station is 4km (2½ miles) from Brockhole. WCs, refreshments and a car park can be found at Brockhole Visitor Centre, just off the A591. More WCs can be found at Townend and more refreshments in Troutbeck village. See www.nationaltrust.org.uk/townend for opening details.

Start point:
Brockhole Visitor Centre – GR NY407023, OS Landranger 90, or Explorer OL7

Distance, terrain and accessibility:
This 6.4km (4 mile) walk, with an ascent of 229km (750ft), will take you across country roads, bridleways, footpaths and a busy main road. The terrain can be uneven and muddy after wet weather. Walking boots or sturdy shoes are recommended.

Route and directions:
1   Leave Brockhole, turn right and walk along the footpath beside the A591 until you see a bridleway on the opposite side of the road. Here you can see Old St Andrew's Chapel (now used as offices). It was built in 1913 by a family who lived nearby, so that their staff would not be away from their duties for too long by going to church in Bowness.

2   Cross the road carefully and follow the track up towards Middlerig Tarn. This track is known as Wain Lane. It is a 10th-century cart lane and was used by packhorses to bring slate from Troutbeck down to the lake where it could be transported by boat.

3   Follow the track past the tarn and continue along it as it veers to the left. You can see the route of the aqueduct along Wain Lane. Look out for single iron gates supported by sandstone pillars, which were used for access.

4   When the track meets a road, turn right. This will take you into Troutbeck village. You will see Townend house to the left of the T junction along the road.

5   Continue along the village road past the barns and interesting houses and up towards the post office. Turn left here.

6   Follow Robin Lane, which will be joined by a bridleway on the left. Continue for 300m (328yd) and then turn left opposite a pillar on the right. This is an excellent spot for a view of Windermere, England's largest lake.

7   Follow the track down to a road. Cross over to Mirk Lane, opposite.

8   Walk along Mirk Lane back down towards the A591. Carefully cross the road again to return to Brockhole.

The Yorkshire Dales

It is perhaps the contrasts of the Yorkshire Dales that make it such a captivating landscape. The high fells are open, wild and remote, dotted with sheep. They are dissected by deep valleys – or dales – and painted green with lush woodland and gentle farmland. Most of the area is part of the Yorkshire Dales National Park – one of the largest National Park in the UK, covering 1,769km² (683 square miles). The bulk of the Dales are in Yorkshire, and although the area attracts around nine million visitors per year, many of these are successfully swallowed up by the landscape.

The landscape of the Yorkshire Dales

Three hundred million years ago, the area that is now the Yorkshire Dales, lay under a tropical sea. The accumulated debris of shell and bones that fell to the ocean floor produced sedimentary rocks of limestone and sandstone, topped with millstone grit, all later subject to lifting, folding and glacial action. The underlying rock in the area is principally carboniferous limestone, which produces such scenic karst features as cliffs, crags, scars, scree and limestone pavements. The latter occur after limestone has been subjected to the scouring action of a glacier; the resulting hairline cracks are further exploited by erosion, leaving a grid of limestone blocks, or clints, and deep fissures, or grykes. Limestone pavements can be seen at Malham and Ingleborough national nature reserves.

Shale, sandstone and slim slivers of coal contribute to the jagged profile of hills and valleys as rock edges and outcrops give way to different seams of rock. To the east of the Dales there are large sections of impermeable millstone grit, which form high, wet expanses of bog and acid moorland. The Three Peaks – Whernside, Ingleborough and Pen-y-ghent – are part of the Pennines, and are all about 700m (2,296ft) high. The walks here reveal wild limestone scenery, including the Norber Erratics, near Austwick – sandstone boulders that have been transported by glaciers.

Above: Malham Cove is a huge, curving, 80m (262ft) high, white-faced cliff in the Yorkshire Dales National Park. On the left-hand side are around 400 irregular steps that lead to the limestone pavement at the top. Here, a tree clings to the sheer rock face.

Right: Sunset and clouds in the area around the tiny hamlet of Halton Gill, situated high up in Littondale, Yorkshire Dales National Park.

The larger southern dales run almost parallel from north to south and are less remote, while to the north the dales run from west to east. The word 'dale' is said to have its root in the Scandinavian word *thal* for valley. Most of the dales get their name from the rivers that run through them – Swaledale for example, is cut through by the River Swale – however there are exceptions, notably Wensleydale, which hosts the River Ure.

Water pours down from the Pennines and vanishes into swallowholes, while caves and gorges further puncture the limestone. White Scar Cave, the longest show cave in the UK, was formed under Ingleborough, one of the Three Peaks. As mildly acidic rain trickles through the limestone rock it becomes in part a calcium bicarbonate solution. Later the solution separates

Above: Glacial erratics – rocks that have been carried by the action of glacial ice often over hundreds of kilometres – litter the limestone pavement at Scales Moor, Upper Ribbleside, Twisleton, seen here looking towards Whernside.

and, as mineral-laden drops of water fall, they leave behind minute rings of calcite (the crystalline form of calcium carbonate), which develop slowly into the classic cave formations of stalactites and stalagmites. These grow at the rate of just 1cm (⅜in) every 200 years.

Deep waterfalls thunder down into the valleys and tumble over rocky ledges. Fine examples can be seen at the Waterfall Walk at Ingleton, that first opened to the public in 1885, and which encompasses a series of spectacular waterfalls. Hardraw Force in Wensleydale, has an unbroken drop of 30m (100ft), and is one of England's highest unbroken waterfalls. The spectacular falls at High Force see the River Tees plunge over Whin Sill, and crash into the basin below. In the south of the Dales is Malham Tarn, an upland alkaline lake – said to be the highest in England – which is ringed by stunning limestone rock formations and home to many dramatic waterfalls, as well as a wetland nature reserve. Grey herons, kingfishers, dippers, grey wagtails and common sandpipers haunt the riverbanks, which meander along the valley floor.

Settlements in the Yorkshire Dales

The landscape is, as is so often the case, essentially man made. Over half of the area is moorland, a sizeable chunk of the remainder is farmland, and just a tiny proportion is made up of woodland, often in minor side valleys or cloughs. Early settlers cleared woodland,

Watch for Wildlife

Upper Wharfedale lies in the valley of the River Wharfe, within the Yorkshire Dales National Park. There are some prehistoric field patterns and remains of old lead mines. Those river valleys that have escaped agricultural improvement support a variety of lime-loving plants, such as **ox-eye daisy**, **yellow rattle**, **betony**, **knapweed**, **sedges**, **self-heal**, **orchids** and many grasses. The gill woodlands are particularly important for their rich bryophyte flora. Historical evidence, and studies of the **lichen** and invertebrate communities, have shown that parts of the valley have been managed as pasture-woodland for centuries. Tracts of ancient meadows remain up in the fells and are studded with wild flowers; **mountain pansies**, **cowslips** and **bird's-eye primroses** grow on high pastures, and many are now formally protected. In the woods, ancient **oaks**, **ash**, **wych elm**, **hazel**, **bird cherry**, **rowan**, **holly** and **birch** can be seen, and the ungrazed ledges on the crags are rich in mosses, ferns and tall herbs. **Primroses**, **wood crane's-bill**, **wood anemone**, **globeflowers** and several species of **orchid** are found in the limestone woodlands, and **sparrowhawk**, **redstart** and **wood warbler** hunt there for food. Above the valley sides the plateaus are peat-covered, with the resulting grassland and peat bogs of particular interest for their plant and bird communities.

Ox-eye daisy

Marsden Moor

Marsden Moor (shown below), owned by the National Trust, is typical of Dales' moorland. It covers around 23km² (5,685 square acres) of unenclosed common moorland, with peaks, crags, a reservoir and valleys. Large numbers of moorland birds including golden plover, red grouse, curlew and twite can be seen moving through the heather and cotton-grass. Tragically the last eagles in the area were shot back in 1851. The moor is a Site of Special Scientific Interest (SSSI) and a Special Protection Area (SPA). Five thousand years of peat has been forming below a thin layer of grasses, rushes, sedges and moss. This can be damaged by overgrazing and trampling and completely destroyed by fire, which exposes the fragile peat, leaving it susceptible to erosion. The Trust has fenced off areas to exclude grazing animals and is reseeding heather.

grew crops in the dales, and grazed their animals on the fen grassland; cattle grazed valley pastureland contained by hedgerow or dry-stone walls, while sheep explored the highest slopes. The Romans drove straight roads through the fells, and in the 9th and 10th centuries Norsemen arrived – their legacy is a collection of distinctive place names: *thwaite*, a common ending to a village name, means 'settlement' and from *fjall*, we get 'foss' or 'force' meaning waterfall. The Normans built castles and abbeys (the monks were the first to make delicious Wensleydale cheese). Minerals, such as lead, were extracted and limestone was quarried, an industry that continues today.

There are almost 1,500km (932 miles) of footpaths in the Yorkshire Dales and the area is crossed by some noteworthy trails. The Dales Way starts at Ilkley and finishes at Bowness-in-Windermere. It follows riverside paths for chunks of its 130km (80 mile) route, covers the full length of Wharfedale, crosses the Pennine watershed and finally heads off to the Lake District. The Pennine Way is a 431km (268 mile) walk, which starts at Kinder Scout in the Peak District, before moving through the southern Pennines and crossing the Yorkshire Dales – it continues right up to Hadrian's Wall. The Ribble Way follows the River Ribble through its valley and on to the sea and stretches over 117km (70 miles).

Below: A beautiful summer evening with stone barns glowing in the meadows near Gunnerside in Swaledale. The meadows run alongside the River Swale and the settlement at Gunnerside was once the heart of the lead mining industry.

Upper Wharfedale

Discover a landscape of limestone pavement, glaciated valleys and flower-rich hay meadows in the glorious setting of the Yorkshire Dales. The farming of this area has created many interesting wildlife habitats, from hillside streams and craggy outcrops to blanket bog and dry-stone walls.

Getting there and facilities:

Off-road cycling is permitted on bridleways and there is a 21km (13 mile) signed on-road cycle route from Skipton to Kettlewell, around 8km (5 miles) from Buckden. By road, Yockenthwaite is 5km (3 miles) north west of Buckden, off the B6160. The Pride of the Dales bus (no.72) runs from Skipton train station to Buckden and there are also buses from Leeds and Ilkley train stations. There is roadside parking at Yockenthwaite and pubs at Cray and Hubberholme. There is a car park, toilets, cafés, pubs and a YHA hostel in Kettlewell. Hill-walking leaflet and other trail guides are available from the Yorkshire Dales National Park Centre in Grassington.

Start point:

OS Landranger 98: SD904790

Distance, terrain and accessibility:

This is a moderately energetic circular walk of approximately 9.5km (6 miles). There is a rather steep climb from Yockenthwaite then it is fairly flat until the descent out of Cray. There is a short stretch of road into Hubberholme.

Route and directions:

1   Start in Yockenthwaite (meaning 'Eoghan's clearing') and follow the footpath signposted to Scar House. Turn right off the farm track at another footpath sign, going through Strans Wood and emerge on to the open hillside.

2   In 1652 George Fox, the founder of the Quakers, stayed at Scar House and converted the farmer. The house later became a Quaker meeting place. A small enclosure with five trees here marks an old burial ground. Continue towards Cray, keeping the

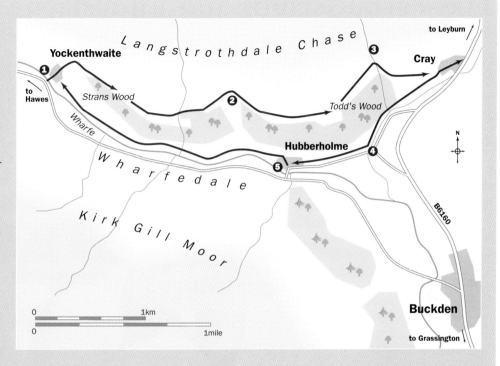

woodland boundary on your right (for a shorter walk, turn right at Scar House and follow the track into Hubberholme). Enjoy the view down Wharfdale's glaciated valley with its wide floor and ice-carved steep sides.

3   Cross Crook Gill and carry on through hay meadows to Cray. Enjoy the wild flowers and lots of birds throughout the spring and summer. Hay is a valuable crop to farmers and it can suffer if trampled by too many feet, so please walk in single file.

4   Drop down to your right when entering Cray and follow a footpath along Cary Gill to a road. Turn right and walk along it for 0.4km (¼ mile) until you reach Hubberholme.

5   Return to Yockenthwaite via a footpath behind Hubberholme church and follow this route beside the river all the way back. There are lots of other interesting places to discover around here. With an optional extra 5km (3 miles) on this route you can visit Buckden, which has an exhibition of the area's history at Townhead Bran. Take the fellside path from Cray to get there, then take a riverside route from Buckden to Hubberholme and rejoin this walk.

The Farne Islands and Lindisfarne

The Farne Islands and Lindisfarne are situated off the north end of the Northumberland coast. There are 28 Farne Islands in total, but some of these are not visible when the tide is high, and many of the islands are off limits. Lindisfarne, otherwise known as Holy Island, is closer to the shore and is linked to the mainland by a causeway. The islands have a rich and colourful history and are famous for nesting seabirds and a colony of grey seals.

The Farne Islands

The Farnes are the most easterly outcrop of the Great Whin Sill; a strip of hard, dark, volcanic rock, dolerite, that stretches across Northumberland. This rock would originally have been surrounded by limestone, but erosion and rising sea levels after the last ice age left the Farnes as a group of tiny islands. The islands are divided into two sections: the Inner Group and the Outer Group. Inner Farne, a serene island with thousands of nesting birds, is the best known of the Inner Group. The principle islands in the Outer Group are Staple Island, an exposed and rugged outcrop with guillemot and razorbill; The Brownsman, which is not open to the public, but is home to a colony of grey seals that can be seen from boats; and Longstone, famed for its association with the lighthouse keeper's daughter, Grace Darling. Grace, along with her father, famously rescued nine sailors from the steam ship *Forfarshire*, which was dashed on the rocks near Longstone Lighthouse in 1838. The Farnes have been owned by the National Trust since 1925.

The islands were inhabited for many years but life was extremely difficult. Locals lived on fish, and seals were killed for their skins and blubber. In 676 St Cuthbert, known for his piety, work with the poor, and gift of healing, took up a solitary life of contemplation on Inner Farne Island. During his time there he had the foresight to introduce laws protecting nesting seabirds – believed to be the first bird protection measures taken anywhere in the world. He was made Bishop of Lindisfarne, but returned to his cell on the Farnes two years later, and died on the island in 687.

Below: A dramatic view of South Cliff on Inner Farne in the Farne Islands, which comes alive with rare seabirds between April and August. Banburgh Castle can be seen in the distance.

Left: The comical puffin is the most numerous bird on the Farne Islands. It sheds the famous, colourful, outer plate of its bill in autumn at the close of the breeding season – what remains is smaller and duller. The beak has spikes inside its mouth, which enable it to carry several fish crossways, allowing the bird to make longer hunting trips.

Inner Farne, Farne Islands

The Farne Islands are one of the natural highlights of the Northumbrian coast. Famed for providing sanctuary to St Cuthbert in the 7th century, Inner Farne is now renowned as a summer haven for nesting sea birds. For a unique wildlife experience, visit between April and July, or explore a more tranquil, historic island after the breeding season finishes.

Getting there and facilities:

Daily boat trips run from Seahouses Harbour to Inner Farne from April to September, weather permitting. The Alnwick to Belford bus service connects to Alnmouth, Berwick-upon-Tweed and Newcastle rail stations. There is a car park in Seahouses, close to the harbour. Seahouses is just off the NCN 1, the scenic coast and castles cycle route. Basic toilet facilities, picnic area, visitor centre selling leaflets, a guide book and postcards are all available. Wardens are on hand around the island to help and answer questions.

Start point:

OS Landranger 75 – NU 230370

Distance, terrain and accessibility:

This is an 0.8km (½ mile) circular route. The boardwalk is slightly uneven and slippery when wet but suitable for most pushchairs. Take care on cobbles and near cliff-top viewpoints.

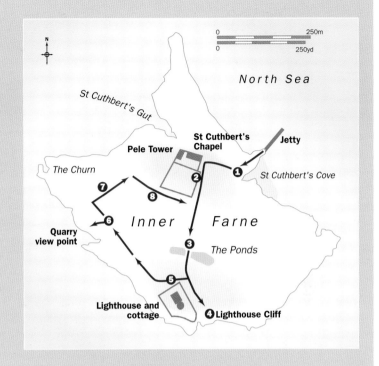

Route and directions:

1 Take care stepping off the boat and on to the jetties and climb up the boardwalk. The small stone building on your left is the 'fishe-house' – it stands on the site of the medieval guest house where visiting monks would stay. From April to July this is the first place you meet breeding arctic terns. They nest near the path and can be very defensive of their eggs or chicks. Expect to be dive-bombed, but don't panic, just slowly wave a hand above your head to discourage them.

2 Visit St Cuthbert's Chapel, see the Pele Tower and check out the information centre, or turn left and start your circuit of the island. Again, this is all an arctic tern nesting zone in early summer and chicks could be dotted around the cobbles so watch where you step and never run!

3 Look left – this is the one spot on Inner Farne where sandwich terns cluster together to breed.

4 Walk up the island to the lighthouse. Before it was built in 1825 a beacon used to get lit on top of the Pele Tower to warn off the ships.

5 Turn left to the Lighthouse Cliff viewpoint, where you can see Dunstanburgh Castle in the distance on a clear day. These are the tallest rock faces on the island. The cliff tops are home to thousands of breeding guillemots, shags and kittiwakes in summer.

6 Return to the lighthouse and turn left past the picnic area. There used to be two more cottages here where the lighthouse keepers and their families lived.

7 Follow the boardwalk through an area filled with puffin burrows and take a quick detour left to Quarry Viewpoint. Bamburgh Castle is straight ahead of you on the mainland.

8 On your left is a large expanse of rocky foreshore. If there's a large sea swell then you might see Churn blow hole spout out water up to 27.5m (90ft) into the air.

9 Return to the start point passing the monks' old vegetable garden on your left.

The cliffs, stacks and grassy tops of this group of islands come alive with seabirds from April to early August, with 20 species breeding here annually, and 290 different species recorded since records began, including a sighting of the now-extinct great auk back in the 18th century. Arctic, common and sandwich terns nest on grassy banks and paths, and are famously aggressive when nesting. Puffins are the most numerous birds, notably on Staple Island and Inner Farne. They dig burrows in the soil and will also utilise rabbit's burrows. Guillemot and razorbill, both members of the auk family, can also be seen nesting in huge colonies on the clifftops. Eider ducks have been on the islands since the time of St Cuthbert; he is said to have allowed them to nest on the altar steps.

Lindisfarne

Lindisfarne is a tiny tidal island, 8.5km (5 miles) north of the Farnes. It is linked to the mainland by a tidal causeway but is cut off for a few hours twice-daily at high tide. It can be reached on foot or by car, via the 5km (3 mile) long Pilgrim's Way, but great care must be taken to follow the guide posts and to check tide times. It has been inhabited since Neolithic times and was principally a fishing community. Lime was quarried on the island and the lime kilns can still be seen.

The island is known for its monastery, founded by St Aidan around 635AD. St Cuthbert, whose life and work was recorded by the Venerable Bede, was Abbot here. In the early 8th century the exquisite illuminated manuscript of the Lindisfarne Gospels was created in honour of St Cuthbert; it represents the earliest surviving old English copy of the Gospels and now resides in the British Museum. A terrible Viking raid in 793AD forced the monks to flee, taking St Cuthbert's remains with them. In fact, he was not laid to rest for another 100 years when the monks settled at Durham

Above: The 16th century Lindisfarne Castle, on Holy Island, was converted into a family home in 1903 by Sir Edwin Lutyens. It is perched on top of a rocky island crag accessible only via the causeway.

Cathedral. The monastery was re-established in Norman times, and became a focal point for Christianity in the north of England, but it was later dissolved by Henry VIII. The remains of this 7th-century monastery can be seen as well as the extraordinary 16th-century castle, remodelled by Sir Edwin Lutyens, which perches on top of Beblowe Crag, now owned by the National Trust.

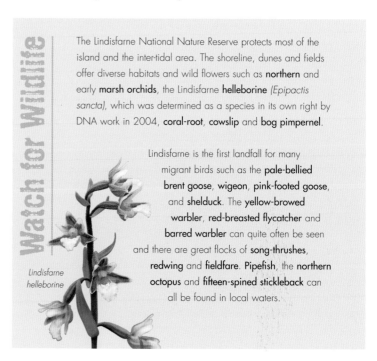

Watch for Wildlife

The Lindisfarne National Nature Reserve protects most of the island and the inter-tidal area. The shoreline, dunes and fields offer diverse habitats and wild flowers such as **northern** and early **marsh orchids**, the Lindisfarne **helleborine** *(Epipactis sancta)*, which was determined as a species in its own right by DNA work in 2004, **coral-root, cowslip** and **bog pimpernel**.

Lindisfarne is the first landfall for many migrant birds such as the **pale-bellied brent goose, wigeon, pink-footed goose,** and **shelduck**. The **yellow-browed warbler, red-breasted flycatcher** and **barred warbler** can quite often be seen and there are great flocks of **song-thrushes, redwing** and **fieldfare**. Pipefish, the **northern octopus** and **fifteen-spined stickleback** can all be found in local waters.

Lindisfarne helleborine

The Northumberland Coast

England's far north-eastern counties of Northumberland, Durham and Tyne and Wear offer magnificent scenery, with a long and dramatic coastline that is arguably one of the finest in Britain. For many years the Durham beaches were a dumping ground for the local collieries, but since their restoration, this unexpectedly beautiful area of coastline now has Heritage Coast status.

Alnmouth

Alnmouth's sand dunes and saltmarshes are worth visiting both for their wild flowers and their birds. The dune plants include marram grass and lyme grass, and also the colourful bloody cranesbill, purple milk-vetch and lesser meadow rue. Where grassland has formed over the sand, it is rich in low-growing plants such as bird's-foot trefoil and eyebright. Biting stonecrop and white stonecrop flourish here on dry ground. Alnmouth's extensive mudflats attract large numbers of waterfowl and waders.

Druridge Bay

In contrast to the industrial might of Newcastle, Druridge Bay is undeveloped. Grassy dunes shelter the sandy beach with a dune system behind. Stretching from Cresswell in the south to Low Hauxley in the north, the area is well known to birders, with golden plover, purple sandpiper, oystercatcher, redshank, pink-footed goose, greylag, whooper swan and lapwing. The grasslands are rich in wild flowers including bloody cranesbill, ragged robin and northern marsh orchid.

Dunstanburgh Castle

Crowned by the dramatic ruins of a 14th-century castle, the cliffs at Dunstanburgh provide an important breeding site for seabirds. Kittiwakes nest here, together with fulmars and shags. Eider ducks breed nearby, nearer to the shoreline. The castle is surrounded by grassland rich in wild flowers, including purple milk-vetch, field madder, spring squill, wild thyme, bloody cranesbill and several species of clover.

Embleton and Newton Links

The glorious beaches on this part of the coast are backed by extensive dunes, rough grazing and freshwater pools. Bloody cranesbill, burnet rose, restharrow and harebell grow around the older dunes, while the slacks between them shelter common

Above: The deserted beach and sand dunes south of the village of Alnmouth, which sits on the North Sea on the Northumberland coastline.

Left: The largest kittiwake colony in the north east can be found on the cliffs at Dunstanburgh, on top of which sits the ruins of what was once the largest castle in Northumberland.

butterwort and tufted centaury. Ducks, waders and seabirds can all be seen as well as migrant species in spring and autumn. Black-headed gulls have a large breeding colony here.

The Leas and Marsden Rock

These limestone cliffs support one of the most important breeding colonies of seabirds in the north east. Over 4,000 pairs of kittiwakes breed here, and herring gulls and fulmars abound, together with some lesser black-backed gulls. Cormorants nest on the top of Marsden Rock. Divers and guillemots can be seen in the coastal waters, and the shore attracts purple sandpipers and turnstones. In winter, migrant birds include the Lapland and snow bunting.

North York Moors

The North York Moors are famous for huge expanses of
open heather moor, the most extensive in England and Wales,
steep-sided dales, originally carved out by glacial meltwater, and
a 42km (26 mile) section of dramatic North Sea coastline fringed
with towering cliffs. The moors are situated to the north and
east of the city of York and cover 1,436km^2 (554 square miles);
approximately one third of this area is designated as a SSSI.

Moorland geology

The rock structure of the area is mixed and dominated by rocks
from the Jurassic era. The foundations were laid down in tropical seas
between 205 and 142 million years ago. Changes in the sea levels
produced a rock profile that included shale, sandstone, limestone and
mudstone. Much later the land was lifted and tilted, cut by glacial
action and topped off by glacial deposits of sand, gravel and boulder

*Above: The 122m (400ft) deep natural hollow known as the
Hole of Horcum, on the North York Moors, has been eroded
over thousands of years by the action of springs.*

*Below: The Brimham Rocks are set within the
Nidderdale AONB. The strange and dramatic rock
formations, such as The Turtle seen here, were
caused by erosion during and after the Devensian
Glaciation – the last ice age.*

clay. There is a domed plateau of impermeable sandstone, and around this, deep-sided valleys have been cut in soft limestone, with streams and rivers rushing through them. Some of the highest cliffs in England can be found just north of Boulby, measuring 203m (666ft) above sea level. The area is shot through with minerals – iron ore, alum shale, coal, limestone, whinstone and the UK's only source of jet – all of which have been mined.

Settlements on the North York Moors

The area has been inhabited for many thousands of years; indeed there are 700 Scheduled Ancient Monuments. There is evidence that the area was inhabited in the Mesolithic period, around 8000BC, when the UK was still part of the European land mass. Neolithic farmers worked the area, leaving pottery and stone implements behind. In the Bronze Age, around 2000BC, the climate was warmer and the whole area was inhabited. The land was worked until it was depleted and then the settlers moved on to new ground. In this way the settlers gradually cleared the area of woodland, and left behind exhausted soil on which only heathland plants could grow, and the moor began to develop. These Beaker people – so called because of the shape of their pottery – left behind around 3,000 burial grounds on the moors. The later pattern of settlement was for isolated hamlets to develop with larger villages around the fringes of the moors.

The wildlife of the North York Moors

Moorland is managed to support grouse shooting and sheep farming – heather is burned on a strict rotation schedule to maintain the essential food supply of young heather shoots, while at the same time maintaining areas of mature growth for nesting. Sphagnum moss bogs are commonplace here, often highlighted by patches of cotton-grass. However in the cold, acidic bog water there is little decomposition of organic matter and the moss accumulates, turning into peat and raising levels so that the bogs dry out naturally. The moors turn purple in August and September when the heather flowers. Three types of heather are commonly seen here: the pink cross-leaved heath, which likes a damp environment; bell heather, which has rich purple flowers; and the pink and purple flowers of true heather or 'ling'. Emperor moths fly by day; their caterpillars feed on heather. Lapwing, curlew and redshank breed on the moor and wheatear and ring ouzels can also be seen. The merlin is a tiny bird of prey that can be spotted perched on look-out points scanning for prey. Encroaching bracken is a problem as few plants can grow in its shade, and it is unpalatable, indeed poisonous, to most creatures.

Above: At low tide on Robin Hood's Bay the 550m (1800ft) of exposed sea floor is wonderful for fossil hunters. The view here looks north to the snow-covered cliff tops.

The moorland plateau is cut by river valleys, crisscrossed with dry-stone walls, and is used for grazing sheep and cattle. Trout, grayling and crayfish can be found in the River Derwent, while otter, kingfisher, heron and dipper haunt the banks. Other areas have more fertile soil and can be used to grow crops. Both forestry plantations and mixed deciduous woodland cover around 22 per cent of the National Park, concentrated in the valleys, and there are both forestry plantations and mixed deciduous woodland. Farndale is famous for its display of wild daffodils in spring. Bluebells and primroses grow along with the rarer wood vetch. The forestry land is home to birds such as siskin, crossbill and nightjar and the damp conditions of the mixed broad-leaved and conifer woodland at Hayburn Wyke favours the development of mosses and liverworts. The woods have a mysterious atmosphere, complemented by a series of waterfalls that end with a double fall on to a beach.

The coastline is home to a fishing community with villages clustered around beaches and rocky bays. Fossils can be found in the rocks around Robin Hood's Bay and Ravenscar, and rock pools contain sea anemones, blennies and crabs, while curlew and oystercatchers pace the shallows looking for food.

Bridestones Moor

The Bridestones Moor nature reserve extends over some 120ha (300 acres) and is most famous for its 'bridestones' – oddly-shaped Jurassic sandstone outcrops. It is also home to a variety of plants that can survive on poor, dry, acid soil. Birch and rowan are common on the slopes, while the woodlands contain oak, ash and larch. Although the reserve is not rich in birdlife, kestrels and sparrowhawks are commonly seen. Lizards can be spotted basking in the sun on warm days.

Other Sites in Northern England

Cheshire and Merseyside

Alderley Edge, north-east Cheshire
Woodland

This wooded escarpment is of both geological and biological interest. The area is rich in minerals, and copper was mined here for hundreds of years. This has left behind many old shafts and quarries. Much of the woodland was planted, but some sections are on ancient woodland sites. Oak, birch and Scots pine make up a varied patchwork of trees that provides homes for many kinds of birds, including the redstart.

Dunham Massey Park, south-west Greater Manchester
Parkland, woodland, pasture, grassland

The 101ha (250 acres) of parkland surrounding the 18th-century mansion of Dunham Massey are an increasingly important haven for wildlife, and a buffer against the intensive agriculture that surrounds it. The estate has been a popular recreational area for the population of Manchester and the surrounding urban sprawl since the early 19th century. The medieval deer park (a SSSI) is of prime importance since it embodies elements of the original forest or 'wild wood'. The current pattern of trees and woods dates from the landscape plantings designed in the 18th century, but these trees are now sufficiently ancient to have adopted the fauna, which has lived in old trees on the site since the last ice age. A herd of fallow deer is protected in secluded areas of the park. The park also provides sites for hole-nesting birds, including all species of woodpeckers. There is an area of unimproved pasture, and there are a number of ancient ponds and water-filled marl pits, which add to the range of habitats.

Lyme Park, north-east Cheshire
Parkland, grassland

Once a medieval deer park, the magnificent Lyme Park surrounds a large historic house. Deer are still very much in evidence today, with both red deer and fallow deer living within the park's perimeter. A visit in September will coincide with the red deer rut, a spectacular and noisy period when rival stags battle for supremacy. Much of the park, which rises to 300m (1,000ft), is covered by grass growing over an acid soil. Fine-leaved grasses – mainly consisting of fescues and bents – dominate the lower levels, but on the upper slopes, purple moor grass takes over. The meadow pipit and skylark are common birds, while snipe search for food in damp areas, and wheatears may be seen on the higher ground.

Formby, north-west Merseyside
Woodland, scrub, dunes, ponds

Formby's sand dunes are a haven for wildlife on the heavily built-up Merseyside coastline. This is one of the few sites in Britain where the natterjack toad breeds. The meadow-like sandy flats abound with maiden pink, harebell, yellow rattle, restharrow, wild parsnip, yellow bedstraw, yellow-wort and both the Portland and sea spurges. Near the main Victoria Road, Formby boasts another curiosity – a colony of red squirrels. These are not native animals, but descendants of red squirrels introduced from the Continent.

Cumbria

Arnside Knott and Heathwaite, south Cumbria
Woodland, scrub, grassland, heath, rock

Arnside Knott is a wooded limestone promontory rising above the estuary of the River Kent and Morecambe Bay. The hill gives spectacular views over the bay, the

Above: The panoramic view from among trees on top of Alderley Edge, a thickly wooded sandstone ridge, looking across the fields to the flat boulder clay of the Cheshire Plain below.

Left: A mature red deer stag roars during rutting to keep his harem of females together, seen here at Coalpit Clough, Lyme Park, Cheshire.

Lakeland fells and the Forest of Bowland. An unusual feature is the fine scree on the south-facing slopes, known locally as the Shilla slopes. The Arnside area is best known for its wide range of butterflies, which includes large numbers of four different species of fritillary, and is one of only two sites in England for the scotch argus. Glow worms also live here. Roe deer are numerous, and the varied habitats attract many different birds, some to breed, others to pass the winter. The plant life is particularly rich – at least six species of orchid grow here, along with several species of fern.

Eaves and Waterslack Woods, Lancashire-Cumbria border
Limestone escarpment, woodland, grassland
Overlooking Morecombe Bay, this wooded limestone escarpment is of great wildlife interest, as Waterslack is known to be an ancient woodland site. Although partly modified by later planting of conifers, the older wooded areas contain a number of plants and insects that indicate continuity of tree cover, such as herb paris, small-leaved lime, wild service tree, lily-of-the-valley, dog's mercury, ramsons and bluebell. Evidence of traditional woodland management is visible throughout the woods, with hazel coppice below the standard trees. Elsewhere, dense thickets of self-sown yew and scrubby woodland grow above areas of limestone pavement and obscure limestone grasslands, which were once grazing land. The limestone grasslands contain anthills, which provide food for green woodpeckers, and associated plants include rockrose,

quaking grass, spring cinquefoil and autumn gentian. Bloody crane's bill and hart's tongue fern grow on the limestone pavement. Butterflies, including high brown fritillary, are abundant and often roe deer can be spotted in the woods.

County Durham

Moor House Woods, north-east County Durham
Woodland
Moor House Woods lie in the valley of the River Wear. The woods are unusual because they contain beech and hornbeam – two species that are generally found wild only in southern Britain. Oak is the most common tree, but small-leaved lime also grows here in some numbers. Bluebells, wood millet, wood sorrel, sanicle and wood avens grow on the woodland floor.

Below: The 152m (500ft) tall limestone hill of Arnside Knott, on the edge of Morecambe Bay, looks down to the estuarial zone of the River Kent. The area is renowned for its woodland.

Northumberland

Allen Banks, south-west Northumberland
Upland oak woodland, natural river system with shingle banks
The steep and sheltered slopes above the River Allen create a favoured environment in the otherwise exposed Northumbrian landscape. Verdant woods of beech, oak, chestnut, sycamore and ash – some species native, others introduced – cling to the sides of the valley, providing food and cover for roe deer, dormice and red squirrels. Dippers and grey wagtails live along the river, while the woods are home to the nuthatch. Devil's-bit scabious and lousewort are found in the small areas of grassland.

Cragside, mid-Northumberland
Woodland, heath, lakes, streams

The woodlands of this impressively landscaped estate harbour woodcocks, sparrowhawks, wood warblers, siskins and pied flycatchers, and tree pipits nest beneath trees on rough open ground. The mammals of the woodlands include red squirrels and roe deer. In the 19th century, thousands of trees were planted on the steep hills, and today mature conifers grow in extensive swathes. Patches of heather, bilberry, purple moor grass and cross-leaved heath mark the remaining areas of the heathland that originally covered much of this area.

Hadrian's Wall, Northumberland and Cumbria
Grass moorland, woodland, lakes

The National Trust owns approximately 10km (6 miles) of Hadrian's Wall, running west from Housesteads Fort to Cawfields Quarry, and over 1,000ha (2,471 acres) of farmland. The Wall was, for a long period, the Roman Empire's most northerly outpost. Built around 122AD, there were 16 permanent bases, of which Housesteads Fort is one of the best preserved. The countryside surrounding the wall, part of the Northumberland National Park, is dramatic and significant in its own right. The lakes are a haven for overwintering and migrating wildfowl; teal and tufted duck are common. The luxuriant, well-developed heathland and fen communities are the remains of shallow glacial lakes, where the high rainfall and impeded drainage has resulted in a patchwork of sphagnum moss, which conceals rare and beautiful plants and invertebrates. The open water, marsh, fen, raised bogs, alder carr and damp grassland

supports an interesting range of plants, such as unusual sedges, grass of Parnassus, early marsh orchids and stag's horn club moss. The crags of Whin Sill contain a rich flora, which includes mountain male and parsley ferns, fir club moss, woodrush and a variety of lichens.

Wallington, mid-Northumberland
Woodland, moorland

This superb estate surrounding an 18th-century sandstone house includes extensive grounds, partly designed by Lancelot 'Capability' Brown, who was born nearby and went to school on the estate. There are extensive views into Redesdale to the slopes of Simonside and the Cheviot Hills to the north. Woodland birds include tree creeper, pied flycatcher, summer migrants and nuthatch (this is their most northerly breeding area). The woods next to the river are of interest for riverside birds such as grey wagtail, dipper and kingfisher. The reduction in grouse shooting has led to the deterioration of the heather moors, but a number of unimproved meadows feature a rich flora, including the melancholy thistle, globeflower and northern marsh orchid.

Yorkshire

Brimham Moor and Rocks, north Yorkshire
Rocky outcrops, moorland, woodland, scrub

The fantastic shapes of its weathered sandstone rocks, together with far-reaching views, attract many visitors to Brimham each year. Those willing to walk a short distance from the

Above: Crag Lough forms part of the Whin Sill, a tabular layer of the igneous rock, dolerite, that runs east to west in the North Pennines and into Northumberland National Park.

famous rocks will discover a range of upland plant life and the animals that feed on it. The drier areas of the moor are covered by heather. Red grouse occur although the moor is not managed for shooting. Curlew and snipe breed where the ground is damp.

Fountains Abbey and Studley Royal, north Yorkshire
Parkland, lowland wood pasture, neutral grassland, ponds

The Cistercian abbey ruins near Ripon lie within the 18th-century landscaped park and ornamental water gardens of Studley Royal. This property hosts several species of bat, including long-eared, pipistrelle, Daubenton's, Natterer's and Brandt's. Old parkland trees, with their abundant dead wood, are host to over 30 species of beetle. Nuthatches, redstarts and green and great spotted woodpeckers use the old trees for feeding and nesting. The woodlands have a rich birdlife, including hawfinches, and in summer they are good places for seeing butterflies, such as the white-letter hairstreak and purple hairstreak. Plant life includes bird's nest orchid, small teasel and lichens. In some parts of the ponds water plants, including brooklime and skullcap, are plentiful. All the British species of newt have been recorded here.

Hayburn Wyke, north Yorkshire
Scrub woodland, rocks, foreshore, cliffs

Hayburn Wyke is coastal scenery at its most varied. It includes a small and beautiful bay with a rocky beach surrounded by cliffs, woodlands and the Hayburn Beck, which cascades over a low cliff in a series of little waterfalls to a pool surrounded by seashore boulders. The woods are broad-leaved – mostly oak – with some holly, ash, hazel, hawthorn, rhododendron and sycamore. The slopes immediately above the beach provide a habitat for the common spotted orchid, kidney vetch and butterwort. Warblers are plentiful in the scrub, and Hayburn Wyke's birdlife also includes the great spotted woodpecker, spotted flycatcher, redstart, woodcock and goldcrest.

Malham Tarn, north Yorkshire
Moorland, limestone grassland, lake, bog, fen, rocky crags
Malham Tarn is a high lake that lies over a bed of limestone. Mallard, tufted duck, coot and great crested grebes all breed on the Tarn, and their numbers swell every winter as more birds arrive to feed in the lime-rich waters. The variety of plants that grow in the bog and fen around the Tarn is quite exceptional, and can be appreciated at close hand from boardwalks that cross it. Away from the Tarn, blue moor-grass, which is confined to northern limestone areas, grows on rocky ledges, and with it green spleenwort, a species of fern. The 'unimproved' grassland is rich in sedges and plants such as wild thyme, mountain pansy and eye-bright. Bird's-eye primrose is a highlight of wet areas, and cranberry, cloudberry and bog rosemary all grow on the raised peat bog. In autumn, kestrels, peregrines and, occasionally, merlins can be seen hunting over the estate. Roe deer are recent arrivals in the area.

Ravenscar, north Yorkshire coast
Cliffs, grassland, scrub
The cliffs of this beautiful part of the Yorkshire coast are composed mainly of soft rocks that are easily eroded by the sea. At Ravenscar, the cliffs have slumped to create a contorted landscape higher up. Herring gulls and cormorants both breed here. The steeper slopes, which are often covered with scree, are generally occupied by heather, bell heather, and some bilberry and crowberry. The flatter areas are good places to see harebell, yellow rattle, devil's-bit scabious, and less common plants such as adder's tongue fern and grass of Parnassus. Meadowsweet, wild angelica, butterwort and sundew grow in the wetter areas. Please note that the cliffs are dangerous, and care should be taken when visiting them.

Hardcastle Crags, west Yorkshire
Woodland, rivers, rocky crags, moorland
The rocky escarpments known as Hardcastle Crags lie in woods on the north bank of Hebden Water. The National Trust owns a total of 175ha (432 acres) of mixed woodland in this area, some of it ancient. There are old millponds in the valley and the bed of the Crimsworth Beck has been designated a SSSI for its unusual geology. Sycamore, oak, ash and beech are the most frequent trees in the broad-leaved woods, which are carpeted with bluebells in spring. Grey wagtails and dippers are common along the river, and the great spotted woodpecker, spotted flycatcher, heron, ring ouzel and short-eared owl inhabit the woods and riverbanks.

Above: Icicles hang from the rocks beside Hebden Water at Hardcastle Crags.

Roseberry Topping, north Yorkshire
Moorland, woodland
The steep climb to the low but dramatic summit of Roseberry Topping, at an altitude of 322m (1,057ft), leads through three contrasting kinds of landscape – woodland, heather moor and bracken-covered ground. Newton Wood is dominated by oaks, but also contains ash trees, wych elms, alders and large-leaved limes. The wood is especially important to wildlife as a haven for breeding birds such as the pied flycatcher, wood warbler, tree pipit, redstart and green woodpecker. The heather on Newton Moor is regularly burned to provide the right conditions for red grouse.

Right: The curiously shaped summit of Roseberry Topping, 322m (1057ft) tall, stands out from miles away. The hill has a sandstone cap which protects the clays and shales below from erosion.

Wales

Brecon Beacons

The Brecon Beacons are a range of sandstone mountains in the south east of Wales. The hills were formed by glaciation, and boast many typical glacial features, including great hollows in the hillsides known as corries. The English name comes from the Welsh habit of lighting fires, or beacons, to warn of attacks by the English – from the summits it is possible to see as far as the Malvern Hills and right across to the Devon coast.

The area forms part of the Brecon Beacons National Park, one of 14 national parks within the UK. It was established in 1957 and covers around 1,344 km² (519 square miles). The park runs from Hay-on-Wye, near the English border in the east, to Llandeilo in the west, and takes in the Black Mountains in the east, the Brecon Beacons in the centre and the, confusingly, similarly named Black Mountain in the west.

There is evidence that man has long battled with the elements to inhabit the area; there are fortifications from the Iron Age, Bronze Age cairns (burial grounds) and single standing stones. The Romans arrived in 48AD, and conquered the local tribes, the Silures and Ordivices, leaving several Roman roads as legacies. On Llangors Lake is an ancient Crannog, or lake dwelling, from around 890AD, while the Normans constructed a string of castles.

Some 60 per cent of the Brecon Beacons comprises great blocks of old red sandstone, mostly from the Devonian period, while in the south there are outcrops of limestone from the early Carboniferous period and pennant sandstone. The layers have faulted and folded since their formation, numerous ice ages have sculpted the bedrock, and meltwater has scoured the valley bottoms and deposited eroded fragments of rock. The highest mountain in the Brecon Beacons, and indeed in South

Above: The sweeping grandeur of the mountain Corn Du, seen from the summit of Pen Y Fan with the Black Mountains visible in the far distance. Characteristic geology can be seen in the anvil-shaped rock outcrop in the foreground.

Left: An adult osprey lands on a log clutching a freshly caught trout. Its diet consists almost exclusively of fish and it nests near water.

Wales, is Pen y Fan, which comes in at 886m (2,907ft). The summit can be reached in just under one hour's walk in good weather.

Llangorse Lake (Llyn Syfaddan), the second largest natural lake in Wales with a circumference of 8km (5 miles), was created by glacial movement. It has been designated a Site of Special Scientific Interest (SSSI) as the lake is naturally eutrophic; it has a high nutrient content making its lower waters deficient in oxygen and resulting in excessive algae bloom in the summer. Legend has it that a town is buried under the waters and that church bells can be heard ringing when the weather is stormy. The rare blue-tailed damselfly

Caves and waterfalls

To the south west of the Beacons is an outcrop of limestone, characterised by caves, gorges swallow-holes and waterfalls, as the water from the Beacons finds its way to lower ground. Near Ystradfellte you will find Porth yr Ogof (Mouth of the Cave), the biggest cave entrance in Wales (shown below), which has the River Mellte flowing through it. It measures 2,250m (7,382ft) in length and presents many challenges for cavers. Ogof Ffynnon Ddu (Cave of the Black Spring) is the deepest cave in the UK and the second longest in Wales. It measures an impressive 308m (1,010ft) deep and is 48km (30 miles) long. The area is known as Gwlad Rhaiadr (Waterfall Country) and there are walks to see some of the most beautiful falls in the area, though it can be wet and slippery, and sensible shoes with good grips are essential. The major falls are Sgwd Clun Gwyn Falls (White Meadow Falls), the 15m (50ft) Sgwd-yr-Eira (Waterfall of Snow), which has a path running behind the water, and Sgwd Gwladus (Lady Falls), though there are numerous other smaller falls to see as well.

Above: Sheep are rounded up on the snow-covered slopes of Pen y Fan, the highest mountain in the Brecon Beacons.

Left: There are a number of beautiful waterfalls along Taf Fechan in the Taf Fechan Forest, a large upland forest in the south of the Brecon Beacons.

breeds here, and the lake is surrounded by extensive reed beds that provide a haven for a huge range of waterfowl. Occasionally ospreys can be seen along with the rare reed warbler and yellow wagtail.

Keen walkers will relish the opportunity to walk the strenuous 161km (100 mile) Brecon Beacon Way which runs from Abergavenny in Monmouthshire to Llangadog in Carmarthenshire and runs more or less east to west across the park. Walking the length, much of which is very isolated, takes around eight days and covers steep ascents and descents; it is not advisable to tackle it in wet weather.

The National Trust looks after some 5,000ha (12,355 acres) of land in the Brecon Beacons, around four per cent of the National Park. Some of the Park's best-known features are under the Trust's care including Pen y Fan, Skirrid Fawr, Sugar Loaf and the Henrhyd Falls. On Pen y Fan fossils of the first land plants can be seen as

dark smudges on the rocks, and near the sandstone summit, ripple marks left by the sea are still visible. It is possible to walk a glacial cirque (an amphitheatre-like valley, typically surrounded by cliffs on three sides, the fourth side being the lip via which the glacier flowed away) that contains the lake Llyn Cwm Llwch (*cwm* is Welsh for a glacial cirque in this context), and the peaks Corn Du and Pen y Fan. The Henrhyd Falls on Nant Llech is the highest waterfall in Wales with an unbroken fall of 27.5m (90ft); it drops off the Farewell Rock into a wooded gorge and is one of a series of waterfalls produced by steep-sided gorges. Sugar Loaf reaches some 596m (1,955ft) in height and has a conical top.

Snowdonia

Snowdonia is a vast National Park covering some 2,170km² (838 square miles) and extending way beyond the mountainous region around Snowdon, Wales's tallest mountain at 1,085m (3,560ft). It ranges from south of the medieval town of Conwy, on the north Wales coast, to Caernarfon in the West, south to Aberdyfi, and east to Lake Bala, the largest freshwater lake in Wales, measuring 6.5km (4 miles) long and 1.6km (1 mile) wide. It is the stunning scenery that attracts visitors, for here there are dizzy mountain peaks, dramatic sweeping valleys, rocky cliffs and sheltered sandy beaches. Snowdonia is the second largest national park in the UK.

The northernmost mountainous area of the park is the most popular with visitors. It includes the mountain ranges of Moel Hebog, which contains Mynydd Mawr and the Nantile Ridge, the Snowdon massif and the steep cliffs of the Glyderau. The dramatic Carneddau contains some of the highest peaks in the country, and encloses lakes such as Llyn Cowlyd and Llyn Eigiau, and the 37m (120ft) drop of the Aber Falls. These areas are inaccessible to sheep, thus allowing arctic-alpine flora to flourish. The rare Snowdon lily, a pretty little white flower and remnant from the last ice age, is a case in point, though it is feared that this may be the first plant to become extinct in the UK due to global warming. Alpine saxifrage, tufted saxifrage and alpine meadow grass thrive on narrow ledges, and attract unusual invertebrates such as the rainbow leaf beetle, which snacks on wild thyme. In the depths of the lakes another relic of the end of the last ice age, a pea mussel, can also be found. Many of the steeper lower slopes are heavily wooded, primarily with oak and ash, though there are also extensive forestry plantations of non-native conifer species.

The geology of the area is complex and diverse, and reveals submersion, lifting and erosion. Mountain ranges were pushed up out of the oceans, confirmed by fossil shell fragments found on the summit of Snowdon. These mountains were then eroded away by the action of glaciers advancing and retreating, forming U-shaped valleys such as Nant Gwynant, and cwms or cirques – large bowl shapes cut out of the side of a mountain, some filled with meltwater lakes or tarns, many with waterfalls dropping from them. Where two cwms have formed on either side of a mountain, knife-edged ridges, or arêtes, such as Crib Goch are created.

Above: A view of Snowdon seen from Glyder Fach and showing Y Lliwedd, the southern arch of the Snowdon horseshoe. Also visible is Yr Aran, Moel Hebog, Crib Goch and on the far right Yr Wyddfa, the summit of Snowdon.

Below: A view of the summit of Snowdon and Crib Goch from the southern slope of the Glyders, Snowdonia National Park.

The area was once industrial with the mountains being exploited for their mineral content. Copper, slate, zinc and lead were all mined, alongside slate, leaving great scars on the landscape.

The Rhinogydd mountain range is formed from hard sedimentary rock and has a folded mountainous structure. The northern end of the range is rocky and heather clad while the southern end has a gentler, grassy profile. The mountains are less well known to tourists, but are popular with hill walkers seeking a more demanding walking experience. In central Snowdonia is a large expanse of moorland and blanket bog known as the Migneint, nearly all of it owned by the National Trust.

In the south of the park is the Mawddach Trail, a traffic-free, relatively flat path for walkers and cyclists that runs between Dolgellau and Barmouth. The Mawddach Estuary was carved out during the last ice age, it is surrounded by mountains, with Cadair Idris 893m (2,929ft) high, to the south, and Llethr and Diffwys to the north. Woodland surround the estuary, mainly comprising oak and birch, which attracts many birds and butterflies – there is reputed to be no better walk.

In the south west of the National Park are the Cregennan Lakes, situated some 244m (800ft) above sea level, and with glorious views of the Cadair Idris massif across the Mawddach Estuary to Barmouth Bay. The streams that run down the mountains form the clear waters of Llanau Cregennan, creating a network of valuable wetland habitats such as Cregennan Bog, which is covered with sphagnum moss and bog myrtle. Further south again, there are sandy beaches backed by valuable sand dunes, right down to Aberdyfi where the rare sand lizard is sometimes found. The entire coastline is a special area of conservation.

The National Trust cares for eleven of the mountain peaks in Snowdonia and large numbers of footpaths, including the Watkin Path, which runs from Hafod y Llan Farm to the peak of Snowdon. The Trust is committed to conservation work to maintain the delicate balance between the need to protect this beautiful landscape and its fragile wildlife habitats, while promoting and enhancing public access, and dispersing visitors throughout the area to preserve the remoteness of the area.

A staggering 500,000 people climb to the top of Snowdon every single year, which, given the wet climate (Snowdon has one of the wettest climates in the UK), means there is a problem with eroding footpaths, gates and stiles. The National Trust is replacing paths with

Above: Slate enclosures, created from slate remnants from the mining and quarrying industry, can still be seen at Cwm Llan on Hafod Y Llan farm in Snowdonia. The South Snowdon Slate Quarry opened in the 1840s and closed some 40 years later in 1882. The National Trust purchased the farm, on Snowdon's steep slope, in 1998 and farms the land itself, carefully, with indigenous Welsh black cattle and reduced numbers of Welsh mountain sheep.

Watch for Wildlife

Snowdonia National Park contains a diverse range of birdlife. In the uplands species such as **peregrine falcon, ring ouzel, meadow pipit, raven, whinchat** and **wheatear** can be seen, while around the lakes and streams the common **sandpiper, grey wagtail** and **dipper** are in evidence. Woodland areas attract **wood warbler, pied flycatcher** and **redstart**, and all three UK woodpeckers nest here. Conwy, with its 13th-century fortress, forms the gateway to the park, and the nearby estuary is home to many ducks and waders. **Osprey** can be seen during spring and late summer, and may be starting to breed in the district.

Osprey

a technique called stone pitching that has been in use since Roman times, it essentially involves building a dry-stone wall horizontally. In addition, the Trust is managing grazing on its mountain farms at Hafod y Llan and Gelli Iago. These estates were bought by the National Trust after a public appeal in 1998. Sheep readily graze out heather, whereas cattle do not, so the numbers of grazing sheep have been reduced and indigenous Welsh black cattle have been introduced to conserve the flora and fauna. Rare species such as the small pearl-bordered fritillary abound as careful grazing has preserved their habitats.

The Aberglaslyn Pass is a beautiful narrow gorge; at its leanest point the River Glaslyn is hemmed in by wooded hillside some 213m (700ft) high. A track, known as the Fisherman's Path, runs along the east side of the ravine from Beddgelert to Port Aberglaslyn where heath, grassland, bell heather and mires can be seen. This is not a straightforward walk and there are some narrow ledges to tackle. The well-wooded slopes of the gorge, with their oaks, ash trees, birches, beeches and sycamores, are rich in mosses, liverworts and lichens.

Above: The lake Llyn Gwynant on the River Glaslyn in Snowdonia was formed by glacial action. It mirrors the magnificent scenery of the Nant Gwynant valley.

Left: Tough and hardy Welsh mountain lambs brave the elements on Hafod Y Llan farm in Snowdonia. The farm is managed by the National Trust, which has halved the number of sheep over the past ten years to help conserve the natural habitat and encourage a more diverse farm plan.

The National Trust has also created a new access path along the riverbank at Beddgelert up to the famous grave. Legend has it that back in the 13th century, Prince Llewellyn the Great returned from a day's hunting to find his favourite hound Gelert covered in blood and his baby's cradle empty. Llewellyn, assuming his dog had killed the child, ran his sword through the hound in fury. As Gelert lay dying, the baby started to cry and was found in perfect health, next to the body of a huge wolf that Gelert had slain. The Prince, filled with remorse, buried Gelert with great honour. The cairn of stones that marks the grave is however, only 200 years old.

Snowdonia

One of Wales's most spectacular valleys, Nantgwynant is encircled by high mountains, with Snowdon rising up to the north. This exhilarating walk explores an historic landscape, rich in Dark Age legend, with the remains of 19th-century copper mines lining much of the route. Enjoy dramatic waterfalls, great views and the chance to spot a variety of wildlife as you climb up through the National Trust's Hafod Y Llan farm, cross the hillside and descend to Craflwyn, a Victorian hall and estate.

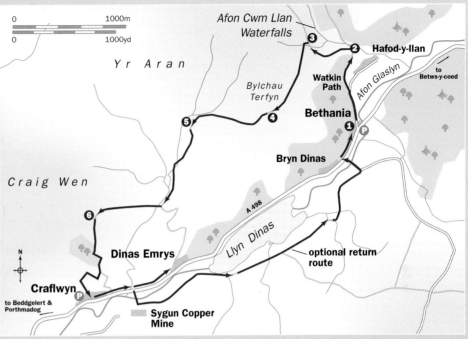

Getting there and facilities:
The walk begins west of Beddgelert on the A498. There are bus stops at the start of walk, on the regular Portmadog–Beddgelert–Betws y Coed bus route. WCs and parking can be found at Bethanaia and Craflwyn, an information point at Craflwyn and accommodation at Craflwyn Hall. There are refreshments and shops in Beddgelert.

Start point:
Bethania – OS Explorer 17 map, or GR SH599489.

Distance, terrain and accessibility:
This is a quite strenuous and exhilarating 6km (3¾ mile) walk with the option of returning via a valley path or taking the bus. You're walking on naturally uneven surfaces with several sections of ascent and descent.

Route and directions:
1   Start at the car park on the A498, near Bethania. Take the Watkin Path (which eventually leads to Snowdon's summit) on the other side of the road heading north, with an oak woodland on your left.

2   Once you rise above the woodland, you are greeted by a wonderful view of the Afon Cwm Llan waterfalls. The ridge to your right is home to many plants, including juniper.

3   Leave the Watkin Path and turn left on to a track. Enjoy a wide panorama of the valley, Llyn Dinas lake and the surrounding mountains.

4   Continue on this track, passing through a wall before entering Bylchau Terfyn. You are now on National Trust farmland, which is managed in an environmentally sensitive way. Welsh black cattle graze this land, keeping it in optimum condition for plants by preventing excessive growth of certain grasses and bushes. A little further on, cross a dry-stone wall using the stile.

5   Walk uphill through the heather until you reach the highest point on this walk at 315m (1033ft). You can see Beddgelert village from here and there are warnings that there are old copper mine shafts still around. Bats inhabit the old mine workings. Descend the hillside, crossing a stream, which has stepping stones, and climb over a stile.

6   Pass a derelict barn (once used to shelter animals) and follow the way-marks to another stile, which leads into the Craflwyn estate. Keep on the path until you reach a T-junction, where you turn left and walk down to the estate buildings and car park. To your left is the historic site, Dinas Emrys. Return via bus or along the valet and around Llyn Dinas.

Pembrokeshire Coast

Pembrokeshire is home to one of the most beautiful stretches of coastline in Europe, and it is the UK's only predominantly coastal national park. The countryside is peaceful, and the coastal scenery nothing short of spectacular, incorporating rugged cliffs, sleepy fishing villages, sandy beaches and lively harbours. Offshore are the islands of Ramsey, Skokholm, Skomer, Grassholm and Caldey, which have changed little over the centuries.

It is the geology of the area that won it national park status for here, dating back some 600 million years to the Pre-Cambrian period, are some of the oldest rocks in the UK as well as many interesting rock exposures and geological features. On the northern side of the park lie the Preseli Hills, where it is thought the Preseli Blue Stones of Stonehenge originated. This area and the rocky volcanic peaks of Pen Beri, Garn Fawr and Llidi, and the moorland on Carningli, have an exposed and mountainous feel. In the west is St Bride's Bay with Skomer and Ramsey Island at each end. On the southern coast there are the limestone cliffs and plateau that make up the Castlemartin Peninsula, the wooded valleys behind Amroth, the tourist resorts of Tenby and Saundersfoot, and the Bosherton Lakes. Finally there is the Milford Haven waterway where the Daugleddau estuary feeds into a deep natural harbour.

Above: The sea broke into a disused slate quarry in the 1930s to produce the Blue Lagoon at Abereiddy on the Pembrokeshire Coastal Path. Graptolite fossils, remnants from the Ordovician period, are found in the area.

Below: Looking down on to the sandy beach at Broad Haven, which has excellent bathing and which falls within the stunning Stackpole Estate.

There are over 1,000km (621 miles) of footpaths and bridleways crisscrossing the Pembrokeshire Coast National Park, including the famous 299km (186 mile) Pembrokeshire Coast Path, which twists and turns through exquisite coastal scenery of towering cliffs, rocky coves, estuaries and glorious open beaches. It runs from St Dogmaels in the north, to Amroth in the south.

St David's Head, the spectacular and exposed headland at the northern end of St. Bride's Bay, is an excellent place for watching seabirds as they travel along the coast and around the offshore islands. **House martins** nest on the cliffs, along with several of the more common species of **gull**, and the **fulmar**. Land birds include **choughs**, **ravens**, **buzzards**, **stock doves** and **rock pipits**. **Orpine**, **wild chives** and **sea spleenwort** grow on the cliff ledges, while wind-clipped **heather** and **bell heather** grow near the edge of the clifftop. The ground near the cliff harbours the rare **hairy greenweed**, as well as **kidney vetch** and **spring squill**, while the heath **spotted orchid** flowers further back among the **gorse**.

Right: A view of St David's Head and the rocky islet of North Bishop and the sea beyond. The area has a profusion of beautiful wild flowers in spring and summer and attracts many butterflies.

Skokholm, Skomer Island and Middleholm lie off the extreme south-west tip of Pembrokeshire. The cliffs are tall, reaching 70m (230ft) on Skomer, and support breeding colonies of chough, petrel, Manx shearwater and puffin. The plant life has to cope with winds, salt spray, nutrient enrichment from guano, and grazing from rabbits. Ramsey Island has been a RSPB reserve since 1992 and contains the largest breeding grey seal colony in the south, as well as birds such as the guillemot, chough, razorbill, raven and peregrine falcon.

The National Trust owns two significant stretches of land in Pembrokeshire, St David's Peninsula and Stackpole. St David's is the smallest cathedral city in the UK. To the north west is the beautiful sandy Whitesands Beach from where the dramatic headland of St David's highlights the southern extremity of Cardigan Bay. From the granite outcrops of Carn Llidi, look down on to ancient field systems, prehistoric settlements, heathland, the cove of Portmelgan and the great stone chambered grave of Coetan Arthur, dating from about 4,000BC.

South west of St David's, and opposite Ramsey Island, is the Tregennis Peninsula where the oldest rocks in Pembrokeshire can be seen. The National Trust is restoring the wet heaths of Dowrog, Tretio and Waun Fawr, which are surviving fragments of an extensive area of common, by grazing the land with cattle and Welsh mountain ponies to create suitable habitats for plants such as the lesser butterfly orchid, and insects such as the marsh fritillary butterfly.

The Stackpole Estate

The Stackpole Estate is situated in the south of the Pembrokeshire National Park, between the villages of Stackpole and Bosherton. The cliffs of Stackpole Head are made of limestone, and many seabirds, including razorbills and guillemots, nest on their ledges. A few puffins also breed in burrows in the turf. Grazing by sheep has maintained the variety of the clifftop flowers, which thrive on the thin limestone soil. Stackpole Court was once a large mansion, sadly demolished before the National Trust took over the land, however there is plenty to see and footpaths radiate from the site; exotic plantings can be seen in the Lodge Park and this gives way to beautiful mixed woodland. Stackpole Quay (entrance shown right) is a tiny working harbour and from here it is possible to walk along the cliffs, via a steep staircase, to the gloriously sandy Barafundle Beach, which is backed by dunes and woods. To the north east of Stackpole Quay is Trewent Point, a dramatic geological feature with numerous caves and arches caused by the collision of continents 290 million years ago. En-route one passes the Iron Age promontory fort of Greenala. Between 1780 and 1860 three narrow valleys were flooded to create Bosherton Lakes, which are dotted with water lilies and ringed with wild flowers and, in summer, otters can be seen here.

The Gower Peninsula

In 1956 the Gower Peninsula was the first part of the UK to be designated an Area of Outstanding Natural Beauty (AONB). It measures just 32km (20 miles) long and only 8km (5 miles) in width, yet it contains some of the longest sandy beaches you could hope to see, with glorious, extensive sand dunes full of specialist plants, and a dazzling array of sea birds and butterflies. The coast is littered with sea shells, razor clams and purple laver – the seaweed from which the famous Welsh delicacy laver bread is made. The area also contains oak and ash woodland, heath, flower-rich limestone grassland, both fresh and saltwater marshes, a mass of archaeological sites, and some 431km (268 miles) of public right of way.

The Gower Peninsula is a relatively low plateau, underlain by carboniferous limestone; folded, lifted, faulted and eroded rocks are on display. In the north there are saltmarshes and dunes, and large swathes of grassland sweep from coast to coast.

The peninsula has been inhabited since prehistoric times, and it contains many ancient sites including Neolithic and Bronze Age features, and a surviving medieval open field system. At Penmaen Burrows there are traces of a large artificial rabbit warren, known locally as the Pillow Mound – this is an example of an early form of rabbit farming introduced by Norman invaders. The area is still farmed traditionally with mixed dairy and arable farming. An agri-environment scheme is in force where farmers agree to manage their land for the benefit of wildlife, conservation and access, and in addition help to maintain traditional landscapes, such as small fields, common land and sunken lanes.

The coastline around the peninsula contains both rocky and sandy bays, such as Langland, Three Cliffs and the larger beaches of Port Eynon, Rhossili and Oxwich Bay. There are fewer beaches on the north side of the peninsula, but here the cockle-beds of Penclawdd are located; the cockles are a local delicacy that have been relished

Below: Three Cliffs Bay, near Penmaen, is a well-loved beauty spot which takes its name from the three cliffs that jut out into the bay. Pennard Pill, a stream, flows into the bay and just inland is the 12th-century Pennard Castle.

Whitford Burrows and Llanrhidian Marsh

The tall sand dunes of Whitford Burrows (shown below), with their 1.6km (1 mile) stretch of golden sand, protect the flat expanse of the Llanrhidian Marsh mudflats from the scouring action of the sea. The dunes, which are managed by the Countryside Council for Wales (Cyngor Cefn Gwlad Cymru) as a National Nature Reserve, are an excellent example of gradual colonisation by plants. The young dunes are dominated by marram grass, while the older, more stable dunes have patches of thyme and yellow-wort growing on them. The slacks between the dunes are rich in wild flowers, including the pyramidal and fen orchids. The saltmarshes to the east are heavily grazed by cattle and sheep, and are dissected by deep creeks, making access difficult. The whole of the estuary area, including the marshes and mudflats, is a very important source of food for birds, especially the oystercatcher, grey plover, redshank, knot and pintail. In winter, a variety of sea-ducks, including eiders, may be seen offshore.

Above: Culver Hole, on the east side of Overton Mere, is said to have been used by smugglers. A masonry wall with 'windows', linked inside by a staircase, rises across a cavern where two rock faces converge.

Right: Whitford Burrows is reputed to be one of the finest dune systems in the UK. The flora is exceptional and includes the autumn gentian, seen here.

since Roman times. The limestone cliffs are dotted with 95 caves, from which the bones of many animals and birds have been uncovered, as well as the teeth of Neanderthal man, flint axes and arrow heads. Perhaps the best known is the Paviland Cave, which in fact is a series of caves. In one, known as Goat's Hole, which is accessible only at low tide, the 'Red Lady' skeleton was discovered in two excavations of 1823 and 1912. Tests later revealed that the skeleton is actually that of a male and tentatively dated at 29,000 years old; the discovery is prized as the oldest ceremonial burial in Western Europe. The skeleton, festooned with a necklace of shells and stained with red ochre, had a mammoth's skull and ivory wands for company, and is believed to be that of a man of some spiritual standing.

Langland is reputed to be one of the best surfing bays in Wales and the West Country producing the prestigious right-hand waves that surfers hunt out, though as these break on to an exposed reef it is considered to be too dangerous for novices. Three Cliffs Bay, as its name suggests, is surrounded by three beautiful limestone cliffs, 20m (66ft) tall that are popular with rock climbers. Its three bays are separated at high tide; Pobbles is to the east, Tor Bay to the west, and Three Cliffs in the centre. Native breed ponies run along the beach and the adjoining fields.

Rhossili Down dominates the western end of the Gower Peninsula, and has long been a popular place for visitors. From its highest point at over 180m (600ft), there are extensive views west along the south Wales coast and out over the Bristol Channel. The down is covered in heathland and grassland, and made up of those plants that can survive both the acid soil and the constant buffeting of the wind. In spring and autumn, many migrant birds make a landfall here, either recovering from their flight across the Bristol Channel, or waiting for good conditions before setting out across the sea. Worm's Head, a National Nature Reserve, is at the south-west tip of the Gower Peninsula and can only be reached by crossing a causeway at low tide.

Other Sites in Wales

Carmarthenshire

Dinefwr Estate, south Carmarthenshire
Parkland, medieval deer park, river
One of the most spectacular vistas in Carmarthenshire can be seen from Paxton's Tower. From the top of the folly, you are rewarded with views of the surrounding countryside. Dominating the landscape is the Dinefwr Estate, with its ancient woodland, deer park and flood pastures that are home to many waterfowl (including ten per cent of the UK's white-fronted geese). The former medieval deer park is now home to more than 100 fallow deer and a herd of rare White Park cattle. The park still contains descendants of the wildwood trees and is a very important site for species of lichen and insects, which are confined to sites with an unbroken continuity of ancient trees. The old ox bows (abandoned river meanders) of the River Tywi include such scarce flower species as floating marshwort, nodding bur-marigold and greater bladderwort. The flood plain and ox bows are part of a site of international importance for wintering birds, including teal, wigeon, shoveler, curlew, lapwing and other waders.

Dolaucothi, north Carmarthenshire
Woodland, heathland, grassland, meadows, rivers, ponds
Famous for its ancient goldmines, the Dolaucothi Estate contains over 1,000ha (2,500 acres) of farmland and woodland. Paths lead from the village of Pumpsaint up the Cothi Valley, past conifer plantations and

Above: The Gold Mine on the Dolaucothi Estate has been worked intermittently since Roman times, reaching a peak in 1938. The entrance seen here leads to a complex of pits, channels and impressive water tanks.

Above left: A herd of rare White Park cattle can be seen at Dinefwr Park, a national nature reserve at Llandeilo, Carmarthenshire.

oak woods, to higher ground. For plants, the richest woodland on the estate is the Llandre Carr alder wood, which is home to an abundance of mosses and lichens. In the valley above Llandre, there are some damp 'unimproved' meadows, rich in wild flowers such as whorled caraway, devil's-bit scabious, heath spotted orchid, petty whin and ivy-leaved bellflower. Red kites may be seen over the estate.

Conwy

Migneint, south Conwy
Moorland, heathland, bog, lakes, rivers
This large, isolated area of upland forms part of the National Trust's Ysbyty Estate, and is one of the best examples of blanket bog in Wales. The most notable vegetation on the high, open ground is mature heather heathland, but there are also large tracts of wet bog with sphagnum moss and cotton-grass. The wet heathland has heather and cotton-grass, which supports the scarce large heath butterfly, while the moorland is covered with grasses, sedges and rushes. Crowberry, cowberry, bog rosemary and lesser twayblade all grow on the hilltops and slopes. There are several lakes and rivers, and common sandpipers, which breed by the rocky streams, can be seen feeding at the water's edge. The high moorland is the haunt of the red grouse and the golden plover, both of which nest in the heather and grass.

Denbighshire

Graig Fawr, Dyserth, north Denbighshire
Limestone grassland, scrub, woodland
This large, craggy hill is a perfect viewpoint from which to look out over the Vale of Clwyd. It is made of limestone, and is famous for its abundant fossils. The summit of the hill is bare rock with some small trees, mostly hawthorn and blackthorn, stunted by strong salt-laden winds blowing in from the sea. The north-east corner has areas of grassland supporting small lime-loving plants, among them salad burnet, white clover, small scabious, sheep's fescue, bird's-foot trefoil, wild thyme and lady's bedstraw. Hoary rockrose, a plant found only on a few sites in Wales and England, clings to the western face. The local dwarf race of the silver-studded blue butterfly occurs here.

Gwynedd

Dolmelynllyn, south Gwynedd
Moorland, heathland, grassland, oak and ash woodland, rivers
The National Trust's holdings at Dolmelynllyn consist of woods and farmland, which rises from the banks of the Afon Mawddach, to merge with the high moors of the surrounding mountains. The woodlands, mainly of sessile oak, together with ash, birch and some small-leaved limes, are an important area for wildlife, providing nesting sites for redstarts, nuthatches and buzzards. Above the woods on the high and exposed mountain slopes, sphagnum moss, cross-leaved heath and bog myrtle grow on the thick and boggy peat. Dolmelynllyn is an outstanding area for woodland ferns and an important site for Lobarian lichens.

The Llyn Peninsula, Cwrt, Mynydd Bychestyn, Braich-y-Pwll, west Gwynedd
Sand dunes, cliffs, heathland
The Llyn Peninsula is one of the jewels of Wales. Multi-coloured beach huts provide a vibrant backdrop to the long, sweeping beach at Llanbedrog. In the sheltered bay at Porthor the sand famously whistles underfoot due to the unique shape of the grains. The coastguards' hut on top of Mynydd Mawr offers one of the best views in Wales. Choughs can often be seen

flying overhead, dolphins swim in the bay and seals bask in the sun. A coastal path has recently been opened around the whole peninsula. Nearby Mynydd Anelog with its precipitous cliffs offers commanding views across to Ireland, the mountains of Snowdonia and south to St David's Head. Further south is the beautiful, sandy beach of Llandanwg, with its views across to the Llyn Peninsula, and a medieval church half-buried in sand. Egryn, a site of continuous habitation for more than 5,000 years, is only a stone's throw away. The wild and beautiful extremity of Braich y Pwll is the point from where the first pilgrims set off during the Middle Ages to Ynys Enlli. During the spring and summer, numerous birds, including the chough, nest on the most inaccessible ledges of the high cliffs. Five per cent of the chough British breeding population is found on Llyn, and this is one reason why the area has been designated a SSSI. It is also an excellent example of coastal heath, one of the best in Europe, where heather and western gorse are the

Below: The view over farmland at Braich-y-Pwll is spectacular. Bardsey Island, a designated national nature reserve just off the Llyn Peninsula and home to Manx shearwater, curlew, shag and cormorant, can be seen through the distant mist.

dominant species and produce spectacular colours in July and August. Braich y Pwll is the only known location on the British mainland for the spotted rockrose. Its bright yellow flower looks like a stem for most of its life, but by catching it at the right time, its beautiful bright yellow petals can be seen. At Aberdaron, the golden hair lichen can be found, growing both on rocks and low on old heather bushes. It is a striking, bright orange lichen which forms a highly branched 'shrub' up to 4cm (1½in) high and is very sensitive to air pollution.

Isle of Anglesey

Cemlyn and Cemaes, north Isle of Anglesey
Farmland, lagoon, beach
This small but varied site, part of which is managed as a nature reserve by the North Wales Wildlife Trust, is of major interest for its bird life. Common and arctic terns breed on the main shingle bank in spring and summer, and in some years they are also joined by sandwich terns. In winter, a number of different species of duck, including the wigeon, teal and mallard, may be seen either offshore, on the brackish lagoon or feeding on the wet meadows. The

beach at Trwyn Cemlyn is home to a good range of plants that thrive on shingle, including sea kale, sea holly and sea radish. Thrift, restharrow, sea campion and spring squill grow on the rocky ground. The coast around is designated a Heritage Coast because of its unspoilt beauty.

Llandona, Bryn Offa, north Isle of Anglesea
Heathland, grassland
This small site on Anglesey's north coast is notable for its plants. These grow in two distinct habitats – lime-rich heathland and maritime grassland. The heathland is dominated by bell heather and dwarf gorse, but is unusual in having many more plants besides these. Over 30 species have been recorded here, including columbine, creeping willow, saw-wort and quaking grass. Some are typical of acid ground, others of alkaline. Animal life includes a coastal species of ant and a whorl snail. The grassland, which lies towards the coast, contains cowslips, and sea spleenwort grows in the cliff crevices.

Below: The sweep of Cemlyn Bay at sunset, on the north-west coast of Anglesey. The brackish lagoon, seen to the left, is home to a large colony of Sandwich terns, arctic terns and common terns. Oystercatchers, plovers and shelduck also breed, while wigeon, shoveler and teal visit in winter.

Powys

Abergwesyn Common, south Powys
Grassland, moorland, scree, bog, heathland, streams, woodland
Reaching an altitude of over 640m (2,100ft), the extensive plateau of Abergwesyn Common provides views northwards as far as Snowdonia. Heavy grazing has done much to shape the vegetation here, something which is noticeable in the places that sheep cannot reach. The sides of the stream valleys have lush ferns and flowering plants, while the crags, rocky outcrops and scree slopes support clubmosses, lichens and mountain melick. Red grouse and waders, such as the golden plover, live on the moorland.

Carneddau, mid-Powys
Rock crevice, moorland, grassland, woodland, farmland, lakes, streams
Covering 6,420ha (16,860 acres), Carneddau contains some of the most dramatic scenery in Snowdonia. It includes Cwm Idwal with its mountain lake Llyn Idwal, 373m (1,223ft) above sea level, and the peaks of Carnedd Dafydd and Tryfan. The high, treeless massif is covered with extensive areas of acid

Above: The grass and heather-covered plateau of Abergwesyn Common is dissected by streams, seen here, leading to a deep river valley. It has many archaeological features including 50 prehistoric cairns.

grassland, bilberry heath, blanket bog and scree. Several important plant species are present, including the Snowdon lily, rose root and dwarf willow. Mosses cover most of the bogs, and alongside them grow sedges, cotton-grass, purple moor grass, heather and cross-leaved heath. Few large animals can be seen on the high tops, but ravens and

buzzards are conspicuous overhead as they scan the open ground for food.

Swansea

Bishopston Valley, south-east Swansea
Woodland, limestone grassland, stream
This deeply incised, winding valley on the Gower Peninsula provides sheltered and pleasant walking as well as considerable wildlife interest. Much of the valley is

wooded, and some parts are home to a wide range of trees. These include oak, ash, small-leaved lime, holly, field maple and the wild service tree. The shrubs growing beneath, among them hazel, spindle and dogwood, were formerly coppiced. The birds that breed in the woods include the blackcap, green woodpecker and buzzard. Many different plants, especially dog's mercury, grow in the areas of older woodland, while meadows in the valley bottom are good places to see wild flowers.

Gower Cliffs, south-west Swansea
Cliffs, limestone grassland, heathland
The tumbling limestone cliffs of the south-west part of the Gower Peninsula are fascinating for anyone interested in birds or plants. Fulmars, kittiwakes, shags, cormorants, guillemots and razorbills breed at Worms Head, and smaller numbers of these birds can be seen along the rest of this rocky shore. But it is not only seabirds that nest on the cliffs. Ravens, barn owls, swifts and stonechats also breed on their rocky ledges. Where the limestone has created an alkaline soil that is safely beyond the reach of the plough, the grass is rich in wild flowers such as kidney vetch, wild thyme and small scabious, and carnation grass also grows here. Juniper is a local speciality.

Northern Ireland

Giant's Causeway

The Giant's Causeway on the north Antrim coast is a dramatic geological feature of around 40,000 interlocking basalt stone columns that were formed by volcanic activity during the early Tertiary Period, some 62–65 million years ago. It has been described as the eighth wonder of the world and is a UNESCO World Heritage Site as well as a National Nature Reserve. It looks like a series of intricately arranged stepping-stones that disappear out into the sea.

The Causeway Coast, on which the Giant's Causeway sits, consists of a series of headlands comprised of resistant lava interspersed by inaccessible bays where grey seals congregate. The cliffs have an average height of 100m (328ft); their stepped appearance is due to a long period of igneous activity that formed the Antrim plateau, the biggest lava plateau in

Left: A diverting feature above the Giant's Causeway is the spectacular basalt cliff-face columns of The Organ, which tower over visitors and are situated above Port Noffer.

Below: The symmetry of the unique rock formations of Giant's Causeway is a window into a bygone volcanic age some 60 million years ago and a prime example of the earth's evolutionary history.

Causeway mythology

The area is steeped in local mythology. Legend has it that the causeway was created after the giant Finn McCool fell for a female giant on the Scottish island of Staffa. McCool is said to have built a pathway across the sea so that he could bring her back to live with him in Ireland. Another legend tells of a Scottish giant by the name of Benendonner who challenged McCool to a fight and built the causeway to get to him. Finn was alarmed by the size of his opponent and hid in his baby's crib. When Benendonner marched into Finn's house and saw the mighty size of the 'baby', he was terrified over the prospect of fighting his father and fled, breaking up the bridge behind him, leaving only its end sections at Giant's Causeway, and Fingal's Cave on Staffa.

Europe. The pattern was formed by rock crystallisation during the accelerated cooling that occurs when molten lava comes into contact with water.

It is generally believed that the attention of the world was drawn to the site after a visit from the eccentric Bishop of Derry in 1692 and a subsequent paper presented to the Royal Society in Dublin in 1694. The National Trust now owns around 70ha (173 acres) of the cliffs and foreshore.

The causeway columns have an average measurement of 45cm (18in) across and 12m (40ft) high, although there are great variations in size. Significant features such as Granny's Rock, the Wishing Chair, the Shepherd's Steps and the Honeycomb stand out. Port Noffer is accessed through Giant's Gate, a narrow pathway between towering columns. On the foreshore is the Giant's Boot, a huge slab of basalt, which has weathered in the shape of a boot. On the far side of Port Noffer is the Giant's Organ, a series of incredibly tall basalt columns.

It is possible to walk a 19km (12 mile) coast path around this phenomenal location on the Causeway Coast Path, part of the Ulster Way. It runs from west of Giant's Causeway at Blackfoot Sand over to Ballintoy Harbour. The views along the walk are magnificent and take you past Port-na-Spaniagh where the galleass (an oared fighting ship) *Girona*, part of the Spanish Armada, met its tragic end. It is perhaps the most famous shipwreck of the many that faltered on this rocky coast.

The *Girona* hit Lacada Point in October 1588 with around 1,300 men on board, many of whom were surviving crew rescued from two earlier shipwrecks. It is not known how many were lost, but it is generally held that fewer than ten of the 1,300 survived. Some 10,000 accumulated treasures were salvaged in the late 1960s and are now on display in the Ulster Museum in Belfast.

A recent extension at the end of the Causeway Coastal Path links Ballintoy Harbour, the limestone cliffs near Larrybane Head, and the island of Carrick-a-rede. To cross over to the island visitors have to navigate a rope bridge originally designed for use by the local fishermen, but now used by visitors to cross a 30m (100ft) chasm; it is only for those who are unafraid of heights! Only two people can cross at one time and the bridge is removed in winter. The area is a paradise for seabirds such as shag, fulmar, petrels and raven, and buzzard and peregrine falcon nest on the rocky cliffs.

Watch for Wildlife

Giant's Causeway and the surrounding area are home to a rich diversity of wildlife, from birds and butterflies, to crabs, plants and lichens. In spite of the harsh habitat, many species of flora have adapted to life here, including the oysterplant, **Scots lovage** (a species only found in Northern Ireland and Scotland), **sea spleenwort**, **devil's-bit scabious**, **bird's-foot trefoil** and **thyme broomrape**. The rocks themselves are coloured with a rainbow of **lichen** species and **tar lichen** has formed black stripes on the columns. Giant's Causeway is a very good spot for birding; commonly seen birds include **fulmar**, **rock pipit**, **wheatear**, **oystercatcher**, **guillemot** and **whitethroat**. Rock pools contain a vast array of marine life including **limpets**, **sea anemones** and **cushion starfish**.

Fulmar

Cushion starfish

Strangford Lough

Strangford Lough is a vast, shallow, sea lough and an internationally important wildlife site. It is the largest Marine Nature Reserve (MNR) in the UK and teems with life both above and below the water. It is the largest inlet in the UK, measuring 8km (5 miles) wide and 31km (19 miles) long, covering a total area of 150km^2 (58 square miles). The deeply indented shoreline measures around 240km (150 miles) in length and accounts for over one-third of Northern Ireland's total coastline. Strangford Lough is virtually landlocked for, on the east side, the Ards Peninsula almost separates it from the Irish Sea; however, a slim, fast-flowing, 8km (5 mile) channel, known as The Narrows, provides the link. One of the first tidal generators has been installed here to harness the power of the tide (see page 19). A third of the lough is inter-tidal, best demonstrated by the expanses of sand flats at the north end of the lough, which are covered with shallow water at high tide. The name comes from the Old Norse *Strangrfjörthr* meaning 'strong ford'.

The landscape was formed by the Ice Age and is indicative of glacial action; the lough contains, and is surrounded by, long, rounded hills, known as drumlins, left behind as the ice retreated. Many of these drumlins form the islands and tiny islets, known as pladdies, that litter the lough. There are over 120 pladdies in total, not, as local legend has it, one for every day of the year. Some are large enough to be farmed, and one holds the remains of an abbey, but many provide important nesting and roosting sites for seabirds or seals. The surrounding drumlins are farmed and crisscrossed with dry-stone walls and wooded margins. The National Trust manages 6,000ha (14,800 acres) around the site, through its wildlife scheme based at the Strangford Lough Wildlife Centre, in the grounds of the Castle Ward Estate.

Below: Drumlins, streamlined hills composed of glacial drift, are submerged in the waters of Strangford Lough, a shallow sea loch a third of which is inter-tidal.

Above: The causeway leading to Mid Island from Ballyurnanellan on the shores of the Lough.

Right: Cormorants nest on Bird Island on Strangford Lough. Nesting birds are at risk from sudden rises in sea level and many eggs, nests and chicks are washed away.

The area is perhaps best known for the birds it attracts and it is said to be one of the best bird-watching sites in the UK, notably so in winter. Over 75 per cent of the world's population of light bellied brent geese, 10,000–12,000 birds, overwinter on the lough, consuming eelgrass. Large populations of wigeon can be seen in the winter months, along with shelduck and teal, and some 45,000 individual wading birds, which either spend the winter or stop off on their spring and autumn migration. Some birds, such as greenshank or common, arctic and sandwich terns, make use of Quoile Pondage, a newly created freshwater lagoon in the south-west corner of the lough. Others, such as plovers, godwits and knot, perform stunning aeronautical displays. Over a third of Ireland's terns nest in colonies on the islands in spring and summer feeding on a plentiful supply of sand eel.

Wildlife under the water is equally exciting; the lough is said to contain some 2,000 species of marine animals, 72 per cent of all the species recorded from around Northern Ireland's coastline, 28 of which are found only in the lough. Maintaining the biodiversity is vitally important, for as soon as any one species goes into decline others inevitably follow. The numbers of horse mussels, which grow in channels throughout the lough, dropped alarmingly in recent years. Horse mussels are not farmed for food and are a different species from the blue mussels we eat. However, they are significant because they provide a hard surface that supports a rich seabed community. Here sea squirts, sea fir, sea anemone, sponges, brittle stars, peacock

Historic buildings

Strangford Lough (shown below) is dotted with interesting ruins and buildings such as Kilclief Castle, Strangford Castle, Old Castle Ward, Audley's Castle and Walshestown Castle. Fortified tower houses like these were built by Irish lords all over Ireland, with the highest concentrations in Down and Limerick. They were built as residences, but at the same time they were constructed for defence – often at the expense of comfort. A typical tower house was a single, rectangular keep, at least 12m (40ft) high and slightly tapered, with two towers flanking the main entrance. Another fascinating ruin is Nendrum, an island monastery. It was founded by St Machaoi and is believed to date back as far as the 5th century AD, to the time of St Patrick. The remains of a church, sundial and a tower can be seen, all ringed by stone-wall enclosures.

Above: Strangford Lough is an important breeding site for common seals and they can be seen resting on the rocks, islands and pladdies – an Ulster word for a small, flat rock.

worms, the queen scallop and the variable scallop may grow or shelter. Without the horse mussels the seabed would revert to mud and few species would be able to survive. In The Narrows lobsters, crabs, conger eels, blennies, pilot whales and harbour porpoises thrive among the wrecks and kelp forests, while basking sharks loiter around the entrance to the lough, hoovering up food.

The sheltered waters are home to Northern Ireland's most important common seal population, which can be seen there all year round. A small number of grey seals can be seen swimming from the shore or on the rocks where they rest and warm themselves; you may even spot an otter in the water.

The shoreline is ringed with seaweed; this attracts sandhoppers and kelp flies, which in turn pull in turnstones and starlings. Areas of saltmarsh are dotted around the lough; eel grasses and samphire build levels to create the marsh, then thrift, sea plantain, sea campion, mayweed, orach and sea lavender move in. Lichens can be found on rocky outcrops and higher up on thin soil wild thyme and beautiful blue squill proliferate, while orchids, knapweed, scabious and sorrel grow in the lime-rich grassland managed by grazing livestock, providing a food source for meadow brown and common blue butterflies.

Mount Stewart, County Down

A walk with exceptional views, beautiful gardens, and beech, mixed and exotic woodland. The mixture of formal and informal gardens provides the perfect sanctuary for one of the few remaining red squirrel populations in the whole of Ireland.

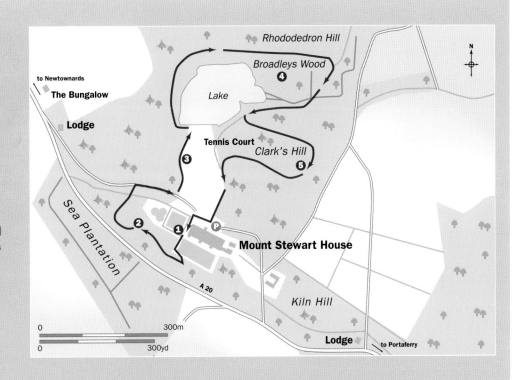

Getting there and facilities:

Mount Stewart is around 24km (15 miles) south east of Belfast on the Newtownards to Portaferry Road, A20, 8km (5 miles) south east of Newtownards. The nearest rail station is Bangor, 16km (10 miles) away. Alternatively, take the Ulsterbus 10 Belfast–Portaferry. The bus stop is at the gates. There are toilet, car park, restaurant, shop, plant sales and baby-changing facilities on the property.

Start point:

OS 1:150,000 sheet 15, GR J553 701

Distance, terrain and accessibility:

A 2.3km (1.4 mile) walk with easy to moderate walking conditions. All areas are accessible.

Route and directions:

1   Start the walk at Mount Stewart House. Notice the exceptionally beautiful formal gardens. The exotic luxuriance of Mount Stewart's celebrated gardens, created in the 1920s by Edith, Lady Londonderry, has helped make it one of Northern Ireland's most popular Trust properties.

2   Informal gardens, including Lilywood and Tir Na'n Og. Nominated as a World Heritage Site, the impressive landscaped garden makes the most of the unique microclimate of the Ards Peninsula.

3   Dramatic views of Strangford Lough and the Mourne Mountains from the romantically idyllic Temple of the Winds.

4   Several different paths can be taken from here, to extend your walk around the lake, into the Broadleys woodland.

5   Again, numerous paths can be taken to explore the woodlands around Clark's Hill before making your way back to Mount Stewart House.

Other Sites in Northern Ireland

Co. Antrim and Co. Londonderry

Portstewart Strand and Bar Mouth, Co. Antrim and Co. Londonderry
Sandy shore, dunes, heath, saltmarsh, mudflats

Portstewart Strand, an attractive and popular beach, is backed by an extensive sand dune spit, which diverts the River Bann. The young dunes provide a habitat for marram grass, sea spurge, kidney vetch and bird's-foot trefoil. Sea buckthorn, a plant that is alien to this area, also grows here, forming dense thickets that have to be cut back regularly. Fourteen species of butterfly breed on this part of the coast, including the grayling and dark green fritillary. Typical birds of the dunes and scrub include the meadow pipit, cuckoo, reed bunting and willow warbler. The muddy sand and saltmarshes of the Bann estuary at Bar Mouth, sheltered from harsh weather by Portstewart Strand, are rich feeding grounds for waders and wildfowl, and the area is now protected as a bird sanctuary. In spring and autumn, Bar Mouth is an important refuge for migrating birds. From November to January, a range of birds including lapwing, golden plover, dunlin, redshank, curlew and oystercatcher come to rest and feed. Offshore, great crested grebe, merganser, shelduck, divers and auks can also be seen. The river also provides a passage in May each year for elvers (young eels) making their way to Lough Neagh for the summer, to return by the same route fully grown in the autumn. In summer, for many centuries, salmon have travelled upstream to spawn. The saltmarsh is covered in typical flora: the grey and green of sea aster, sea milkwort, common saltmarsh grasses and sea rush.

White Park Bay, Co. Antrim
Chalk grassland, scrub, cliffs, dunes, sandy shore

At White Park Bay, chalk cliffs rich in fossils give way to a sandy beach. Between the beach and the surrounding cliffs is an extensive area of grassland and scrub. The narrow band of sand dunes is home to dune plants such as fragrant agrimony and both sea and Portland spurge. The turf is herb rich, with thyme, devil's-bit scabious and broomrape. The site is particularly rich in orchids, with eight species, including pyramidal orchids on the dunes, frog orchid, fragrant orchid, and the very rare small white orchid. Butterflies are also plentiful, with the dark green fritillary and wood white being the most notable. Breeding birds found here include eider ducks and oystercatchers that breed on the shore, and swifts that nest on the cliffs.

Fair Head and Murlough Bay, Co. Antrim
Cliffs, heathland, bog, grassland, woodland, shore

Fair Head overlooks the north channel of the Irish Sea, with Rathlin Island and the Mull of Kintyre in the distance. On its eastern side, the wooded slopes of Murlough Bay contrast with the bleak rocky plateau above. The vegetation above Fair Head consists of a mixture of wet and dry heath, and acid grassland. Creeping willow, crowberry and bog myrtle can be seen, as well as the insect-eating sundew and butterwort. The heath near the cliff edge is a favourite feeding place for choughs, while ravens and peregrines nest on the steep cliff face. Fair Head is an excellent vantage point for watching pilot and killer whales in the summer and autumn.

Left: Buttercups strew the fields leading down towards the rocks and the sea at Carricknaford as seen from Dundriff, Co. Antrim.

Right: Wild fuchsia grows profusely in Ireland, here framing the sides of Coolranny Waterfall. This area of County Antrim is a wild stretch of coastline situated between Fair Head and Murlough Bay.

Rathlin Island, Co. Antrim
Dry and wet heath, wetland, grassland, cliffs

Northern Ireland's largest offshore island, Rathlin is 13km (8 miles) long and less than 1.6km (1 mile) wide, and is located 10km (6 miles) off the north Antrim Coast. It is heaving with seabirds, and boat trips can be taken out to see the vast colonies of razorbill and guillemot; shag, puffin, eider duck and Manx shearwater can also be seen. Two hundred plant species have been recorded on a range of habitats from shore to cliff, heath, marsh and scrub. Among the island's rarities are hare's-foot trefoil, sea fescue, frog orchid and the parasitic plant red broomrape. Marram grass puts down roots to bind loose sand and attracts the burnet moth. Kelp pits are reminders of the kelp industry that died

Above: A stunning view of Attacory Bay, Rathlin Island, viewed from Ballyconagan. The East Lighthouse is just visible in the far distance.

out in the 1930s. The ash produced from burning wrack was used in the soap and glass industries, which provided a living of sorts for the local population.

Co. Down

Murlough National Nature Reserve and Slieve Donard, Co. Down
Beach, sand dunes, lichen heath, heath, scrub, woodland, saltmarsh

Murlough was the first nature reserve to be created in Ireland. Its sand dunes lie in a superbly scenic position across Dundrum Bay with the Mourne Mountains in the background. The dune sand is acidic and supports a whole spectrum of plants, from those that flourish on young dunes, such as marram grass, sea bindweed and viper's bugloss, to those that favour more stable dunes, such as wild thyme, restharrow and bird's-foot trefoil. Sea buckthorn forms dense and spreading thickets in the youngest dunes to the north, while blackthorn, hazel and spindle grow on the older dunes. Murlough is especially rich in insect life, and home to many thermophilic (warmth-loving) invertebrates including mining bees, ants and hoverflies. The rare marsh fritillary is abundant in the heathland areas, while the Réal's wood white breeds in the dunes. The sea buckthorn scrub is very attractive to birds, though the National Trust is clearing areas of this invasive shrub, often with the help of Exmoor ponies and black Galloway cattle, which graze the heath at certain times of year and keep the bracken at bay. Large numbers of wildfowl and waders can be seen on the sea and estuary in winter.

Slieve Donard's summit slopes, which overlook Murlough, are home to a rare montane heath habitat, containing a mixture

of heather, bilberry, crowberry and some mosses and lichens. A little lower down is upland heathland habitat, which contains heathers, rare mosses and liverworts. These habitats are so important that Slieve Donard has been designated a Special Area of Conservation (SAC). But they are under pressure, struggling to survive, partly because of the trampling of human feet, but mainly because of too much grazing by sheep. The National Trust is working to develop a restoration programme to ensure that grazing on the mountain is reduced, thereby enabling plant communities to recover in the long term.

Co. Fermanagh

Crom, Co. Fermanagh
Oak and wet woodlands, parkland, lowland meadows, rush pastures, fen, lake
This extensive estate on the shores of Upper Lough Erne is of international importance for its wildlife. All eight bat species found in Northern Ireland have been recorded at Crom, including the rare Nathusius' pipistrelle. The area is home to many scarce species, with the Irish hare and

blue-eyed grass among them. Many wading birds breed on the estate, and the rare corncrake has nested in the hay meadows. Large numbers of wildfowl spend the winter on the lough, and whooper swans and white-fronted geese from Greenland may be seen grazing in the meadows at this time of year.

Belfast

Divis and the Black Mountain, Belfast
Mountain, heathland, peat bog
On 27th June 2005, the National Trust celebrated the opening of Divis and the Black Mountain. Now that Belfast's famous backdrop is open to the public, the people of the city and beyond have access to a mountain landscape that has been in military ownership for decades. Divis at 478m (1,562ft) and Black

Mountain at 390m (1,275ft) offer spectacular views across Northern Ireland. The Mourne Mountains, Strangford and Belfast Loughs, the Castlereagh and Holywood Hills and the Sperrins are all visible, as are the coasts of England, Scotland and the Isle of Man. Purple moor grass and rush pasture are common on the mountains and are priority habitats for Northern Ireland. Badgers and hares are often seen alongside upland breeding birds such as snipe, stonechats and red grouse. Many waxcaps often grow in autumn, and in spring the lower slopes support the rare marsh fritillary butterfly.

Left: Five per cent of the world's whooper swan population overwinter on Upper Lough Erne in County Fermanagh, making the long journey annually to escape the cruel Icelandic winter.

Below: The view from Divis Mountain across Black Mountain to Belfast City beyond. Red grouse, snipe, stonechat, skylark and other upland breeding birds can be seen here.

Index

Picture Credits